THE COLLECTED WORKS

OF

JAMES I. WEDGWOOD, D.Sc.

St. Alban Press

Publishers to the Liberal Catholic Church, International
741 Cerro Gordo Avenue
San Diego, CA 92102

James Ingall Wedgwood

THE COLLECTED WORKS
OF
JAMES INGALL WEDGWOOD

Docteur (Sciences) de l'Université de Paris

Edited by

The Very Rev. Tony Jack Howard, M.A, M.L.A.

All Saints Day 2004

Second Printing 2007

This is not an official
publication of the
Liberal Catholic Church

ISBN: 0-935461-99-X

FOREWORD

James Ingall Wedgwood was born in London in 1883 and died in Farnham in 1951. He was a member of the well-known Wedgwood family, famous for china among other things. When he was a young man he studied church music and organ construction and later received the degree of Docteur (Sciences) de l'Universite de Paris for a textbook on organ stops, a work that I understand is still being used. In 1904 he attended a lecture on Theosophy given by Annie Besant and in that year joined the Theosophical Society. In 1911 he became the General Secretary of the English Section. As detailed in "The Beginnings of the Liberal Catholic Church," included in this publication, he was consecrated in 1916 as the first Bishop of the Liberal Catholic Church, a movement devoted to liberalizing Christian thought. In the early years of the Church he was its "missionary bishop," traveling throughout much of the world spreading the news of a Catholic Church with new freedoms. In his writings, Bishop Wedgwood had the capacity to explain traditional Christian theology in a clear and understandable manner while explaining where the teachings of our Church have reverted to earlier Christian usage or have grown beyond the limits of traditional theology.

The Introduction to this collection is contributed by The Very Rev. Tony Jack Howard. Father Howard is Professor of English and Comparative Religion at Collin County Community College located near his home in Frisco, Texas. He is also the Dean of the St. Alban Theological Seminary, the denomination's religious training center. As Father Howard makes clear, Bishop Wedgwood was a primary author of *The Liturgy of the Liberal Catholic Rite* and his writings on that subject are of particular interest to all Liberal Catholics.

✠ **The Most Rev. Dean Bekken**
B.S., M.S., J.D., D.D.
Presiding Bishop Emeritus
Liberal Catholic Church, International

TABLE OF CONTENTS

Page

INTRODUCTION

To Begin...

As originally conceived, this book was to be simply a reprint of two of Bishop Wedgwood's seminal works: *New Insights into Christian Worship* and *The Presence of Christ in the Holy Communion*. Both are required reading for students at St. Alban Theological Seminary, and both had been difficult to obtain of late. When the editor at St. Alban Press suggested that we go further and offer a more complete edition of our founder's writings, it remained only to gather them and make them accessible to all who might be interested in the Liberal Catholic Church. Most of what follows comes from the denominational journal, *The Liberal Catholic*, during the early years of the church, 1927-1929. At that time, the Liberal Catholic Church was, perhaps, more heavily influenced by the teachings of the Theosophical Society; both Founding Bishop Wedgwood and the church's second Presiding Bishop, Charles Leadbeater, were ardent Theosophists, yet they staunchly advocated the church's prime directive, as it were: that we honor the freedom of conscience of *all* her members.

The Liberal Catholic Church International publishes this collection of Wedgwood's works respectful of the freedom of her members to adopt a Theosophical interpretation of the material or a more traditionally Catholic interpretation—all the while insisting that neither position becomes a litmus test for spiritual worthiness. For a more explicit explanation of this ideal, readers are encouraged to read *The Statement of Principle of the Liberal Catholic Church International*, which reads, in part, that we allow "entire freedom in the interpretation of Creeds, Scriptures and Traditions, and of the Liturgy, [asking] only that differences of interpretation be courteously expressed, [holding] strongly that belief should be the result of individual study or intuition, not its antecedent."

As Dean of the seminary, I would like to focus my remaining remarks on the two required works mentioned earlier since they offer not only a glimpse through the historical window which brought our branch of the One, Holy, Catholic, and Apostolic Church into existence but they serve also as a template for our current understanding of the ecclesiology, liturgics, and sacramental theology of the church. The other works provided will no doubt be of use both to our seminarians and the general populace, of course, but most likely more as reference material rather than as applied theology, and so I will not analyze them with the same rigor.

Nothing New Under the Sun...

In the late 1920s, when Bishop Wedgwood compiled his observations on the Liberal Catholic Liturgy, the Roman Catholic Church still used Latin in the Mass, and the Protestant Episcopal Church in the USA had but recently approved its revised Book of Common Prayer, the 1928 version still loved by traditionalist Episcopalians to this day. Wedgwood and Bp. Charles Leadbeater had created a truly novel liturgy of which they could be proud, and their legacy continues today as Liberal Catholics worldwide continue to worship in the stately, joyous manner envisioned by their founding bishops. However, the reforms of Vatican II and of the Liturgical Movement in general have made many of the innovations documented in Wedgwood's *New Insights into Christian Worship* somewhat anachronistic, if not simply quaint. Here, I am thinking primarily of using the vernacular during the liturgy, the prevalence of the dialogue mass, the encouragement of frequent communions, etc. Nonetheless, as a reference guide for those seeking an understanding of Liberal Catholic liturgics and as a companion text to Leadbeater's formidable *Science of the Sacraments*, Wedgwood's little collection of essays remains essential reading.

Throughout the text, Wedgwood maintains that his observations may be more fully appreciated by reading Leadbeater, so if the text may be faulted for occasional omissions of detailed explanations, one is always aware of Leadbeater's tome as an antidote. What Wedgwood does emphasize, though, is the importance of worship beyond the concerns of the individual on his or her knees, as it were, and the necessity for having an informed, engaged congregation, those actively involved in the "work of the people," which is the root meaning of the Greek for "liturgy."

Whereas it had been the custom at the time for those worshiping in Roman Catholic churches to be focusing on their individual piety rather than interacting with the sacred drama to which they were present, and while many Protestant churches emphasized the dynamic between the preaching from the pulpit and the audience in the pews, Wedgwood maintained that Liberal Catholics believed that "every time the Holy Eucharist is celebrated great spiritual forces are sent out over the world around, which operate to change the thought atmosphere of the neighborhood." So that rather than go to Mass to say one's rosary and receive communion when the bells chime or to go to Morning Prayer to hear the pastor's sermon and focus on one's individual salvation, Wedgwood's "new idea" was that "[a]mong the various Churches, the Liberal Catholic is probably the only one which teaches its people that they go to Church not primarily to help themselves, but to help the world outside." That insight proves especially fruitful when weary parishioners ask me why they should bother to come to mass week after week; I insist that not only are they doing *themselves* a favor, but more importantly, *they are helping to build the spiritual edifice into which all may be admitted.*

The most interesting section of the text is that focusing on the Holy Eucharist, and in two points especially: that mentioning the "Act of Faith," co-authored with Leadbeater, and also the section on "the Epiklesis." Of the former, Wedgwood writes:

> Curiously enough, [the Act of Faith] is the only section of our Liturgy that must plead guilty to the charge of teaching heresy! The frank proclamation that "all His sons shall one day reach His feet" is "universalism" or "*apocatastasis*." It can claim, however, a list of very presentable protagonists, notably Origen, Clement of Alexandria, S. Gregory or Nyssa. It is, of course, very widely held at the present day, and our Church is not likely to have qualms of conscience about this particular heterodoxy.

And while I may prefer saying the Nicaeno-Constantinopolitan Creed—both because of its historicity and because of its uplifting effect within my soul—I am aware that many will prefer this brief affirmation. More pressing, however, is my desire to go to Origen and Clement and Gregory so that I may have more solid reasons to defend the universalism implied by the Act of Faith. I have had and will continue to have ample opportunities to speak on this issue. One priest acquaintance of mine tried to circumvent this universalism by suggesting to me that 'all His sons' means that God knows whose are His and whose are not. I did not venture to inquire what may become of 'whose are not.'

On the matter of the Epiklesis, I was disappointed that Wedgwood and Leadbeater did not follow the example of their Eastern Orthodox brethren in giving precedence to the action of the Holy Spirit. As Wedgwood mentions, in the Orthodox tradition, the "priest recites the words of institution, as in the West, then praying that the bread and wine may become the Body and Blood, uses the formula, 'changing them by Thy Holy Spirit.'" In the Liberal Catholic rite, the formula echoes that of the Episcopal Church—"by Thy Word and Holy Spirit"; however, Wedgwood's explanation seems fitting: "Ours...is an epiklesis of the Holy Trinity—for the invocation of the Logos is another primitive use—the prayer, that is to say, is addressed to the Father, and we then invoke both the Holy Spirit and Logos." I can live with that.

The section on the "Benediction of the Most Holy Sacrament" is clear and helpful—as is that on "The Service of Healing" (though one chuckles at Wedgwood's fastidiousness in his insistence on the cleanliness of those who present themselves for this service). The least satisfying section is the "Work with the Dead." Perhaps my lack of complete sympathy with matters theosophical are at work here or, perhaps, Wedgwood truly is as vague here as it appears. I would like to have seen a more developed theology of the dead.

For a thorough grounding in Liberal Catholic liturgics, one must peruse Leadbeater's *Science of the Sacraments*—no question about it. But for those interested in an abbreviated version of that work, they might do well to give Wedgwood's *New Insights into Christian Worship* some attention. And although these "insights" are no longer truly "new" seventy some-odd years later, their appeal comes from the balanced, gentle eloquence expressed in their author's tone and by the fact that they are penned by our first Presiding Bishop. May God grant him continued growth in God's love and service, and may God grant us, Wedgwood's successors, the courage and joy in keeping the vision alive.

Wedgwood's Sacramental Theology...

The celebration of the Holy Eucharist forms the central act of worship for catholic Christians, and though its form has varied through the centuries, its objective has remained constant: to nourish the recipients with the Body and Blood of Jesus Christ. In *The Presence of Christ in the Holy Communion*, Bishop Wedgwood suggests how we might best understand Christ's presence in the sacrament today.

Not surprisingly, the narrative for the event Christians have called by various names-- the Lord's Supper, the Mass, the Divine Liturgy, the Holy Eucharist—is explicitly expressed in the synoptic gospels and theologically expressed in the Gospel of John. The relevant passages are as follows:

> While they were eating, Jesus took a loaf of bread, and after blessing it he gave it to the disciples, and said, 'Take, eat; this is my body.' Then he took a cup, and after giving thanks he gave it to them, saying, 'Drink from it, all of you; for this is my blood of the covenant, which is poured out for many for the forgiveness of sins.' (Matthew 26:26-28 NRSV)

> While they were eating, he took a loaf of bread, and after blessing it he broke it, gave it to them, and said: 'Take; this is my body.' Then he took a cup, and after giving thanks he gave it to them, and all of them drank from it. He said to them, 'This is my blood of the covenant, which is poured out for many.' (Mark 14:22-24 NRSV)

> Then he took a loaf of bread, and when he had given thanks, he broke it and gave it to them, saying, 'This is my body, which is given for you. Do this in remembrance of me.' And he did the same with the cup after supper, saying, 'This cup that is poured out for you is the new covenant in my blood.' (Luke 22:19-20 NRSV)

> 'I am the living bread that came down from heaven. Whoever eats of this bread

will live forever; and the bread that I give for the life of the world is my flesh.... Very truly, I tell you, unless you eat the flesh of the Son of Man and drink his blood, you have no life in you. Those who eat my flesh and drink my blood have eternal life; and I will raise them up on the last day; for my flesh is true food and my blood is true drink. Those who eat my flesh and drink my blood abide in me, and I in them. Just as the living Father sent me, and I live because of the Father, so whoever eats me will live because of me.' (John 6:51, 53-57 NRSV)

From these scriptural passages and through the teachings of the apostles, the Church enshrined the memory of her Master in this sacred meal and claimed that in it Christ is truly present. But how is this presence to be understood? Indeed, can it be understood at all? What does it mean to say that Christ is truly present in the sacrament of the altar?

In *The Presence of Christ in the Holy Communion*, Bishop Wedgwood outlines four different views of the Eucharistic presence: 1.) The Real Objective Presence, 2.) Receptionism, 3.) Virtualism, and 4.) Zwinglianism. He then offers thorough interpretations of these views, followed by a Liberal Catholic perspective. Of the first view, Wedgwood affirms that it is the "belief that after the words of consecration have been pronounced by a duly ordained priest or bishop, the Body and Blood of Christ are present on the altar under the veils of bread and wine." Three sub-categories of this view are 1.) what I would call the ineffable: the idea that the Real Presence cannot be defined; only appreciated. This view approximates that of most Eastern Orthodox theologians who are less inclined to dogmatize upon the issue as in the following view, that of 2.) Transubstantiation, the doctrine of the Roman Catholic Church from the time of the Council of Trent (1551) to the present Catechism of the Catholic Church (1994):

> Because Christ our Redeemer said that it was truly his body that he was offering under the species of bread, it has always been the conviction of the Church of God, and this holy Council now declares again, that by the consecration of the bread and wine there takes place a change of the whole substance of the bread into the substance of the body of Christ our Lord and of the whole substance of the wine into the substance of his blood. This change the holy Catholic Church has fittingly and properly called transubstantiation. (Qtd. in *The Catechism of the Catholic Church*. Liguori, MO: Liguori Publications, 1994)

Finally, Wedgwood mentions 3.) Consubstantiation, which was "the doctrine of Luther who believed that the substance of the bread and wine remained, together with the real Body and Blood of Christ, in and under the bread and wine."

The remaining three views were (and continue to be) held by various Protestant bodies in that they protested against, among other doctrines, the Real Objective Presence. According to Wedgwood, Receptionism means that "[i]t is at the reception of the sacrament that the communicant partakes of the sacred Body and Blood, and then only by virtue of faith." Therefore, it is the act of *receiving* the sacrament *in faith* which determines its efficacy. Virtualism means "that Christ's Body and Blood are not present in literal fact, but rather their virtue and effect." This view was an attempt to argue against Christ's being, for lack of a better term, imprisoned in the elements. Since He now reigns in heaven, how could He also be on earth? Or so the "reasoning" went. Zwinglianism, named after Swiss Reformer Huldreich Zwingli (1484-1531), means that the "consecrated elements are figures or symbols of the Body and Blood.... The sacraments bring and dispense no grace, but are a public testimony, the badge of our profession as Christians." Against these three views, Bishop Wedgwood amasses considerable arguments, the essence of which is that they deny the explicit warrant of scripture and, at the time of the Reformation, the nearly fifteen centuries' cumulative experience of the Church.

These views amount to a near denial of the central doctrine of Christ's Incarnation, and they reveal a kind of Gnostic fear of matter. If Christ is present in the sacrament only by faith, does that mean the Incarnation is not a fact? If Christ is present in the sacrament only virtually, does that mean He cannot be with us as He promised He would be? What would these adherents say of the Mystical Body of Christ, His Church? And finally, if Christ is present in the sacrament only as a sign—as a wedding ring is but a sign of marriage—, what is one to make of what Wedgwood calls the "remarkable change of consciousness or experience of spiritual things that overtakes so many people at the Eucharist? Clearly, Bishop Wedgwood wants us to understand that to deny Christ's Real Presence in the Eucharist is to undermine the principal means of grace available to us through the Church. To deny Christ's Real Presence in the Eucharist is to deny us access to our own potential divinization.

The process of divinization, or *theosis*, as it is called in the Eastern Orthodox Church, has its roots in scripture and in the Mystical Tradition of the Church. Bishop Wedgwood clearly articulates this doctrine when he writes:

> Mankind lives in illusion and separateness until it awakens the Light within so that it becomes one with the Universal Light without and is reintegrated consciously into the mystical Body of Christ. Our Lord is ever thus scattering the fragments of His Life upon the altars of His holy Church, so that we, participating in that Life, may quicken and fan within ourselves the flame of our own inner divinity.... That Divinity that was fully manifest in Jesus Christ is being gradually unfolded in each one of us until we come "unto a perfect man, unto the measure of the stature of the fullness of Christ."

Wedgwood therefore subscribes to a view of Transubstantiation, which he describes as follows:

> Substance is the reality, force, or ensouling Life, or *noumenon*, which lies behind a physical object. It is that which stands under (Latin, *sub* = under; *stans* = standing) or behind the outer physical object, and of which that object is the expression or epiphany. Transubstantiation (Latin, *trans* = across) on this principle, means that the essence, substance, or superphysical reality and counterpart or creative force of the bread and wine is transmuted, or changed across, and replaced by a similar ensouling Life coming direct from Our Lord Himself.... [T]he consecrated Bread and Wine become a vehicle or channel directly connected with Our Lord, through which He expresses His Life and blessing.... [T]he purpose of the Sacrament is to quicken within us the manifestation of His Life so that our efforts towards self-realization may be aided.

This interpretation is true to the sacramental view of life expressed in scripture and in Holy Tradition wherein God uses matter as a vehicle for Spirit. From Genesis we learn that God's creation is essentially good; from the Incarnation we learn that God was pleased enough with Man to dwell with him as Man (Emmanuel = God With Us); from Bishop Wedgwood we learn that in the Holy Eucharist Christ offers us a means to reconnect with the divinity He came to bestow upon us, and He does so by using matter—bread and wine—just as when He came to Earth He did so by using matter—the flesh from the *Theotokos*.

A Personal Note…

I am not a cradle Liberal Catholic. Most of us aren't; most of us come to the Liberal Catholic Church as a terminus (and for some a way station) on our spiritual journey. I was raised in the Anglo-Catholic tradition, and I learned from boyhood that Christ is truly present in the Eucharist. Serving as a young acolyte brought me into proximity with the holiness emanating from the altar; at times it was nearly palpable. When I was older, I served as a Lay Chalice Bearer, and I was ever mindful of the awesome gift I carried from communicant to communicant—at times nearly weightless with the sheer joy of being an instrument of Christ's blessing, at times nearly crushed by the perceived unworthiness to hold even a drop of His precious blood. When I entered upon a period of hyper-rationalism as a Unitarian, I was always cognizant of a vacuum in my soul, having traded the sacraments for the lofty ideals of the mind. When that vacuum became unbearable, I found solace within the Eastern Orthodox tradition; their reverence for the Eucharist is nearly unmatched, and the splendor of their liturgies is beyond telling. But the weight of their theology too often oppresses, making one feel more like a worm than a man; and their xenophobia too often alienates, making their Christian charity too often apparent, rather than genuine.

I hope I may not be misunderstood: I treasure my experiences as an Anglo-Catholic, and as a Unitarian, and as an Orthodox Christian, for they have been steps in my spiritual journey, which have brought me thus far. All of which is a way of saying that I am blessed in my discovery of Liberal Catholicism, for it embodies the best of these traditions. I do not have to abandon my foundational understanding of Christ's presence in the Eucharist established in my Anglo-Catholic years; nor do I have to check my mind in at the church doors, thus salvaging what was good about Unitarian-Universalism; nor do I have to abandon the beauty of liturgical worship and the sense of mysticism present in Orthodoxy.

If this experience were unique, I wouldn't be telling it. Most likely, though, it mirrors the journey of my colleagues, and that of the seminarians under my care, and that of the parishioners in Liberal Catholic churches throughout the world, and, perhaps more importantly, that of the many thoughtful, searching souls reading these words right now. *All* of us can profit from the essays contained in this volume—those of us seeking the history and teachings of the Liberal Catholic Church as expressed by its founding bishop, a true visionary; those of us curious about its unique approach to theology, whether we be Theosophists or Traditionalists or neither; and, indeed, those of us simply aspiring to the time-honored dictum, *fides quaerens intellectum*, "faith seeking understanding."

The Very Rev. Tony J. Howard, M.A., M.L.A.
Dean, St. Alban Theological Seminary
Professor of English & Comparative Religion
Collin County Community College
Frisco, Texas

THE LARGER MEANING OF RELIGION

CHAPTER I

INTRODUCTORY

THE object of this little work is to remove prejudice and misunderstanding that exist plentifully in regard to religion. It seeks to do this by explaining what religion really is. It is evident that numbers of people are growing up with little sympathy for Churches. And this is largely due to a change of focus, which has led much idealistic thought that was formerly devoted to God to be centred on problems of human welfare. It is also partly due to the age of materialism through which we have passed, for religion is largely concerned with aspects of man's being which are not of this physical world.

The aim of this book, then, is to study the purpose and meaning of religion, presenting to the reader a number of facts and points of view which are not usually taken into account. It tries to show that religion has a scope and appeal much wider than is commonly in these days attributed to it—in fact, that it pertains to every department of life. The book submits that it is a specialised section of religion which now remains as the chief occupation of the Churches, rather than religion in its entirety; but that public worship, so far from being antiquated, may have far-reaching results. And it points out that aspects of religion that are usually seen as hostile and antagonistic to one another can be regarded as complementary and as meeting the many-sided requirements of the human temperament. If the churches could be brought to see this point of view, much of the existing conflict and antagonism between them would vanish automatically.

THE ATTITUDE OF THE ORDINARY MAN TOWARDS RELIGION

Religion is a word that covers a number of ideas. It concerns our understanding of God and our relation to Him. And, more and more, as people are recognising the Life of God in their fellow-men, religion is being understood also to comprise the science of our relationship with those fellow-men. We shall deal with these various aspects of the subject later on. At the moment it is only necessary to point out that religion is acknowledged to be one of the strongest and most innate elements in human character. In fact, if we were asked to say what is the most fundamental influence in the life of a man, it would, I think, be a question of deciding between religion and the ties of family and other affection. In some people the one would be found to be the strongest factor, in some the other.

It is only at a comparatively advanced stage of human development that people begin to think for themselves about religion and about the larger problems which bear upon the purpose and meaning of life. In the greater number of our fellow-men God is still slumbering, or, at the best, dreaming. They are not yet awake to the significance of life. There are thousands of our fellow-beings in whom selfishness or the love of personal pleasure are stronger than any feelings of religion. It would be idle to pretend that the influence of religion is either dominant or constant in the lives of ordinary undeveloped people. Most of these take no interest in Churches, or even in learning and the more serious pursuits of life. They are superficially antagonised by official religion and by the want of human feeling and sympathy in so many departments of learning. Many of them find their chief happiness in the society and friendship of their fellows. They are not what the world calls " religious," but they nevertheless often have in them pronounced ethical and moral instincts which tend to orient them towards right and kindly dealing with their fellows.

The majority of such people view the world chiefly from their own self-interested standpoint. Their friends, and the experiences with which life provides them, are expected to minister to their personal happiness and satisfaction. They are born into the world and grow up accustomed to being where they find themselves, and they view life from the point of view of its reaction upon themselves, not at its intrinsic value. It does not occur to them to look at it objectively from the standpoint of other people. Burns, no doubt, had this limitation of the ordinary man in mind when he wrote his famous lines:—

> Oh! wad some power the giftie gie us
> To see oursel's as others see us!
> It wad frae monie a blunder free us,
>   And foolish notion.[1]

There are plenty of other men who go regularly or occasionally, as the case may be, to places of worship, of whom it would be true to say (as I have written elsewhere) that they would have been just as good Hindus, if the accident (so-called) of birth had taken them to India. The majority of them get their religious formation, just as they do their political affiliations, not from individual study and careful reflection at all, but from heredity, environment, custom and convention. They were brought up "Church of England," it may be, and they remain "Church of England" by force of habit, and because it has never seriously occurred to them to be anything else.

In spite of all this, the assertion made above that religion is one of the strongest and most innate elements in human character holds good. We have to consider what is fundamental in man, to think, in terms of quality and not of quantity, of that which reaches up to his innermost nature, to the source of his being. Desire for pleasure and selfishness are the strongest instincts in a good many people, but they belong to the surface expression of life and human nature, and not to the more fundamental part of man which is at that earlier stage of his development largely impeded from self-expression.

---

[1] For the sake of our many readers of other nationalities, it may be useful to put this into ordinary English:

> Oh! would some power the gift give us
> To see ourselves as others see us!
> It would from many a blunder free us,
>   And foolish notion.

The Larger Meaning of Religion
Page 3

THE AWAKENING OF MAN TO LIFE

There comes a stage in the life of every man when he awakens to the existence of the world around him. He begins to ask what is the nature of the scheme of which he forms part. Why is he here? What is the purpose of life? His origin? His destiny? The search for an answer to these questions, which have been dubbed "the riddle of life," is often long and sometimes painful, but he eventually gives his allegiance—maybe a temporary allegiance only—to some theory of life which enables him to see himself as an integral factor in the whole, and with his own purpose to be fulfilled. Up to this time his consciousness has been mostly inward-turned, he has been living mainly in the subjective world of his own sensations and his dreaming thoughts. Now he grows to be outward-turned, he sees himself as a unit in one vast organism, and addresses himself to the task of discovering and fulfilling his right relationship to that whole. In the language of religion the word "conversion" is generally used in another connection altogether; but it accurately describes this turning-point (Lat. *cum* = with, *vertere* = to turn) in a man's life. He turns himself round into the flow of life's evolutionary purpose, and henceforward seeks to unite himself with the current of the Divine Purpose and Will. One writer has put the situation concisely when he says that the world is divided into two classes of people— "those who know" and "those who do not know."

It is at this stage that an intelligent grasp of religion can be of great service to a man. And the more many-sided and satisfying the scheme of religious thought, the more fruitful will be his efforts at co-operation. If he can be shown in what direction it is most profitable for him to bend his efforts, and how he can learn to give expression to the various sides of the complex nature with which he is endowed, it is evident that his way will be made much clearer for him. All this is really part of what is called religion, and if we view religion from this standpoint, its importance is seen to be paramount.

CHAPTER II

WHAT IS MAN?

RELIGION has been described as "God's message to man." Whatever view we may choose to take about religion, what it is and how it came into the world, we shall not dispute the fact that it is in any case concerned with man. Before we can usefully discuss its scope and purpose—which is really the object of this little book—we must come to some kind of understanding as to what we mean by man. It is not necessary that we shall go at all deeply into the question, but there are a few points which have to be made clear before we can pass on to the main subject of our enquiry. Man is evidently a complex being, and it is not possible to discuss him in the entirety of his being without some complexity at least of language if not of thought.

It is often the earlier conceptions of religion that came to be formulated which now hold the field as the orthodox ones. The older outlook viewed the creation of man rather too much perhaps under the overshadowing sense of the greatness and majesty of God. Man was made at the pleasure of Deity, though we need not associate with this idea the imputation of whimsicality made by later anti-Christian writers. There is not much attempt, however, to indicate what goal or purpose was in view so far as man, the unasked product of this creation, was himself concerned. We read in the *Catechismus Romanus*:—

Q. Why did God make you?
A. God made me to know Him, love Him, and serve Him in this world, and to be happy with Him for ever in the next.

At its face value, this may seem a little puerile, especially when we read it in conjunction with the traditional view derived from Genesis ii., 18-20, that the birds and beasts were made, on their part, for the pleasure of man, and the flowers also as it is generally assumed. Experience lends added weight to the conviction that few people ever gain from their religion any really large view of the purpose and meaning of life. Granted a more adequate view, it is possible to read much more into the answer quoted above. "To know God" assumes a development of the spiritual organs and faculties which makes such knowledge possible. "To love Him" implies possibilities in the way of giving and receiving love that are illimitable. In God's service we are told in the wonderful phraseology of a Collect of the Church of England, "is perfect freedom," at any rate when that service is rightly understood. "To be happy" with God is the satisfaction of our deepest nature. Says a Hindu Scripture: "Brahman (God) is Bliss." (*Brhadaranyaka Upanishat*, IX., 24)

MAN AS A SPIRIT

There is what I have above called "a more adequate view" finding wide acceptance in these days, which is closely connected with the doctrine of the Immanence of God in His world—that doctrine which, together with its inference as to the essential nobility of man, the late Archdeacon Wilberforce did so much to spread abroad in our contemporary religious thought.

Conventional religion speaks about man having a soul and a spirit. It derives this idea, of course, from orthodox tradition. St. Paul, for example, makes use of the three terms, body, soul and spirit, and in one text (I *Thessalonians* v., 23) the three terms are used side by side. It often uses the two terms interchangeably, making no distinction in practice between soul and spirit. And there is little clear thinking about either of them, or on what may be their distinctive functions. The soul is thought of as the immaterial part of the man, standing, so to speak, at the back of his physical doings, and religion has made people vaguely familiar with the thought that the leading of a good life is the means of the soul's ultimate salvation. If it be true that man has a spirit (as we were taught at our mother's knee), that spirit must be the real and most important part of him. It is more fitting, obviously, to say that man is a spirit using a soul and a body.

The "more adequate view" of man's purpose of which I have been speaking has the advantage of suggesting a noble and dignified *raison d'être* for his pilgrimage. According to this view of things the world is not separated off from God, but owes its existence to the inbreathing of the Divine Life, by which it is continually vivified and maintained. God does not interject Himself into a world held perpetually separate from Himself in order to work miracles or manifestations of Divine Providence, but the manifestation of His Will in the world is what we call "Natural Law." Miracles, so-called, are wrought by the knowledge and application of forces higher than those usually in action. In just the same way, man is not a creature separate from God. The human spirit is a spark of the Divine Flame, divine in essence and potentiality, one with God. This doctrine is not to be confused with that of "pantheism" as commonly defined. The common objection to that is summed up in the phrase "the helplessness of God." The view that we are now propounding does not imply that God is wholly identified with and limited by His universe. It acknowledges His transcendence as well as His immanence, and is wonderfully well and majestically expressed in a phrase from the Scriptures of another religion:—

I established this universe with one fragment of Myself; and I remain. (*Bhagadad Gita*, X., 42.)

THE DEVELOPMENT OF HIS LATENT POWERS

This doctrine of the essential divinity of man enables us, as I have said, to see a wonderful purpose being worked out in life, and gives us illimitable hope and encouragement for the future. It is held that the spirit of man is like a seed of Divinity; it contains within itself in germ all the qualities and attributes of its Divine Parent. As the acorn is sown in the soil of the field, and, passing through various intervening stages of growth, eventually developes into the giant oak tree, so the spirit of man is sown in the soil of a universe, and, passing through an infinite variety of experiences, emerges with all the divine qualities, that had been latent or germinal in it, fully developed and manifest.

Man is brought into the physical world and surrounded with the many sensations of life in order that he may react to those surroundings and profit by the many experiences with which they supply him. He meets and talks with a friend, for instance; there is an interchange of thought and emotion by which he becomes richer in experience. In fact every thought and emotion, which is awakened by his fellow-men or by contact with the outer life in general, strengthens somewhat his power to use his mind and emotions. This is true even of the most trivial experiences of life, and we know well from our own experience how the deeper events of life make real changes in our character. It is in this manner that the Divine powers latent in us are gradually brought out into expression, and come to form part of our permanent equipment of character. We can see this process of development going on around us on all sides, and it accounts for the differences and inequalities that we observe among human beings.

FURTHER THEORIES OF IMMANENCE

It is sufficient for our purpose to say that this ultimate achievement of perfection is worked out in one manner or another from the time of man's entrance into a universe of manifestation until his egress therefrom, by which time he has learned the various lessons with which the universe can provide him.

But there is an extension of this teaching which I may mention in passing, though the discussion of it would not be altogether apposite here. It involves the theory of reincarnation, and goes even further.

We have already referred to the passage in the book of Genesis which speaks of the creation of the beast and the bird. The original is as follows:—

And the Lord God said, It is not good that the man should be alone; I will make him an help meet for him.

And out of the ground the Lord God formed every beast of the field, and every fowl of the air; and brought them unto Adam to see what he would call them: and whatsoever Adam called every living creature, that was the name thereof.

And Adam gave names to all cattle, and to the fowl of the air, and to every beast of the field; but for Adam there was not found an help meet for him. (*Genesis* ii., 18-20.)

In the preceding chapter, also, it is said:—

And God said, Let us make man in our image, after our likeness: and let them have dominion over the fish of the sea, and over the fowl of the air, and over the cattle, and over all the earth, and over every creeping thing that creepeth upon the earth.

So God created man in his own image, in the image of God created he him; male and female created he them.

And God blessed them, and God said unto them, Be fruitful and multiply, and replenish the earth, and subdue it: and have dominion over the fish of the sea, and over the fowl of the air, and over every living thing that moveth upon the earth.

And God said, Behold, I have given you every herb bearing seed, which is upon the face of all the earth, and every tree, in which is the fruit of a tree yielding seed; to you it shall be for meat.

And to every beast of the earth, and to every fowl of the air, and to every thing that creepeth upon the earth, wherein there is life, I have given every green herb for meat: and it was so.

And God saw every thing that he had made, and, behold, it was very good. And the evening and the morning were the sixth day. (Vv. 26-31.)

The hypothesis with which we are at the moment occupied endeavours to review the purpose and aim of creation in general. Not only does it give a *raison d'être* to man and to the fact of his creation, but it contemplates the lower kingdoms of nature not only in the legendary and poetical sense detailed in Genesis, but as vehicles of the Divine Life in its earlier stages of manifestation. It goes so far as to include the mineral kingdom within the category of animate matter—an adventure of thought which is by no means foreign to the latest outlook of science. The protagonist of this theory of the mineral kingdom is the well-known Indian scientist, Sir J. C. Bose, D.Sc., M.A., F.R.S., and others have followed in his wake. He has shown that metals can be made to give a response to electrical stimulation, similar to that of vegetable and animal tissue, and have been caused to show appropriate reactions to the effects of poison and its antidote. Metals also give signs of fatigue, but can be restored to normal action by repose. People who use a razor blade constantly can observe this last fact.

It may be interesting if I quote here a passage indicating a similar belief from the writings of a Sufi-mystic, Jalaludin Rumi (1207-1273) in a book entitled *Mesnavi-i Ma'Navi* (Book III.):—

I died from the mineral, and became a plant;
I died from the plant, and reappeared in an animal;
I died from the animal, and became a man.
        Wherefore then should I fear?
        When did I grow less by dying?
Next time I shall die from the man
        That I may grow the wings of the angel.
From the angel too must I advance: all things shall
        Perish, save His Face.

Exponents of this doctrine of evolution (seen from the life side as well as that of form) argue that there is progressive freedom of expression for the indwelling life, as it becomes expressed through the higher kingdoms. And reincarnation reconciles with the idea of Divine Justice the existence of the savage, through whom the earliest and crudest human experiences are to be realised. The memory of past lives is said to be stored up in the real man—the Ego—and to show itself as aptitude for different kinds of work in each new body, and in the innate tendencies of character with which it is endowed. It is held that by this sequence of many lives, rising gradually, as they do, in culture and usefulness, the admonition of our Lord may literally be carried out: "Be ye therefore perfect, even as your Father which is in heaven is perfect." (*Matthew* v., 48.)

MORE SPHERES OF LIFE THAN ONE

There is another line of thought to be pursued before we return to our main subject. This growth and development of man takes place not in one world alone—this physical world—but in several worlds. There is a large gulf to be bridged over between man's manifestations as a physical body and his manifestation as a spirit. This conception of several worlds or planes or spheres of being is not foreign to the most orthodox traditions of religion. The teaching on the subject of the life after death speaks of different conditions or regions of the soul's existence, such as purgatory, the intermediate world, hades, heaven and so forth. We can carry the idea further, and reason that, since psychical research bears out the teachings of religion by showing good evidence for the continuity of emotion and thought and will after the death of the body, those functions of consciousness do not have their seat in the physical brain, as is supposed by materialists of the extreme school, but in the higher being of man. We may think of various worlds intervening between the physical plane and the world of pure spirit, in which these different aspects of man's consciousness find their special and appropriate bodying out into expression. The intermediate part which forms the connecting link between the spirit and the body is called popularly the soul.

CHAPTER III

MAN AND HIS PILGRIMAGE

HAVING finished this cursory examination of the different aspects of man's being, we are now concerned only to point out that the Christian religion is repeatedly asserting that we are living in a world of exile. "In my Father's house are many mansions.... I go to prepare a place for you." (*John* xiv., 2) "Lay not up for yourselves treasures upon earth...but lay up for yourselves treasures in heaven." (*Matt.* vi., 19-21) This recurrent idea finds even more common and often poignant expression in the language of Christian hymnody.

> My spirit homeward turns,
> And fain would thither flee;
> My heart, O Sion, droops and yearns,
> When I remember thee.

In this particular hymn we are reminded of a lost birthright; but the ailment of most people is not so much nostalgia for a home whose attractiveness still lingers like a fragrance in the memory of man, but a sense of loneliness, of separation from something yet unknown, a feeling within oneself of being perpetually incomplete. And if human love and friendship fail and disappoint us, as they too often do, it is perhaps to bear witness that we shall never find our true happiness save in that union of the lower and higher selves to which the mystics of old referred as the "heavenly marriage" or the "spiritual nuptials of the soul."

The same idea is portrayed in one of the most dramatic of our Lord's parables, that of the Prodigal Son. But Christianity is not alone in this view of man's pilgrimage. Freemasonry tells of a Great Secret that has been lost, of the search for the Lost Word, of the loss of the "genuine secrets of a Master Mason," "till time or circumstances shall restore the genuine ones." Hinduism is every whit as explicit. Man is living enwrapped in a world of *maya* or illusion, and it outlines for him a science of *yoga* or the attainment of union or oneness, by which he gradually divests himself of this *maya* and reaches the goal of self-realisation or the recognition of reality. The Buddha similarly proclaimed the Noble Eightfold Path that leads to *Nirvana*.

The explanation of all this current of teaching is quite simple. Man in his lower waking consciousness is no longer aware of his own essential divinity. The recovery of this lost knowledge—but knowledge in the sense of true inner realisation—is the re-discovery of the Lost Word or of the Great Secret. It is freedom from the bondage of *maya*. It is the attainment of Reality. It is Fulfillment or Accomplishment or Liberation or Freedom. It is the Vision Splendid of the Heavenly Jerusalem—the prototype of all celestial beauty and perfection.

CHAPTER IV

WHAT IS RELIGION?

IF one wishes to get to the heart of a subject, it is often useful to examine the etymology of its chief technical terms. It is well known that words tend to change their meaning in the course of time, and this sometimes involves the loss of ideas that are precious. Especially is this true in regard to the study of religion. Religions arise in an atmosphere of living spiritual experience, and from time to time within the organisation men of vision spring into prominence and contribute richly to the heritage of its thought. But as the teachings become formalised in their transmission by men who lack the spiritual illumination of their predecessors, the terms of speech are apt to lose their vividness and life, and convey to a later age ideas different from those which originally informed them.

We penetrate straight to the essential core of religion if we study its etymology. The word itself has a wonderful significance. There is a little doubt amongst authorities as to its origin, but opinions reduce themselves to two likely derivations, with the balance of probability resting on the former. Both are capable of the same interpretation. These are (i) *religare* = to bind back (2) *relegere*, which bears the sense of "sailing back over the same waters."

THE "BINDING-BACK"

From what has been said in the previous chapter about the nature of man and about his pilgrimage in matter, it will be quite clear in what sense religion is for him a "binding-back." Its object and purpose is to restore to man the knowledge of what he really is. In whatever fashion we interpret the story of the "Fall of Man," the experience of descent into physical life involved for him loss of realisation of his Divine origin and birthright. The remembrance of that origin is wiped away from the tablets of his mind. The poet might equally thus have adapted his imagery of the waters of Lethe. It is worth noticing the special significance of the prefix "*re-*" in "*religare*." The *Concise Oxford Dictionary* gives a number of meanings which the prefix bears, of which the ninth is:—"Back, with return to previous state after lapse or cessation or occurrence of opposite state or action." What could be more apposite?

It is the purpose of religion to "bind us back" to God, the source of our being; to bring us back into conscious relation with our spiritual self and to open for us the resources of our own higher and spiritual consciousness. I cannot better bring home what I have been trying to say than by quoting a passage of wonderful power and beauty from a book entitled *Esoteric Christianity*, by the famous lecturer and writer, Dr. Annie Besant:

Next comes the question: In what way do religions seek to quicken human evolution? Religions seek to evolve the moral and intellectual natures, and to aid the spiritual nature to unfold itself. Regarding man as a complex being, they seek to meet him at every point of his constitution, and therefore to bring messages suitable for each, teachings adequate to the most diverse human needs. Teachings must therefore be adapted to each mind and heart to which they are addressed. If a religion does not reach and master the intelligence, if it does not purify and inspire the emotions, it has failed in its object, so far as the person addressed is concerned.

Not only does it thus direct itself to the intelligence and the emotions, but it seeks, as said, to stimulate the unfoldment of the spiritual nature. It answers to that inner impulse which exists in humanity, and which is ever pushing the race onwards. For deeply within the heart of all—often overlaid by transitory conditions, often submerged under pressing interests and anxieties—there exists a continual seeking after God. "As the hart panteth after the water-brooks, so panteth" humanity after God. The search is sometimes checked for a space, and the yearning seems to disappear. Phases recur in civilisation and in thought wherein this cry of the human Spirit for the divine—seeking its source as water seeks its level, to borrow a simile from Giordano Bruno—this yearning of the human Spirit for that which is akin to it in the universe, of the part for the whole, seems to be stilled, to have vanished; none the less does that yearning reappear, and once more the same cry rings out from the Spirit. Trampled on for a time, apparently destroyed, though the tendency may be, it rises again and again with inextinguishable persistence, it repeats itself again and again, no matter how often it is silenced ; and it thus proves itself to be an inherent tendency in human nature, an ineradicable constituent thereof. Those who declare triumphantly, "Lo! it is dead!" find it facing them again with undiminished vitality. Those who build without allowing for it find their well-constructed edifices riven as by an earthquake. Those who hold it to be outgrown find the wildest superstitions succeed its denial. So much is it an integral part of humanity, that man will have some answer to his questionings; rather an answer that is false, than none. If he cannot find religious truth, he will take religious error rather than no religion, and will accept the crudest and most incongruous ideals rather than admit that the ideal is non-existent.

Religion, then, meets this craving, and taking hold of the constituent in human nature that gives rise to it, trains it, strengthens it, purifies it and guides it towards its proper ending—the union of the human Spirit with the divine, so "that God may be all in all."[1]

THE MEANING OF REVELATION

Before we turn to consider in the next chapter the bearing of religion, in the meaning we have given to the word, upon different departments of man's work, it may be well to direct our attention to some points connected with revelation as a factor in religion.

I do not intend to discuss here the theory that religion is nothing but elaboration of primitive superstition or nature-cults. The contrary theory seems to account for the facts far better, namely, that from time to time great religious teachers have appeared in the world who, out of the fullness of their own spiritual knowledge, have given both instruction and a great impetus towards spirituality to the race. We may go even further, and say that the periodic appearance of these teachers may well be part of a scheme, on the part of Divine Providence, for the helping of the world. Instruction of this sort is so admittedly above the intellectual and spiritual level of the day that the term "revelation" is commonly applied, at any rate in the specific instance of the Old and New Testament Scriptures. An impartial judgment would see no difficulty in applying it also to the origin of great religious schemes like those of Hinduism and Buddhism. The day has passed when the other great faiths of the world are attributed even by missionaries to the Devil, and quite conservative thinkers are now willing to consider them at least as "partial revelations."

It is not our purpose here to discuss comparative religion, but rather the implications of this term "revelation." Revealed knowledge is commonly regarded as being beyond the capacity of human faculty. It is given by or through highly developed beings. It has to be accepted on faith, because it transcends the limitations of our minds. Now this is perfectly true as a general statement, and particularly in regard to the more abstract notions, such as those pertaining to the Deity. I want only to point out that the problem becomes modified somewhat if we accept the view about the nature and destiny of man outlined in our second chapter, namely, that man is a being undergoing a process of gradual perfecting. In that case the distinction between revealed and human knowledge is not one of kind, but of degree. As man unfolds and exteriorises the powers latent within him, he gains access to knowledge and phases of consciousness beyond the ken of the less developed man. Is not this the obvious explanation of the famous experience of the Apostle Paul (for it is thought generally that he is referring to himself) narrated in II *Corinthians* xii., 2, when he was "caught up to the third heaven," "whether in the body, or out of the body, I cannot tell," and "heard unspeakable words, which it is not lawful for a man to utter?"

---

[1] Pp. 3-4, Theosophical Publishing House.

People in these modern times[1] are interesting themselves a good deal in the faculty called "intuition," of which Bergson has so interestingly written. It is said that in some of the newer countries a new type of child with unusual body and head characteristics and measurements is springing up. These children are said to arrive at results less by process of slow reasoning than by direct intuition. The mistake that has been made in our generation is to regard a faculty like intuition as a divine gift, to be viewed and admired at a distance, so to speak, rather than as a quality capable of development, like every other human faculty. Intuition is just such an aspect of consciousness as I have been mentioning above, which comes into operation as man sensitises himself to spiritual things. It must be within the experience of a good many priests that they get flashes of intuitional knowledge about the persons to whom they are about to administer the Holy Communion—even when they are strangers. Reasoning on these premises, it is easy to see that "revelation" is a word of relative signification. People who are more developed are able to know for themselves at first hand some of those truths which would ordinarily be grouped within the category of revelation.

[1] 1929 [Ed.]

CHAPTER V

THE SCOPE AND AIM OF RELIGION

WE have already drawn attention to the fact that man is a complex being. He has many different sides to his nature, and through these he expresses himself and makes relationship with the world about him. Religion in its larger and truer meaning is concerned with all of these many different aspects of his being and with the various levels of consciousness at which he works.

Religion is not only an affair of devotion and religious aspiration. It is concerned with the awakening of those higher powers of consciousness which are still chiefly latent within man, with the instruction of his mind and even with the fashioning of the physical body. The perfected man who would be the finished product of religion, rightly understood, would have a physical body trained to express as adequately as possible the whole gamut of emotions, thoughts, intuition, creative energy and so forth. It is evident, therefore, that religion is concerned even with the good health of the bodily vehicle, and with fashioning it into a proper expression of the indwelling spirit.

Art is conventionally called the handmaid of religion, but art is an integral part of religion because so indispensable in the training and refining of the emotions and the widening of the outlook. The mind, too, must be a keen instrument in the pursuit of truth and available for the instruction of other people. And there are higher faculties, as we have just seen, appertaining to the synthetic use of the mind, the imagination, the intuition, the naked power of the will, which go to the equipment of the developed man. In every aspect of his being, man has to be "bound back" to the ideal state of existence which lies at the source of each of these faculties.

If we accept this larger meaning of religion, we get rather a shock when we turn to the limited views that are apt to be encountered in the ordinary church, which claims to be the organ of religion. The view that we have just been examining has something vast and noble in its sweep of thought; and it certainly is apt to produce an unwelcome contrast to this wider horizon of thought when we think of the *odium theologicum* and the rancour that are still so prevalent between those who worship the same God.

RELIGION-SECULAR AND ECCLESIASTICAL

What are we to think of the situation? Is there any solution to be offered? I think myself that the Churches have unduly narrowed down their view of the scope of religion. They are the victims of circumstance, in that many lines of activity which used to be regarded as religious and the work of the Church have in the course of time become separated off and transferred to the civil administration. Education is a case in point, and offers a good illustration of the march of events to which I refer. It was at one time the prerogative of the Church. Medicine, too, was at one time much more connected with religion than it is now. We are told that in Greece patients were taken to be healed to the temples of Aesculapius, where there were beds provided for them. So with the drama. The Church had a great deal to do with the drama in the Middle Ages. It was much concerned also with philanthrophic work and social organisation.

It does not matter much in principle whether it is the State or the Church which now administers these departments of work for the aid and upliftment of the people at large. It is still part of the scope of religion. We may assume that no one will quarrel with the existing arrangement by which these special divisions of religious work, and similar ones, are now under State administration. But there are two deductions to be drawn from this *fait accompli*. First, that the more work of this kind is transferred from the patronage of the Church, the more frankly must the remaining elements of the Church's heritage be regarded as specialised departments of religion—and not as religion in its entirety. Secondly, Church members should be encouraged to feel their responsibility for these transferred sections of work, to take a real and personal interest in them, and to be satisfied with the existing arrangement only when it is being satisfactorily and efficiently carried out. Only then can their consciences be free in the knowledge that this department of religion is being properly cared for. Let us just realise in passing that international relationship is essentially a religious question, for it is based on the principle that we are all sharers in the One Life, and that that which is harmful to one member injures the whole body.

No useful purpose would be served by going into details with regard to the work of these different departments. They have acquired a position of dependence upon the civil arm, because they belong to the comparatively-speaking more secular side of religious work. That which is left to religion is concerned more with the development of qualities of character and higher aspects of consciousness, than with the more concrete and better understood sciences, in taking care of which the State ought to have no insuperable difficulty. Hygiene, physical culture, education and art are aspects of human life for which there are plenty of experts, who are capable of looking after their development and organisation and their useful application.

The public can well appreciate the usefulness of people interesting themselves in public health, the advancement of knowledge and matters of social order, but those aspects of religion which still are attached to the ministration of the Church belong to categories of thought and experience which are less commonly understood. I propose, therefore, to devote the remainder of this book to explaining their *raison d'être* and the part that they occupy in the religious life of man.

SCHOOLS OF RELIGIOUS THOUGHT

The student of religion will find plenty of material with which to interest himself when he surveys the various Churches and denominations of Christendom, and discovers the reasons for their existence in a state of separation from one another. Some coalescense of these institutions could be effected without much difficulty if questions of principle alone were involved, but the situation is hugely complicated by questions of vested interests, of tradition and pride. Federation and even coalescence of some of the so-called Free or Nonconformist Churches have been brought about in overseas countries, and a sweeter temper in regard to this kind of thing is coming more and more to prevail.

But there are divisions between Churches which consist not simply of minor difference of usage but which turn on much deeper issues. The Roman Catholic Church, for example, considers itself alone in holding the Divine Commission of our Lord; it insists upon the recognition of the Papacy as the visible centre of unity, and upon a faith which is Divinely inspired and not therefore to be questioned by the individual. The system as such is perfectly logical, and the only question that applies to it—one of supreme significance—is whether one can bring oneself to accept it. There are other Churches, like the Eastern Orthodox, Old Catholic and Anglican, who differ from Rome on some matters of belief, and to some extent from each other, but who stand in a camp quite different from the Free or Nonconformist Churches, and from the Protestant Churches of the Continent of Europe, on the question of the nature and meaning of Holy Orders. The Church of England itself is a comprehensive body, and therefore, as recent events have shown, a quite unworkable one in regard to unity of faith and to any logical consistency on questions of discipline, of organisation, and of worship. It contains within itself representatives of a number of quite different schools of thought, ranging from one extreme to another.

It will show readers, not acquainted with the technicalities of the situation, something of its difficulty, if I tabulate roughly some of these schools of thought within the Anglican communion.

Extreme Catholic Party.—Some members of this school accept in a modified form the Papal claims, and can even conceive of conditions under which Papal Infallibility could be accepted.

Anglo-Catholic or High Church Party.—Many of these accept most of the Roman Catholic theology, and differ little, if at all, on the theology of the Sacraments.

Broad Churchmen.—These believe in avoiding extremes; they are often Liberal and even Modernist on questions of dogma. They are likely to be enthusiastic about the genius of the English race and its National Church, and are of opinion that the Church should hold together by compromise on extremes and by the satisfaction of the natural religious instincts of the majority of citizens.

Modernists.—Difficult to distinguish from Broad Churchmen, but more free in their rejection of traditional doctrines and systems, and eager for collaboration with accepted scientific and philosophical thought.

Erastians.—These hold that the Church is a department, so to speak, of the State, intensely national and subject to State regulation.

Low Churchmen.—These base their teaching on a Protestant interpretation of the Bible. Many believe in salvation by faith ("Believe on the Lord Jesus Christ and thou shalt be saved" (*Acts* xvi., 31)), and some irrespective of any recognition of the validity of good works.

I take these divisions as typical of the Anglican Communion, though the question of State control does not apply in countries like America. I need not specify the distinctive tenets of the Nonconformist bodies. Occasionally there are set Liturgies in use, but more often the interest centres round the preaching, often excellent, and there are prayers, hymns, sacred songs and Scripture readings. Dr. Parker, of the City Temple, thought that the Anglican Prayer Book was "steeped in Popery," and even nonextreme Anglican views on the Sacraments are not on the whole acceptable to Nonconformists.

UNITY IN DIVERSITY

Now a person who wants to understand the religious situation, confused and complicated as it is, and to come to an opinion about the tenets of these differing schools of thought, will do well to bear in mind one fact. And that fact is the complexity of human nature, and the enormous difference that may exist between man and man. This is a difficulty which confronts every religion at the outset. There are people of unevolved mentality and there are people of developed mentality. What is suitable by way of teaching and ideal to one group will not be at all apt for the other. We can find a parallel to this difficulty, and an attempt at its solution, if we turn to the caste system of India. It has no doubt its disadvantages and is perhaps no longer suitable in these days of easy communications and the democratisation of knowledge. Some people, in fact, argue the same of the marriage tie, which may have been all very well when people were brought up and lived in the same village all their lives. We find in India the four castes in Hinduism the *Shudra* or menial caste, the *Vaishya* or merchant caste, the *Brahmana* or religious and teaching caste, the *Kshattriya* or warrior caste. Apart from those who belong to no caste, the people are divided under these four headings. The outlook on life of these four groups is each different; their duties are not the same and what is intensely illuminating is that their ethical duties and requirements are not coincident. The ideal of the religious teacher is harmlessness to man and beast alike. Not so of the warrior. The precepts of the Sermon on the Mount would justly apply to the *Brahmana*, but nobody would dream of applying them to the merchant, who is justified in the pursuit of wealth.

I will not attempt to gainsay the fact that there are difficulties in carrying this out into practice, especially in modern times. But there is a good deal that is valuable in the principle. There is perhaps greater difficulty in carrying out the teachings of the Sermon on the Mount. The solution probably lies in some compromise. It must be remembered that the Sermon on the Mount was given not to the multitude but to the disciples, and may, therefore, quite legitimately be held as applicable to the Christian counterpart of the *Brahmana*, but not to that of the *Vaishya* or *Kshattriya*.

As in ethics so in regard to doctrine, it does not seem helpful to attempt to impose one code or standard on all alike. And one finds in actual practice that people select that presentation of religion which they imagine most to fit in with their tastes—which they easily mistake for their requirements. This is true everywhere. I have seen outside the entrance of a Hindu temple, a collection of small and scarcely recognisable iron images. These were the tutelary deities of the village and received from the general populace much more *puja* or devotion than the larger and much finer images within the temple, appertaining to the more philosophical cults. Anyone familiar with the habits of the peasantry in Roman Catholic Countries will recognise that in practice there are grades of cult in that institution. I have seen processions of Roman Catholic worship in a little native fishing-village in India where the treatment given to the images of the Saints was on all fours with that given to the Hindu deities.

When, therefore, we find variety of usage amidst the denominations of Christianity, we need not assume that this is an unmitigated evil. For in this way people at different levels of intelligence and general growth, to say nothing of difference of temperament, can find satisfaction. It would be much better, however, that this divergence should be intelligently arranged for these differing types of men and women. It is too much to hope that order may at the present time come out of this haphazard promiscuity. What is evidently needed is instruction—and much of it. That instruction must deal with the composite nature of man, so that the different aspects of his being should be explained to him, their proper use and the way of gradually improving them.

There is the additional complication that those religions which have come down from the past do in point of fact make provision for arousing and bringing gradually into activity the higher realms of man's being. The man himself naturally knows nothing of all this, and if left to his own free choice will quite likely choose some form of religion whose attractions are more obvious than they are necessarily deep.

It is true that our Blessed Lord prayed "that they may all be one." (*John* xii., 21) We do not know precisely what He meant by this or what exactly were His intentions in regard to the sheep "of other folds." There has been much earnest work done for the reunion of Christendom. It has tended to soften down asperities, but has not yet accomplished much in the way of definite results. The question of diversity of temperament is never seriously faced. Moreover, if there is one lesson that our generation has learned, it is that unity and uniformity are utterly different. There may be great unity of spirit consistent with outer diversity in the form of cult. "Live and gladly let live" is a motto, the realisation of which may involve more of real unity than some artificial measure of uniformity.

POPULAR RELIGION

It happens from time to time that there comes into prominence a clergyman who captures the allegiance of a large section of the public by the type of sermons he preaches. Such people are usually gifted with the charm of personal magnetism and have a very real feeling of sympathy for the masses or for humanity at large. They are usually large-hearted and they preach a kind of religion which, whether consciously or unconsciously on the part of the author, is calculated to attract the man-in-the-street. There were cases of padres of this sort who made their mark during and after the war. The Rev. "Dick" Sheppard, late of S. Martin's-in-the-Fields and author of *The Impatience of a Parson*, is a case in point. Such men are deservedly popular. They are by nature humanists; they have a natural love for their fellows, which is more than can be said for hundreds of stiff-backed clergymen. At the same time this freedom with people is a form of genius. There are many clergymen who have a real love for humanity in their hearts, but who nevertheless find it difficult to overcome their natural shyness, and to meet people of all kinds and classes with freedom and an absence of reserve. What attracted people at one time to S. Martin's was that the crypt was thrown open as a "doss-house" during the war, as an *asile* or refuge for wanderers and stragglers, and for soldiers on leave. We may well admit that during a great war conditions may rightly and advantageously be relaxed. An action such as this makes a moving appeal to the public, who straightway think that "the parson must be a decent fellow." So, under the circumstances, was this particular one. The same public would not so easily realise the difficulties and disadvantages of the scheme. Difficulties of dirt and cleaning, of possible misbehaviour and drunkenness around the church. Nor would they understand that a church is a building with its own appropriate functions, among which is not the housing of derelicts. A church is a place for the worship of God and for training in spiritual development. The little shoots of growth that take place in the higher nature of man may be compared to the delicate shoots of a rose-tree. They are easily damaged and repressed by adverse conditions. A church is a building set apart specially for these purposes, and it owes its atmosphere of calm and peace and devotion to the fact that it is used for worship almost exclusively, and not for secular purposes. As I have said above, one does not criticise what is done during the emergency of a war time, but a church is a church and a "doss-house" a " doss-house," and their functions were never intended to be interchangeable. But one can well imagine that some people would argue that this would be an excellent use for churches at all times.

What is not usually understood by those who set out to criticise religion and churches is that a whole science is involved, having to do with this higher spiritual development of man of which I have been speaking, and of which the public at large is mostly ignorant. Nor, indeed, can it be said that the real scope of this is often realised at all consciously by the clergy. I propose, therefore, to take up the consideration of this more specialised aspect of religion in our succeeding chapters.

CHAPTER VI

AN EXPLANATION OF CHURCH WORSHIP:

(I) *OUR RELATION TO GOD*

THERE is a very familiar passage in the Gospel of S. Luke (x., 27), in which a certain lawyer asked our Lord what he should do to inherit eternal life. And our Lord referred him to a passage in the Law which said :—"Thou shalt love the Lord thy God with all thy heart, and with all thy soul, and with all thy strength, and with all thy mind." (*Deuteronomy* vi., 5). And then the text goes on to say "And thy neighbour as thyself." (*Leviticus* xix., 18) People in many ages have found this sublime, and will, I dare say, for ages to come. But I am not sure that the youth of our day would not put the second injunction first, arguing that we at least know something about our fellow-men and little, if anything at all, about God, and that love had better begin at home, so to speak, with those we do know. In fact, if he knew his Bible (which in the case of the modern youth is improbable) he might quote from I *John* iv., 20 :—"If a man say, I love God, and hateth his brother, he is a liar: for he that loveth not his brother whom he hath seen, how can he love God whom he hath not seen?" I am going to be a little venturesome and say that S. John seems to me to miss the point here, and that there is a very real purpose in the sequence in which the earlier statement that I quoted is put.

We hear much about human brotherhood in these days. In fact, twenty-four years ago I joined a society whose first object is "To form a nucleus of the universal brotherhood of humanity, without distinction of race, creed, sex, caste or colour." I am proud still to be a member of it. One learns in this society to meet with people of many nationalities and races, oriental as well as occidental, of different interests and temperament, and of many different levels of culture and learning. It is not so easy to love all our brothers as some people in the pursuit of their theories demand. We find in many of them things that are repugnant and that arouse antagonism within us; and the more we are able to see and understand of life, the greater do we find the differences and inequalities between man and man. People of similar tastes and interests tend to group themselves together and to become more cordial to each other than to less interesting people. This is quite natural, and it has been pointed out that Jesus had His John, and Buddha His Ananda.

But Christianity insists on this sense of brotherhood—the modern name for neighbourliness. So do other religions—in fact, the verse quoted above is Jewish. "Hatred ceases not by hatred at any time, but hatred ceases only by love." (*Dharmpada*, 37) is a saying attributed to Gautama, the Buddha. Hinduism also is rich in this conception. Here are some inspiring quotations:

Knowing the Supreme to be in all beings, the wise extend love to all creatures undeviatingly. (*Vishnu Purana*, I., xix., 9.)

He who seeth the Self in all beings, by his own Self, he realises the equality of all, and attaineth to the Supreme state of Brahman. (*Manusmriti*, XII., 125.)

He who seeth all beings in the Self and the Self in all beings, he hateth no more. (*Isha Upanishat*, 6.)

How are we to realise this brotherhood? If we ask what it is in other people that antagonises us, we find that it is invariably something that we recognise as a fault. There is a view of man which sees him as a divine spirit inhabiting an animal body—a body, that is to say, evolved from that of the animal. We understand that certain instincts and qualities adhere to such a body and express themselves through it. There are brute instincts in practically everybody. We are not asked to feel brotherly towards the animal propensities. The basis on which we find and found our fellowship with one another is that of the Divine Life in which we all share. In so far as that is realised by us and is expressed through us, we are able to recognise its expression through others. It is this recognition of the Divine Life which is the basis of our sense of brotherhood. Hence in the attempt to live the brotherhood of man we look for that which is highest and best in our brothers. That we can appreciate. For the time being we pay as little attention as possible to the animal form and its traits of character. When we are sufficiently firmly rooted in a realisation of the Divine Life in ourselves and are thus able to see it clearly in others, we can afford to be tolerant of their weaknesses and are no longer antagonised by them. We simply note that people stand at various stages of development, and that faults that we perceive in others to-day were exhibited by us in the past. We love our fellow-men in so far as we are able to find and to answer to the Divine Life in them. It was therefore with very good reason that the old precept of the Law told us first to learn to know and love God. For, that once accomplished, it becomes less difficult to "love our neighbour as ourselves."

WORSHIP AND ITS PURPOSE

In all countries people are losing the habit of going to church. Where the older generation was brought up to the habit of attending church on Sundays at any rate, numbers of the younger generation never, or only on the rarest occasions, go to church. The reason for this is many-sided. It is partly that people have grown to disbelieve the more old-fashioned presentations of religion. It is partly due to the spread of pleasure and of facilities for getting enjoyment—all this is linked up with the growth of cheap and rapid transport. It is partly due to the greater pressure of business life and the need felt for relaxation. It is partly due to the spread of humanitarian ideas, and the ethical satisfaction gained by many people in work for these rather than in the more technical area of religion.

In regard to all this, it is difficult to forecast the future. It may be that people will come increasingly to feel the need of religion and of worship, that they will more and more look for a theory of things adequate to explain life and the world in which they find themselves. Or it may be that technical religion will appeal to a select few, who by deeper instruction and greater earnestness may be able to replace in terms of quality what has to be sacrificed in terms of quantity. It is useless to prophesy: let us "wait and see."

I feel very strongly that a new *apologia* has to be framed for the kind of worship that is rendered in church. I have myself come as the result of logic and deliberate reason to see the huge importance of church worship. One may doubt whether the masses, as they grow progressively emancipated, will see this need; but I am convinced that good reasons can be laid before those who are prepared to accept a spiritual philosophy of life and to work for the good of their fellows.

If one puts the question, What is the use of going to church? the answer that can be given is threefold:—

1. It is the duty and privilege of man to worship God.
2. It is for man an exercise in spiritual training and development.
3. It is an act of service to the world in which we live.

THE WORSHIP OF GOD

It was of set purpose that this chapter opened with a little disquisition on the relation between the love of God and of one's neighbour. The age of reactionary religion, that has been left behind by our generation, was one which talked much about God and which often tended to separate Him off completely from man, except for odd notions of covenants and mercies. This generation concerns itself much more with human relationships and with the service of one's fellows, and so tends to give to the ideal of humanity that importance which our forefathers gave to God. Both tendencies are exaggerated. I know of no better approach towards God than along the lines that have been indicated at the beginning of this chapter. It gives us a reason for learning to know God, and because of that inspires us in a way that the dogmatism of our fathers fails completely to do.

Many people in these days will frankly confess that they know nothing of God. And it is often because the language of church services refers so constantly to God, and that the singing of psalms and so forth is felt to be unnatural, that they drop away from church attendance. They cannot put much meaning into the formularies that are commonly used. I suppose we may take it for granted that the first contact that we establish with God is likely to be an intellectual one. I am leaving out of count, of course, the traditions and memories of one's childhood days, which are strong in a good many people and were, indeed, intended to be formed strong by those whose tender solicitude implanted them. I do not attempt in these few pages to prove or argue at all fully any of the ideas that I am bringing before readers. Those ideas can be studied in detail elsewhere, and I am wishing rather to suggest a line of linking these ideas. I will not attempt, therefore, to state the case for the existence of God. I do care personally for the exercise of the mind. And its exercises tells me that there are many problems in life about which we can arrive at no certain solution for ourselves in the present undeveloped stage of our faculties. I find very reasonable on many points the claim that teachings on the higher things have been given to the world sufficient for our understanding by the great teachers of religions, and I find much in the idea of revelation in Christianity. Within the orbit of such ideas it is not difficult to frame for oneself what one conceives to be a general but intelligent conception of the nature and being of God. Any open-minded man who looks out on the world around him and who studies the course of events in life, must, it seems to me, be convinced of the existence of some plan which has shaped the universe and which guides and directs our lives. Hence I have no difficulty in believing in God. The marvels of science and of nature are sufficient to render that inescapable.

I have already in Chapter II given utterance to the belief that the universe owes its existence to the Divine Life. Religion speaks of God as being above His universe—or, in a word, "transcendent"—and also as putting down His Life into the universe—"immanent." There is a wonderful symbolism worked out in the *Apocalypse* or *Book of Revelations*, which speaks of this outpouring of the Divine Life from the Second Person of the Trinity as from "the Lamb slain from the foundation of the world." (xiii., 8) It is on this primal sacrifice that the whole conception of sacrifice in religion is based. The highest sacrifice that man can make (especially in conjunction with the Sacrament given to him by our Lord) is the sacrifice of "ourselves, our souls and bodies." And so in the course of the Holy Eucharist we are admonished in the words of the ancient liturgy to lift up our hearts, and to give thanks unto our Lord God. And we respond that to do this "is very meet, right and our bounden duty." It is the God within us reaching out towards union with the God without, a union which at our stage is capable of realisation in some measure, but will never be completely realised until we have achieved the purpose of our appearance on earth.

We need not pursue this idea further here. The validity of what I have been saying is not demonstrable by further argument; it is demonstrable only from that experience which has to my knowledge in many cases crowned an earnest and persistent effort. In studying the liturgies of the traditional Churches there is a distinction to be noticed, say in the Eucharistic rite, between that praise and prayer addressed generally to Almighty God and referring from time to time to Persons of the Trinity, and that addressed to Christ through the Blessed Sacrament. Each brings a different response and I want at the moment only to touch on the former. There are sensitive people who feel a mysterious influence in a church. The downpouring of Divine Grace is traditionally symbolised by the dew or the rain. There are sensitively-framed people who, in response to whole-hearted praise or prayer to God—worship which is devoid of selfish motives and self-interest—can apprehend some downpouring of power, which they come eventually to identify with the answer on the part of God to any unselfish act of praise or adoration.

Let me say in leaving this aspect of our subject, that while people may argue that God has no need of our praise, or that our wishes in regard to prayer are already known to Him, the question of this does not arise. The question is rather one of our own conviction. Worship means the giving of "worth-ship" to God. We feel and know that it is right and meet for us to lift up our hearts in praise and adoration to God, and to strive to unify ourselves more completely with the Divine Will. To do this gives the greatest satisfaction to our natures, and is found to be the most productive means that we have for drawing nearer to Him. Further, in proportion as we awaken to appreciation of the greatness and splendour of the Divine Majesty, so are we unfolding the godlike qualities in ourselves and fulfilling the purpose for which we were created. And, secondly, there is also the question whether God does not make use of our co-operation with Him and even count on that co-operation more and more as man grows into spiritual maturity

CHAPTER VII

AN EXPLANATION OF CHURCH WORSHIP:

(2) *ITS VALUE TO THE WORSHIPPER*

IN the last chapter we outlined three points of view from which it is possible to approach the study of church worship, and we dealt at once with that aspect which has to do with man's attitude to God. The second point of view concerns man and his own training and development. We shall understand better the special position occupied by the Church in this respect, if we first glance at some general principles underlying the acquisition of knowledge on the part of man.

KNOWLEDGE THROUGH EXPERIENCE

In the first two chapters of this book we studied the theory according to which man's contacts with the experiences of life awaken the powers latent in him. We saw this growth taking place at two stages—unconsciously and consciously. As soon as a man understands the scheme in which he is taking part, he can use his intelligence and newly-awakened independence to seek out for himself experiences that he thinks may be profitable for him.

Now there are two ways in which a man can learn a lesson. He can learn it by direct practical experience. He puts his finger in the fire, for example, and discovers that fire burns. Or he can learn it by theoretical study, on the authority of others. In this case, he is warned that fire burns. He can verify this either by putting his finger in the fire as in our case just mentioned, or by approaching his finger gradually near the fire till the heat becomes insupportable. In the latter case, of course, he does not get the complete sensation of burning. It is doubtful whether lessons are learned to any great extent exclusively on a theoretical basis. A man usually resorts to some minimum of practical experience in addition, but the theoretical instruction reduces the amount of this that is necessitated. There is a subtle thought involved in the statement that education helps man to anticipate experience. It gives him the advantage of the collective experience of mankind, and thus enables him better to understand the whole experience in its true context. And if he does get practical direct experience for himself, he is able to appreciate its significance more fully, that is to say, more of the whole content of the experience.

Belonging to what may be called "higher factors" in education are science, art, religion and travel. Science, useful as it is in many ways, has one special value in regard to the point we have under consideration. By bringing people into touch with the infinitely great and the infinitely little in nature, it can work enormously to stretch the horizons of the student's mind. Art provides a rich and concentrated environment of beauty, the creation of human genius. Religion provides a rich and concentrated environment of spirituality, calling out the highest instincts in man. Travel brings contact with phases of life and of nature not found over a smaller area in the same abundance and diversity. I do not want to digress further on this subject, but just to point out that a church service is of extreme value in that it provides an environment of religious influences which it would be difficult to find for purposes of reaction elsewhere and otherwise.

MAN AND HIS SPIRITUAL TRAINING

Let us now study this process of man's development more in detail. We have already pointed out that man is by no means a simple creature, and that progress for him means attention to many different sides of his nature. All work of this sort is usually divided into two categories. One has to do with the refinement and getting under control of his existing powers, and the other with the development of new powers or of higher phases of those already in expression. It is convenient to begin with work upon three sections of his being—(i) the physical body, to which is related especially action; (ii) the emotions and passions; (iii) the mind. The kind of discipline or training into which man puts himself for this work implies in the first place a certain general attitude towards life, and secondly some special exercises with a definite end in view. The general attitude is one to which we have already given our attention, namely, to be always on the look-out for and to profit by whatever experiences the daily round may bring. There come occasions when we can put our ideals into practice. We are apt to get over-strained and irritated by constant interviews or interruptions in our work, for example, and have in such an event an opportunity for practising patience and for learning to put aside our own regrets and complaints, thinking rather of the interests of the other people concerned. This attitude can be summed up in the simple phrase that our life should be purposeful.

As I have already pointed out in Chapter II, there is one secret the understanding of which transforms life. We grow up used to fending for ourselves. At the earlier stages of evolution this is necessary. It is obviously unavoidable in the position of the savage. It belongs also to a great extent to the life of commerce. But it is an anachronism so far as the spiritual life is concerned, and those activities of the daily life in which it is possible for us to act as aspirants towards spirituality. We understand at this later stage that we are not in the world simply to get pleasurable sensations for ourselves. And we learn to view our physical body, for example, not from the standpoint of ministering to our own pleasure, but as a vehicle of kindliness, strength, and so forth towards others. It has to be a channel of beneficent influence. Similarly do we learn to deal with our emotions and thoughts. We realise that they are not intended merely to minister to our own self-satisfaction, but to be instruments of helpfulness to others. In short, we learn to be self-disinterested in the three sections of our being that I mentioned—the physical body, the emotions and the thoughts.

All this relates to the general attitude towards life of which I spoke. What about the special exercises? These can be of various kinds. One point of great importance is freedom of self-expression in regard to the body. Many people are stiff and awkward in their bodily movements and gestures. Physical culture, especially of the type spoken of as eurythmics, is exceedingly valuable in helping to make the body a flexible instrument and a ready channel for noble and beautiful influences. Opinions may differ on the subject of social intercourse. There are people who think we chatter too much, and I have heard the suggestion that before saying anything we should habituate ourselves to discriminating whether it is (i) true, (ii) kind, and (iii) necessary. This is a practice which has its great utility, but in my own opinion in its appropriate place. I am afraid that house-parties would be dull under such circumstances. Small conversation is a great art, and carries with it the power of putting strangers at their ease and making them feel at home.

When we pass to consider the training of the emotions and of the mind, we are struck by one curious fact. The system of normal education hitherto prevalent has addressed itself almost exclusively to the mind and practically ignored the emotions. As a consequence, people when they reach adolescence are often quite "at sea" in regard to the control and useful expression of their emotional impulses. For the refinement and uplifting of the emotions, art and religion are the two sovereign influences. Art is still envisaged as a luxury and as reserved for the few. Our modern towns have been allowed to amass themselves, utilitarian and economic considerations mainly regulating their construction. People do not realise that the money they save by ignoring the claims of beauty, they soon lose in consequence of the atmosphere they encourage and bequeath. A generation born and bred amongst ugliness and industrial strain grows up with savage instincts, and social antagonism, strikes and class war are the natural outcome of this policy of ostracism in regard to beauty. Much that is similar might be said in regard to religion, and the fault has been largely on the side of institutional religion.

MEDITATION

There is one other exercise in spiritual training to which attention may be drawn, before we pass on to the real subject of this chapter. I mean meditation. Meditation can quite well be included in the category of church worship. I myself take a meditation class weekly in my church. But we lead busy lives in these days and there is not much time for going to church. So the churches chiefly concern themselves with public worship, and these other activities of the larger sphere of religion remain in the category of those that are little, if at all, concerned with the specialised area of church work. Moreover, meditation may be practised collectively, but it should be done also quietly in the sanctuary of one's own heart.

Meditation is based on the idea that thought is a creative power. "As he thinketh in his heart, so is he." (*Proverbs* xxiii., 7) And an Indian Scripture puts the case with extraordinary wisdom "Man verily is desire-formed ; as is his desire, so is his thought ; as his thought is, so he does action ; as he does action, so he attains. So indeed the desirer goes by work to the object in which his mind is immersed." (*Brhadaranyaka Upanishat*, IV—iv, 5-6). By taking qualities of character in meditation it is possible to build them into our character. Let us say, for example, that a man lacks courage. He would take this as his subject for meditation day by day. He would begin by defining courage to himself, by examining it in its different aspects and in its bearing on his life. He would picture himself in surroundings which required the display of courage and himself as acting courageously. Presently, such an opportunity might present itself in real life, and courage would at once come to his mind, as he would have made it a habit of thought and built up, as it were, a line of least resistance. The difficulty with most of us is that in an emergency we do not think to act in time. It requires only a little application of will to put into practice an idea already strongly in the mind. Moreover, the constant reflection upon courage, and the accustoming of oneself to its contemplation, breaks down complexes that may exist in the character and which tend to impede the expression of a particular quality. One has to be careful, of course, not to allow feelings of gratulation and self-conceit to creep into exercises of this sort. But it is easy to avoid this, if one's attitude is high and one of idealistic aspiration.

ARCHETYPAL IDEAS

There is a school of philosophy which holds that "thoughts are things," or, to put it more philosophically, that the world came into existence as the result of the creative thought of the Logos. It is held that there is a world of Archetypal Ideas, and that all manifestations in the lower worlds of phenomena are the outcome or expression of these Archetypal Ideas. In meditation the mind seeks to find union with these great centres of life and creative energy, and, in concentrating steadily on ideals, the mind may receive great illumination and a realisation of some supreme spiritual power. Hence we come to the view that, apart from practical considerations of the moment, it is more important, as far as the future is concerned, what a man thinks than what he does. His actions are the product of his past thoughts; his thoughts are the creators of his future actions. Meditation, therefore, helps us in the first place to control and to refine our nature. It enables us to build new qualities into the character, and in its more advanced practice to unfold in the higher nature, and bring down gradually into expression through the physical body, higher phases of consciousness. A faculty like intuition can be awakened and cultivated through meditation.

THE CHURCH'S SPECIAL CONTRIBUTION

Readers may have been thinking that all that I have just been saying is irrelevant to the subject of this chapter, which is the influence of church worship on men's spiritual development. In reality, it is not possible to understand the action of worship upon its devotees without this preliminary *exposé* of thought.

Let us first see what special advantages and aid the church system has to offer us. Up to the present I have contrived to avoid what are sometimes called sectarian issues and to speak of the churches in a collective sense. Of course, one has one's own point of view in regard to what the church is intended to be and to do. I am personally a devout and convinced believer in the Sacraments, and see certain great advantages in what is called liturgical worship. These beliefs do not make me exclusive or unsympathetic in regard to other churches. I am prepared to admit that Nonconformist churches can do a great deal more with some people than I could ever hope to do. Nonconformist friends of mine have agreed that the Salvation Army does much for people that they cannot reach. I have my own views of an ideal church which would grade her services according to the temperaments of the worshippers. Some of what I shall have to say will not apply to churches which do not use the methods that will be considered, but much of it will apply to most churches, and readers can extract as much or as little from my remarks as they feel disposed to accept.

I take it that the object of church worship is to "bind back" (Lat. = *religare*) man to God, and to his spiritual nature which represents what is godlike in himself. The church services are designed to this end, and we have already spoken of the instinct natural to man to give praise and to lift himself up to God. There is a point of practical significance which comes up for our attention at the outset of this enquiry. We have to realise that this effort in the direction of religion is in marked contrast to the attitude of the average man throughout the day, and I suppose it is not impolite to say that many of my readers will naturally have to group themselves into this class. The daily life is much occupied with material pursuits, cares, and pleasures, and this occupation carries man's attention and thoughts in certain directions. These may be innocent enough in themselves, but they do not usually flow in the direction in which flow thoughts of religion. If we do not make rapid progress in the spiritual life, we have here at least one common sense reason.

It is difficult for a man to keep his thoughts concentrated on religious topics for any length of time. His thought is working at an unaccustomed level of his nature, and the man finds it hard work and experiences often a natural reluctance to keep on at it for a sustained period. This brings me incidentally to an explanation in regard to meditation. I have spoken above of a natural trend of our activities during the day towards worldly interests. In the same way, our activities are habitually outward-turned. Meditation reverses this process and carries our thoughts inward. The scheme is to render oneself oblivious of all outer happenings, and to use the consciousness turned in upon ourselves. We find it difficult to continue this for more than quite a short time. Indeed it is dangerous to do so, for we may easily overstrain the brain, and lesions of the brain may be produced without warning. In the early stages, serious concentration is usually limited by teachers of the science to a quarter of an hour. What is even more serious in the way of difficulty is the deliberate withdrawal from all outer stimuli. If a great friend suddenly comes into one's presence, feelings of friendship and love rush out spontaneously to him. But if we take our friend in the solitude of meditation and try to send him love, the process is vastly less successful; it is often cold and intellectual—the reason being that we are used to working in obedience and response to external stimuli and not to originating activities of consciousness within ourselves. All this is a matter of practice. I have been working for some time with a congregation at meditation and similar exercises, and have a group of people who have learned to turn on the tap, if I may use a homely illustration, of a certain number of fundamental virtues at will. And let me add that there is a vast difference between thinking and meditating about love and *becoming* love at a moment's notice.

But to return to our original point. The church service demands an attitude of mind that is still to a large extent outward-turned and yet which draws plentifully on the spiritual resources of one's inner nature. And the fact that the work is not a solitary one, but is done in common, and that the worshipper is in an environment suggestive of religion, enables him to keep his attention concentrated on the work in hand for much longer periods of time than would be possible under other conditions. I can conceive of a person becoming similarly absorbed in a book about religion. We may regard the case as parallel in some respects, only in the service he is working with far greater intensity than is the reader. If we think of the duration of a Church service, which may be anything from half-an-hour to two hours under normal conditions, we realise that it must be of immense value to the worshipper to have his thoughts and emotions raised to the high level that is attained for so continuous a period.

THE USE OF A LITURGY

Among the various points at issue between the Nonconformist churches and those of the older tradition is the question whether the services shall include a certain proportion of extempore prayer and praise of God or be conducted according to a fixed liturgy. There are arguments of some validity on both sides of the question. There is certainly something to be said for spontaneity in worship, and, on the other hand, there is much in favour of the objection that the standard of such extempore utterance is apt to fall rather low except in the case of a few real masters of thought and speech. Such objectors prefer the stately and ringing language of experts, hallowed by centuries of constant usage. The English tradition has been singularly fortunate in that its Bible and Prayer-Book represent the finest period of the English tongue and bear the stamp of extraordinary genius. In fact, there is some truth in the remark that the English translations of some of the *Psalms*, and especially of the *Apocalypse* or *Book of Revelation* often read better than the original.

FORM AND LIFE

In examining the arguments for and against liturgical worship there are certain considerations that should not be overlooked, and which we have already to some extent considered. Liturgical worship is one part only of the whole content of religion and a part that still belongs to the ministrations of the church. If the church looked after the whole content of religion there would be other religious exercises that were less formal and more flexible or spontaneous. The liturgical form is specially useful for the particular work that the service has to do. It is easy to talk about disembarrassing ourselves of forms and so obtaining freedom, but talk of this kind is usually rather light-headed and only relative. We cannot get away from form so long as we live in a universe of manifestation. In manifestation itself duality is implied—God and the universe into which He manifests, spirit and matter, life and form. No life can be expressed apart from a form. So long as we inhabit physical bodies or other bodies we must use forms. We cannot escape from forms, but ought to see that the forms we use are made adequate to express the life. A liturgy, as we shall further see in the next chapter, uses a special form for a special purpose. The way to overcome prejudice or dislike towards it is so to familiarise oneself with the form that one can devote one's attention to making it a channel of life. It will not then be found difficult to reconcile oneself to its use.

LANGUAGE AND SELF-EXPRESSION

Apart altogether from questions of literary merit, there is another view of the liturgical question which is not widely recognised, but opens up a vista of great significance. A liturgy is not merely a form of prayer or praise, but it has the marks also of a form of meditation. Two possibilities lie before the man who is called upon frequently to use a liturgy. Either the words will grow formal to him and come to be repeated in a mechanical fashion, or the mentality will delve beneath the phrases of stately language and live in a world of thought and sentiment beautiful and holy in the extreme. Let us for a moment examine the significance of language. There are still nomadic peoples in the world who trade with one another in produce and kind for a livelihood. The world at large has adopted another system of barter, and uses coins or counters of metal and paper vouchers. These represent a certain value for the purchase of natural produce or for the remuneration of human labour. Words, in a similar way, are a kind of currency by means of which we exchange thought with one another. We are not yet at the stage when we can communicate directly from mind to mind by process of telepathy. We have to "step down" our thoughts into language, vocal inflexion, change of facial expression and gesture, and so hold communication with one another. A word, therefore, is a symbol of thought. It is related to a thought or an emotion, which is to be regarded as its ensouling life. People can use language quite casually and express through it very little of this substratum or "substance" of life. On the other hand, words can be made the vehicle of strong and rich emotion and thought. We can go further still in our ideas, and take our minds back to those Archetypal Ideas of which we spoke earlier in this chapter. If a man's consciousness be sufficiently developed and attuned to these Archetypes, language may be so wielded as to release a great downflow of spiritual power. It is in this attitude that we should approach a liturgy. The words themselves, if properly chosen, are "Words of Power;" they unlock the entry to this universal reservoir of power. Moreover, behind such a liturgy in many cases is the accumulated devotion of centuries. As the leading key-ideas are brought before a congregation, the collective thought of the people can work wonders, and a liturgy becomes a marvellous instrument of self-expression.

MODERN REQUIREMENTS

These reflections lead us on to another. A liturgy has to be carefully compiled by people who know to a reasonable extent what they are doing. The liturgy of the church in which I am privileged to work has been carefully revised, so as to exclude a number of features that we feel to be defective in the older liturgies and to present difficulty to sincerely-minded modern worshippers. We have cut out petitions for temporal benefits, and all passages which indicate fear of God, of His wrath and of everlasting hell; all expressions of servile and cringing and exaggerated self-abasement, appeals for mercy, imprecations of the heathen and cursings, and the naïve attempts that one sometimes finds to bargain with the Almighty. The evil of all this is patent to anyone who pauses to look at it. One may take two illustrations from the Roman Mass as typical of this objectionable element in the older liturgies:

We therefore beseech Thee, O Lord, to be appeased, and to receive this offering...; grant that we may be rescued from eternal damnation.

Hear us, O God of our salvation, and deliver Thy people from the terrors of divine anger, and make them secure by the bountifulness of Thy mercy.

It ought to be impossible for thinking people of our generation to have to repeat this crude anthropomorphism. Such elements are disfiguring to a liturgy, and derogatory alike to the idea of a loving Father and to the men whom He has created in His own image. In place of all this it is possible to insert passages of joyous aspiration, and we thus eliminate any element of darkness and malignancy from the worship of our Divine Father. It is difficult, of course, for the older churches to adjust themselves to the reasonable demands of progress for fear of discarding points of value. But such changes as I have been indicating are inevitable.

Enough has been said to show that the church has much of instruction to offer to its members, and much of help in their spiritual development to give to them in its services. If I have not dealt with the Blessed Sacrament of Christ's Love, nor with various other features of worship, it is because these matters come up more conveniently for consideration in the subsequent chapters of this book.

CHAPTER VIII

AN EXPLANATION OF CHURCH WORSHIP:

(3) ITS INFLUENCE ON THE SURROUNDING WORLD

IN this chapter it is proposed to study a view of church worship quite unfamiliar except to a body of students holding certain special ideas. It is the third aspect of worship that we have mentioned, in which it is seen as an act of service for the world in which we live.

CONGREGATIONAL WORSHIP

I want to begin by discussing the principles which underlie the old custom of congregational or collective worship, and may mention in passing that much that will be said in this chapter may be regarded as a continuation of the subject dealt with in the last, namely, the opportunities that worship offers for the training of the individual. For, after all, the congregation consists of a number of individuals working together in a corporate capacity.

Christianity is essentially a religion of fellowship. It took over the idea of corporate worship from the Jewish usages, and from the beginning it practised it. Except for gatherings at great festivals, Hinduism and Buddhism have nothing in common with this, and neither Hinduism, Buddhism nor Islam have the same corporate singing and liturgical worship. Moreover, Christianity is a sacramental religion, and the principle underlying not only the rite of Holy Communion, but prototypes of it which existed in earlier mystery-cults in the shape of sacramental meals, is that of uniting the fellow-devotees together in the bonds of brotherly love and common aspiration. This may be called the spiritual basis of such collective work. Humanity is one great brotherhood, depending on the fact that we are all sharers of the one Divine Life. That brotherhood exists as a reality in the world of pure Spirit, it does not have to be created there. It has to be brought down into realisation in the lower worlds of being, and this process is gradually being achieved as man rises to the height of his spiritual heritage.

There is another point of view which gives us to see a great plan underlying congregational worship. An old motto tells us that "In union is strength." People have a perfect right to make what use they like of their individual freedom. Of course, if they choose to live in inhabited territory in the community of their fellows, they subject themselves to certain general regulations which are not on the whole burdensome or tyrannical. But this measure of sacrifice they make of their own free will and accord in order to reap the benefits of civilisation. It occurs sometimes to a man to take up a piece of work which he is unable to do by himself, and he enlists the aid of his neighbour. If the object is to their mutual benefit, they willingly co-operate together, without any complaint as to the sacrifice of their personal freedom. It is sometimes necessary that this co-operation shall be close and perfect. A crew of oarsmen, for example, have to work together as though inspired by a single will. Among sailors there are some traditional songs called "chaunties," which they sing while weighing anchor. They serve to increase the jollity and sense of fellowship amongst the men, they divert the men's thought from the severity of the labour, and the rhythm of the music set the time, so to speak, at which they would pull at the rope or chain together.

Exactly the same principle underlies congregational worship. The people working in collaboration together do so of their own free will and accord and produce a cumulative result which is much more powerful than would be the haphazard contribution of the same number of people each following his own temperamental bent.

I have emphasised this voluntary basis of co-operative work, because there exists in these days a curious tendency to rebel at this form of worship. People cry out for the spontaneity of religious self-expression, or they grow romantic about the beauties of contact with nature. The point really is that these are all different sorts of worship. Each has its own great value and it is only shortsightedness to set up one as antagonistic to the other. They should be mutually complementary, and they work upon different sides of the human character and accomplish different ends. Christianity allows plenty of freedom for communion with nature as well as for private prayers and devotions whether in the home or in the church. The want of vision arises from the state of confusion that we have noted in a previous chapter, which has led so much that is essentially religious to become separated off from the oversight of the church, and that which remains to be carelessly regarded as the whole content of religion. The churches are themselves partly to blame for any diminishing interest in their services. Many people find difficulties in repeating from a liturgy sentiments that they have outgrown—but we have already discussed this. But there would be less of this critical and shallow talk about the services of the church, if people were taught what those services really accomplish and how tremendous an influence they can have on the world. It is to this subject that we will now address ourselves.

ANOTHER IDEA OF WORSHIP

The theory of worship that I am now going to offer for consideration presupposes certain views in regard to man, to the origin of religion and to the objective power of human thought, emotion and other activities of consciousness. We have already dealt with the make-up or constitution of man. He is to be seen as a spiritual intelligence inhabiting a physical body. Between these two extremities of his being, so to speak, is a certain intermediate section of his being, which we sometimes call the soul. We need to understand that he has a number of different aspects of consciousness, such as will, intuition, creative thought, concrete thought, emotion. These are thought of as manifesting at different levels of his being and as expressing themselves in intervening worlds or spheres or planes of being. It is unnecessary for our purposes to enter into this question of man's psychology at any length, only we have to understand clearly that religion is intended to minister to man in his entirety and at all levels of his nature.

The next point to be grasped is that a liturgy invented by ordinary human beings and written from the standpoint of this world in which we live is likely to be deficient in providing for action upon the higher reaches of man's being. There is a striking similarity in the Eucharistic rites that have descended to us from the distant past, and it is thought that probably our Lord Himself indicated certain central points in the ritual, the intervening portions to be filled in at the discretion of His followers. It is thought that some of these extemporised the ritual in much of what they said. Students of this higher psychology of man can only point to the fact that the sequence of action and thought in the Eucharist gives evidence of a definite scheme lying behind that service, built upon great understanding of what is required.

Thirdly, we have to accustom ourselves to the idea that the various aspects of man's consciousness, as they are brought into play, produce results not only in a subjective sense within the man himself, but produce radiations of force which can act upon other people, that is to say, those radiations can influence and affect other people in an objective fashion.

It is difficult to formulate these ideas without some complication of language. But we can put one illustration of what I mean into language that is quite clear. When a man uses thought, what takes place is not only a subjective impression within himself but there passes also from him a wave of thought power which will impinge upon other people in the area of its activity, at the thought level, and will tend to awaken and to set going similar thoughts in those people. Naturally, at the ordinary level of human thought, this is often likely to be one thought only amongst a thousand other jostling thoughts. But people can train themselves in the control and use of thought, and can learn to send out thoughts which not only are very powerful but, being noble and elevated in their character, operate at a higher level than that touched by the thought of ordinary people.

It is difficult to hold the mean between over-credulity and over-conservatism of temperament. The public in general is a little conservative about new ideas. Sometimes it is justified, sometimes it is made to look foolish. I think I am not exaggerating when I say that most thinking people would in these days be willing to accept the possibility of telepathy or thought-transference. It has been vouched for by many great scientific men, of whom Sir Oliver Lodge is one. And so many people have themselves experienced or known of flashes of telepathy in the intercourse of ordinary life. The view that I have been submitting is mainly covered by the theory of telepathy.

A SERVICE TO THE WORLD

This view of what is taking place makes bold to say, then, that worship is something which does not concern the individual alone. It is not entirely a question of giving "worth-ship" to God, or of deriving strength, encouragement, love and illumination for oneself. It is also a matter of working for the outside world, and, let me add, of working very hard, if one really understands what a prodigious work one is enabled and entitled to do.

We could use no better word than "service." A church service is a "service" rendered to the world in which we live, and it is equally a "service" rendered to God because we are privileged in being able in that way to co-operate with Him, and to take our share in His great work of pouring out strength and blessing upon the world.

I have spoken of telepathy in order to justify to readers, to whom ideas of this sort may be new, that which is a matter of wonderful experience and knowledge to myself and to a number of my colleagues and co-workers in our various congregations. Let us enquire a little more closely into what kind of influence actually is sent out. Telepathy is usually translated as "thought-transference." Actually the word is derived from the Greek "*tele*" = afar, "*pathos*" = feeling. On this principle it ought to mean rather transference of feeling. The *Concise Oxford Dictionary* defines it as the "action of one mind on another at a distance through emotional influence without communication through senses." (The word "emotional" may conceivably be used here in its etymological sense of "*e*" = out or forth, "*movere*" = to move). Another dictionary says: "The occult communication of facts, feelings or impressions between persons at a distance from each other." When one comes to examine the various elements that figure in a service, we find that the whole gamut of human faculty is really at work. As I have already pointed out, the Liturgy is "the plan of the work." It suggests a number of key-ideas to the people, and it is through these that they express themselves according to the possibilities of their temperament. There are intellectual conceptions, there is a great variety of emotion. Underlying everything should be a sense of devotion and aspiration, a glad joyousness and the deepest reverence before Almighty God. Between the members of the congregation there should exist a real feeling of brotherly affection. Moreover, the musical accompaniment and embellishment of the service, the influence of the architecture and decoration of the church, should combine to awaken the sense of beauty and artistic appreciation within ourselves. And underlying all is a deep resolve to attain that which is destined for us and to persevere amid the storms and tumult of our earthly life, which calls out the sovereign power of the will. This is a rough *résumé* of some of the chief influences that will be poured out upon the world by a congregation in church.

THE NEED FOR REALITY IN WORSHIP

I have in the last chapter stressed the fact that this output on the part of the individual worshipper represents an expression of faculty at a much higher level than that at which ordinary worldly affairs are affecting the world. And for this reason what is done is really powerful and useful. It is, in fact, on this principle that good is bound eventually to triumph over evil, for an amount of energy working through good thought produces a far greater effect than the same amount working through lower thought, which can express itself only in grosser and more inert matter. If we examine the thinking of the ordinary man of the world on spiritual matters, and indeed on most matters, it does not go very deep; in fact, it is apt to be vague and not at all clearly-defined. I am reminded of a delightful story told of the Governor of one of the smaller American States. He was somewhat addicted to the use of bad language, and the local preacher thought it his duty one day to reprove the Governor openly from the pulpit on account of the scandal caused by his language. On hearing of it, the Governor only smiled and remarked : "Oh, never mind, I swear a little, and Mr. Jones, he prays a little, but we neither of us mean much by it!" I am afraid that that applies to many, many churches. People listen idly, indifferently, or with vague and faint emotion, to the prayers, but only rarely is there anything approaching real spiritual activity based on understanding. I am perhaps too exuberant about the possibilities of a church service. In many churches, unfortunately, the type of thinking is much like that of the ordinary man who does not go to church. Still, it does work at a higher level, and has that much (and it is a good deal) to its advantage. Personally, I am used to working with a highly-trained congregation—not of any special intellectuality, but who have seen the possibilities of this work and are afire to do justice to it. And I can see that if church-goers could be awakened to think with definiteness, and to give free scope to their love and devotion, a church would become a veritable centre of help and blessing to the neighbourhood in which it is placed.

THE ANGELS

Thus far I have been taking into account only the contribution of the worshippers, the human participants in the service. And what they can do is by no means to be despised. If one were to ask the ordinary more or less orthodox Christian if he believes in angels, it is probable that he would answer in the affirmative but without any great display of enthusiasm. Our conception of the "worlds invisible" may well include the idea of these gracious ministrants, swift and active in carrying out the Divine Will or watching patiently over tasks that take a life-time or even centuries to bring to fruition. There is one delightful side to the religious thought of the East; it is that they have a vivid conception of nature being instinct with life. And perhaps this may not be so foolish as the West in its superiority is apt to assume. They go so far as to personify the forces of nature. It is held that the operation of these forces is carried out through the agency of such angelic beings. The traditional idea of Christianity is that in the worship of God men and angels sing in concert, and that angels are winged messengers of mercy who spread abroad blessing and who accomplish good deeds, and who delight to co-operate with man when he pauses to render that possible.

THE DIVINE GRACE

Nor should we forget that God Himself is concerned with our worship. Religion is constantly speaking of the down-pouring of Divine Grace. Perhaps the most spiritual and at the same time the most reasonable explanation that we can frame of the action of this divine power, is to picture ourselves as living perpetually within the sphere of the Divine Omnipotence, Omniscience, and Omnipresence. Every flicker of our consciousness must be reacting within His consciousness, and every aspiration that is not turned in upon oneself, but is selfless and impersonal, brings its immediate response and recognition from the Divine Omnipresence. A worship that is single-hearted and sincere must, it seems to me, call down from on high untold blessing over the place where it is being held or, in other words, through the channel that is being made. In addition to this, again, we have to make note of the special blessing of the Christ which pours through the sacramental channels. The Holy Eucharist is thought of as being "a propitiatory sacrifice, which may be offered for the living and the dead, for sin, punishment, satisfaction and other needs." (*Canons of the Council of Trent*, Sess. XX II., cap. i-ix.) It is held, in other words, to be capable of wiping out part of the accumulation of sin in the world.

SPIRITUAL TRANSFORMATION

When we add together these different sources of spiritual power, we shall agree, no matter what may be our special view of the constituent factors, that the resultant blessing to the world may be really great. I am one of those who look upon work of this kind as fundamental. We know that different elements have to be taken into account when dealing with problems like the upbringing of children and the amelioration of the lot of the masses. There are those who set great store by environment, and others who are rather fatalistic about heredity; and there are others who hold that there is in man an inner power which can enable him to rise superior to both environment and heredity. Faith in this innate power does not excuse us from efforts to improve slum areas and the heredity of the coming generations. But to arouse that dormant power within a man is recognised as the surest of all methods, if it be feasible. I regard the work that the church does as doing the equivalent for the district, the country or the continent. It appeals to me as vital to the spiritual welfare of our civilisation, and I believe that if this could be made more efficient and properly organised, we should have at our disposal an immense power for social and political regeneration, and for changing the whole atmosphere of public opinion. A single church sending out thoughts of brotherly love, of altruism and understanding, could neutralise in its environment much of the turmoil of lower thought.

THE BODY-CORPORATE AND THE LARGER CONSCIOUSNESS

There is one other reflection which calls for attention before this chapter can close. There is an attitude on the part of the worshipper which begins to shape itself when he realises this objective reality of the work that he is doing. He is perhaps justified in thinking that he can as usefully serve God in ways other than that of singing or praying to Him in church. But when he realises the extraordinary help that he can be to the outer world—to people who never enter a church door—he may quite easily develop a sense of duty towards this work of public worship. To my own way of thinking that work is quite fundamental, and I rank it as one of the most useful that can be done for the world at large. Presently another idea grows upon him. He realises that one person can help another in worship. We do in fact stimulate one another, so that half a dozen people working together are likely to produce a greater effect than if they were to work at the same thing apart from each other's company. Moreover, each person has his own special contribution to bring. One is strong in devotion, another in thinking, and so on. And eventually a congregation can be trained to work, not as a number of separate entities, but as a single body. What each member does in the way of thought, or feeling, or devotion, is done on behalf of the whole body-corporate by one of its aspects. It is not his feeling that the individual offers but his feeling blended with that of the whole. It is not useful to talk much of all this; the method has to be practised for it to be understood and its significance realised. The congregation acquires a new characteristic, and this close union of consciousness makes it a much better channel for the reception and outpouring of the divine power.

In writing of the value of worship to the individual, I have already stressed the necessity for impersonality and self-disinterestedness in worship. If to this we can add this sense of corporate work, not only is the work improved, as I have just been pointing out, but the congregation themselves often grow into new experiences of consciousness. They learn to escape from the prison-house of their own separated personalities, and find themselves enjoying and experiencing a larger consciousness, which is that of the body-corporate. Gradually in this way do they grow into a larger outlook towards God and humanity; they become conscious of the over-shadowing Presence of God, and they are increasingly able to identify their consciousness with that of other people and with the race as a whole. It is this power to put oneself into the position and outlook of another which gives to a person real sympathy and largeness of spirit. It would be difficult, I suppose, to exaggerate the help that may be derived from such practices and the complete transformation of character that can be effected in a short space of time.

CHAPTER IX

THE HOLY EUCHARIST

AN INTERPRETATION FOR THE WORSHIPPER

I FEEL that it may give substance and reality to the ideas that I have been trying to present in the last chapters of this book if a concluding chapter be devoted to an examination of the Holy Eucharist. We can find in that most sacred of services practical exemplification of these ideas. Of the public services of the Church it is the only service prescribed, to our knowledge, by the Lord Himself. Consequently, it is often spoken of as "the Lord's own service," and the older Churches of Christendom—the Roman Catholic and Eastern Orthodox—together with others who follow the tradition, treat it as the central act of Christian worship and surround it with all the solemnity of symbolic ceremonial.

THEOLOGICAL THEORIES

I do not want to enter here into any long review of the disputes which have arisen about this rite. The Reformers were faced with abuses in the Church which were undoubtedly grave. There are those who agree with what was done by one or other section of the Reformers ; there are others who hold that "in emptying the bath water, they threw the baby out with it," to use a descriptive phrase that I once heard. That is to say, that in getting rid of abuses they succeeded in some cases in discarding things that were essential and many others that were at least desirable. The Episcopal Succession, upon which depends the transmission of Holy Orders, in the original sense, is a case in point. In many post-Reformation churches the Eucharist has been relegated to a secondary place. It is not looked upon as an act of worship in at all the same way as the morning office that has replaced it.

As there are different ideas about the nature of the Holy Sacrament, so there are different names used to describe it.[1] The portion of the rite relating to the administration of Holy Communion is well described by the name of Holy Communion. But many people prefer for the rite as a whole the title "Holy Eucharist," derived from the Greek *eucharistia*, meaning "thankfulness," as representing "the giving of thanks." Objectors have whittled away the sacrificial characteristics one by one from their conception of the service till in the extreme position it comes to be regarded only as a commemorative supper, representing in the sphere of religion what an Old Boys' dinner represents in the sphere of education. Some admit not a propitiatory sacrifice, which makes atonement (or literally "at-one-ment"—this is the derivation of the word), but a sacrifice "of praise and thanksgiving" only. The Protestant view generally is that Christ's sacrifice on the Cross, "His one oblation of Himself once offered," to quote the words of the Anglican liturgy, is "a full, perfect, and sufficient sacrifice, oblation, and satisfaction for the sins of the whole world," and that Christ "did institute, and in His holy Gospel command us to continue, a perpetual memory of that His precious death, until His coming again." The fuller idea is that the rite is not simply a memorial, but is a representative sacrifice. Priest and Victim are the same, but the sacrifice is different in the manner of its representation, for Christ in the

---

[1] The popular name "Mass" is one about whose derivation scholars have not always been agreed. At the close of the present-day Roman form there is a phrase of dismissal, *Ite, missa est*," which is usually interpreted as meaning, "Go, the Sacrifice is sent." It seems that this dismissal was used formerly at other places, and that catechumens were enjoined to depart with these words. Objection is therefore sometimes made that the name has no special or accepted significance.

Eucharist is offered under the sacramental species and not under His own flesh and blood. Some writers have pointed out that the Eucharist *applies* the graces of Christ only and does not originate them as was done according to the Catholic theory on Calvary. But in every celebration of the Holy Eucharist there is involved a real outpouring of Life from the Second Person of the Blessed Trinity into the lower worlds. Of this Christ is the *origo* or source, so that it is true in this sense to say that grace is continually originated.

The mists of confusion which surround the whole problem would be greatly clarified if theologians would bethink themselves to take the conception back a stage further altogether, and call to mind the wonderful symbolism in the Apocalypse of "the Lamb slain from the foundation of the world," (*Revelation* xiii., 8) the cosmic sacrifice. It is no more then a question of repetition of the sacrifice, of re-accomplishment of the sacrifice of the Cross, but rather of constant re-presentation in terms of time and space of that primal sacrifice out of time and space to which the world and all created life owes its existence. Christ, the Second Person of the Blessed Trinity, is also in this conception at once Priest and Victim, for the sacrifice is always considered as an act of self-oblation, made voluntarily.

A RITUAL-DRAMA

The service of the Holy Eucharist takes the form of a ritual-drama. It begins with preliminaries of purification, praise and prayer. There then follows a series of actions and ideas which typify the cosmic process of the descent of the Divine Life into matter, and the re-ascent from matter to spirit. This cosmic process is in its turn re-enacted in the gospel story of Christ, of which the Eucharistic drama makes use. A number of different conceptions lie behind the whole process and a great wealth of mystical thought. An outsider not familiar with this would find it difficult to understand what is taking place, and when we add to his difficulty the natural bewilderment occasioned by the surrounding ceremonial, it is evident that some measure of explanation is required before he can hope at all adequately to understand and to appreciate such a service.

I propose, then, to summarise the general procedure of the service and to explain the purpose and meaning of its more important parts.

PRELIMINARY PURIFICATION

The Eucharist begins with a process of purification and consolidation of the people. We must bear in mind that there are great differences among such an assembly of people collected together according to no premeditated plan—differences of age, of intelligence, of temperament, of occupation in life and so on. The immediate task in hand is to consolidate this heterogeneous crowd. They have come from many different walks of life, full of different influences and interests, and they have to be freed as far as possible from worldly influence and even contamination, to be united as far as may be for the great piece of work that lies before them. Hence the use of Holy Water to purify them from evil influence, to spread a particular influence and vibratory rate over the congregation. The procession of the choir and clergy round the church, if it takes place, sends out also a steadying body of influence, and the opening hymn and canticles turn the thought and aspiration of the people to a uniform direction, while the rhythm of the music helps to effect this necessary preliminary unification. This is further promoted by the general confession and absolution, which have also the effect of clearing away within the worshippers themselves the obstructions, caused by sin and wrongdoing and inattentiveness, which impede free access to the spiritual life within them.

INCENSE

Incense is now offered at the altar. It symbolises the rising of our aspiration before the throne of God, and the prayers of the Saints. It has also its practical side. Scientists will tell us that when we perceive the fragrance of a perfume, it is because a crowd of infinitesimal particles is liberated over the intervening space, some of which are impinging themselves on the olfactory nerve in the nose. What is here involved is a mechanism of rapid and widespread dispersion. It is considered, by experts on this science of ceremonial, that the incense itself when made of the right components, has an uplifting influence (just as there are other perfumes, such as musk, whose influence is much less elevated), and can serve also as a physical basis and vehicle for the spiritual power poured upon it at its benediction by the priest in the Name of God. This, then, is another steadying and uplifting influence upon the congregation.

THE PROGRESSIVE STIMULATION OF OUR FACULTIES

Various prayers now follow, expressing the "intention" or special thought-ideals of the day. With the reading of Scripture the mental element is stressed and is added to the devotion and feeling previously called out, this portion of the ceremony concluding with the sermon and the recitation of the Creed, which calls out more abstract thought. The Creed, moreover, is hallowed by centuries of usage and goes back to the original instruction of our Lord—to certain original archetypal ideas, so that it is a veritable talisman of thought-power, when said with confidence and reverent understanding, causing great illumination and quickening of our higher mental faculties.

TWO KINDS OF FORCE

Up to the present, the Eucharist has been following what we may call the general course of worship. It has made use of scriptural and other passages for praise, of versicles and responses, of prayer and of Biblical readings. Thus far it has not differed in the nature of the material used from the evening service called in the Roman Church Vespers, or from the Devotional Hours, from the Anglican Morning and Evening Prayer, and from much that figures in Nonconformist churches. This type of service may be regarded as calling upon what we may term the cosmic power of God. It is difficult to characterise what I am attempting to convey here. This kind of power flows down in response to human aspiration, and if this latter can be divested of self-interest, the down-pouring becomes proportionately intense and perceptible to people of sensitive temperament. There is another kind of power which flows through the sacramental channels; it appears to flow through the intermediation of our Blessed Lord, and to have this characteristic, that it is more amenable to direction towards specific ends—the relief of personal distress, the healing of sickness or trouble, the purifying and ennoblement of life.

THE OFFERING

With the Offertorium we pass on to a new phase of the work. Bread and wine, to be used in the sacrament, are now offered. This offering will repeat itself in various phases. At the moment, they are offered as representative of the fruits of the earth. Few people understand that this much of nature-worship, if we may use that expression in its literal sense (worship = "worth-ship," the giving of worth—friendly consideration and co-operation in this case) lingers in our Christian usage. Why not? Nature is instinct with life. We know little of the conditions of consciousness in the sub-human kingdoms; but need we deny that there may be some instinct towards God in the blade of grass or the tree of the forest? And so we thus dedicate the life of nature in this act of offering. We speak on nature's behalf.

The same "creatures of bread and wine" are next to be offered as a token—in the mediaeval sense of an external mark—or symbol, of our sacrifice of praise and thanksgiving. We offer ourselves, our souls and bodies, to be a holy and continual sacrifice to God.

After the singing of the *Sursum Corda* ("Lift up your hearts"), the Preface and *Sanctus*, in which we invoke the hierarchies of angels and offer our praise and the sacrifice of ourselves once more in union with them, comes the opening of the long and important Prayer of Consecration. We specify the special objects and intentions for which the sacrifice is to be offered. We commemorate the civil and ecclesiastical hierarchy, those present, friends in "trouble, sorrow, need, sickness or any other adversity," and finally our special cases among the company of the dead.

The offerings of bread and wine are now purified from contact with lower influence, and so retain only the most noble and worthy side of our previous offering; they are first blessed by the priest for their sacred destiny, and then at the time of consecration are changed in all that is essential, in what lies behind the outer forms, and by the power of God become the channel or vehicles of Christ's Presence.

THE REAL PRESENCE

This heritage of holiest love bequeathed by our Lord has become the battle-ground of the theologians. I have dealt with the subject elsewhere[1] and will not attempt to resume the whole discussion here. The belief that there was a real Presence of Christ in the hallowed elements does not seem to have been widely disputed before the time of the Reformation. Luther indeed testified that all Christendom believed in it. Various glosses on the idea grew into partial acceptance. One school asserted that the bread and wine were only symbolical, in the later sense of the word.[2] The elements are made into a kind of reminder of the Body and Blood of Christ which was shed for us. Another theory, called Receptionism, taught that the Presence was not objective, that the bread and wine were unchanged, but that the Presence became effective in the faithful receiver of the Sacrament. There was also discussion as to how the Body was taken. Calvin bluntly affirmed that Christ's Body was in heaven and nowhere else, and that "a power emanating from the Body of Christ, which is now in heaven only, is communicated to the spirit."[3] Others, called Virtualists, held that the faithful received not the Body but Its efficacy.

---

[1] *The Presence of Christ in the Holy Communion*, included in this volume.

[2] Greek *sumbolon*—throwing together, means really a correspondence between a *noumenon* and a *phenomenon*, between a reality in the higher archetypal world and its outer physical expression here. Symbol and figure came later to acquire the sense of denying the very reality they originally affirmed.

[3] *Explanation of the Thirty-Nine Articles*. Bishop Forbes, p. 499.

Others held that it was not the earthly Body but the glorified or heavenly or spiritual Body that was given.

I have discussed this Babel of theories in the book mentioned, and have ventured an interpretation that is less cumbersome. The crux of the matter does not turn on the word "IS," as is the tendency with theologians to assume, some of whom want to substitute "signifies" and some to interpolate "not." The crux of the question is what we mean by "Body" and "Blood." What is our own physical body? It serves for us to receive impressions from the world outside, and to express our life or consciousness to the same outside world. Why not see the consecrated Host in this way? A body is a vehicle for consciousness. In this case it is the Vehicle of Christ's direct Presence and Blessing. The word "Blood" can be explained along similar lines, and in the light of the mystery-tradition of antiquity. The blood is the life-force; it is symbolised by the juice of the grape, the symbol of plenty and joy and gladness. Christ's Blood is His Life poured out into the world and into us for our nourishing and sustaining. We live on His sacrifice.

One other question arises. Is not the doctrine of the Real Presence contradictory to that of His Omnipresence? To this it is simply necessary to answer that there are degrees of presence. Christ's Life is in everybody, but is certainly more manifest and more expressed through some people than through others. The degree of presence depends on the object which expresses it. I regard the Eucharist as bringing a special intensification of His Presence, in other words a greater immediacy, for our helping and spiritual awakening and a great outpouring of spiritual power.

Other theories of Receptionism, Zwinglianism and so forth, do not account for the fact that numbers of people feel before the Blessed Sacrament an objective Presence which is not dependent upon their reception of It nor upon any subjective working of their consciousness. I have met several cases of people who had the capacity to detect this Presence. And in one case where I was on the spot, a person walked into an Anglican Church where there was no sign of reservation or any apparent likelihood of its practice, and immediately recognised the Presence of the Blessed Sacrament. I had myself previously done so in the same place and under the same conditions.

To assert as some do that such an idea is materialistic is to reverse the facts. It is the people who deny the Real Presence and wish to shift It to some heavenly or abstract "spiritual" locality who are materialistic. To hold that matter is the vehicle of spirit is a spiritual theory and tends to spiritualise our conception of life, and to carry this to the extreme of believing that the power of God can so spiritualise the densest physical matter is the acme of spirituality.

AFTER THE CONSECRATION

There is still one further offering of the now consecrated Elements that takes place. No sooner are they bestowed upon us than we offer them back in deepest devotion and gratitude to God. Before, it was bread and wine that we offered as a token of our sacrifice of ourselves, our souls and bodies. Now it is the Sacred Host and Chalice that we offer—an immediate gesture of response to God—with all our gratitude and joy and adoration behind Them—the complete and single-hearted offering of ourselves. We ask that this may be borne before the throne of God, "there to be offered by Him Who as the eternal High Priest for ever offers Himself as the eternal Sacrifice."[1]

[1] Words which I have quoted in this chapter are from the Liturgy of my Church. The sequence can easily be followed in the Roman Missal, but certain points were clarified in our revision.

We come now to that portion of the Eucharist concerned with the diffusion of the Divine Blessing over the world. We take our Consciousness to the highest pitch, to the divine spirit within us or to whatever reflection of that we can touch. We pass into the world of intuition, of the realised experience of the Oneness of Life, and we recognise our fellowship and unity in Christ. Here in the tradition of the Eucharist comes the Salutation or Kiss, or Embrace of Peace. After a prayer follows the Communion of the priest and later of the people. This outpouring of power from the Church over the outside world may be exceedingly intense, especially if the congregation work with that end in view. There is a great flood after the final Benediction.

THE COMMUNION

The priest's act of communion is what is technically known as the "confection" or "consummation" of the sacrifice. The old notion of a sacrifice included the destruction of the victim. The gift is offered fully and completely in the sense of being put beyond the possibility of subsequent usage by the sacrificer on earth—except, of course, in respect of additional Hosts consecrated for the service, emergency or regular, of the people. In the Eucharist this ancient condition is technically fulfilled at the communion of the priest, but there is a highly spiritual significance attached also to this act. For the whole assembly communicates vicariously through the priest, such is the unity and intimacy of contact established between priest and people. The power is brought right down to this physical world for distribution and radiation.

The congregation who partake of the Blessed Sacrament receive a very precious gift indeed. The Host is a radiating throbbing centre of life and love. It is the Vehicle of the most direct blessing from our Lord that we can picture to our imagination and hearts. How priceless the gift is known only by those who grow into intimacy and kinship with Him in the Blessed Sacrament of His love.

In conclusion, and in the wish to bring home to readers the greatness of the Holy Communion, I venture to quote some sentences from the book of mine already mentioned.[1]

I like to go back in thought to that scene of the Last Supper, the outlines of which we recapitulate in the Prayer of Consecration at each Eucharist. Our Lord had been giving hints to the little band of disciples of the parting that was impending, as we learn from the Gospel story. We can picture them gathered together in the upper room and the final intimation being given them of the calamity that was to take place. How deep the grief that must have fallen at the thought of the separation, the anxiety, the sense of helplessness, the thought of awful and utter loneliness. Can we not picture His tender sympathy with their distress, the endeavour to rehearten them and to inspire them for work they yet had to accomplish. For the disciple must not think of himself, but of the constant note of the world's great need. And He speaks to them of His love and care for them, of His power that will sustain them and support them in all their difficulties. Presently He tells them of the plan that He has devised for them, a rite that shall incorporate His very being, that shall keep the sense of His living Presence perpetually in their hearts, and shall help them to maintain that realisation of their fellowship with one another, that holy and all-possessing unity which they had gradually found in their common devotion to Him. How wonderful must have been those moments as in solemn thanksgiving He brake that Bread, and as He blessed that Cup. How sweetly tense the peace and stillness of that greatest of all moments. What a panorama in the inner worlds, what hosts of angels and Great Ones to do homage to that memorable occasion! And above all the sweetness of His love binding them perpetually to Him with ties that should never be broken.

---

[1] Op. cit., pp. 150.

It was not only once in the history of this sad world that so marvellous an experience was given to men. The rite still lives on; His love still binds men's hearts together, and we take comfort and strength in His marvellous promise, "And lo! I am with you alway even unto the end of the world."[1]

ACCENDAT IN NOBIS DOMINUS IGNEM SUI AMORIS, ET
FLAMMAM AETERNAE CARITATIS.

[1] *Matthew* xxviii, 20.

NEW INSIGHTS INTO CHRISTIAN WORSHIP

THE PLACE OF CEREMONIES IN THE SPIRITUAL LIFE

SINCE the Liberal Catholic Church began its work, it has evoked a good deal of discussion as to what value and worth are to be attached to religious ceremonies. Undoubtedly there are large numbers of people who are out of sympathy with existing religious institutions. They mostly lean to the idea that religion in its essence consists of the Sermon on the Mount. It is constantly asked: 'What has true religion to do with forms and ceremonies? Is it not rather a matter of the free soaring of the spirit, untrammeled by dogmas and rites and by formalism of any sort whatsoever?' 'God is a Spirit: and they that worship him must worship him in spirit and in truth' (John iv, 24). 'Do we not bewilder and confuse people by our elaborate theories on spiritual matters; does not all true spirituality make towards simplicity and freedom from artificial bonds and restrictions?'

Needless to say, these views represent conception of things which has much of reality and truth behind it, and because of that they commend themselves to many people. Their validity need not be disputed, but we do need to see to what stage of the spiritual life they apply and exactly where they fit in and belong in the domain of religion.

Unfortunately, people who discuss religion often do not take the trouble to give to it the same thorough and all-round study that they do devote to the mastery of any other science. The sciences are understood to involve study and training for their acquisition, but religion—the science of ultimate things—is the one upon which the man in the street so often considers himself competent to speak without any preliminary training. In place of this study, for which abundant material exists, people seem to think that in religion we are concerned simply with how they feel about things, and so their vague sentiment is made to pass muster as an opinion of value and authority. The fact is: religion covers so wide a field of thought and effort that its understanding demands a good deal of deep thinking, and requires that in many aspects of the question we shall discriminate and not confuse issues which are separate and distinct.

The Purpose of Religion

If we are to bring order into our, thinking on the subject of religion we need at the outset to understand what religion is and what duty and function it has to perform. We often get a good basis for broad generalisation on such subjects by taking a little excursion into the etymology of the words we use. In this case, the most generally accepted derivation of the word is from the Latin word *religare*, meaning to bind back. (Some derive it from *relegere*, which carries the similar sense of 'going over again' or 'sailing back over the same waters.') Hence religion is that factor in our lives which binds us back to the source of our being, to God, or to the Individual Monad, from Whom we derive our existence. We need not elaborate the point here. The Gnostic Bardesan saw in a parable akin to that of the Prodigal Son an allegory of humanity in its state of pilgrimage, lost at first in ignorance and in the darkness of materiality, and finally seeking the Father's home (c.f. *The Hymn of the Soul*).

Why Religion Cannot be Simple

We need to understand, first of all, that there are different spheres or departments of religion, all of which have their share to contribute in the helping of humanity. Religion cannot be the simple affair that idealists would like to have it be, because humanity—individually and collectively—is so complex; and religion is intended for humanity. Religion has to be operative at all levels and in all departments of our being. Hygiene, in so far as it makes for the well-being of our physical bodies, is a department of religion. To be hale is to be whole, that is, in a state of physical healthiness and of at-one-ment with the remainder of one's self. Social activities which make for the physical and moral well-being of the race are a part of religion. Yet hygiene and political economy are complicated and difficult sciences, involving theories which are abstruse or difficult of comprehension; and this aspect of religion—incontestably true religion!—does not at first glance seem to have much in common with the 'free soaring of the Spirit' or the elimination of theories and systems. System and theory of the right sort, in fact, are of its essence. Transcendental ideas relating to the mystic union of the soul with God belong to another department of religion, and we should avoid confusing the issues by supposing that all branches of religion are concerned with this kind of thought.

The human being, furthermore, finds himself endowed with emotions and the ability to think. The training of this emotion and thought towards higher things is part of the work of religion. It is no common sense to ignore the mind and say that it has nothing to do with religion. We exaggerate the importance of some aspects of mental activity in these days and sometimes we still tend to deify reason, but the remedy is not to cast off the mind and all its works, but to purify and raise it until it becomes illumined and permeated by the intuitional reason. I have heard people boast that they never read books. Obviously a nice discrimination in the choice of reading is to be commended, but to pretend that one can afford to ignore the accumulated knowledge and experience of others is sheer silliness. In the case of a street accident, for example, the superiority of one who has taken the trouble to learn 'First Aid' is so obvious that the subject simply does not lend itself to discussion.

From all this emerges the reflection that since man, himself is an exceedingly complicated being, so also the religion which seeks to train and minister to the many-sided activities of his consciousness cannot escape from being likewise a complex and many-sided affair. One has only to think of the many lives in which we have been working and gathering experiences in the past to realise 'what a wonderful piece of work is man.' And when it is understood that religion is confronted with the task of providing not only for a single one of these complicated individuals who have been wandering through innumerable incarnations, but for masses of them in the aggregate, one sees that as a practical proposition religion cannot be the simple affair that people would have it be, if it is to do its work and minister to the highly varied types and temperaments of humanity. It has to deal with many sides of man's nature and with the many-sided nature of many differently-made men.

The Question of Ceremonies: A Discrimination

Much of the objection that is made against rites and ceremonies arises from misunderstanding of what they are intended to accomplish. There are two sides to the work of the Church. On the one hand, it is intended to minister to the spiritual development of its members as individuals. It does this in a variety of ways, into which we need not enter here—by religious and moral instruction, by methods of prayer and meditation, by the training in good works. On the other hand, a Church is intended to be a centre of spiritual influence for the helping of the world at large. Its public services, when rightly understood, are intended more for this purpose than for the helping of the individual, though the individual may derive much help from them. It is obvious that the man-in-the-street knows absolutely nothing of all this side of the work, and he is certain therefore to have erroneous and confused ideas on the subject. A ceremony which is intended to group a mass of people together for the purpose of sending out a great flood of thought influence on the outside world will naturally be quite a different thing from the exercises in meditation which may be given to one who has in view some purpose connected with his own inner development. People who have to be grouped together for a given work have necessarily to be subjected to a discipline—which means, of course, limitation in a form. They submit themselves, gladly and freely, to the conditions which are found best for the work in view. 'Nature is conquered by obedience.'

To contrast this collective work with 'the free soaring of the Spirit, untrammeled by limitations' is foolish, and betrays a want of understanding of the situation. Let me repeat again, that religion has many different departments of work. We saw just now that hygiene and political economy are two of these departments. The raising and stimulating of the thought and feeling and spiritual faculties of the outside world is another of these departments of work, and its methods and requirements ought not to be confused with those appertaining to the department of mystical experience. Difficulties need not arise if only people will not confuse issues which are separate and distinct.

Objections to Ceremonial: Materialistic

The objections that are made against rites and ceremonies can be grouped under two headings, needing separate treatment. Under the first we can combine all those which speak of religious ceremonies as being meaningless or superstitious, or as 'putting the clock backwards.'

I do not intend to deal here with the first group of objections; it does not really belong to our subject. Neither the ceremonies of the Church nor those of Freemasonry can be understood without the aid of the Theosophical teachings. For the ceremonies of both these systems are designed to affect the man as a whole, and not simply that part of him which lives on the physical plane. When it is understood that man is a spiritual intelligence, divine in essence, and that there are higher worlds of being in which he is living contemporaneously with his physical existence, the perspective of the problem changes. These ceremonies are not planned from a standpoint which sees the physical plane as the one reality; but they take into account the super-physical worlds, and the working of natural forces in those worlds. And their aim is to lift us up into conscious communion with our higher Self, and thus to make possible the recovery of the 'Lost Word,' the 'Great Secret' of the Divinity hidden in the human heart. I do not propose to deal further with this side of our subject, as I have already said; but those who are interested can study this new outlook on religion in Bishop Leadbeater's great work, *The Science of the Sacraments*.

Buddhist Objections

The second class of objections to ceremonial to which I referred are of quite a different order, and take their source in certain traditions of Buddhism. I remember speaking some twenty years ago on this very subject with Ananda Metteya, a Scotsman by birth who belonged to a group of Buddhist monks in Burma. He then told me that attention to all phenomenal manifestations, whether to psychic faculties or to rites and ceremonies, was in the nature of a deviation from the direct way to Nirvana. They were not in themselves wrong, but they were like dallying by the roadside.

There was much discussion on the question some years ago in the Theosophical Society when the ceremonial movement, which has now grown so strong, began to develop. And as there are periodical recurrences of the same questioning, I propose that we should deal with the matter in some detail. In the earlier days the teaching that dependence on rites and ceremonies was one of the fetters to be cast off at the stage between the first and second of the great initiations was apt to be misunderstood. It was supposed that all use of ceremonies was condemned. It may not be out of place to quote the words employed in the earlier books. In *The Path of Discipleship* Mrs. Besant speaks of the last of the three fetters that have to be cast off at this stage as superstition. She says: '...it means the reliance on external, sectarian rites for spiritual help.... The man has risen above exoteric forms and ceremonies.' (page 87)

C. W. Leadbeater says in *Invisible Helpers*:

The third fetter to be got rid of comprehends all kinds of unreasoning or mistaken belief, all dependence on the efficacy of outward rites and ceremonies to purify the heart. He who would cast it off must learn to depend upon himself alone, not upon others, nor upon the husk of any religion. (pages 116-7)

At a later date came Alcyone's *At the Feet of the Master*, which said:

You must feel perfect tolerance for all, and a hearty interest in the beliefs of those of another religion, just as much as in your own. For their religion is a path to the highest, just as yours is.... You must...be free from bigotry and superstition. You must learn that no ceremonies are necessary; else you will think yourself somehow better than those who do not perform them. Yet you must not condemn others who still cling to their ceremonies. (pages 46-7)

It is clear from a close study of the above passages that what is treated as undesirable is DEPENDENCE upon outer rites and ceremonies, and the idea that their use can replace individual effort. As is well known, these instructions of the Brotherhood are based upon the teaching of the Lord Buddha, and we shall better understand the whole situation if we put ourselves back into the circumstances under which He promulgated them. It was a German historian, Leopold von Ranke, who introduced what are called the exact methods of historical criticism, which insist upon the idea that events in history cannot be judged in the setting of modern conditions into which most people are liable to place them, but have to be viewed amid the circumstances under which they occurred. The Lord Buddha came into India at a time when Hinduism was greatly overburdened with rites and ceremonies. Probably many of them had already in His time become changed and distorted. That is still the state of affairs today, and one often finds the letter of the law observed in entire defiance of its spirit. People are told to wash the cloth which forms their raiment before entering the temple, but the water of the tanks which are provided in the temple precincts for that purpose may be green with the slime of ages. Hence we can quite well understand that part of His mission was to discourage the idea that the mere performance of these ceremonies could in itself achieve liberation for those who performed them. We have an excellent illustration of what is meant in the naive use of the prayer-wheel among the Tibetans. The continual spinning of a wheel engraved with certain prayers replaces the utterance of the prayers by the worshipper.

The stress which the Lord Buddha laid upon one aspect of truth at a certain period of the world's history and amid special conditions does not necessarily apply with equal force to another period and set of conditions. Anyhow, when His great successor founded the Christian faith He chose to institute within it certain rites which have been the well-spring of its life through the centuries that have since elapsed.

Our Attitude

What bearing has all this on our Liberal Catholic Church and its work? I do not think that any of us is dependent upon the ceremonies that we do, or looks to them as an end in themselves. Even if we were so, it is worth noting that such dependence is an obstacle that has to be surmounted only as we are preparing to take the second of the great initiations. There need be, for most of us, no burning hurry to disembarrass ourselves of ceremonies!

You all know how in the training through which we pass in this particular Church at Huizen[1] we try to make self-disinterestedness the foundation of all our work. People are for the most part wrapped up in their own ideas and in pursuit of their own likes and pleasures. The first step in our training here is to teach people to turn outwards, and to learn to take more interest in other people and in great world movements and events than in their separated personal attachments. And so it has always been an understood thing in this Church that people come here not primarily for their own spiritual benefit, but to join in an act of service for the helping of the outside world. We believe that every time the Holy Eucharist is celebrated great spiritual forces are sent out over the world around, which operate to change the thought atmosphere of the neighbourhood, and to give a spiritual stimulus to all who come within the sweep of this outpouring. Many people who never come to a church are thus helped, and receive from time to time some impetus in their spiritual growth. If you study closely one of our services, in which every person present in church is encouraged to express himself as earnestly and at as high a level of aspiration as he can reach, you will realise that for a protracted period of time you have a number of people in a state of great concentration, working at a level of thought and feeling that they seldom touch at other times, and that other people seldom touch at all, unless indeed they are working along parallel lines. When you add to this the blessing of Our Lord that flows through the sacraments and all the spiritual help from other sources, it will be realised how magnificent this outpouring may be. The quality of thought and of emotion is so much more elevated than the ordinary thinking and feeling of the outer world, that with its greater potency and having a clear and uninterrupted field of action, it really can do much to melt away the hatred and distrust and unhappiness all too prevalent in the world. That is the attitude in which we in this Church work. To tell those who are working in this purposeful attitude to "throw away their crutches" seems hardly a counsel of understanding.

To use ceremonies as a means of working for other people is quite a different thing from being dependent upon them. A business man may find it convenient to use an automobile or a stenographer in order to economise time and strength. These things are instruments that he purposely uses, and nobody is so foolish as to ask why he has not outgrown them. A spiritual

---

[1] This chapter is the substance of two sermons given at the Church of St. Michael and All Angels, Huizen, in 1927. [Ed.]

teacher may use the printing press to disseminate his ideas. It does not occur to us to tell him that spirituality is concerned with 'the free soaring of the Spirit' or with 'the heavenly marriage of the soul' rather than with printing presses. We have the good sense to see that the two things belong to different orders of thought and to different departments of the work, and the printing press may enable him to reach people in larger numbers.

Let me finally point out, in this connection, that however much we profess to have outgrown ceremonies, we cannot really escape from them. The manifestation of God in His World implies the fundamental duality of spirit and matter, or life and form. Ceremony is the science of form. Our bodily movements throughout the day are one long ceremonial. There is an elaborate process of eating, of dressing, of locomotion, and our relations with one another all require self-expression through form. The Quaker who objects to forms and ceremonies only substitutes his own simpler, and perhaps, therefore, less effective, set of forms for those he disapproves of in others. In fact, it will generally be found that people who inveigh against these things really mean that they dislike the forms that other people employ (generally because they have not studied or tried to understand them), but are quite prepared to substitute others of their own making and within the measure of their comprehension in their stead.

'The religion of spirit' is an attractive and captivating phrase. But the religion that the spirit would impart and the religion that the man-in-the-street can receive are poles apart. St. Paul, when he speaks of the gifts of the spirit, emphasizes the diversity of their distribution among men. One has the gift of wisdom, another of healing, another of the discerning of spirits, another of the interpretation of tongues. Not any one has them in their plenitude and entirety. Religion has to deal with people as they are—much enveloped in the world of form. Before one can occupy oneself with a religion that appertains to the realm of pure spirit, one must have accomplished a long and strenuous ascent through the realms of matter.

Ceremonies not necessary to Salvation, but Useful

There is, of course, a sense in which the value of religious rites may be exaggerated. The Roman Catholic Church, for instance, teaches that the Sacraments are necessary for the salvation of mankind[1] and the Church of England in her Catechism speaks of two, Baptism and the Supper of the Lord, as being 'generally necessary to salvation.' Hence the Church was regarded as the ark of salvation, and in mediaeval times churches were sometimes built in the form of an ark, with the walls sloping outwards, symbolizing the belief that as the ark of Noah saved its occupants from the waters of the great flood, so salvation was to be found only within the shelter of the Church.

This is one of the points on which most members of the Liberal Catholic Church would find themselves unable to follow the teaching of the older Churches. We do not believe that Baptism is actually 'necessary to salvation.' We believe that the world is the theatre of an ordered Plan, and that humanity achieves Salvation, Nirvana, Liberation, Fulfillment—whatever word one likes to use—through the cosmic processes. No particular Church and no particular religion is necessary to this, though it may be questioned whether a man could entirely dispense with religion in the broad and general sense of the term. But Churches and religions may be of great help in the accomplishment of this process. We say, therefore, in our own particular orbit of work, that the Sacraments, while not necessary to salvation, are extraordinarily useful.

---

[1] Though not all of them for every person, e.g. Holy Orders and Matrimony.

What We Really Believe

I should be conveying a false impression if I did not add that while we do not regard the rites of the Church as 'necessary to salvation,' we feel that we have still untold riches of spiritual experience to gain from the Church. Let me ask you to consider with me what the Church offers to us. Why do we celebrate the Holy Eucharist? We do so because Our Lord himself said to His apostles and their successors: 'Do this in remembrance of Me.' We can picture how the disciples were sad and perplexed as on the eve of His Passion He told them of His impending departure. And we can see Him breaking the Bread and blessing the Cup as He told them that He was bequeathing to them a rite which should keep His presence perpetually among them and help them to maintain that unity and sense of fellowship which they had found in their common devotion to Him. 'As oft as men shall do these things,' He said—if we may slightly paraphrase the utterance—'they shall do them in remembrance of Me.' How wonderful the gift that He has left to us only those know who day after day seek Him in the silence and peace of their hearts. How exquisite the thought that by His incorporation in ourselves and the merging of our consciousness into Him, we grow more and more like unto Him Who is our Sun of Righteousness, the very life and nectar of our being.

People often fail to realise what is involved in the doctrine of the unity of life. It means that the whole of creation is interdependent, linked together in one chain of being. And as we help those who stand below us on the ladder of evolution (so that the domesticated animals, for example, owe their progress to our association with them), so are we in turn helped by those who stand above us. It is part of the scheme that Those who remain on earth to help forward struggling humanity by Their very sacrifice gain the mighty power that They can use in that work. To refuse to profit by Their blessing, from a mistaken idea of spiritual independence, is to deny the unity of the One Life. This is the truth which lies behind the old theological idea of the 'free gift of grace.' Because of this unity of life, the Elder Brothers of the race can pour out upon us blessing altogether surpassing in measure that which we can earn or merit for ourselves. It is through this law that Our Lord, as the 'first among many brethren,' can give us His Divine Life through the Sacraments that He instituted for this purpose.

The student will be familiar with the idea that all rightly designed ceremonies are in the nature of allegory, and in terms of physical action represent the divine drama of the heavenly worlds. In the symbolism of the Eucharist, as so magnificently outlined for us by Bishop C.W. Leadbeater, we have a picture of the descent of the Second Aspect of the Deity into matter, of His glorious Resurrection and His triumphant Ascension. And since in that sublime Mystery we not merely commemorate the heavenly processes so portrayed, but verily take part in them and re-enact them, so is it given to us to work with that degree of self-awareness we can attain in those processes of the higher worlds in which the Spirit of man has his place of dwelling. Let me put what I mean for you in language that is clear and unambiguous. Bishop Leadbeater describes for us as part of the celebration of the Eucharist an activity taking place at those levels of consciousness which we qualify with the technical names of atmic, buddhic, causal, etc.[1] The blessing which comes with the consecration of the Host and the subsequent movement of the rite, is strongest at the buddhic level. Part of the action takes place at the atmic level, and much again at the causal. It is at this last that we are able to respond best, because of our present lack of development of the higher vehicles of consciousness. Do you not see the possibilities which

[1] According to Bp. Leadbeater in *Science of the Sacraments* these refer to Sanskrit terms for "spirit, intuition and intelligence—exactly as the Three Aspects of the Trinity manifest as the Father, the Son, and the Holy Ghost." (302) [Ed]

lie before you in the unfolding and exercise of the powers of your higher consciousness, and how foolish it is to talk of 'outgrowing' the Eucharist until you are as much at home in those higher worlds and in the consciousness of Our Great Lord as you are at present in this physical world of shadows that we consider real?

People sometimes think the Eucharist complicated. Of course it is. But think what a great achievement so to arrange the material objects of earth and to compass the forces of heaven that Our Lord is physically incarnate with us. How could so mighty an achievement be wrought otherwise than with difficulty and elaboration? And yet in the sense of His Presence all becomes simple and elemental. Forms no longer bind; they have served their glorious purpose; and we soar aloft in the freedom of the spirit into the everlasting arms of His love, there to know that we are one with all that lives and moves.

A great spiritual teacher comes but rarely into the world. He can accomplish marvels simply by the magic of his presence. It all seems so simple, so easy. But he is not simple. He is the product of many lives and of innumerable experiences in the past. He can do what he sets himself to do with ease and freedom because of long experience from the past. Such teachers are rare, the efflorescence of an age. In His Church we compress the elaboration of many lives into one great ceremonial act, and lo! He is with us upon a thousand altars daily and the whole world is blessed by His Presence.

A NEW IDEA OF WORSHIP

AMONG the various Churches, the Liberal Catholic is probably the only one which teaches its people that they go to Church not primarily to help themselves, but to help the world outside. There are, of course, services—like those of Baptism, Confirmation, Prime and Complin—which are arranged chiefly for the helping of the people who take part in them. Religion is intended to lead us to self-knowledge, to aid us in realising our higher Self and the power of the God within us, and for that purpose the Church should give instruction and training in spiritual development to its members. But its chief services, and especially the Holy Eucharist, aim also at supplying a constant spiritual stimulus to the outside world. It is this idea which explains certain features in the ceremonial setting of these services, and which, when properly appreciated, gives a new zest and incentive to Church-going.

That a Church 'service' can in the literal sense be a service rendered to the outside world is an idea which ought not to be difficult of acceptance in these days, when scientific achievement has brought about so great a change in our ideas. The discovery by Roentgen of the X-Rays proved that there exist in Nature forces which surpass the range of our normal physical perception, and the marvellous development of radiotelegraphy has inured people to the idea that these finer forces can make their influence perceptible at a distance. Thought-transference has now become axiomatic. From all this it is but a short step to the well-known Theosophical teaching that thought and emotion are forces which affect not only those who express them but others also who come within their range of influence, so that there rests on us a moral responsibility for their existence.

It is, of course, true that the desultory thinking and feeling of the ordinary man is not a very serious factor in the sum total of the world's thought activity; but there has existed in the East from time immemorial a science called yoga, teaching man how to control and steady down his thoughts and emotions and how to develop their intensity until they become a veritable power in the world. These exercises are called, in the tradition of Western religion, meditation. In the monastic Orders of both the Roman Catholic and Eastern Orthodox Catholic Churches this science has been studied and practised. There can be no doubt that the early hermits of the desert must have devoted themselves to such practices, and they still form part of the daily routine of some religious Orders, different methods being in use. Amongst these *The Spiritual Exercises of S. Ignatius* are well known.

The principles underlying such practices, being based (especially in the case of the *Yoga Aphorisms of Patanjali*) on a deep study of human consciousness in its working, are unchanging; but each age has its own particular needs, and not the least among them our own age. The mediaeval setting of the religious Orders is quite unsuited to the general thought of today, but here again the literature of Theosophy interprets and satisfies the need of our time.

Definite Thought

The special utility of a Church to the outside world rests in the fact that it is a centre for the distribution of thought and emotion of an unusually high nature. If the thought atmosphere of the world is to be changed, certain conditions must be fulfilled. If we examine the thought of the ordinary man on spiritual matters, even on most matters, we find it to be vague and superficial. He does not probe deeply into such subjects. Religious ideas call up some vague emotion within him; and he usually satisfies himself with that much of reaction and carries his thinking no deeper. Thinking which is as vague and indefinite as that of the average man cannot be expected to accomplish much. It is useless to talk about changing the world, and then to employ the same spiritless and ineffective kind of thought that passes muster as thinking amongst most people. Our thought should be stronger, more sustained, more clear-cut and purposeful if it is to accomplish its purpose. But if, in addition to this, we can work at a higher level of consciousness, then much can be done to effect changes in the world about us. For thought which is above the average level has a freer field and encounters less "jostling," as it were, from thoughts of the same crowded level; moreover, working in matter of greater rarity, its effect is correspondingly greater. It is, in fact, on this principle that good is bound eventually to triumph over evil, for an amount of energy working through good thought produces a far greater effect than the same amount working through lower thought which can only express itself in grosser and more inert matter.

We see, then, that a Church, because of the high level of consciousness at which it works, can be a source of great help to the world. The world, shall we say, is largely filled with thoughts of business competition and rivalry. These are selfish and materialistic, and tend to produce a like state of mind in those upon whom they play. Rival thoughts working at the same level of materiality and self-interest are simply pitched against one another, and those will prevail which are the strongest and the most sustained. A single church, sending out thoughts of unselfishness, of altruism and brotherly love, could neutralise much of this lower turmoil of thought, because it works in a less impeded medium and at a much higher level. But for this it is necessary that the thought of the church shall be strong and real—that the faithful, in other words, shall be full of conviction. I remember once hearing a delightful story told of the Governor of one of the smaller American States. He was somewhat addicted to the use of bad language, and a local preacher deemed it his duty one day to reprove the Governor openly from the pulpit on account of the scandal caused by his language. On hearing of it, the Governor only smiled and remarked: "Oh, never mind! I swear a little, and Mr. Jones, he prays a little, but we neither of us mean much by it!" I am afraid that that applies to many, many churches. People listen idly, indifferently, or with vague and faint emotion, to the prayers, but only rarely is there anything approaching what I have above called Yoga in the services of the Church. There is a Sanskrit word which expresses exactly what I mean: the word *tapas*. It occurs frequently in the Hindu Upanishads, and its root meaning is "to burn." *Tapas* has in it the creative fire, the fire of intense devotion and enthusiasm, guided by the directive power of sustained thought and energised by the sovereign power of the will. Speaking of this word, Annie Besant says:

> There is no one English word which expresses its meaning; the various translations given: austerity, penance, asceticism, devotion—all are in it, but it is more than all of these.... It may be defined as "a sustained strenuous physical activity, sternly controlled and directed by the will to a given end, and dominated by concentrated thought." By *tapas* Brahma created worlds; by *tapas* Vishnu won his lofty rank; by *tapas* Mahadeva became the Jagat-Guru. By *tapas* every Rishi won his superhuman powers, and forced boons from the hands of even unwilling Devas.

At our humbler level of achievement, it is *tapas* that is needed in the Churches, if they are really to influence the world and to be efficient in spreading abroad the blessing of their Divine Master.

The Catholic Tradition in Worship

People often want to know why our Church has adopted so much of the Roman Catholic type of worship, and why it goes out of its way to arouse prejudice and opposition by using the word "Catholic" in its name. To this it may be straightly replied that it is not so much the practices or name that need to be changed as people's ideas about these things. The question of the name is not in itself important, but the practices are. The word "catholic" means "universal"—a harmless enough designation, even though it has acquired associations which in the minds of some people are sinister. In times of dispute in the early Church it became customary to make appeal to the universal belief of the Church, as exemplified in the famous maxim of St. Vincent of Lerins: 'That do we believe which everywhere, always and by all has been believed; for that is rightly and truly Catholic.' The word thus came to designate the solidarity of the Church. The Eastern Orthodox Church, which has been separate from Rome since the XIth Century, also calls itself Catholic, as again do the Old Catholics. But as our Statement of Principles points out, the word has now come to stand for the outlook and practice of the historic Church as distinct from that of the later sects, who gradually repudiated one essential after another. The Liberal Catholic Church allies itself with this historic tradition, but qualifies itself quite justly with the twin adjective "Liberal." It would have been easy to take some guileless and less provocative name, but our Church would then have been open to attack as "a wolf in sheep's clothing," appearing before the world in a garb of harmlessness to spread Catholicism. At some stage or other it has to explain and justify itself, for its type of worship is too far removed from the understanding of the ordinary person in these days. This justification is quite an easy task before really unprejudiced and open-minded people, and its promoters preferred to issue the challenge at the first meeting. The Liberal Catholics, moreover, have been a clearly recognizable school of thought within the Church.

The reason why the Liberal Catholic Church has adopted so much of the Roman Catholic type of worship is that it stands for what is true and real, regardless of popular misconception and prejudice. It believes that the form of worship it uses is that best designed to help the world in the particular way it chooses, and that the way it chooses is the most generally advantageous. Many of the practices which are popularly objected to as Roman Catholic are really of an universal nature; they are common to other great religions of the world and to those of antiquity. The use of incense is an example. The Liberal Catholic Church does not adopt practices like the use of incense simply because they are Roman Catholic, but because they are scientific and effective. Other bodies which observe the same things were no doubt originally animated by the same good reason.

All this brings us to a consideration of what we may call the science of public worship. There is such a science, in the sense that there exist certain laws upon which public worship is founded, partly having to do with human psychology and partly with the hidden working of forces of nature. The man in the street cannot be taken seriously as an authority or arbiter upon these matters. Even the historic Churches have lost the knowledge underlying their rites; and had the mediaeval Church been able to explain and to justify the traditions it had inherited, it is doubtful if that dismemberment of the Church which men call the Reformation would have eventuated on anything like the scale that it actually assumed. Most of the Churches which have grown up in Protestant Christendom since the Reformation have missed the mark, because they remained in the same ignorance as to what really underlay the Catholic tradition. The man in the street has gradually come to assume that religion must be adapted to suit his own outlook, as witness the many articles of newspaper editors and journalists who have taken upon themselves the role of interpreting and even of instructing the public on questions of religion and theology. There is some truth in the claim, for conditions obviously do change from one generation to another, and great changes have marked the last hundred years. But there are some institutions founded on the Divine Wisdom and not merely on human assumption, which are intended to change people and even peoples, rather than to be changed by them, so far as their fundamentals are concerned.

There are two grounds for this persistent failure to grasp the true function of a Church since the Reformation. Of these the first is summed up in the words rationalism and materialism. That tendency reached its climax as a positive assertion in the century past, but it always arises from a want of vital conviction or living experience in things spiritual. "Where there is no vision, the people perish." (Proverbs xxix, 18) Where people themselves have spiritual experience, they are able to speak with conviction and first-hand knowledge. When this fails a Church, its teachings become narrowed down and hardened, dogmas are enforced by outer authority rather than discerned by inner illumination, and the revolt of rationalism follows speedily in the wake. Religion will never be rightly apprehended so long as it is allowed to centre round the idea that man's life is bounded by the physical plane, and that the spiritual world is a realm which he enters only at death. It must be understood, clearly and definitely, that man is a Spirit, and that his spiritual and soul life are proceeding contemporaneously with his activities in a physical body. Religion is something which influences the whole man, and is intended to minister to his entire being. It is, therefore, intended to be operative in all those worlds in which he is living, and not to be planned solely in reference to part of his physical life. A religion which takes only the physical plane into account, and is rational in the sense of having been created by people who believe that the physical plane is the only world of which we can have any cognisance, is obviously incomplete and futile, however much it may commend itself to the many who judge solely by physical plane standards.

Catholicism is not a religion founded on ignorance and bounded by the physical plane. It takes into account the other worlds of man's being and concerns itself largely with the operation of natural forces in those worlds. Hence it is misunderstood by many, and rejected because it cannot be compassed in its plenitude by their intelligence.

I said that there was a second respect in which the Post-Reformation Churches had failed to grasp the true function of a Church. It arises out of the point I have just been urging. People have forgotten what I pointed out at the outset of these remarks—that a Church service is intended to help the outside world and not only to edify the worshippers within its walls. The Catholic form of ordination of a Subdeacon and Deacon empower them to read respectively the Epistle and Gospel in the Church of God "both for the living and the dead," and the Priest has the same mission in offering the Holy Sacrifice.

As soon as the idea of the spiritual worlds, the company of the dead and the host of angelic assistants is divorced from the conception of worship, people's minds are focused within the four walls of the building, and henceforward worship becomes a matter of self-interest and self-centredness. The Reformation introduced the era of subjective pietism. This is unfortunate, inasmuch as all real growth in spirituality is gained at the price of unselfishness and impersonality. It is obvious that a service intended to work for the world outside is not likely to be planned according to the ideas of those who do not understand that such a possibility exists.

I have made it sufficiently plain, I trust, why the Liberal Catholic Church does not use a form of service likely to commend itself at first acquaintance to the uninstructed person. The Old Reformation did much for the people by winning for them, however unintentionally, freedom of conscience. But it cut itself off from a vast amount that is vital and real in Catholic tradition. Thanks to the clear and broad generalisations of Theosophy, the New Reformation inaugurated by the Liberal Catholic Church will at least be based on a wider survey of the field of religion than was possible in the XVIth Century.

CONGREGATIONAL WORSHIP

AS soon as it is realised that the chief work of a Church is to help the outside world by pouring out upon it spiritual influences, the custom of worshipping collectively, or "congregational worship," as it is usually called, becomes intelligible. When a number of people meet together to work according to an appointed plan, the result of their efforts is naturally more powerful and effective than if they work in isolation and without organizing themselves. There is an old motto which tells us that " In union is strength," the under-lying truth of which is seen in many departments of life. No crew of oarsmen could hope to win a race who did not co-operate and learn to work as inspired by a single will, and among sailors it is an ancient custom to work to the tune of a nautical "chaunty," so as to gain this unity of effort. Acting on this principle, the Church arranges that her workers shall meet and work together in co-operation when the blessing of the Lord is to be distributed over the world. By this community of effort and by working according to a plan, unity of purpose is achieved, and the work done is more effective than anything which would be accomplished without such collaboration. This is the real reason for congregational worship, though the explanation usually given in support of the practice has also its significance—namely, that in so meeting together we give expression to our sense of Christian fellowship, in that we are all children of the one Father.

It has already been explained that not all of the services of the Church are primarily intended for the outside world. There are some rites, like Baptism, Confirmation, Marriage, which are concerned with the individual, and there are Offices like Prime and Complin, which are performed chiefly for the edification of those assisting, or which at any rate do not make any use, except an indirect one, of the sacramental channels in what they do for the world outside. But apart from all this, the collective work on the part of a congregation is not intended to be their sole spiritual activity. Some practice of private meditation is a very necessary feature of training in spiritual development; but this also can often be made more fruitful and easy if done in a consecrated building and in the presence of the Blessed Sacrament. In the public offices of the Church we make use of the prescribed forms and enter wholeheartedly into them, because we are working for others.

It is the duty of the Church to give instruction and training in the work of individual development; and in proportion as people develop their higher faculties under such training, so will they be of greater service in the work of the church. This is peculiarly true; for whilst congregational worship is based on the principle that combined effort directed towards a given end is more effective than unorganised effort, it is also the case that the power generated in such an assembly is not simply the sum total of the effort on the part of those present. The effect is not to be judged only in terms of addition. There is also another principle at work analogous to what in electrical science we call induction. The more developed people in a congregation stimulate those who are less developed, and by the influence that they radiate help others to reach a higher level of consciousness than is normal with them. Hence the enormous value to an ordinary congregation of the presence of some who are trained in meditation and who have an understanding of theosophy. Nor is it only this principle of induction of stimulation that is at work. People who are more advanced spiritually are able to be used as channels for great spiritual forces, which can thus safely be poured upon the whole body of worshippers and greatly enhance their contribution to the outside world.

The Body-Corporate

From the consideration of these various principles which underlie congregational worship, there emerges a rule observance of which is of prime importance in the performance of the Liturgy. It is that the congregation shall do their work not as separate and isolated units, but as a body-corporate. They should, in other words, recognise their fellowship with one another, and strive to do all that they have to do as one body. This is an ideal difficult to achieve. To begin with, most people are habitually centred upon themselves. They are more interested in themselves and in their own experiences than in their fellows. Especially is this so in the domain of religion. As the doctrine of hell and everlasting punishment darkened the fair vista of Christianity, religion became a matter of "saving one's soul," and the Reformation, too, ushered in a period of exaggerated subjectivism.

This self-interest has to be avoided, and the first lesson to be learned by any congregation that would achieve something is to forget themselves and to think rather of God, of great ideals and of their fellow-men. It is difficult for the ordinary person to realise how persistently he thinks of himself. He judges events and things in general by the particular reaction which they have on him. People are loth to face unpleasant realities, and will prefer to burke their very existence. As a first step, then, the worshipper must free his work of this persistent self-interest.

But it is more even than unselfishness that is needed in congregational worship. An intense and active interest in others is needed, a real sympathy, and a habit of going out towards them. The opportunities to cultivate this in the church are unsurpassed. In general, people are at their best when engaged in worship, and therefore easier to deal with; moreover, if there be any one special characteristic which may be said to represent Our Lord's influence, it is the sense of great unity and sympathetic understanding. Difficulties which previously loomed large, melt away in the sunlight of His Love, and it is perhaps easier to realise our fellowship in the One Life before the Blessed Sacrament of His Love than anywhere else. We must then learn to fill our hearts with this Love and uniting ourselves in thought, in sympathy and in action with our fellows do all that has to be done in the service as members of one body—"grafted into the mystical Body of Christ." There is a deep reality underlying those words, and in the administration of Baptism. For the person who is baptized is linked with the Lord who is the head of the body, and becomes part of that body-corporate which is the vehicle of His blessing to the world.

It is the condition of really successful work on the part of a congregation that they should feel this unity, not only in theory but in practice. Everything that is said or sung should be so rendered as by one aspect or facet of this Body, that is, on behalf of the Body, the individual being simply the mouthpiece of the entire congregation for the time being. It is a good plan to work consciously with the aura—that sphere of influence created by the expression of all our faculties, which surrounds and radiates from each one of us. The student would do well constantly to work in his daily life at the realisation that this sphere of influence is around him, affecting his environment. And in church he should practise enfolding the whole of the congregation in this aura and so aim at working as a collectivity. If all will constantly remind themselves of this during the service, the necessary unity of consciousness will be attained. It is of little use to assert in writing that the worship becomes quite a different thing if carried out in this manner. Experience alone can show the student how important is this attitude in the work. One of the purposes of worship is to lift us up into the consciousness of the higher self, that is to say, into Self-realisation. And if our work be really impersonal, outward-turned and unselfish, carried out in an attitude of unity with our fellows, we shall find ourselves rising into a larger consciousness, and able to escape from the prison house of the separated personality. As before said, it is useless to try to depict these experiences of the larger consciousness in words. Words can but serve as a signpost to the great reality which is above formal description.

Religion and the Larger Consciousness

The attainment of this larger consciousness is one of the objects of worship, viewed as an aid to the spiritual development of the individual. It is a definite realisation of the unity of all life. The word "religion" is usually held to be derived from the Latin religere, meaning "to bind back," and it is the purpose of religion to bind us back to God, the source of our being. There are various stages in the process, and so far as the ordinary man is concerned, the first stage is to unite the personality with the soul. This process is later repeated at a higher stage, when the soul in turn is carried up into union with the Monad.[1] To reach the consciousness of the soul is to escape from the imprisoning limitations of the personality, from the illusion of these lower worlds of pilgrimage. For this unselfishness and impersonality are required—as has already been explained—the habit of looking outwards and allowing one's forces to ray out upon the world. Worship gives unparalleled opportunity for the expression of high and noble thoughts. Obviously there are such opportunities in daily life. But they are not ordinarily such as to allow of the same intensity of effort carried out over so long a period of time. To reach self-consciousness at the level of the soul, much cultivation of these higher qualities is needed; they can be awakened and strengthened only by being brought constantly into use. All this is part of the work of the Church, part of the training it gives; and the Church provides both for the private and collective practice of these methods of development, so that we may realise the divinity both in ourselves and in others.

The Liturgy

The Liturgy may be regarded as the "plan of the work," for it is by common working according to this plan that the unity of worship is maintained. Objection is sometimes made to the kind of worship which involves the use of a Liturgy, on the ground that it lacks the spontaneity of extempore worship. The Society of Friends goes even further and, apart from extemporisations on the part of its worshippers, spends much of the meeting in silent meditation. All these objections come from a view of worship which is partial and incomplete, as we shall realise from what has already been said on the subject. Solitary effort or individual meditation is useful and to be encouraged in its own place, but is not the appropriate method to be practised when people meet together to send blessing over the outside world. Similarly it will be evident that extempore prayer and praise may have its value and due position, but cannot replace a ritual based on highly expert and technical knowledge, intended to work in the special way that has already been indicated.

It is hardly necessary to say that a Liturgy ought to be compiled only by those who know to a reasonable extent what they are doing, for a Liturgy is not merely a sequence of beautiful words and actions. It calls into play great forces of nature and it quickens into activity various faculties of man: These processes must follow an appointed order, with due regard to their effect; and the ideal Liturgies are true to type in that they portray in the physical world processes which appertain to the archetypal worlds, the "Intelligible world" of Greek Philosophy.

---

[1] Greek Monos, a unit. An individual spiritual; essence. [Ed.]

Language and Self-expression

The Liturgy is intended to be a vehicle for self-expression on the part of the people. As it moves along stage by stage certain ideas are presented before the people who use it, and emotions of one type or another are called forth from them. Generally, this language is followed more or less carelessly, but to a congregation trained in concentration and able to draw upon the deeper resources of mind and emotion a Liturgy, if it be a good one, offers incredible opportunities. We shall better understand them if we pause for a moment to examine the inner significance of language. Words are a sort of currency by means of which we exchange thought with one another. We are not yet at the stage when we can communicate directly from mind to mind by process of telepathy, and we need consequently to formulate our thought in terms of language and use that as the means of communication. A word is therefore a symbol, that is to say, it is related to a thought, a feeling, which can be regarded as its ensouling life. People can use language quite carelessly, in which case the words embody only a minimum of the life-force. On the other hand, words can purposely be made the vehicle of strong and rich emotion or thought. Our examination of the subject can be carried deeper still; for there exist archetypes of thought and feeling in the higher worlds, and if the consciousness be sufficiently active, it may be so wielded as to touch directly and draw upon these archetypal sources of power, the word being thus a key which unlocks the entry to this universal reservoir of power, and releases a flow of it for our use. It is in this attitude that we should approach the Liturgy. The leading key ideas, as they are successively brought before us in the language of the Liturgy, are an opportunity for collective thought on the part of the people and, so used, the Liturgy becomes a vehicle of self-expression.

The Liturgy of the Liberal Catholic Church has been very carefully compiled with this end in view, and given agreement with the leading ideas of the service. Nothing is put into the mouth of priest or people which they cannot honestly and reasonably be asked to say and mean. They are not asked to take vows or to make promises of an impossible nature, but rather (as in the case of the Confirmation service) to say that they will strive to do certain things which are generally regarded as good and desirable. Moreover, the language is that of joyous and glad aspiration. Expressions of fear and wrath and hell, which so disfigure most liturgies, have been carefully eradicated. We see, then, that what is called congregational worship, combined with the use of a Liturgy, provides a mechanism by which spiritual power can be flooded out upon the external world at the various levels on which men's consciousness is capable of functioning.

CHURCH MUSIC

THE use of music in Church worship is quite primitive in the historical sense of the word. The music of the Jewish Temple appears to have been elaborate and to have filled an important place. The earliest Christians, converts from Judaism, attended the Temple, and their public worship would have been Jewish—save that they met in suitable places for the "breaking of the Bread." Later, as converts from other sources came in, they developed their own Liturgy, which included readings from the Old Testament and the singing of Psalms, after the manner of Judaism. Through force of outer circumstances their ritual manifestations and music would have been restrained; but it is quite evident that they took over the use of music current in Judaism and in the Mystery-cults of the Mediterranean. Tertullian tells us that Holy Scripture was read and Psalms sung, and Pliny that they honoured their Lord before dawn by the singing of a hymn. The chanting of the Liturgy was a universal custom, so far as we can judge, in the religions of antiquity. To this day, the Orthodox Eastern Church enjoins[1] this chanting of the Divine Liturgy in its entirety, maintaining that it is not seemly that the speaking voice employed in secular life should be heard in the Liturgy. The early Church did not permit the use of organs or other instruments, as savouring too much of paganism; and to this day the music of the Eastern Church is purely vocal and the organ is unknown in its churches.

Gregorian Music

In its primitive form this chanting is simple, the inflections of the voice being few and free from elaboration. Such music is in the West called "Plainchant" or "Gregorian" music. It is quite possible that the primitive chant is based on the inflection of the human voice which is natural to people who speak in the open air or before large gatherings of people. Such conditions demand a special technique of speech. As the chant develops it becomes more ornate and the inflections are more frequent and more elaborate. This enriched form of chant was called melismatic (Gr. *melos*, a song), as opposed to the syllabic chant, in which a single note was attributed to a syllable. Especially did this tendency towards elaboration show itself in the singing of the word "Allelluia"—the ancient acclamation of the Divine Majesty—in which the final *a* was made the occasion for an outpouring of purest and ecstatic melody. We eventually get specimens of melismatic chant in which over three hundred notes are attributed to one syllable, and there is, I have been told, one instance of seven or eight hundred notes being so allocated. The syllabic chant is supposed to have been the expression of western taste, which liked directness of utterance. The melismatic chant is thought by some to have been derived also from the Hebrew cult. This is quite possible, and certainly this element of ecstatic vocalisation is to be found in the traditional synagogue music, much of which is of the purest splendour. Others think rather that the melismatic chant was the product of Eastern temperament, which has less appreciation of the exigencies of time and space, and issued from the monasteries of Syria and Egypt in the fourth century. It is even said that the melismatic chant was borrowed from Gnostic heretics, who after the manner of the Egyptian hierophants elaborated their sacred chants to the sounds of the seven vowels (the two forms of *e* and *o* in the Greek alphabet were included). There are still some fragments of these Gnostic chants extant, in works dating from the fourth to the seventh century—a period contemporaneous with the development of the melismatic chant in the West. Authorities in the domain of occultism suggest that some of the traditional music comes down to us in broad outline through Egypt from Atlantis. However this may be, there is a

---

[1] In the meaning of requiring. [Ed.]

strong family resemblance between the chanting that is common to the religions of the East and the Gregorian tones of the Christian Church. As a young man, my life so shaped itself that I was brought into close personal contact with one of the few exponents of this traditional music in England, and with a church where much of it was performed. I made some study of it, and eventually grew to appreciate even the more elaborate and archaic specimens of Plainchant. Visiting India some years later, I found myself fairly well at home with the music of that country, and not at all needing the gradual process of acclimatisation to Indian music necessary to most Europeans. Some of the mantras that one hears chanted in India bear a close structural and melodic resemblance to certain of the Gregorian Tones.

This earlier music of the Church, as already said, is called "Gregorian" or "Plainchant." There is a tradition and some evidence that may be called historical that Pope Gregory I edited the body of liturgical music extant in his day and brought it into order. He lived from 540-604; therefore much of the music that is popularly known as Gregorian was written after his time. It is called Plainchant (*cantus planus*), not because it is necessarily simple and unembellished, but because it flows evenly and smoothly like the landscape that we call a plain.

The Choice of Music

The question as to what music is most suitable for the services of the Church is one on which there has been much difference of opinion. We find, in consequence, very different types of music being employed in churches, both in our own country and abroad.

There are many advocates of what is called "the Cathedral service," in which the people are expected to listen reverently to high-class music well rendered by a trained choir. Music has great power to uplift people, and a better sermon is often given from the organ loft or choir stalls than from the pulpit. It may be employed as an adjunct to church worship with good effect. At the Eucharist it may be so used during the Second Incensing and the Communions of the people, or after the Gospel or Creed. But the kind of music in which the congregation participates by listening is not what is desired in the worship of the Liberal Catholic Church, except as an adjunct to the service. To go to the heart of the matter, it is not so much music that is required, as sound as a vehicle of self-expression. Greater intensity of effort is required when a service of words is sung than when uttered in the normal speaking voice; consequently the output of power is greater. A great deal lies behind the conception of the voice as the organ of the creative word, and much greater effect is produced in the surrounding area when a person sings a thing than when he says it. The effect of which I speak is not simply the dynamic one of the physical plane, but there is also a greater intensity of emotional and mental effort. The process is largely concerned with the vivifying of the elemental essence.

Consequently, that type of music is best which gives the people most scope for self-expression. The standard will naturally vary according to the people with whom one has to deal, it will vary according to nationality and to the extent to which they can give the time and energy to practice and instruction. Music that is too "highbrow" is obviously unsuitable, but it need not be too "lowbrow." It is well to keep at a good standard for the people concerned. For some churches and in some countries revivalist hymns of the Moody and Sankey type may be quite useful. Many of the hymn tunes (and words) which find popular favour in England cannot possibly be used on the Continent of Europe, where musical taste is generally different.

The Structure and Rendering of the Gregorian Chant

I have gone into the subject of Plainchant at some length because much use of it is made in the Liberal Catholic Church, and it is well therefore that our members should understand something about it. The simpler forms are peculiarly suitable for congregational singing. Their compass lies within convenient bounds, they have much to recommend them aesthetically and in regard to their working upon the psychic part of man's nature, and they have the right character and produce the proper "atmosphere" for liturgical use.

But Plainsong differs in many respects from music of the more usual modern type. It is not difficult even for those who have no musical training to grasp the special characteristics of this music, and a congregation that has learned to understand these special features of Gregorian music can easily sing it as it should be sung.

In the first place, it is intended to be taken in free rhythm. We all understand that the ordinary hymn has the metre of poetry, and the music divided into bars, with so many beats to each bar, has a fixed metre. The Psalms are not poetry but prose. All good prose has a certain rhythm, not the regular metre of poetry, but none the less a certain balance. The so-called Anglican chant, used in most English Churches, is written in fixed metre with bars, and tends to bring the words into the same strict metre. An example of such a chant is found in our service of Vespers for the *Te Deum*, though this is a quadruple chant instead of the more usual double variety. The drawbacks of this variety of chant can be modified if the chant is treated freely and adapted, as far as may be, to the flow of the words, and especially if the words allocated to the reciting note be not hurried. It may be pointed out in passing that the words of the *Te Deum*, as well as those of the *Nunc Dimittis*, are wrongly divided in the traditional setting of the Anglican Prayer Book (which we have for good reasons followed). Those of the first two verses should in reality form the two halves of one verse. The existing arrangement shortens unduly the halves of the verses, with the result that the musical rendering of these two canticles is difficult. The *Te Deum* will be more effective if care is taken to speed up the first and third sections of the chant, especially the third, in which people tend to drag.

The Gregorian chant, on the other hand, is not meant to be taken in strict rhythm or fixed time. It is flexible and is meant to follow the words. It cannot be pretended that this is always possible. The music is bound in certain cases to preponderate over the words, the more so when it becomes elaborate. Still, in the simple Gregorian chant this distortion is reduced to a minimum. It should always be remembered, then, that this music is in free rhythm and intended to follow the flow of the words. Let us take as an example the phrase: "I said to the King." The accent here comes on the two words "said" and "King." As we speak the sentence, "to" and "the" are barely touched, "the" less so even than "to." In reciting this according to the ordinary music, the choir will dawdle on these two words. But in Gregorian music, the accents should be given to "said" and "King" and the other two words sung very rapidly, the two together occupying about the same time as "said."

In order to illustrate the structure of a Plainsong Tone, the melody used for the opening canticle of the Eucharist is here printed:—

First half of verse

Second half of verse

4   5

The part numbered 1 is called the Intonation. It is used for the opening of the first verse and of the two verses of the Gloria. For solemn, festival or ornate forms of the canticles, it is used for every verse. Then follows the Reciting Note, marked 2. The singers should begin promptly with this, but it need not be hurried or "gabbled." The tendency is to do this and then to take the Mediation or Inflexion, marked 3, slowly. People are usually unfamiliar with the Mediation and are more or less anxious about the pointing or distribution of the words. Also they are perhaps used to the Anglican chant where these notes are sung in fixed measure. Exactly the contrary should be the case. The words should be uttered deliberately on the Reciting Note, with stress on accented words in the case of a long recitation; then the Mediation should be sung very rapidly, freely and easily, without preliminary hesitation. There follows here a pause represented by the colon printed in the middle of the verse in the Liturgy. This colon marks the antiphony, or point of balance between the two halves of the verse, which is characteristic of Hebrew poetry, and which is recognised in the traditional way of rendering these psalms. In some English Cathedrals the two sides of the Choir (*Decani* and *Cantoris*) each take a half-verse, and thus sing antiphonally. The pause at the colon should be well marked; in fact its observance enables one to chant at a brisk tempo without giving the appearance of irreverent hurrying. Then follows the Reciting Note of the second half of the psalm verse, marked 4, and the Ending, marked 5.

According to the structure of the individual Tone will be the notes demanding accent. In the above Tone the A in the Mediation takes an accent and the following B should be subordinated; and in the ending the first A receives an accent and the last A an even stronger one.

Another peculiarity that is sometimes encountered is what is called technically an "interrupted" or "broken" Mediation. An instance of this occurs in the Tone that we use for the Asperges and for one of the Vesper psalms. This Mediation is marked by a wavy line or dots:

to   be   mov   –   ed
day   by   day

The rule is that the note following the dots is omitted when the last word of the half-verse is a monosyllable, but sung if it comprises more than one syllable. Our musical Liturgy does not always observe this rule. The last verse of the Gloria, for example, ends its first half with a monosyllable—"shall be." The word "be" should be sung to the note B, before the break of the Mediation. In practice the word "shall" is attributed to the B, and "be" to the following G. There are two reasons to account for this, namely, that the word "ever" falls awkwardly on the first B of the inflexion, and secondly that if the "be" ended on the ascending note it would tend to receive an accent, whereas it should be subordinate to "shall." A similar case occurs in one of the Vesper psalms, where the half-verse ends with the words "Holy One." Our Liturgy instead of breaking the Mediation here according to rule, places the word "One" on the lower note, so as to avoid accenting the "One." The more correct method would be that the singers should lower the voice on this word, even though it be sung on the note of the ascending scale.

Plainsong Notation and the Accents

There is one other feature of plainsong the understanding of which is of great importance. That which distinguishes music of the ancient world from modern music is that the former relies for its effect chiefly upon the rhythmic element and the latter on the harmonic. Jazz is an attempt to re-introduce the older method in conjunction with the newer. How the transition took place is easily to be seen. With the introduction of harmony, or rather of counterpoint, the unaccustomedness of the singers and the crudity of the organ mechanism then existent required one note to be laid out flat as it were, against the other. It was not until a much later period that choirs attained sufficient virtuosity to sing melodies with complicated rhythm against one another, as for instance in some of Wagner's marvellous part-writing. He who would understand the old music must learn to appreciate this rhythmic complexity. The Plainchant music had a notation all of its own, and this involved certain rules as to its rendering, based on a scheme of primary, secondary and even other subordinate accents. The wondrous poise of this music with its recurrence of accents sweeps the listener into the influence of its rhythm; arid, as much of it was evidently written with knowledge, the effects produced are most remarkable. It is useless, however, to write about this. Such things belong to the Mysteries, and must be experienced by the individual.

The two examples of "neumatic notation" which now follow will serve to illustrate this principle of accentuation. The first is from the well-known hymn, "*Urbs Beata Hierusalem*" ("Blessed City, Heavenly Salem"), Hymns, Ancient and Modern, No. 396.

Of pure gold are   fas-hion-ed

The joining of two or more notes together is called a note-group or "*neum*." The rule is that the first member of such a simple note-group is to be accented—whereas the tendency of the modern musician is to accent the second of such a group. In the more elaborate music one finds a number of notes grouped together, some requiring a secondary accent, and *neums* themselves are linked together in lengthy sequence. In the above illustration the figure to which the word "gold" is sung is a "*clivis*." That corresponding to "are" is a combination of a "*podatus*" and a "*clivis*." The lower note of the *podatus* is sung first and accented, and the other notes tailed gently off. Notice the four-lined stave, and the clef mark indicating that the line on which it is placed corresponds to F. The clef is movable, and the system is a kind of tonic sol-fa, the whole thing being susceptible of transposition.

The next illustration is a sentence from the *Sursum Corda*:

Ha-be - - mus ad   Do-mi-num
We lift them up   unto the Lord

Again it is the first member of each group that is firmly accented. Finally an elaborate grouping is subjoined.

I - - - te - - - - - - - - - - - - - - - - - -

. . . . **mis-sa est**

The clef in this case is the C clef, so that the line on which it occurs may be taken as corresponding to C.

The Musical Tempo

Next to the Celebrant, the Organist is the most important official of the church, for rhythm is the foundation of all collective work, and it is the organist who has control of the rhythm. I have my own very decided views on the question of musical tempo; it is a question which involves a number of different issues, and I will endeavour to deal with them here. In the first place, I think that the musical rendering of the Liturgy is not first and foremost a question of music at all. The real Church music is the rendering of really good music by a trained choir or a very trained congregation. This is fitly so called; and as I have said above, this is to be treated as an adjunct to the Liturgy, like the sermon. What we are concerned with during the rest of the service is to get the people to express themselves joyously and whole-heartedly through sound. This may not produce very good music, though it should not produce bad music. The production of good music is not the aim that we set before ourselves; the aim is rather the working upon and stimulation of human character, and the blending of the congregation into an organic unity.

The first task with the ordinary raw material of a congregation is to wake them up. The consciousness of most ordinary people is largely in the vegetable stage. They are the people who have, perhaps, been in the habit of attending church and listening to the prayers being said, with little or no attempt to put anything of their own will or effective devotion into either prayers or singing. Such people have to be transformed into active and intelligent collaborators.

Hence, I believe in setting the music to a *tempo* to which they are entirely unaccustomed and which rouses them with a shock when they first hear it. That is the first step in the training of such people. They are encouraged of course to participate in the singing, and their first experiences leave them breathless and bewildered. Presently they master the technique of what is wanted of them, and when once you have got them alert and awake and made them into active workers, there is no harm in slowing down a little and adding refinements of light and shade to what is being done. One must not, of course, overdo this kind of thing in public worship. Still, the fact remains—the music has to be employed for the shaping of human character. The greatest care must be taken that the congregation do not get sleepy and drag the music. A few *staccato* chords on the organ are a good animating influence, and recall people to their work.

There is more involved in this training than meets the eye. People complain at first that they cannot feel devotional when the music is taken quickly, and this in many cases simply means that they have not time to feel the effects of their own emotions. It should be explained to them that the singing is not intended as an occasion for emotional self-gratification—and, as for real devotion, they have plenty of time for it at the more silent parts of the ceremony. The singing is part of the collective work done less for the edification of the participants than to provide the "raw material," so to speak, for the great spiritual outpouring that is to help and uplift the outer world. The secret of the work is that people should learn impersonality or self-disinterestedness. Gradually their personal idiosyncrasies disappear; they merge themselves into the body-corporate, working now as individuals rather than personalities, and a great unity of consciousness is achieved. The congregation is then a willing and pliant instrument ready to answer to the inspiration and special character of the service—for there is infinite variety in the Sacraments of Christ's Church.

It is when this stage is reached that collaboration with the higher Angels becomes possible. They work on a basis of rhythm, and they are themselves untouched by thoughts of selfishness. A congregation that can work rhythmically, no longer hampered by the forms and technique of its work, but using them as the means of its unity, and which has learned to be self-disinterested, can work not only as a unity in its own consciousness, but can blend their human consciousness with that of the Angels, and enter into the peace that passeth understanding.

Our own efforts at devotion are feeble and poor. The offering that we make is not worthy to be borne by our great High Priest before the Divine Throne. But let it never be forgotten that we are not alone in this work. The whole of Nature joins with us in our Eucharist of thanksgiving, and our feeble offering is purified and embellished by the more perfect devotion and love of those who gather round our altars, and with friendly encouragement join with us in the commemoration of that Eternal Sacrifice by which the world is nourished and sustained.

THE HOLY EUCHARIST

IN the preceding chapters I have dealt with certain general principles underlying Church worship. I propose now to apply these to some of our services, and to suggest to worshippers how they may co-operate actively and intelligently in our beautiful rites. I feel some hesitancy in setting about the task, because guidance of this kind tends to create a fixed orthodoxy of procedure. But so many people are entering our movement who have had no previous experience of Catholic worship, and the more definite use of emotion and thought of which I have previously been writing is so foreign to congregations in general, that some such *vade mecum* is needed as a kind of foundation for their instruction.

The Procession And The Asperges

We will begin with the Holy Eucharist, and proceed at once to discuss the 'why' and the 'how' of the procession and the Asperges. Whenever numbers of miscellaneous people gather together for a religious ceremony, the first stage in the process must always be one of purification. It is necessary that the people shall be brought into a similar direction of thought and emotion; they should be helped to feel their unity with one another, and should be purified of those discordant elements produced within them by their contact with ordinary life, its worries and irritations.

The procession around the church, combined with the singing of the introcessional hymn, tends to steady down their thoughts and to weld them into a more uniform and united body. Great attention should be paid to the formation of this procession. It is headed by the censer with its purifying influence, and the processional cross which follows serves as a distributing centre for the spiritual power built up by the procession. The clergy come last in the procession sending their greater contribution of blessing through those in front. People are so little accustomed to team-work that the carrying out of such a procession is usually found difficult. Gaps are likely to occur in it, because people are so little used to thinking of themselves in right relationship with others; those ahead often fail to consider or to observe those at the rear, and often people will be so intent upon themselves that they pay no heed to the movement of the general body.

A well-formed procession symbolises the unity at which the participants in the worship should aim; and if it moves as one body, maintaining uniformity of distance between those who compose it, it serves as an embodiment and channel of this sense of unity as it moves through the church. Gaps mean a leakage in the power flowing through the procession from back to front, and break the homogeneity and efficiency of the vehicle.

The Asperges now follows,[1] and this may be described as the marking out of the field of operations. It is not necessary for the priest to fling the water; rather he projects the influence which has been instilled into it at its blessing over the area that he intends to delimit. The effort he makes should be positive, not apologetic, and he should aim at clearing the atmosphere well above the heads of the people. During all this time the dominant thought of the people should be one of purification.

During the *Antiphon* the intention of great purity should be linked with the words 'clean' and 'whiter than snow.' The latter words are usually sung rallentando.[2] The Psalm

---

[1] When the Full Form is used. [Ed.]

[2] "Gradually slower." [Ed.]

should be sung in a clean and clear-cut fashion, not too slowly.

Great attention should be paid to the versicles and responses which follow. It is the usual custom to make a smaller cross over the lips with the thumb at the words 'O Lord, open Thou our lips.'[1] This gesture is an invocation to the Divine Power to kindle our speech and to awaken within us the sense of sanctity. The idea of Christian worship is largely founded on praise; praise and thanksgiving are part of the sacrifice that we offer. Worship means the offering of 'worth-ship' to almighty God.

We may safely say—to quote from the preface to our Liturgy:

> that God Himself does not need our praise, and certainly would not appreciate anything in the nature of adulation from those who might be expected to know better. We feel and know, on the other hand, that it is good for us to lift up our hearts in praise and aspiration, and to strive to unify ourselves more completely with the divine will. But we may go further, and say with all reverence that God does make use of our co-operation, and in his plan counts on that intelligent and energetic co-operation more and more as man grows into spiritual maturity. The Liberal Catholic Church aims at making its members strong and efficient workers in His service.

And in another part of our Liturgy—the service for the Admission of a Singer—it is said:

> Man is endowed with many faculties, and all of them should be used, in the service of God. From time immemorial, however, the voice has been regarded as the especial instrument for rendering praise and glory to almighty God. It is indeed very meet, right, and our bounden duty that we, in company with the angelic host, should give thanks unto Him whose name is holy and who filleth the whole earth with His majesty and glory. And as you come before Him with a song upon your lips, see to it that you also make melody in your heart, joining in the great song of life which is the ceaseless hymn of all creation. Let your work, then, be done in the spirit of service, not with vainglory and pride of self, but rather in singleness of heart. So shall the blessing of the Christ rest upon you, and inspire both your voice and your heart.

Such are the ideas of praise and worship that we are bidden to recall to our minds as the priest sings: 'O Lord, open Thou our lips.' And the congregation bursts forth in response 'And our mouth shall show forth Thy praise.' It may be well here to draw attention to the fact that in all well-rendered services—as in all operations of ceremonial—the participants should always be turning their attention to the various points of their work slightly ahead, so that when the right time comes they shall be ready and prepared for the piece of work. So the first note of this particular phrase should be the signal for the release at the psychological moment of a vast body of pent-up praise and reverent adoration. If the responses are planned out and worked up beforehand in this way, they give intense vitality and power to the ceremony.

The last of these versicles and responses is the Minor Benediction and its response. The priest lifts himself up into the consciousness of the Lord and sends out His blessing over the people. If the priest be loved and respected by his people, there will come a glad response of love as they sing: 'And with Thy spirit,' and in any case there should be the reply of glad and lively co-operation, not only at the physical level of co-operation, but at all levels of consciousness, up to that of the highest that can be touched.

---

[1] This custom was disapproved by the Third General Episcopal Synod and is not practiced today. [Ed.]

The Angel who is to take charge of the preliminary work of preparation and of the building of the eucharistic edifice is then invoked, and the congregation should go out in their thought to welcome him with courtesy and with the same loving co-operation that is given to the priest.

The Invocation

The introductory ceremony of the Asperges being over, the Eucharist proper begins with the invocation of the Ever-Blessed Trinity. In the case of the shorter form [of the Asperges, included in the Shorter Form] of the Eucharist and of most of the other ceremonies, the Invocation introduces the ceremony. It is a dedication of all our efforts to the Trinity, and an acknowledgment and reminder that all is being done in Their power. The 'Name' in the ancient sense of the word represented the power flowing from the essence of a being. It is so used in the old and well-known traditional Irish hymn called 'St. Patrick's Breastplate,' which begins with the words:

> I bind unto myself to-day
> The strong Name of the Trinity;
> By invocation of the same,
> The Three in One and One in Three.

When the Invocation is said the worshipper thinks of the triune Godhead, and awakens into activity the three primary centres of consciousness within himself (for man is made in the image of God) or whatever reflection of them he can touch.

The Canticle

This Canticle, with its Antiphon, is still in the nature of a preparation for the ceremony to follow. During the singing of it the Priest remains at the foot of the altar steps, and he does not ascend them until after the *Confiteor*. The key-note is joy and gladness. The intention of the Canticle is to inspire the worshippers with a glad spirit of praise and aspiration, and references are made to the majesty of God amid the grandeur of the universe, all with a view to enlarging and widening people's minds and lifting them out of the pettiness and sordidness of ordinary life. These passing comments will serve to indicate to worshippers how to use their thought in the rendering of the Canticle. Words like joy, gladness, strength, peace, should be thoroughly meant, and our praise should be thought of as uniting with that of all Nature and of the 'heavens that declare the glory of God.'

More versicles and responses follow this, designed with a view to reminding us of the God within, the Inner Ruler Immortal, and to stirring us to call upon His Omnipotence.

The Confiteor

The process of preparation by self-purification leads on finally to the *Confiteor*, one of the noblest pieces of writing in our Liturgy, which is literally a surrender of the heart before God. It continues the process by which we lift ourselves out of the personality into the individual or egoic[1] consciousness. In some Churches it is chanted; but the occasion seems apt for the

---

[1] *Ego* is used here as in theosophical literature in the sense of the higher side of man, the soul, as against the lower everyday self, the personality (from *persona*) mask. [Ed.]

use of the speaking voice, for in the recitation of this it seems as though we pay less attention to the collective consciousness that we have been trying to build up, and make our own personal and free intercourse with the Divine Love; and for this the use of the natural speaking voice is perhaps more appropriate. The beautiful phrase, 'Thou, O Lord, hast made us for Thyself, and our hearts are ever restless till they find their rest in Thee,' is from St. Augustine (Conf. Lib. I., cap I.). During the concluding words we should be glowing and uplifted in our egoic aspect.

The Absolution

The Absolution sets the seal as it were, upon all this effort in the way of purification, upliftment and ego-realization. That may be regarded as the upward moving flow of force rising from the people. It calls down its contemporaneous response from on high, as does all true aspiration. But the Absolution represents another special outpouring from above, the effect of which is to hold and maintain the bodies in their opened attitude, and in their capacity to transmit a fuller flow of life.

The Censing

In the use of incense we make a varied appeal to human consciousness. We appeal to the imagination through the familiar medium of symbolism, for the world without and the world within are intimately correlated. The smoke of the incense as it rises upwards before the altar is beautifully associated by our holy mother the Church with the prayers of the saints rising before the throne of God. The offering of incense is to us an outer expression of the sacrifice of ourselves, our souls and bodies, a sacrifice offered in union with that of the whole Church past and present, militant, expectant and triumphant, and with that One Great Sacrifice—the great offering of the Second Person of the Blessed Trinity—by which the world is nourished and sustained. This appeal to the imagination through the sense of sight is heightened by the rhythmic movement of the servers which satisfies our sense of order, by the perfume which makes its own appeal through the appropriate sense, and even by the clanking of the chains which through a third sense marks certain points of the rhythm. Besides all this, the incense serves another purpose; it is an instrument as well as a symbol. The scent which it diffuses has in itself an influence which is normally beneficent and tends to devotion and purity of feeling; and the incense spreads this abroad wherever its perfume may pass, as well as the spiritual power poured into it at the blessing by the priest.

It may be mentioned in passing that care ought to be taken as to the composition of the incense burned in our churches. To mix a satisfactory incense for oneself is not at all an easy matter. It is generally known that *gum benzoin* supplies the cathartic element, and *olibanum* the devotional, and that for a cultured and enlightened congregation the latter should be in decided preponderance. A little *gum thus*[1] is sometimes added to give vigour to the etheric action, sometimes also myrrh and various essential oils, such as rose, cloves, lemon, geranium, sandalwood. But the correct proportions of these are largely matters of experience. Moreover, there is a great range of difference in the quality and price of the gums indicated, and there are processes of mixing the ingredients under heat in the case of the gums and by gradual absorption in the case of the oils. Much may depend also on the nature of the embers that are employed. It is perfume

[1] The exact nature of *Gum Thus* is a matter of some speculation, it is generally taken to be the dried, ground sap of pine or fir trees. [Ed.]

that should be aimed at, not smoke. The best effect is obtained the moment the incense is spread upon the charcoal, and care has to be taken that the incense is not such as at once to take over the embers with a layer of malodorous used material.

How should the people think during the censing? They may use their imagination along the symbolic and aesthetic lines indicated above. But other lines of work also suggest themselves, for as the candles are taken in rotation, our thoughts may well turn to the Rays[1] and the special influences that they represent. As the priest censes each candle in turn, he should gather up from the congregation their contribution of the quality of the Ray concerned and, uniting that with his own contribution should offer it with love and devotion to the Lord of the Ray.

The chief purpose of the censing is to prepare the altar and its surroundings for the spiritual operations that are to follow, and of which it is the central focus. Finally, the priest is himself censed. He then turns to the people with the Minor Benediction, to renew and refurbish the link between himself and the people, and to permeate them with the higher degree of sanctification produced by the ceremony of incensing.

The Introit

The initial part of the Eucharist concerned with the purification of the people and of the theatre of their work is now finished—though the process of purification naturally continues right up to the reception of the Holy Communion. There now follows a good deal of hard work in the way of praise and adoration. The latter word means really 'speaking to' God (Latin: ad—to, orare—to speak), and adoration here is quite literally a speaking to God. Similarly, the word worship (Old English; weortkscipe) means the giving of 'worth,' or that which is His due, to God.

Our worship and 'speaking to God' begin, as is fitting, with the ascription of praise to the Ever-Blessed Trinity. Our thoughts should be carried up as high as possible, and the practice of contemplation upon the Divine Being will eventually open up for us a wider expansion of consciousness. For many people who have grown up with little instruction or thought upon religious matters, God is little more than a name, and certainly the thought of God does not in such cases call out any feeling of love and self-dedication or any passion for righteousness. It is not that the modern generation lacks idealistic conceptions, but it has transferred them from so seemingly remote an abstraction as God and contrived to fasten them round intermediary characters. To sing, therefore, of the Holy Trinity which is yet 'the Undivided Unity' is to use an idiom not generally understood. It is not always well, however, to make concessions to the passing ignorance of a generation or group of generations.

There are some institutions rooted in the immemorial past, whose task it is, while welcoming new aspects of Truth, to preserve certain things which are fundamental and which, because they are eternal, are changeless. These are institutions not to be changed and modified by generations or by races, but rather to change them. Is it not true, as say the Scriptures, that 'in Him we live, and move, and have our being.'[2] His is the all-embracing life; and could we but know it, we are closer to God than we can possibly be to any of our fellow-men, or even to Those Greater Ones, to Whom we look up with love and veneration.

---

[1] A Theosophical typology envisioning divine characteristics; as a prism reflects light so each of us refract some aspect of God. [Ed.]

[2] Acts, xvii, 28.

One very suggestive book which presents God under the thought of the Numinous is Rudolf Otto's *The Idea of the Holy*. He speaks of the *mysterium tremendum*, that sense of the awe-fulness of God, which can seize upon man with almost paralysing effect, and make itself felt in a thousand different ways. This sense of awe of the Divine Majesty has deteriorated into the familiar sense of fear, whereas the underlying idea is much more that of something stupendously over-powering, because so infinitely richer in all characteristics than ourselves.

I cannot here enlarge upon this very fascinating theme, but the Liberal Catholic Church has as one of its tasks, it has always seemed to me, to restore to the technical language of religion the wealth of meaning which originally underlay that terminology. In the course of the Introit we presently come upon the words 'honour' and 'glory' in the phrase 'to Whom be honour and glory for ever and ever. Amen.' Honour is a word of many meanings, including: high respect, reputation, nobleness of mind; and glory similarly may mean: exalted renown, praise and thanksgiving, resplendent majesty, beauty or magnificence, effulgence of heavenly light. The 'glory of God' is that sense of overmastering power and beauty and bliss which we sometimes are privileged to sense on occasions of great spiritual experience. When the catechisms tell us that we are here on earth 'to glorify God,' the inner meaning of the phrase is to make glorified and effulgent the radiance of the divine light within us. And we speak further of this Divine Glory which 'covers the earth as the waters cover the sea' when we hymn the Supreme with the words, 'How excellent is Thy Name in all the world,' the Name having here the usual technical meaning of the essence, the power or the life.

The music to which the Introit is set in our Musical Liturgy is one of the Parisian tones, one of those melodies written on the model of the Gregorian tones which grew up in the later usage of the diocese of Paris, as others grew up in other dioceses.

The Kyrie

I cannot do better than quote some words of Bishop Leadbeater upon the use of the Kyrie:

> …this ninefold invocation corresponds to the ninefold offering of spirit, soul and bodies at the censing; that opened up the man at those three levels, and the response which comes to this appeal fills the opened vessels. As he sings the first petition, the worshipper, reaching up with all his strength towards the All-Father, and trying to realize his absolute unity with Him, should think: 'I am a spark of Thee, the Living Flame; O father, pour Thyself forth into and through Thy spark.' Holding the same realization, as he sings the second, he will feel: 'Father, flood Thou my soul, that through it other souls may be nourished.' And at the third: 'Father, my bodies are Thine; use Thou them to Thy glory.' At the fourth, fifth and sixth recitations, he will repeat these thoughts, substituting the realization of the Son for that of the Father; and in the third series he will offer the same petitions to God the Holy Ghost. Yet in all this he must not ask anything as for himself alone, nor take pride in being chosen as a separate vessel for God's grace, but rather know himself as one among the brethren, a soldier among comrades.[1]

The Kyrie provides a very wonderful opportunity for out-pouring of love on the part of the congregation. It is not easy, of course, to do this straight away—to order, as it were. The majority of people are not used to producing emotions directly by their own efforts. Emotions are more usually called forth by some event, or by the presence of some person, in our outer

[1] *The Science of the Sacraments.*

surroundings. The sight of a little child, or of someone dear to us, evokes our feelings of affection. We are more used to working in this way of reaction to our environment, and most people find some difficulty in producing any kind of strong emotion directly from within. And yet we are called upon to exteriorise one emotion after another all through the rendering of the Liturgy. It is one of the accomplishments that we learn through the practice of meditation. To be able to feel a rich warm glow of love, such as is demanded of us in the Kyrie, requires long effort and practice. We do well to begin by thinking of some person whom we love, and to dwell upon him, intensifying our sense of affection as we proceed. We then take this glow of love, refine and ennoble it in every way—so as to make it pure and fitting for divine worship. And then, substituting the Source of all love, direct our efforts to reaching up towards Him. As the congregation learns to do this during the Kyrie, the floodgates of heaven are opened, and the Divine Love pours down upon the group of devoted worshippers.

The Gloria In Excelsis

The Gloria opens with an expression of praise to God and the sending of a wave of peace over the outer world. The phrases which immediately follow can be coloured differently with shades of meaning according to the disposition of the worshipper. To 'bless' God is an archaic expression; not strictly logical perhaps, since blessing is given by superiors. As contrasted with the preceding word 'praise,' it carries perhaps the idea of blending love and warmth of feeling into our action. The special significations of 'worship' and 'glorify' have already been indicated when considering the Introit. 'We give thanks to Thee for Thy great glory' is a quaint but wonderful phrase. We then pass on to extol the kingly aspect of God, the aspect of power and omnipotence.

In the second paragraph the phase of thought changes, and we pass especially to the consideration of the Second Person. The music should suddenly grow much softer at the words 'Indwelling Light,' as we think of the great mystery of the Christ who dwells in the human heart, 'the Light which lighteth every man that cometh into the world,' and our thoughts turn at once in reverence to cherish and revere that Divine Presence within. We then apostrophise the well-known Trinity of Wisdom, Strength and Beauty, pouring forth a great stream of love, of strength and of splendour, as we lift ourselves in aspiration. The prayer that God is asked to receive is our outpouring of strength.

The third paragraph is a final paean of praise addressed to Our Lord, concluding with an ascription of praise to the Blessed Trinity.

The congregation will do well to keep very active and vigorous during the Gloria, and should beware of dragging the music. Up to this point the singing has entailed very hard work; but the most strenuous part is now accomplished, the outlines of our building are complete, and our coming task is concerned with the enriching and embellishment of our labours.

The Collects

Not much need be said about the collects. In fact, it should suffice to say that they are intended to collect the thoughts of the people and offer them before the heavenly throne. The collect of the week often expresses the special intention of the season, the subject round which our spiritual efforts for the week are to turn. The congregation have it within their power to make the last collect for peace a very powerful determination towards world-peace. The thoughts that are presented in the collects are usually cast into the form of supplication or prayer, partly because that is traditional, and even more because it is so extraordinarily difficult to write affirmations in language that is graceful and fitting. The effort has been that they shall have the character of aspirational utterances. There is an old saying that 'God helps those who help themselves,' and although this proverb is often made the starting-point for demonstrations of human wit, it is none-the-less very true in this case. Supplication, in which a person asks for something, may be beautiful if uttered in a spirit of devotion and earnest faith, and will, we believe, receive its response; but more worthy of a potentially divine humanity is surely the attitude of co-operating with the Divine Will in evolution. In our prayers, therefore, we do well to create by our own efforts the qualities for which we ask, knowing that as those positive efforts are offered to God, they will be increased and made fruitful by His power.

The Epistle And Gospel

These serve the purpose, not only of instructing and exercising the minds of the people, but also of contributing mental matter to the eucharistic edifice. The Liberal Catholic Church may be said, on the whole, to have what may be called 'modernist' ideas on the subject of the scriptures. Popular opinion, at large, is rapidly moving away from the idea of their being inspired in the literal or verbal sense; or that, except in a very general and romantic sense, they can be called the 'Word of God.' There is in them much that is the product of the highest inspiration, and we cannot reverence and treasure too highly the sayings of Our Lord or of some of the prophetic passages of the Old Testament. But the fact remains that the scriptures are very unequal, and in many cases difficult or even impossible to understand. As in the case of many ancient documents, passages are capable of various interpretations, and isolated as we are from the correspondence or thought which called them into being, we have no means of deciding what was the intended meaning of their authors. How much easier would our theology be if it were possible to re-awaken and question our authors, or to travel back through the ages and place our minds in close contact with theirs!

Now that people have made the acquaintance of the scriptures of other religions and have learned to appreciate magnificent passages that they also have to offer, we are sometimes asked why we did not include some such passages amongst our epistles. The answer is that such mixing of streams of religious influence seems often to produce a clash of influences. It must be added that difficult as it is to provide consecutive passages of edifying scripture from Jewish and Christian sources, it seems even more difficult to do so from other sources.

There is one fact which invests the reading of the Epistle and Gospel with considerable additional interest. It would seem that the scriptures of all of the great religions have attached to them great angels, who use the scriptures during their reading or public recitation as vehicles of their influence. Consequently, it often happens that the actual blessing poured out over a congregation during the reading of a gospel is a good deal more than can be accounted for by the intrinsic value of the passage read.

The Gradual

The beautiful words of the Gradual, in praise of wisdom and understanding, tend to awaken the higher reaches of our mind-activity. They form a useful basis for meditation.

The chant to which these words are set in our Musical Liturgy is by an organist named Richard Redhead, who was prominent in the Anglo-Catholic movement in the latter half of last century. It is written in the Gregorian style.

The Credo

The Liberal Catholic Church works in over thirty different countries and chiefly amongst people who had ceased from Church attendance. Some of these countries find in history and tradition a sense of stability and of anchorage in this world of change; others are 'forward-looking,' and care more about the shaping of a noble future than dwelling on the past. A few of the wiser people manage to combine the two points of view. It can quite well be understood that a document like the Creed finds a mixed reception. This is an age of popular religion, when it is fashionable to decry 'worn-out creeds and dogmas,' and the rather superficial utterance: 'No creed, no dogma,' is a popular slogan. I say superficial, because the affirmation that creed and dogma are taboo is in itself just as much a dogma as to say that they are useful or necessary. People who have listened to the Creed from childhood are wont to weave around it a good deal of romantic association, and even more is this the case with those of scholarly inclination, whose devotion to this ancient statement of the universal faith only grows as they study its passage down the ages.

> Faith of our Fathers, living still
> In spite of dungeon, fire and sword,
> O how our hearts beat high with joy
> Whene'er we hear that glorious word!
> Faith of our Fathers, holy Faith.
> We will be true to thee till death!

Very different is the impression which the Creed may make in a newer country like America or Australia, where people have not been brought up in the same atmosphere of religious tradition, and where such a succession of dogmatic utterances does not accord with the popular feeling for undogmatic religion so-called. To such people the Creed may even seem ominous with persecution from the past, and suggests a bondage to ecclesiastical authority which leaves a decidedly unpleasant impression behind it.

There is a good deal to be said on both sides of the question, and, the Liberal Catholic Church wisely leaves its members free to use the Creed or the alternative Act of Faith. There can be no question but that a Church must have instruction to give to its members, and that that teaching must be systematised and defined. Hitherto its dogma has been the test of a Church. Dogma obviously cannot disappear but the question arises whether it cannot take its appropriate and necessary place and yet allow added emphasis to be placed on other aspects of Christian life, such as the sense of our common fellowship and our common desire for the betterment of humanity. Our Church retains the Nicaeno-Constantinopolitan Creed, because by all churches of catholic tradition that is regarded as one of the fundamentals of the faith, and is a bond of fellowship between those churches. But, as is expressly stated here in a footnote in the Liturgy, the Liberal Catholic Church leaves to its members perfect freedom in the interpretation of Scriptures, Creeds and Liturgy. And there is then quoted a paragraph from a book by a modernist Anglican clergyman, now deceased, saying that 'the ancient Church altered the language of the Creeds from time to time, in order to meet the advance of religious thought. The modern Church has retained the words but altered their interpretation.' Such re-interpretation does become necessary from time to time, and if it be justified in the case of one clause; it is justified in the case of any. Several years ago I became involved in a controversy on this very point with the bishop who ordained me. He wished me to assure him of my adhesion to the doctrine of the resurrection of the body in the literal sense. I told him that in the light of modern science it was impossible to do so. I explained that a man died, his particles passed into the ground, thence into the verdure, a cow ate the verdure, and another man ate the cow. Whose particles were they at the day of resurrection? Similarly, the clause in the Creed 'and sitteth on the right hand of the Father' came up for discussion. Of all of its clauses it is the one which most obviously requires interpretation and is least likely to disturb people's feelings in the process. Is Our Lord to be thought of as needing to take a sitting posture in heaven and are the spatial relations of heaven like those of earth? Obviously the phrase means simply that He took a position of dignity and power in the spiritual worlds. So also with the phrase 'He ascended into heaven.' Are we to think of an upward movement in space? When poets talk about the strings or the petals of their heart, we do not assume that they are writing anatomical treatises. We give them what is called 'poetic licence.' If people who use the Creed are troubled by the fact that they cannot regard all the clauses as literally true, they can in the Liberal Catholic Church take comfort in the knowledge that this is not asked of them. A little 'poetic licence' may be allowed in dealing with such a venerable document. It can be treated as poetry—and wonderfully significant poetry—rather than as expressing scientific accuracy in every clause. It is not the business of a few obscure bishops to re-write the Creeds. They are fundamental documents to be changed only by Ecumenical Councils of the Church.

Reasoning in this fashion, we soon see that the advancing knowledge of one age may often require a re-interpretation of the language of a more primitive one, and those who have studied a book like C.W. Leadbeater's *Christian Creed* come presently to realise that the Creed is not so much intended to give historical data relating to Christ's life on earth as to summarise certain great cosmic processes. Bishop Leadbeater advances in that book a theory that the biographical details of Jesus Christ are the outcome of a materialisation of the original document, which was an ancient formula of cosmogenesis given by our Lord to the Essene community in which for two years He dwelt. Also some matter relating to the ceremonial of the first of the great initiations in Egypt became. mingled with this.

The significance of all this is not generally appreciated. When a congregation says the Creed with devotion and fervour, and with an attempt to reach with the intuitive mind into the great spiritual facts therein portrayed, they touch a variety of influences. First of all, the recitation of this mighty profession of the Christian faith over century upon century has built up around it a marvellous atmosphere of thought and devotion, the influence of which is enhanced by great angels who ensoul such things, and is utterly and indescribably grand and wonderful. Secondly, they have the power to touch something of the atmosphere appropriate to the great initiation spoken of above. This may be more potent if a congregation can bring themselves by a sufficient elevation of thought into direct touch with the thought of the Christ himself, with the archetype of the Creed, as it was given originally by Our Blessed Lord. No wonder that sometimes the heavenly worlds seem to be ablaze with light and glory as the congregation have wielded this talisman of holy thought. I have often seen the bishop's crozier flaming with fiery power at the recitation of the great mystery of the faith.

The information that has been given us about the origin of the Creed has its own peculiar interest and significance at the present time. Of the three years' ministry of Our Lord,

> two...were occupied in instructing the heads of the Essene Community in the Mysteries of the Kingdom of Heaven, and one in preaching to the general public among the hills and fields of Palestine. It is of this last year's work only that some traditions are preserved in the Gospel story.... The heads of this Community were already in possession

of fragments of more or less accurate information—possibly obtained from Buddhist sources—with regard to the origin of all things. These the Christ put together and rendered coherent, casting them for the purpose of ready memorization into the shape of a formula of belief which may be regarded as the first source of the Christian Creed.[1]

Teaching similar in character and similarly illustrated by symbol was given by Him with regard to the work of the Logos in His First and Third Aspects, though comparatively little of it has been preserved to us.[2]

Further, occult investigators are well aware that after the death of the body, Our Lord continued to give His disciples the private instructions He had given them when on earth,[3] and, that amongst these were some detailed instructions as to the ceremonies, ritual and even vestments of the Eucharist and the relation to that ceremony of the Angelic Orders.

It is well to take note of all this, for in these days people talk glibly of 'the religion of Jesus' as though it envisaged nothing further than the Sermon on the Mount, and they set that aspect of His teaching in contradistinction to anything in the nature of systematic teaching or the institution of religious ceremonies. In point of fact we never in the Gospel narrative find Him opposing the worship of the Temple; on the contrary, He taught in the Temple, He made havoc with the money-changers and upheld the Temple to respect.[4] The religion of Christ is founded upon love for God and for one's neighbour; but in the tradition of the Ancient Wisdom knowledge has always been held to be as necessary as goodness, and a close study of Christian origins seems to show that provision was made both for definite instruction and for rites which were to purify and ennoble the worshipper and to keep the presence of Our Lord in perpetual realisation.

Those who are not well instructed in the meaning of the Creed are recommended to study some book on the subject. It would obviously be out of place to give an exhaustive interpretation here. They will find much of interest about the original sense of some of the clauses in Bishop Leadbeater's book mentioned above. In the Liberal Catholic Church we use the pronoun 'We' instead of 'I' at the opening of the first and last paragraphs. This is the original form. So phrased, it emphasises the fact that it is the collective utterance of the Christian Church, and it reminds us of the corporate nature of our worship. The earlier passages in the second paragraph dealing with the procession of the Godhead can be used most effectively to enlarge the scope of the mind. The accent in 'God of God' and in the two subsequent phrases is on the word 'of.' The sentence does not mean that the one is God above the other, but God coming forth from God. The genuflection at the *Incarnatus* is a very touching incident; we express in that act of humility our recognition of all the marvel and loving condescension involved in the primal sacrifice of the Logos, and those other sacrifices of Our Lord and of other Great Ones, which in their turn are part of that One Eternal Sacrifice which is the law of our worlds. Then follows the glory of the resurrection, and a number of other beautiful conceptions are brought before us in the concluding paragraph. Here the influence of the Holy Spirit is very real. The Creed is intended to stimulate our consciousness to work at the causal level, so that influence of that type may be garnered by the Angel of the Eucharist for the great outpouring.

---

[1] *The Christian Creed*, pages 15-16.

[2] Ibid., page 19.

[3] S. Mark IV, 10, 11, 34.

[4] S. Matthew, XXI, 13.

The Act Of Faith

The glowing statement of belief called An Act of Faith was written by Bishop Lead-beater, and sums up in a few clear succinct sentences a great and noble philosophy of life. Curiously enough, it is the only section of our Liturgy which must plead guilty to the charge of teaching heresy! The frank proclamation that 'all His sons shall one day reach His feet' is 'universalism' or 'apocatastasis.' It can claim, however, a list of very presentable protagonists, notably Origen, Clement of Alexandria, S. Gregory of Nyssa. It is, of course, very widely held at the present day, and our Church is not likely to have qualms of conscience about this particular heterodoxy.

The Act of Faith has not behind it the same inner power as the Creed; but it is direct and to the point as the expression of the most cherished convictions of most of us, and therefore calls out a great warmth of feeling, besides carrying our minds into relation with that great body of thought that we call the Ancient Wisdom.

There is a second version of the Act of Faith, for which I am personally responsible. It is less suitable for recitation at the Holy Eucharist, but is well adapted as a basis for meditation. Each section begins with the words 'We place our trust in,' rather after the manner of the buddhist 'refuges,' and the whole is intended to be in the nature of an affirmation.

The Offertorium

At this time a hymn is often sung, and a collection of money is taken. On the principle that a phrase sometimes catches the eye and awakens the conscience of a reader, let me say that the custom of putting as little as possible into the bag as it passes is one which has nothing to commend it! It is based on the theory that church-going is a bore rather than a privilege; but people often perpetuate such customs unthinkingly. Our congregations are as a rule extremely generous but there still may be people who have not faced the question of what is their glad opportunity in this respect.

The *Offertorium* marks the beginning of another section of the Mass. In older times, when the discipline of the Catechumenate, i.e., of those who were preparing for baptism, was still in existence, the Catechumens were dismissed from the service before this stage began. Hence this part is sometimes called the Mass of the Faithful. The earlier part is more exoteric and in the main is adapted from the Jewish worship; but now begins the celebration of the Mysteries.

The priest makes the offerings of bread and wine as representing the fruits of the earth, so that the offering of nature is here blended with the offerings—formerly in the way of raw material and produce, but now usually of money—that we human folk make. The inner side of this process is more far-reaching than would generally be supposed. I am not sure how far what I am going to say applies to the ordinary town church. I have had the privilege for some years of helping at a daily sung Eucharist in the Centre where I live,[1] right out in the heart of nature, where the influences of nature are strong and unusually active. At this part of the service we count upon a definite collaboration on the part of the nature spirits. Powers of fire, earth, air and water join in at this stage and make their own offering in the heavenly sacrifice, and to the chalice-like form which is now being built up on the altar a good deal of distinctive 'nature-influence' is contributed, into which we blend at the prayer following the *Orate Fratres* our own sacrifice of devotion—ourselves, our souls and bodies.

[1] St. Michael's, Huizen, Holland at the time of writing. [Ed.]

The complete circle that is made by the priest as he turns around for the *Orate Fratres* enables him to sweep with him in the requisite direction the response on the part of the people, which sets this chalice-like form on the altar spinning round, so that a kind of vortex is set up in subtler matter. This forms the basis of the 'tube' which is spoken of by Bishop Leadbeater in *The Science of the Sacraments*, the isolated area wherein the process of consecration takes place. This is further contributed to by the censing which precedes the *Orate Fratres*. The point to be noticed is that there is a delightful collaboration here between humanity and nature, and that the Eucharist is offered not only on the part of humanity, but of the lower kingdoms of nature, the nature-spirits and the angels also. There is plenty of scope here for work on the part of the people. They can feel their oneness with nature; and let it always be borne in mind that though the spirits of nature are invisible to most of us, they are in close touch on such occasions with our thought and emotion, and that the surest way to work in union with them is to intend to do so.

The prayer which follows the *Orate Fratres* gives the congregation opportunity for a very sincere act of self-dedication. The reference to their fellowship in the mystical Body of the Lord aids them to realise their common life and therefore unity in one another, and the phrase about possessing 'the kingdom which is prepared for, you from the beginning of the world' is a reference to the destiny that may await all earnest seekers, that of entering the great Brotherhood of Initiates, the Kingdom of Heaven, whose members realise themselves consciously as members of the mystical Body of Christ, through the attainment of the intuitional consciousness.

The version of the Shorter Form, 'May our strength be spent in Thy service, and our love poured forth upon Thy people,' is pleasantly direct and has the merit of saying exactly what it means.

The Sursum Corda And Preface

We revert again to a series of Versicles and Responses, the rapid interchange of which between priest and people re-knits their close relationship and intensifies the general flow of the forces. The music of these passages is wonderfully potent, and as the ancient plainchant resounds through the church it is as though the summons goes forth that men and angels shall unite together to give, 'as is very meet, right and our bounden duty,' praise and glory to God. The summons goes forth not merely in the physical world but in higher worlds also. Proper attention, on the part of both priest and people, should be given to the due accentuation of the note-groups in this chant, as has already been explained in that section of these comments devoted to Gregorian music. The rhythm is important here. The congregation should also bear in mind what was said on the subject of the Versicles and Responses which occur at the beginning of the service. Their Responses are intended to be a release of energy—the right thought, the deep earnestness of devotion, a great burning enthusiasm for the praise of God, all that is marshaled in the mind beforehand, ready to be liberated as the moment comes for the people's response.

These sentences and the *Sanctus*, and probably also the Preface, are most likely of Jewish origin. The Jewish grace before meals says: 'Let us give thanks to Adonai our God.' 'In the *Sanctus* the words 'Lord God of Hosts' ran originally 'Lord God of Sabaoth,' and are so retained in many liturgies. This form of Versicles followed by a Preface occurs in other portions of the Liturgy, apart from the Mass. It is to be found, for example, in the Roman ordination form, at the consecration of a church and in the case of other benedictions. It is employed for purposes of great solemnity, and gave scope originally for great fervour, and also length, of utterance, in which were rehearsed a multiplicity of reasons for praising God. It introduces the Canon of the Mass, for as Our Lord in the first Eucharist gave thanks to God, so is it fitting for us before all things so to do when following the rite He instituted. The phrase 'Let us give thanks unto our Lord God' is held by many to carry the connotation, 'Let us make Eucharist.'

The melody to which all this and the Preface is sung is traditional; or, to be quite accurate, there are different versions of it, but all evidently built on the same model and containing certain characteristic inflections. It is, in the secondary sense of the word, a *mantram*. The Preface calls the angels, or shall we say the angels come, whether the Preface be said or sung, and in no matter what language, or with what variation of the melody.

We should at this stage of the ceremony be specially fervent in our praise, and reach out towards our angel collaborators with intense courtesy and goodwill, remembering that all that is harsh and unrefined in human nature is discordant to them.

The Prayer of Consecration

In the present-day Roman rite the Canon of the Mass begins here, but the Liberal Catholic Liturgy reverts to the older custom of marking the Canon from the *Sursum Corda* and Preface. Canon is a word of many meanings, some of which are peculiarly technical (e.g., the canon of architecture). It means in one sense a rule or formula. And the Canon is the sacred formula, or rule, or usage, according to which the supreme act of the consecration is effected. Note that the prayer, in accordance with usual custom, is addressed to the Father, and ends just before the recitation of the Lord's Prayer with an ascription to the Trinity. The hymns which we sing after the consecration are really an interruption in the one long Prayer of Consecration. The elevation at the consecration and attendant formalities are a later introduction, made as the idea of Eucharistic adoration developed. Bishop Gore, in *The Body of Christ*, points out that the absence in the early Church of Eucharistic adoration as we now understand and practise it is part of a larger problem, 'that what Dr. Hort called "Jesus-worship" as a whole—the distinctive feature alike of Protestant evangelicism and Catholic sacramentalism—is not at all prominent in the theology of the first five or six centuries.'[1]

It developed later, in all probability as a wave of emotional self-expression swept over Europe—due to the culmination of the Sixth Ray influence—and also as a reaction against the attacks on the doctrine of the Real Presence which began at about the time of the Reformation. Dr. Gore goes on to say that we cannot reasonably separate the worship of Jesus from our whole attitude towards Him. If the early Church had been in the constant habit of singing such hymns as "Jesu, lover of my soul," is it not very likely it would also have sung "Jesus, I adore Thee on Thy altar throne?"[2]

The Consecration Prayer, called in Greek the *Anaphora*, begins with a petition for the purification and hallowing of the elements. They have served first as tokens of the offering of nature, then of our human self-oblation; now they are to become the vehicle for the blessing of the Lord. The first cross made by the priest thus 'breaks the link with us and with all lower things,' and the bread and wine are magnetically isolated and set apart for their holy purpose. The action is now full of interest and significance for the congregation, in that a number of special suffrages or intentions for the Mass are now formulated.

---

[1] Page 106
[2] Op. cit., page 109.

For The Holy Catholic Church

We begin by recognising our fellowship with Christ's Church as a whole, then pass on to a succession of other ideas—the civil authority of the country, the hierarchy of our Church and its membership; then special cases needing help, and the company of the departed. Bishop Leadbeater has explained the working of this in his book, *The Science of the Sacraments*, and I shall therefore limit myself to certain accessory aspects of the process. He does not mention one fact which was discovered during the investigations he made many years ago when gathering together material for the book which was destined to form so wonderful a contribution to our understanding of these things. It was noticed that the outpouring upon the Church connected with our petition at this part of the service linked up in various intimate ways with churches of similar character. There was but a general influence upon non-episcopal churches, similar to that shed abroad generally. The radiation from our little oratory in London, situated in Upper Woburn Place, was being studied. It was found that we contributed specially to the neighbouring Anglican churches of St. Pancras, to a High Church in the vicinity of King's Cross, and some others. The connection thus set up is of a two-fold character. We receive from sister churches and we also give to them. I have noticed that the Liberal Catholic congregation that is really trained can do a great deal for other churches. Training of the sort that I have in mind means a strengthening of the power of thought and emotion, and also the ability to work at higher levels of consciousness than those levels usually reached. There are thus special qualities of influence radiated out from such a church. These are often carried by the angels to other churches, but also, where the Blessed Sacrament is reserved, as in Roman Catholic churches, the power of the Host can be used after the manner of a relay, so that the special influence that we are considering can be spread still further abroad. Thus it is possible for the work of one small congregation to be extended to a degree that would normally be quite unforeseen and un-expected.

For the King

The ruler of the country is next mentioned. It is not generally understood that there is a hierarchy of the First Ray, a hierarchy of government, as well as that of the Church on the Second Ray. Actions performed in a country in the name of the King call upon the power of that hierarchy. I remember once standing before the Speaker's Chair in the Senate House at Melbourne in Australia, and noticing to my surprise how strong was the sense of the Presence along this line. I sometimes tell my friends of that Ray that, scoff at the episcopal hierarchy as they may, their own is unhappily even more set in faded glories, for its work, its influence, its significance, goes almost unrecognised. It is this idea which lies behind the tradition of the divine right of kings. A king who, like our English sovereign, is solemnly crowned by the archbishop and anointed with oil, receives the consecration from the Head of the Hierarchy which he represents in his land, and is a real channel for that power. The judges, magistrates, His Majesty's forces, and even the police officer, are part of this hierarchy and work in its power. And the national angel who co-operates with it is sometimes a very wonderful and glorious being. The association of Church and State, it has often been pointed out, is not to make the Church secular and Erastian, but the State truly religious, ordering all things 'upon the best and surest foundation' for the eventual good of humanity. It is along this line that our contribution from the Eucharist is intended to be effective. In the case of the temporary head of a republic, the link does not exist in the same way, but the representative headship is still an office of great importance and has also its inner significance. Even universities have their hierarchy, and one who takes a degree receives some spiritual blessing, however slight, as he is incorporated in the graduate fellowship—the mystical body—of his alma mater.

For The Episcopate

Next on the list comes the Presiding Bishop, and following him the Ordinary, or bishop of the province or diocese. The bishop exercising jurisdiction is called an Ordinary, whether the jurisdiction is territorial, as in the case of those who take the title of territorial sees, or as in the case of our Church over those persons in a given area who voluntarily submit themselves to the general internal discipline of the Church. He holds his spiritual powers *jure ordinario*, by common right, as successor of the apostles. There is no order in the Church higher than that of the episcopate, but there are grades on the administrative side of the organisation, such as archdeacon, canon, dean, which are higher than the ordinary rank of priest, and archbishop, patriarch, cardinal, in the other churches, superior to the rank of bishop. These grades of administration do not involve more spiritual 'character' (in the technical sense of the term) than a priest or bishop, but their occupants do receive additional help for the work they have to do from the side of the governing administrative hierarchy. All this, it is to be understood, concerns the office as such irrespective of the person who occupies it. The bishop has a very heavy burden to carry, for the charge of the Church within his jurisdiction is an existent factor with which he is inwardly associated as well as outwardly, and priests who derive their ordination from him are linked with him spiritually. In consequence of this, he can appreciate the prayers of the faithful being offered for him, and the help that is given to him from every Eucharist said within his area of responsibility. Others in positions below him of derived jurisdiction, like auxiliary bishops, parish priests, and so on, receive their help and support both from the direct thought and prayer of the faithful and along the channels of hierarchical attachment to the bishop. What has here been said of the bishop of the diocese applies in corresponding measure to the Presiding Bishop, who has a still greater responsibility upon him, in addition to being usually Ordinary of a province or diocese.

In the very early days of our Church, whilst it was still attached to the Old Catholic tradition, we made it a custom to pray for the Pope as our Patriarch. This led to an extraordinary storm of criticism in the United States of America and in Australia. In fact, in the former country, elaborate brochures were issued to show that we were Roman Catholic—although a few moments' attention to any religious encyclopaedia *sub tit.* 'Old Catholic' would have demonstrated the absurdity of this idea. But religious fanaticism is a curious phenomenon; it springs from the most intense and uncontrolled emotion and seems in some odd fashion to throw out of action the mind of people who in other respects are often quite lucid and intelligent. Any one at all acquainted with ecclesiastical history would have recognised that the use of the term 'Patriarch' ranged the Church on the side of those who denied the later papal claims. The three original Patriarchates, or sees of primary rank, were Alexandria, Rome and Antioch. There are several Patriarchs in Christendom, and the historical Patriarchates of the East are of the Orthodox Eastern Church and not Roman Catholic, though the Roman Church, after the schism between East and West, later appointed its own Patriarchs of the Uniate Churches, who usually reside at Rome. There has never been any dispute as to who is Patriarch or occupant of the Apostolic See of the West; it is the Bishop of Rome. This position was accepted by the Anglicans who took part in the conversations at Malines, who were willing to accord to the Roman See a primacy of honour.[1] All this is simply acceptance of the historic position of the Roman See. What is denied is the claim to universal jurisdiction and the infallibility of the Pope. However, when our Church took the name of 'Liberal Catholic,' it decided to emphasise the 'forward-looking' aspect of things and to leave aside a good many of the problems which occupy the historic Churches and have been the cause of so much perplexity and strife in the Christian Church. Hence the prayer for the Patriarch of the West disappeared from our Liturgy, and its place was taken by that for the ruler of the country. Controversies naturally sort themselves out into different epochs of history. Nobody could raise much enthusiasm in these days by reviving the *Filioque* controversy. The question of the position and authority of the Pope is in these days not one of purely archaeological importance and does not turn simply on the early usage of the Church; it concerns very vitally international political relationships and the sovereign rights of each country.

For Those In Need

The next clause of the prayer directs our attention to "all who in this transitory life are in trouble, sorrow, need, sickness or any other adversity (especially...)." How the help is sent out to these different classes of suffering people and to any others in special need of help in fully explained in *The Science of the Sacraments*, and I need not repeat the information here. Of the reality of the help given those of us who have to deal with these things get abundant testimony. I recall the case of a young man who incurred the hostility of a worker of magic in the Dutch Indies. The Dutch colonists there are so used to objective evidence of the reality of magic—such as the production of sickness or poltergeist phenomena—that one has no need to argue on the subject with the generality of them. I was asked by the parents to protect this young man against the obsession that was being practised on him, and I therefore included him in the list in use at our Church at Huizen of those to be remembered at this part of the Mass. Later the name was removed, as the list is always long and there are fresh cases. Soon afterwards I received an urgent appeal to the effect that the obsession had again occurred after a long interval of quietness and freedom. One may usefully take this opportunity of pointing out that people should have a due sense of reverence and responsibility in asking for the help of the Church in these things. Cases of trivial indisposition should not be inflicted on those in charge, and the latter should exercise due censorship and remove the names after a reasonable time. To see people who are being prayed for as sick attending Church in the condition of being quite "hale and hearty" comes as rather a shock.

For The Dead

Next, in regard to the dead. It is important for us to avoid the traditional attitude towards them. Those who have studied Theosophy will not make the mistake of contaminating the dead with our own thoughts of sorrow and grief. It is difficult for people not to be upset at their own loss and the outward sundering of ties of affection. Our theosophical writers have often pointed out that this attitude is selfish and concerned with the state of our own feelings rather than with the well-being of the dead person. It is in the dead person's interest that we should send him influences of peace and happiness which will help to reconcile him to his new surroundings and to recover from the shock and disturbance often occasioned by sudden change of conditions that

---

[1] The Conversations at Malines, 1921-1925. Oxford University Press.

has befallen him and the changes that gradually pass over him. There are many amongst us who can do this, but we feel awkward and heartless when we appear at a funeral controlled and exhibiting no signs of grief, before others who have not the same beliefs. For this reason, perhaps, or because we have not been able to free ourselves entirely from a false tradition, many of us who ought to know better still relapse on such occasions into a sort of deteriorated sentimentality, which is really a sinking down from the greater refinement of emotion which should be normal to us. It is all connected with what passes for piety in the English character, and is like the long-faced mien that English people assume whenever the religious instinct is evoked. Church people talk about the blessed, or holy, dead and think of them with the thought-equivalent of a sort of hushed unnaturalness of manner. Dead people soon get accustomed to their new conditions of life, and this exaggeration and unnaturalness on the part of their friends on this side is in fact rather displeasing to them; and it colours unfavourably our prayers and the loving thoughts of goodwill that we send towards them. Many of the dead are a good deal happier in their new life than they were ever able to be in the other, and they find our sentimental patronage, however well meant, out of place. We can help them a great deal at the stage of transition, and often they then have need of help; at other stages our attitude should be exactly the same as our attitude to living people. It was Bishop Leadbeater who inserted the *Te Deum* at the beginning of our Funeral Service. I was a little shocked at the time, not so much for myself but having in mind the ordinary mourner who had never heard of Theosophy. But I see now and quite plainly how that canticle really strikes the right note, and produces the very influence that ought to be produced in the best interests of the dead person—and, if they only knew it, also in the best interests of the mourners.

Our attitude towards the dead, then, should be one of glad and courteous co-operation. Great masses of them often congregate at our church services, for the invisible helpers attach much importance to the fact of those who are being specially brought on in their evolution in preparation for immediate reincarnation, being thus bathed in a spiritual atmosphere. There is no better manner of awakening and fostering the higher faculties of the being and the higher reaches of mental and emotional consciousness than by this permeation by the great spiritual forces working in and through a well-conducted Church service. The action of these forces seems to be analogous to that of the sunlight on a bud.

The Great Sacrifice

The words which now follow on before the consecration of the offerings begins are the memorial of the cosmic sacrifice of the Second Person of the Trinity. There has been much dispute over the question of the Eucharistic sacrifice, whether it is a repetition of the sacrifice on the cross or only a memorial of it. In Protestant evangelical tradition very much centres round Christ's death on the cross. In Catholic tradition it is rather the Incarnation that constitutes the great mystery. The real mystery and sacrifice is the self-limitation of the Son of God in matter, and the coming forth of the World-Teacher into the rude haunts of men. The Eucharistic sacrifice gives no occasion for controversy, if it is related to the great cosmic sacrifice. There is then no question of the repetition of the sacrifice in time, for that primal sacrifice is in the eternal now, outside of our conceptions of time and space, and we do but perpetuate it within the limitations of time and space which veil our earthly eyes from the excess of His glory.

The intention in all this is to unite the thought of the people with that supreme Sacrifice. First, to carry them up through the Person of our Lord to that omnipresent aspect of the Deity of which He is the special epiphany or manifestation to our world, and then to the historic Christ who left us the wonderful memorial of His love. In a few moments the supreme act of consecration is to take place. Hence we re-present our offerings, cleansed and purified and freed from worldly attachment, to the Father. We do this in union with His "whole household"—"the household of faith" of which S. Paul speaks, (Galatians VI, 10.) and "uniting with His holy Church throughout all the ages," as our Liturgy has it. And our Eucharist is offered "in obedience to the command of Thy most blessed Son. As oft as ye shall do these things, ye shall do them in remembrance of Me." (Luke XXII, 19; 1 Corinthians XI, 24-25.)

The Epiklesis

The sentence which now follows is in the nature of what is technically called an *epiklesis*. There are different traditions from the early Church as to the manner of consecration. The custom which has prevailed in the West is to effect the consecration by prayer followed by the use of the words of institution. But the Eastern custom is different. The priest recites the words of institution, as in the West, then praying that the bread and wine may become the Body and Blood, uses the formula, "changing them by Thy holy Spirit." There is no difficulty in believing that both of these methods of consecration are effective. It is a little difficult to follow the changes in the case of a strange rite and a foreign tongue, but on the various occasions when I have been admitted as a bishop within the *ikonostasis* or sanctuary screen of Russian and Greek churches, it has seemed to me that the change took place previous to the invocation of the Holy Spirit, but that the power remained in abeyance, as it were, till the invocation. The older attitude—which is still that of the East in regard to most things—was different from ours. Our forefathers made less attempt to define with clearness and precision the exact moment that changes took place. They lived more in the world of the timeless, and for them the Liturgy was one long action.

In compiling the Liberal Catholic Liturgy we followed another tradition, and placed the *epiklesis* before the words of institution. Ours, moreover, is an *epiklesis* of the Holy Trinity—for the invocation of the *Logos* is another primitive use—the prayer, that is to say, is addressed to the Father, and we then invoke both the Holy Spirit and *Logos*.

The Western theory is that the words attributed to our Lord remained as words of power and that the priest who repeats them in personification of our Lord accomplishes by His grace the same change as He.

The Act of Consecration

The part of the congregation at this most solemn moment of the service is not, however, to trouble themselves with details of mechanism and theory, but to unite themselves with our Lord, and to carry themselves back in the imagery of the mind to that undying scene of the Last Supper celebrated in the upper chamber. The priest is now to become merged in His Master, to impersonate Him in the offering of bread and wine; the faithful are to become one with that little band of disciples before whom this sublime act was consummated.

It was at the institution of the Eucharist that our Saviour began to offer Himself to His Father for the sins of all men. The sacrifice which He then offered was His natural body and blood, as separate from each other, because His body was considered as broken, and His blood as shed, for the sins of the world. But because it would have been unnatural for Him to have broken His own body and shed His own blood, and because He could not as a living High Priest offer Himself when He was dead, therefore, before He was so much as apprehended by His enemies, He offered to the Father His natural body and blood voluntarily and really though mystically under the symbols of bread and wine mixed with water; for which reason He called the bread at the Eucharist His body, which was then broken, given, or offered for the sins of many, and the cup His blood, which was then shed or offered for the sins of the many. All the sacrifices of the old law were figures of this great one of Christ; and the Eucharist or sacrifice of thanksgiving, which we celebrate according to His institution, is a solemn commemorative oblation of it to God the Father, and procures us the virtue of it.[1]

So wrote a bishop of the Nonjurors, Thomas Deacon, in 1747, and I know of no more uplifting version of the doctrine. It is the people's part to enter into the mystery and tenderness of the scene, and by their purest devotion and love to make it live again in the house of God.

The Anamnesis

It is unnecessary to treat of the hymns which follow upon the consecration. There is nothing recondite about them. It is only to be desired that the congregation should sing them with realisation of the meaning of the words. A few moments' complete silence should intervene between the homage of the bells and censer and the opening notes of the first hymn. This is impressive; and it reminds us of the words occurring in our service of ordination to the priesthood: O Lord Christ, Whose strength is in the silence. The Holy Spirit manifests Himself in the Kindling of our speech, in the gift of tongues, in the splendour of self-expression. The Son is the still small voice heard in the stillness and purity of our hearts.

The section of the Prayer of Consecration which now follows is called the *anamnesis*, meaning "memorial," referring to the injunction: "This do in remembrance of me." It summarises the various points of the mystery-drama of the Lord's Life. Liturgies differ as to what they mention. Fortescue says: "All Eastern Liturgies name not only the passion and death, but also the resurrection and especially our expectation of the second coming." He mentions a case where the nativity was included.[2] The *epiklesis* is the appropriate reference to the descent of the Holy Spirit. Our liturgy speaks of the incarnation, the resurrection and the ascension, to portray the descent of the Divine Life into matter, the conquest of matter, and the re-ascent from matter to spirit, in the heavenly drama.

Having now "the most precious gift" that has been bestowed upon us, we hasten to lay It at the feet of God, using It, as before we used the bread and wine, as a "token of the perfect devotion and sacrifice of our minds and hearts" to God. But it is not merely this gift that we offer; we blend with it our whole nature. The priest makes here the five crosses which are by Bishop Leadbeater explained to represent the fivefold Hermetic man, (a) spirit, (b) intuition, (c) intelligence, (d) the lower mind, (e) the emotions. And we offer our entire contribution of devotion to God through these different aspects of our nature, opening ourselves thus completely and unreservedly before the Divine Presence, and praying that our offering, so stimulated and quickened by the power of the Host, may be borne by the Angel of the Presence to the heavenly altar. Then follow two series each of three crosses. The priest in the former re-forms the threefold

---

[1] *A Full, True and Comprehensive View of Christianity*, Part II, Lesson xxvii, quoted in *A History of the Doctrine of the Holy Eucharist.* by Darwell Stone, M.A., Vol. II, page 482. Longmans, 1909.

[2] The Mass, by Dr. Adrian Fortescue, page 346. Longnians, 1922.

link with the Christ, himself taking the place of the now departed Angel of the Presence, the other two principles being represented by the consecrated Host and Chalice; and the second set of crosses draws out power from the consecrated elements which quickens into flame the three-fold reflection of the Blessed Trinity in the souls of the congregation. Finally he concludes the Canon with the ascription of praise, the crosses here drawing down "the holy influence from the monadic level...into the ego in its three-fold manifestation of spirit, intuition and intelligence; and then as he makes the two crosses between the Chalice and his own breast, he draws that influence into his own mental and astral bodies, that through him it may radiate fully upon his people."[1]

At the close of this ascription the celebrant raises the Chalice and Host in what is called the Minor Elevation. As Fortescue says, it suggests rather the lifting of the holy things to God than the showing of them to the people.

The Communion

There is difference of opinion as to whether the portion of the Liturgy following upon the Prayer of Consecration belongs to the Canon or not. The heading *Canon Missae* is continued in the missals till the end of the Mass. Fortescue maintains with some citation of authority that it does end here, and explains the difficulty by pointing out that in mediaeval times a distinction was made between the Canon of consecration (Canon *consecrationis*) and the Canon of communion (Canon *communionis*).[2] The Roman Ordinal, and ours also, warns the newly-ordained priest that, as what he has to handle is not without its mischances, he do diligently learn the course of the whole Mass, and that which regards the consecration, breaking and communion of the Host, before he attempt to celebrate Mass. The Canon, or rule of procedure, would seem from this to extend at least to the Communion. The continuation of the Liturgy after the Prayer of Consecration has all the marks of a Canon, as is only to be expected from a ritual which deals with the Host present upon the altar, and we may call it the Canon of Communion.

The Lord's Prayer

This occurs in every traditional Liturgy of the Holy Eucharist in Christendom. Bishop Leadbeater points out that its clauses are pre-christian.[3] It contains some very beautiful thoughts. The first clause is a recognition of the fatherhood of God and the reverence that is due to Him. We can also think of the Father, the monadic power which is the essence of our being. The next two clauses pray for the coming of the Kingdom of God upon earth—the prayer "*Adveniat Regnum Tuum*," which has been taken as the motto of our Church. It refers to the state of utopian anarchy on our earth, of which Dr. Besant has spoken when there will no longer be need of outer legal compulsion because the Divine Life will be so awakened in all men that they can have no other wish than to cooperate for the good of the whole. That Will which is ever done in the heavens above will then be perfectly accomplished on the earth beneath. The prayer for our daily bread refers to the spiritual sustenance given to us for our daily work, and, in the opinion of many commentators to the Holy Communion. The clause about our trespasses has much the same purpose as the *Confiteor* at the beginning of our Liturgy. The next clause

[1] Bishop C. W. Leadbeater, *The Science of the Sacraments.*
[2] Op. cit., page 325.
[3] *The Science of the Sacraments.*

presents so much difficulty to some that they prefer to abstain from the use of the prayer. It is awkward to change traditional documents, such as this, without oecumenical authority; but the French translation at once solves the difficulty—"*Ne nous laissez pas succomber á tentation* (Do not suffer us to fall in temptation)"—and refers us to the sustaining power of the divine principle within us. The final ascription has a Kabbalistic flavour.

Some years ago a well-known Anglican liturgiologist, The Rev. Dr. Percy Dearmer, reminded us of the psychological value of the use of the speaking voice from time to time in the service. It gives a welcome contrast to the continued chanting, and I have always made it a point where I have had control of the use in a church to have the *Confiteor* and the Lord's Prayer thus spoken. It gives an effect of great sincerity, and the contrast and naturalness allows of such sincerity being more readily expressed. I feel that the Lord's Prayer comes at a psychological point in the service. The long Prayer of Consecration is said solo by the priest; moreover it carries the consciousness of the officiant and of trained worshippers very high, so that other less practised and less developed members get, perhaps, rather left behind. Here is an opportunity to come back to effective touch with ordinary thought once again, to pick up the threads which have slipped, as it were, to unify once more the thought of the body-corporate; and the homely recollections of childhood, of early prayers at the mother's knee, of the family circle— all this, it seems to me, so touches the heart as entirely to counter-balance the little jar caused by the one phrase I have just mentioned, and the necessity of putting some poetic gloss on it.

The Symbology of The Eucharistic Drama

We have already had occasion to study much of the symbolism of the Eucharist in its various stages, notably the successive offerings of the bread and wine at the *Offertorium*, after the *Orate Fratres*, and during the Prayer of Consecration. Another phase of this symbolic drama opens here and works out its significant course till the kiss of peace and the Communion. This is all explained in great detail in *The Science of the Sacraments*, but the thought of this part of the book is so high that it escapes most people. A Church member who has been using his opportunities regularly would receive a kind of revelation in re-reading these passages, for his understanding would have been prepared by his work to receive the teaching given. The symbology here is a real symbology.[1] In the early days of the Church when the Fathers spoke of the consecrated Bread and Wine as symbols, they used the word in the correct sense. The word comes from the Greek *sumbolos*—thrown together; a symbol is a correspondence, i.e., a state of attunement, between heaven and earth, a vehicle or channel through which spirit can be expressed. The reformers used the term in the sense which it later acquired. To them a symbol was not the mark of objectivisation of a reality; it marked, on the contrary, the absence of the reality. The bread and wine portrayed a Christ absent from the physical world, whose body was in heaven, as Calvin affirmed, and nowhere else.[2]

The symbolism here is real because the outer action with the symbols, the paten, the Host, the chalice, the Wine and the Water, is indicative of a real change which goes on in the higher principles of man, which those objects are used to symbolise or portray. The changes

---

[1] "The art of expressing symbols".

[2] Zwingli, the Swiss reformer, expressed himself quite to the point: "Nor do we think that those are to be heard who say, 'We indeed eat the real and bodily flesh of Christ, but after a spiritual manner.' For they fail to see that to be a body and to be eaten after a spiritual manner are inconsistent with one another; for body and spirit are so different that, whichever you take, the other cannot be."

involve in part very high levels of consciousness, and they proceed at those levels in so far as the development of the person makes them possible; at the lower levels the efficacy of those changes depends largely on the receptivity, the earnestness and the positive co-operation of the worshipper.

To co-operate with the Mass requires a considerable amount of occult development and definite experience in meditation. I have already pointed out that all through its Liturgy the Mass involves the constant interaction of the worshipper with the several Persons of the Blessed Trinity. We are told that as God is a triplicity, so is the Spirit which is His reflection in man. And we attribute to this triplicity various aspects of consciousness—will, wisdom-love, and creative activity or intelligence, is one such attribution. The student has to learn in his meditation to distinguish and identify these three fundamental aspects of his consciousness in himself. And he can be helped enormously in doing so by the Church services. For these provide periods when one aspect or another is in predominance, and by accustoming himself to these changes of phase, it becomes much easier for him to orient himself aright than in unaided meditation. The frequent passages which have to do with strength, power, the omnipotence of God, give emphasis to the aspect of the Father. Other passages having to do with wisdom, compassion, the indwelling light, give us opportunity to recognise the influence of the Son—and most of all, of course, the influence of the Blessed Sacrament. And thirdly, at ordinations during the singing of *the Veni Creator*, and at Whitsuntide, we have a predominance of the fiery power of the Holy Spirit, less easy to define and to describe in words, but none the less distinctive and characteristic. To familiarise oneself with these three lines of influence is the elementary work for one who would penetrate the *arcanum* of the Christian Mysteries, for there are riches of spiritual experience to be discovered on each of these paths.

Another task which the student has to master is the identification of his various principles, and the bodies or planes through which those aspects of consciousness express themselves. The symbolism that we are now to consider turns upon this, and the more one works at this inner side of the Eucharist, the more marvelous does one see its possibilities to be.

The Commemoration of The Saints

All through this portion of the Eucharist we have a double signification in the ritual. We refer at this stage to our Lady, the World-Mother, and naturally we offer her our reverence and devotion. We then pass on to think of the saints and, uniting ourselves with them, we offer worship before the heavenly Throne. That is the outer layer of the meaning and sufficiently lofty in itself. But the inner layer of symbolism gives the clue to the action of the heavenly worlds. Our Lady is the personification of the whole matter or form side of evolution. The real Saints—those made holy, hale or whole—are the Masters, just men made perfect, whose consciousness is normally at the *nirvanic*[1] level. The symbolism here is that the paten, withdrawn at this stage from its veiling beneath the corporal, is placed under the Host—the Host representing the Monad, and the paten its vehicle, the triple Spirit, at the *nirvanic* level. We are concerned with the manifestation of spirit in matter. As the cross is made with the paten, our consciousness concentrated at the atmic or *nirvanic* level (or whatever reflection of that we can touch), and turned upwards to the glory of the Deity, there is a great flashing out of atmic power. This gives a great stimulation at that level to all who can respond, and tends in some measure, we may suppose, to arouse those who as yet cannot.

---

[1] Similar to the Buddhist notion of that supra-mundane existence to which all aspire. [Ed.]

At the next prayer the centre of action is at the *buddhic* or intuitional level. We speak of the unity of the One Life and we pray that we may ourselves realise this unity through our common fellowship in the mystical body. The breaking of the Host represents the descent into matter, into diversity, and the three crosses made with the particle of the Host the brooding of the Divine Life over the atma, buddhi, manas,[1] with the descent into the threefold soul or ego symbolised and effectuated as the Particle is dropped into the chalice—uniting with the Sacred Wine, the chalice representing the ego in the causal body.

As the greater portion of the Host remained on the paten, and only a particle has been blended with the contents of the chalice, so with the Monad; and so again at a higher level with the transcendence in relation to the immanence of God.

The Salutation of Peace[2]

This symbolises and continues the idea of the *buddhic* unity which has already been expressed in the previous prayer. The physical contact makes for a closer rapport down to the etheric[3] level, and welds the body-corporate together to serve as a vehicle for the power that is to be brought into effective physical application at the act of Communion. The prayer which follows is intended to kindle our devotion and raise us into the love of Christ.

The Act of Communion and The Rationale of Worship

I have explained elsewhere[4] that a religion may be studied under three special aspects; namely, those of philosophy, morality and worship. The philosophic teaching is intended to make its approach through the avenue of the mind and to explain to us man's relation to God and to the world in which he lives. Morality explains to us the sum total of man's working experience in regard to conduct, illumined as it has been from time to time by the wisdom of great Teachers; and worship represents a system of training intended to help man in his spiritual growth. Through the long course of evolution the spiritual qualities which are latent in him are gradually awakened from their state of latency and externalised in self-expression. The earliest lessons are learned in what we call the backward races and the cruder conditions of human existence. Passing through many lives, man gradually learns to respond to a cultured environment, and it is in this stage that religion, at the level at which we are familiar with it, can be most useful to him. The man at this stage is awakening to the existence of higher impulses within him, prompting him to unselfish action and to the higher expression of mind and emotion. He is no longer intent only upon the attainment of his own personal ends, upon wealth or possession, upon the gratification of his own desires and passions. It is here that religion offers him certain help and training in the expression and strengthening of these higher impulses, and in the rendering of them more and more permanent. When they begin to assume this condition of permanency, the lower instincts and appetites are gradually sloughed off from the nature, because

---

[1] Sanskrit terms for the three aspects of the human soul. [Ed.]

[2] The original position for the Kiss of Peace in the Liturgy was at the beginning of the "Mass of the Faithful" where it served to reconcile any enmity among the members. Dix, *The Shape of the Liturgy,* Page 105-110. [Ed.]

[3] The finer, invisible part of the physical level. [Ed.]

[4] *The Distinctive Contribution of Theosophy to Christian Thought.* Page 151 et seq. of this book. [Ed.]

something that is more permanently satisfying has replaced them. It is no longer a question of forcibly suppressing the lower nature; it has been outgrown and rejected as unsatisfactory and leading invariably to unhappiness in comparison with the higher.

The helping of a man to realise the beauty of the higher life and its reaction of happiness upon the nature is the especial task of religion and art. Art has often been called the hand-maid of religion, but rightly seen and in its high achievement, art is religion. Worship is intended to help man in the gradual realisation of all this. It is one of the contributions made by the Great Teachers and by his fellow-men to his helping. He has gradually to be taught to understand and experience the higher things, and in thus experiencing them to grow to appreciate them. In the Christian religion, Christ has instituted various rites called sacraments to help a man at every stage "from the cradle to the grave." The Holy Eucharist is planned to work upon the whole nature of the man. Its action at the higher spiritual levels at which the ordinary man is not as yet awake, is equivalent to that of sunlight as we are able to study its action. As the sunlight quickens the life within a flower and brings the flower to self-expression, so with the life dormant in the higher reaches of our spiritual nature. At the levels at which we are awake, those of thought and emotion, the influence of the Eucharist purifies and ennobles, and it tends always to awaken man to higher levels than those at which he has been accustomed to express himself. *Le culte*, as the French call the practice of worship, is constantly helping man to new and higher experiences of consciousness, and as all these give a sense of greater happiness and of the opening up of the consciousness into "moreness," into a larger and wider life, man reaches these experiences of his consciousness as a kind of new revelation, superior to anything he has known before, and is therefore stimulated and inwardly urged to attempt to reproduce them by his own self-initiated effort. We have in all this an illustration of the co-operation that is intended to exist between the outer and the inner worlds, between the God without in the many stages of His perfect manifestation and the God within still struggling to reach unity with His primal source. Nor should I omit to say that in this work the due mean has to be observed between "self-interested" and the "other-interested" aspects of the work. We do not call a young man selfish because he goes to school or to the university to carry through his education instead of going out to work in the world to help other people. A man who is well educated and properly trained becomes at the later stage a more efficient and trustworthy worker. So also if we are to help humanity, some training and the requisite knowledge are desirable; and time and thought given to such training are not to be classed as selfish. The question really turns on which self it is that is being considered; is it the lower self or the higher self? The lower selfishness is to be avoided, but not the higher selfishness. So in worship, we may legitimately work at our own self-development, though in practice we shall find that we achieve this better if we offer ourselves, spirit, soul and body, to God. But there is the other aspect of worship on which our Liberal Catholic Church lays so much stress, namely, that we go to Church less for our own sakes than for joining together in a scientifically-planned ritual for spreading higher influences abroad over the world, offering ourselves for this purpose to be used by the Lord as units in the body-corporate.

I have gathered together and formulated these various ideas as to the underlying purpose of church worship because the thought of the Holy Communion comes as a fitting climax to them, and because the understanding of them enables us better to understand the purpose of Holy Communion and to realise how wonderful is the gift that our Lord makes to us therein.

Holy Communion means nothing less than the incorporation of Christ in us. As we seek in thought and in our soul's highest flights of aspiration to unite ourselves with Him, to share and partake of His life, so through this means does He bring Himself into effective contact with us even at the level of the physical body. The gift is so intensely real that, as we have seen, many people shrink from the thought as too audacious an adventure into realism.

We cannot wonder that those who feel this Presence to be true have surrounded the ceremony with every exterior mark of respect and holiness. Experience has shown that such an environment of strict and regulated ceremony guards a truth that is precious from the attacks of scepticism and ignorance, and we cannot be too grateful to the great Churches of the West and the East who have guarded for us this priceless heritage.

The Communion is very much a personal matter, and I prefer to leave the inward manner of its reception to the worshipper, suggesting only that he should think out for himself how best to approach this great blessing. As regards the outer manner—that is a different matter, for the comfort and convenience of other people depend on it. It may not be out of place to refer to the matter here, as so many of our people have not been in the habit of attending churches which have inherited the Catholic tradition. A well-conducted church appoints certain people to regulate the approach to the altar rails and the return. People are often curiously sensitive about being managed by their fellows, and there is probably less likelihood of annoyance being caused if acolytes, young and vested as they are in robes, are sent out into the various approaches to take charge of this.

The exact arrangements to be made will depend on the shape of the church, but it is well to avoid the advancing and returning streams of communicants meeting in one gangway, unless it is sufficiently large to permit of this. It is better that they should advance by one gangway and return by another. The waiting queues should not block up the space around the communion rails. The people kneel in a row along the rails; they need not remain kneeling till the whole rail is communicated, but should be careful not to disturb neighbours who are receiving Communion. It is a good plan not to rise till the priest has passed the person next to you. People are unconsciously very selfish about this kind of thing, and a person will often rise immediately after having received, careless that his neighbour is actually receiving, and even, perhaps, in his awkwardness jolt him. In the same way people will squash into a row of communicants where there is really not enough room, or one person by placing himself awkwardly will take up too much room.

A little consideration should also be had for the priest. The priest ought not to be expected to find his way to a lady's mouth under the rim of a large hat. The head should be held erect at the time of Communion, and it is most convenient if (as our Liturgy asks) the tongue be protruded slightly beyond the lips. The priest should make the movement to the mouth, not the communicant, otherwise there is sometimes contact of the mouth with the fingers. The observance of these details facilitates the work of the priest—a work which must always demand his careful attention, considering the sacredness of That which he handles. It is only fitting that the congregation on their side should do what they can to adapt themselves to the correct procedure. I may close these remarks by saying that it is the tradition of the Catholic Church that the Sacred Host should be swallowed without manducation of any kind. If the tongue be slightly extended, as suggested, the Host can then be lodged on its tip, and no difficulty will be experienced in the swallowing. The regulation is prompted by reverence; it is not thought fitting that the Host should be pierced or torn by the teeth, and there is the possibility of particles lodging in the interstices of the teeth.

After The Communion

The paragraph beginning "Under the veil of earthly things" is an attempt to render articulate some of the joy that we experience in consequence of our Communion, and the hope with which it has inspired us for the future. The being brought into the presence of the Father's glory can be interpreted as the attainment of initiation, which the Father in us—the Monad—irradiates for one brief moment the Ego or Soul.

The *Communio* directs our thoughts once more towards the outer world, and ourselves fortified by our participation in the communion, we pour out our praise to God and so share with the outer world the blessing we have received. The *Post-Communio* reminds us of the duty that we have to make manifest in our lives the spiritual help that has so richly been proffered.

As the priest sings the *Ite missa est,* announcing the conclusion of the sacrifice and dismissing men and angels, we send out gratitude and brotherly feeling to the angels who have helped us in the service and who now go to make fruitful our share of the work done for the world.

It will be noticed that the priest has used the minor benediction twice in succession in a brief space of time. This is in order to keep intact the intimate sense of unity resulting from the Communion, and this unity renders specially effective the two benedictions with which the Eucharist closes. The former is the benediction appropriate to Christ's Church. At the mention of the Trinity the congregation should lift themselves up, as individuals and collectively, into the special power of each of the three Persons. The second, that of the First Ray, is a formula borrowed from another institution with the consent of the Head of that Ray.[1] It bears with it the blessing of the Great White Brotherhood[2] and its King, and foreshadows in its language and in the nature of the power that it conveys, the ceremony of Initiation into that Brotherhood.

---

[1] The Second Ray Blessing is not authorized for use in parishes of the Liberal Catholic Church International. [Ed.]

[2] The Communion of the Saints. [Ed.]

THE LONGER AND THE SHORTER FORM

Each form duly serves the sacred purpose in view, namely, the consecration of the bread and the wine into the Body and Blood of Christ, the offering of the Holy Sacrifice before the throne of God, and the ministration of Holy Communion to the worshippers. Two other factors, however, call for consideration. There is, first of all, the edification of the faithful, the lifting of them up into effective spiritual self-expression. Secondly, what may be called the field of action, namely, the area and the degree in and to which the service may work to uplift and bless the world.

The Short Form used with an intelligent, devout and trained congregation may be more effective than the Long Form used by less developed and less trained worshippers. People vary much in their spiritual calibre or make-up. Most people are still largely dependent for their reactions on stimulus from outside, on people with whom they meet and the general environment with which they are brought into reaction. As a result of this age-long process qualities of character are built into us as permanent assets. It is the mark of the developed man that he can spontaneously and at will give outlet to these different qualities of thought and emotion, to intuition and to will, without needing the stimulus of external provocation. Such developed and alert people will be on their mettle when the Short Form is used, and can use it with efficiency.

For ordinary people, less trained in such work, the Long Form lends itself far more naturally to the calling out of devotion, for there are high sentiments in it which arouse the imagination and aspiration of the worshipper. The opening Canticle is longer, and people get better settled down to their work at this initial stage. The symbolism of the additional paragraphs of the Canon is wonderfully uplifting. It is only fair to add that the opening Canticle of the Short Form, though short, is a masterpiece of symbolism. Its concrete imagery holds the mind and recalls somewhat the methods of Freemasonry. It has the merit of carrying on through the entire six verses. The trained congregation of which we have above spoken will, of course, find fuller scope for self-expression in the Long Form.[1]

Those familiar with the Mass as celebrated in the Roman Church[2] know that the congregational side of the worship is not stressed. Many people will be engaged in private devotions, some will be telling their rosary. The music being sung is not sequential with what is taking place at the altar. The detachment from the congregation is the more evident because the service is not in the vernacular and much of it is said "in secret." The priest, moreover, is trained to say his Mass in an impersonal manner. It is often taken at great speed and the sign of the cross is made as rapidly as can be. What underlies this impersonality is the idea that the Holy Sacrifice owes its existence and effectiveness to the Divine Grace alone. The priest is but an unworthy instrument. There is a movement afoot on the Continent, showing itself more especially in Belgium, to unite the people in singing certain passages of the Mass in the vernacular. There may be something to be said for the scheme of training the priest to be impersonal in his administration of the sacraments and in the recitation of the Office. Thousands of men are involved in the scheme, many of them of peasant origin, though all carefully trained for their work.

---

[1] As stated in the introduction to the Shorter Form, "The shorter Form may be used by Priests at their regular daily Celebration, at services for children and whenever the fuller version is found too long for practical convenience." The difference in length between the two versions, when said instead of sung, is approximately 25%. A Brief Form is also authorized for private use; it is approximately 45% shorter than the Full Form. [Ed.]

[2] It is the Roman Tridentine Mass (pre-1969) that is being discussed. [Ed.]

In our movement the method of procedure is different. We have stressed the idea of "the priesthood of the laity." Our Liturgy is so phrased that it can be used by the worshipper without scruple and so that he has scope for the noblest ideals and aspirations. Our services are made as "congregational" as possible. And our people are encouraged to open themselves in thought and feeling to the great powers of which language is in our physical world the token and symbol.

Theology has always consistently asserted that the unworthiness of the minister hinders not the efficacy of the sacrament. We may assume that there is a certain irreducible minimum of spiritual power transmitted when the Mass is said inattentively, mechanically and formally, and with perhaps only one server present as congregation in this physical world. Christ is the true minister of all sacraments. His world stands in need.

It is not unreasonable to assume, and in all reverence, that He also takes advantage of human co-operation. Experience seems to bear this out. A congregation filled with devotion, seeking to serve Him, provides a body-corporate through which His Blessing can pour forth in fuller measure over the world. The greater intensity of the power will depend on the competency and understanding and dedication and size of the congregation. Such achievements need not affect only the neighbourhood of the building where the worship is being held. It is possible to link up in thought with friends and centres of work in different parts of the world. We do not sufficiently realize that Our Lord, stands waiting to pour forth His blessing wherever opportunity is offered for Him. And one has sometimes glimpsed another technique at work. The special quality of worship offered by a small Liberal Catholic Church is sometimes blended with the worship, of much greater volume but of different quality, coming from a nearby church of another denomination, the two being thus merged and contributing to the welfare of the world. It may even be that the work of many churches is thus amalgamated.

THE BLESSED SACRAMENT

(From an early talk by the author)

Students of the hidden side of Christianity know that when the Consecration of the Bread and Wine takes place in the Mass, the substance—SUB STANS, that which stands beneath or behind that bread and wine—is changed by the Angel of the Presence who comes from the Christ, and that there flows through the Sacred Elements a direct ray of light, a line of living fire, from Our Blessed Lord, and through Him, we are told, even from the Second Person of the Blessed Trinity Himself. That is what is meant when it is said that the Bread is the Body of the Lord; for a body is that which is a vehicle of life or consciousness or power, that which expresses the life. Our physical bodies are the instruments that we use in this physical world for expressing ourselves, and so also in this Sacrament the Bread is the Body of Christ in the sense that the life and the blessing of Christ pour through that Bread as their vehicle on the physical plane.

Whenever that Consecration takes place a great stream of influence pours forth from the Church over the surrounding neighbourhood, and there is a second manifestation of power when anyone who is present at the Service sends a thought of aspiration, of devotion, of worship to the Christ. A ray of living light connects him with the Sacrament upon the Altar. The adoration that he outpours calls forth from the Consecrated Host a great response, far greater, of course, than the effort he puts out. That wondrous manifestation occurs whenever a thought of aspiration is sent up to the throne of God in the Presence of the Blessed Sacrament, and upon that great fact in nature the service of Benediction of the Blessed Sacrament is based.

There are Catholic countries where this worship is allowed to take place publicly, and on certain great festivals of the Church the Host, the Consecrated Wafer, is carried through the streets in a magnificent procession, with all the pomp and splendour that the resources of the place can command, in the presence of thousands of people on bended knee offering worship and adoration. The power called forth in that way is tremendous. In non-Catholic countries such processions are very seldom seen, but in Sydney, for example, there is a Procession of the Blessed Sacrament which takes place on the Sunday after the feast of Corpus Christi in the college grounds of the Roman Catholic Seminary at Manly. I remember going there myself on one occasion; there were hundreds of people gathered together and the power called forth from the Blessed Sacrament as It was carried in procession was very great indeed. After the procession, Benediction of the Blessed Sacrament is given. In Catholic countries the Benediction is often given several times in the course of the procession, occasionally they give it from some old ruined church, and it is altogether an exceedingly beautiful and awe-commanding ceremony.

This outpouring of the power of the Christ over thousands of people, the kindling of the spiritual principle within them, the fanning of the spirit into flame, is really a very wonderful thing; and in this Benediction of the Blessed Sacrament we have one especial feature which causes it to differ from other benedictions. When a priest is ordained, he is ordained more along the line of the Holy Spirit than along either the line of the Father or of the Son. At the Second Imposition the Bishop's hands are laid upon his head with the words, "Receive the Holy Ghost for the office and work of a Priest in the Church of God." He is opened up as a channel more along the line of the Holy Spirit than along the line of either of the other two great Streams of Influence in nature. The blessing, therefore, that he gives personally draws more along that line; but in this Benediction of the Blessed Sacrament we have a different worship altogether. That draws upon the Second Person of the Blessed Trinity, upon the Wisdom aspect of God rather than upon His aspect as Creative Activity. An Angel comes from the Christ Himself in this service, and it is through that Angel, as well as through the Sacred Host, that the blessing is given to the people.

When the Blessed Sacrament is exposed upon the altar, every thought of devotion that we send out brings to us response a hundredfold. That is literally true, and so in this Service we have an opportunity of enormously quickening our spiritual growth. We have this tremendous power available for our use, and in proportion to the effort that we make, to the force that we send out, to the lifting up of our hearts and minds in devotion to the Christ, so will be this response that flows from Him towards us. That is one reason why in this service we have a somewhat lengthy, though very beautiful Litany of twenty-two verses, in addition to the two other hymns that are used, the *O Salutaris Hostia* and the *Tantum Ergo*. That is arranged so that all those present may gain the greatest benefit possible from the service. Various sentiments are expressed in the course of the Litany: sometimes it is one aspect of the Blessed Trinity, sometimes another aspect that is invoked. Various ideas are placed before the people; different conceptions are brought before their minds. Everything is done that can be done to rouse and enkindle the fire of their devotion, in order that every person in the congregation in some way or another, through one sentiment or another that is expressed, may have his devotion stirred and enflamed, and so may gain the full benefit of this quickening Life that is outpoured upon us, the blessing from the Christ Himself.

All who join in these services should put forth all the effort that they can. In Roman Catholic churches we find many people who are full of deep devotion, but their devotion is individual rather than congregational. During the Mass, for instance, they are mainly occupied with their own private devotions, except at certain great moments in the service. What we are trying to do in the Liberal Catholic Movement is somewhat different. In the first place, we have the Liturgy in the vernacular, in our own tongue, in order that everybody may understand what is being said. It is quite true that many people in the Roman Catholic Church do understand what is being said, because the English is written alongside the Latin, but in actual practice not so much attention is given to the service as might be. For that reason amongst others, with us the service is put into English. It is quite true, too, that where the Latin language is used we have a greater sonority of sound, so that more power flows out from the sound of the words than in the English. "DOMINUS VOBISCUM" is certainly a more powerful sound than the English, "The Lord be with you." But much greater power is gained if we can have the mental co-operation of the people who are taking part in the worship.

What we desire to ensure in this particular Movement[1] is that the people shall understand what is being done and shall be able themselves to co-operate intelligently with it as a body corporate. Our people are expected to take every sentence that is sung in the Liturgy and to try to mean that sentence with their whole heart, with the full power of their understanding; and if we pour out the irresistible power of the will into what we are doing, we shall feel the tremendous response that will come from above. We must try to mean with the whole of the power that we can summon to our assistance every word that we say in the service. In order that that may be done we have inserted such sentences only as can under normal circumstances be said by any member of the congregation. Perhaps it is too much to hope that every sentence shall be entirely acceptable to everyone. But we have done our best to ensure that. We do not

---

[1] In a sense, the Liberal Catholic Church is a movement within Catholic Christianity and not a new Church. Bishop Wedgwood reflects that here by speaking of "The Movement." [Ed.]

ask the obviously impossible of our people, nor do we require them to express exaggerated sentiments to which they cannot live up; it is all made as straight-forward as it can be, in order that we may in this way have the full power of the co-operation of the congregation in what is taking place.

In the service of Benediction we approach the living Presence of the Christ. Let us make our offering to Him a worthy one. In the Roman Catholic Church a number of people show the utmost reverence and devotion. They kneel when they enter the church, where the Host is ever reserved. We may know where It is kept in a church by the light before or on the side of the Altar. They genuflect in adoration and worship. Where the Blessed Sacrament is exposed, as it is during Benediction, they go down on both knees in adoration, and that which they do with their body is done also with the heart and the mind. When they go to communion they always genuflect before the Blessed Sacrament before they receive It, and before they depart. I would like our people to do the same, so that it might never be said that we were behindhand in devotion and reverence. We who have studied more deeply the hidden side of Christianity ought to show even greater devotion than those who live more upon faith perhaps, than upon knowledge.

Let us strive to enkindle the same deep enthusiasm in our hearts for these holy things that those in other churches have, so that we may offer to Our Lord in this Blessed Sacrament of His Love an offering which is worthy, a great stream of love and of devotion ascending before Him, which can be used by Him for the helping and uplifting of those in the world who are in sorrow or distress. That is one great object of our worship, that the power which flows out from us to Him in our Services of praise and thanksgiving (for we serve not only by action but also by the use of our feelings and thoughts), may be such as can be used by Him for pouring out upon those who need help, who need power, thus bringing into their lives the spiritual benediction that flows from Him, and which is augmented and distributed by our own co-operation with His mighty purpose.

Let us try, then, to mean every sentence in the Liturgy with the whole of the power, the whole of the will, the whole of the thought, the whole intensity of devotion and feeling that we can summon. Many Christian people have an untrue view of the Master Jesus, the Master of the Christian Church. They do not realise that His main characteristic is not so much gentleness as burning power, ardent devotion; that the mighty power which streams forth from Him burns up all the impurities, the dross of our lower nature, and kindles an intense response in our spiritual nature. That is the kind of devotion that we should offer to the Christ, a devotion that is strong and fiery and burning, a devotion that can be usefully employed for the uplifting and helping of our brethren.

BENEDICTION OF THE MOST HOLY SACRAMENT

Benediction is, perhaps, of all the Church services that most liked by the ordinary worshipper. It has the merits of simplicity and brevity and it gives immense scope for expression and devotion. I have heard people say that they preferred it to the Eucharist, as being less tiring and a more direct and natural expression of worship. But a little reflection shows that it is quite invidious to compare the two services. Benediction could not take place without the Blessed Sacrament, and that presupposes a previous celebration of the Holy Eucharist. Like the giving of Communion with the Reserved Sacrament, the service of Benediction is really an extension of the Eucharist. The Eucharist necessitates a good deal of hard work and some complicated procedure—a fact which is easily understood and accounted for when one realises what it sets out to achieve. And Benediction is only simpler and more direct because it represents the comparatively leisurely and facile use of the fruits of this supreme achievement.

Benediction and Christian Development

Benediction is a comparatively modern service—in the main a development of the last four hundred years—though there is reason to think that the blessing of the people with the Host held in the hand during the Eucharist may go back to early times. It is probable that the rite began to develop round about the thirteenth century and made headway under a two-fold influence; namely, the intensification of the devotional phase of consciousness in the Middle Ages, and later a reaction against Protestantism, which challenged the doctrine of the objective Presence of our Lord in the Eucharist at the time of the Reformation and onwards. We need not suppose that Christ intended His religion to remain fixed and unresponsive to development. The Roman Church seems to have set her face against a good many practices which tended to spread in mediaeval times and which she checked as abuses, but Eucharistic adoration and the rite of Benediction took their natural course of development. Curiously enough, this process of development does not seem to have been at work in the Eastern Church. Reservation is practised presumably for the sick, but the Host is not usually made a centre of adoration. I remember how in one cathedral of the Russian rite that I visited, the sacristan pointed with his finger to a silk bag that was hanging in a room at the back of the altar, in response to my enquiry as to where the Host was kept. A theory is current that away from Communion the Presence is dormant. Nor is Benediction practised.

There are a few churches of the Anglican communion where Benediction is to be found, sometimes under the name of "Devotions." But as the rite is virtually a post-Reformation one, it is difficult to smuggle it in within the covers of the Prayer Book. Conservative Anglican theologians, even of the High Church order, often follow the example of Luther who, convinced of a Real Presence, held nevertheless that It was *in usu, non extra*.

I do not find myself able to agree with this view. In the Holy Eucharist Christ is at once Priest and Victim. In the Cosmic Sacrifice the Life of God is both transcendent and immanent. "I established this universe with one fragment of Myself, and I remain."[1] As I have pointed out in a book,[2] this reluctance to accept the doctrine of the Real Objective Presence in itself, is a survival of the old heresy that matter is evil. One understands that the intention of theologians

---

[1] *Bhagavad-Gita*, x, 42.
[2] *The Presence of Christ in the Holy Communion*, now part of this volume at page 121 et seq. [Ed.]

of this school is to preserve the holiness and mystery of the great ideal, and one respects them for that sentiment. But they do so by wrapping the process in cloudiness and by vagueness of thought and utterance instead of by rightly understanding matter. There is nothing crass or degrading in the idea of the Real Presence if matter is exalted and sanctified as the vehicle of spirit. Does not the Divine Life slumber even in the mineral?

There is only one voice that may decide between those who hold that the Christian faith and practice must explicitly find its warrant in Holy Scripture or primitive custom, and those more romantic souls who believe in development under the living guidance of the Holy Spirit. That is the voice of first-hand spiritual experience. And the test that we apply is not necessarily that of Scripture or primitive usage, but that of the pragmatic method applied to religion. No one who has trained his spiritual faculties to right discernment can doubt the radiant outpouring of our Lord's blessing through the Reserved Sacrament or in the rite of Benediction.

Ritual Directions

People who visit Roman Catholic churches in different countries will be surprised to find a good deal of diversity in regard to ritual usage and to what is included in the service. As has been pointed out above, in its present form Benediction is a comparatively modern service. It does not figure in the liturgical books of the Roman use. It is otherwise fully authorised, but with a good deal of variation of usage. The method of celebrating it at Rome is said to be rather different from the order to which we are accustomed in English Roman churches.

The Liberal Catholic Liturgy gives us an arrangement which is followed as the norm in most of our Churches, though it allows of some curtailment and of something else replacing the Litany. Ritual and ceremonial directions covering all this appeared in the May 1928 number of *The Liberal Catholic*.[1] As I stated in introducing those directions, they differ in one or two points from the directions given in the Liturgy. The proposed points of slight variation were, of course, previously submitted to the Presiding Bishop and approved by him. It should be remembered that the directions given in the Liturgy were drawn up at an early period of our Church, before we had had much experience of work under all sorts of conditions to guide us, and may occasionally be open to improvement. It is intended that Benediction should follow the order given in the Liturgy under all normal circumstances. The one variation that it may be desirable to make relates to the position of the Collect for Peace. This was inserted in the second edition of the Liturgy in obedience to a hint given that at all public services there should be a prayer of peace. The beautiful prayer which was then composed was written by a Buddhist, Mr. Jinarā-jadāsa. It is evident that the flow of thought is intended to be kept on the Lord's Presence through the Blessed Sacrament from the time of the Litany until the Ascription which precedes the act of Benediction. Roman Catholic usage is very particular about this, and no prayer may follow the *Tantum Ergo* except the one prescribed. Our short Collect for Peace does not seriously disturb this flow, though it is better, perhaps, to transfer it to the interval between the *O Salutaris Hostia* and the Litany.[2] But the situation becomes more difficult if other collects are to be inserted, for which there may sometimes be quite a reasonable case to argue. There is a rubric at the close of the Service of Healing in the second edition of the Liturgy, which permits the giving of Benediction with the special intention of healing. This was authorised as the out-

---

[1] The former journal of the Church, now replaced by *Community*. [Ed.]

[2] The Third Edition of *The Liturgy* makes provision for optional Collects at this point, although it is not required that the Collect for Peace be one of them. [Ed.]

come of some investigations that our Presiding Bishop made when I was with him in Sydney. He found that the spiritual outpouring in Benediction could be used effectively in this way. And there are quite a number of good earnest people who feel a special call to work of this kind.[1] These permissive uses are not meant to replace to any extent the normal use of the service, but where Benediction is frequently held and where special work has to be done, the Presiding Bishop saw no difficulty about sanctioning slight variations. The rubric in question authorises the inclusion of the Prayer for the Sick. Again, there are special Centres which exist for doing a particular work, like my own at St. Michael's, Huizen. We have since the beginning of our work there made a point of using at every public liturgical service the collect for St. Michael and All Angels. Personally, I think it quite desirable that every church should include in the services the collect of its Patron Saint. His patronage is thus brought before the congregation and made living and real instead of being a mere formality. If, then, the rite is to include the Collect for Peace, that of the Patron, and perhaps that for the Sick, it is certainly much better that these shall precede the Litany than interrupt the special devotion to our Lord which is to culminate in the giving of His blessing. But there is no need for any of these extra collects if Vespers precede Benediction, for they take their place there.

It gives a more finished effect if the *O Salutaris Hostia* does not begin until the Host is exposed and the censer ready for use in the Officiant's hand, and if the second censing is made between the two verses of the *Tantum Ergo* to the accompaniment of soft extemporisation on the organ.

The Thought Intention

There is no need to comment at any length on the constituent features of Benediction as they succeed one another. The opening hymn, *O Salutaris Hostia*, is intended to bring the worshippers into special relation with our Lord. Bishop Leadbeater tells us that "the Angel of the Presence" again appears as at the Eucharist. The Litany continues the devotion, emphasizing different aspects of our Lord's relation to us and of our dependence upon Him. Of this I will speak later. The fine old hymn, *Tantum Ergo*, increases and intensifies this devotion. The Collect tells us that the one way to real conscious union with the Lord is to identify ourselves with the one great Sacrifice by which the world is maintained. So long as a person looks out on life from the standpoint of his personal interest or gain or gratification he misses the underlying rhythm of the universe. When he can rise to the condition where life in itself and as a whole, and the interests and well-being of other people, interest him naturally more than himself, with his personal desires and ideas and gratifications, then only can he merge his consciousness into the larger Self, which knows itself to be one with all that lives.

The Ascription relates the consciousness of those who follow it as an act of *Yoga* with various great centres of the spiritual Hierarchy, and the Benediction comes as the culmination of all this self-offering, identification and devotion. The final singing re-establishes the unity on all planes, and provides the opportunity of further vocal self-expression, which brings down the great benediction to effective self-expression even at the physical level.

---

[1] Use of Benediction with the special intention of healing is still authorized by the *Book of Ceremonies,* although the Third Edition of *The Liturgy* no longer includes the statement cited. [Ed.]

The Two Kinds of Power

All this has its own place in the general scheme and purpose of worship. The student who wishes to understand this scheme should realise that where the Blessed Sacrament is the centre of the worship, at the Holy Eucharist and at Benediction, he is dealing with the influence of the Second Person of the Blessed Trinity brought down through the direct and personalised channel of our Blessed Lord, the especial manifestation or epiphany of that Person. At Vespers, on the other hand, in the various Offices, and in the earlier part of the Eucharist we are dealing with the more impersonal influence of the Blessed Trinity as a whole. This force has perhaps more of a cosmic aspect about it. The sacramental channel can be used in a very special way for self-development, and for directing spiritual power for specific purposes—for helping people in sickness or difficulty, for promoting and vivifying righteous causes in the world. The other is more general in its action, and, being less specialised, works perhaps on another aspect of the consciousness. The wise student will not neglect this more general aspect of the Divine Power. There are many passages in the Psalms and in the Scriptures generally which extol the Deity, meditation upon which will aid him in the realisation of this. Especially potent, too, are some of those texts of majestic splendour to be found in the Upanishads. Too much attention cannot be given to this sterner (shall we call it) side of our work, and it proves an excellent corrective against exaggerations and distortions of the devotional nature into which the neophyte may sometimes lapse.

There are dangers along the line of devotional expression familiar to religious psychologists. But *usum non tollit abusus*, and these cannot be used as any argument against the right use of devotion. A common tendency, into which people may all too unconsciously slip, is to seek satisfaction of their own emotions in that type of worship which invokes the aid of an aesthetic setting in the way of music, of colour and form in vestments and embroideries, and in perfume of incense. Worship means of giving of "worth-ship" to God. Devotion means "to vow oneself away from." The "peace which passeth all understanding" bears with it a feeling of bliss and elation, beautiful beyond the power of words to describe. "Brahman is Bliss," says an Indian Scripture. Such happiness comes as the natural result of true worship and devotion, but its place should be left to continue as incidental. The moment a worshipper seeks to reproduce for his own pleasure and self-gratification such a feeling of psychic well-being, his work becomes tinged with selfishness and sinks on that account to a lower level. The sensation that he is seeking will probably then elude him, but there are cases when the will can force an entry thereto, and the resulting process is dangerous in the extreme. We should learn to make our worship single and pure, that is to say, detached from all self-interest—from interest in the *lower* self. It is not for us to dwell upon our own happiness as an end and aim in itself—that is the distortion of the hedonist school of philosophy. We need rather to realise how natural it is that the Self in us, seeking union with the larger Self without, should pour itself out freely and in gladness without thought of recompense or return. "It is very meet, right and our bounden duty that we should at all times and in all places give thanks to Thee, O Lord, Holy Father, Almighty Everlasting God."

Singleness of Purpose

Such should be our attitude during the Benediction Litany. It rehearses before us a number of different attributes of our Lord, and it brings before us certain qualities of character through which we are to fashion ourselves into His adorable likeness. There is no limit to the possibilities that here open out before us. But there are certain facts about our own habits and methods of thought that need to be appreciated before we can work efficiently in the vineyard of our character. Human evolution has been long and slow, and it has taken life upon life for us to learn to control and direct the mechanism of body, emotion and mind. If one asks the ordinary person to meditate upon love, he usually thinks about love instead of becoming love. His colour is the yellow caused by the expression in the intellect of an idea rather than the rose of that quality. He needs not to think about love, but actually to become love. We are accustomed for the most part to express emotions as the result of interaction with environment. The sight of a loved one or the receipt of a letter evokes a great glow of love from within us. But it is much more difficult to do the same thing by effort self-initiated from within, where an external stimulus is lacking.

One of the great advantages of Church training, rightly understood, is that it develops this ability to modify our consciousness as we wish in response to the demand of the Liturgy with its constant flow of key-ideas and in the fellowship of the other members of the Lord's mystical body.

We best learn to accomplish this by the use of the imagination—the image-making power of the mind. If love is asked of us, we picture ourselves as being with some loved one. The thought evokes a natural reaction of love, and we work upon this to intensify it, to purify and refine it, and eventually to divest it of all self-interest, with a view to making the finished product of our consciousness worthy as an offering before the throne of God. Let us take another example. The two words "hail" and "adore" occur frequently in the last line of the verses of the Litany. We have only to cast our minds back to some great patriotic function when a sovereign or a leader has been hailed or acclaimed by the multitude. How grand and thrilling a spectacle! Need we offer less in our Litany? So, too, with the word "adore." It is an attitude such as this which puts life and reality into a service, and under the conditions thus produced it is not difficult to get one's own assurance as to the truth of the doctrines which underlie the worship of our Church. How close can be the union with our Lord in this service of transcendent beauty only those know who have found in this greater realisation the sure means of forgetting themselves.

The Effect on The World

I ought not to close on that aspect of the work to be done in this service which relates to ourselves and our self-development—though there is. nothing discreditable about the development of the higher Self. We should not forget to realise how marvellous is the effect of a good service of Benediction in the neighbourhood and far around the place where it is celebrated. There may be masses of the dead present to bathe in this wonderful influence of love and purity, as well as many who are only temporarily separated from their bodies. Hosts of angels are also there. And as the great wave of peace and utter beauty sweeps around the horizon when our Lord acclaims His people, many a sorrowful soul who knows nothing of the Church hard by is cheered and consoled, and the whole world is lifted a little nearer to its final destiny by the blessing of the "First among many brethren."

THE SERVICE OF HEALING

During the last half century there has been a great awakening of interest in the subject of spiritual healing. The discoveries of the X rays and of radio-activity have turned people's thoughts and hopes towards the employment of subtler methods of research and healing, and psychology has come to occupy an increasingly important sphere in the domain of medicine. With the spread of these ideas, people have begun to ask whether it is not part of the Church's work to heal the sick. They point to the example of Our Blessed Lord and ask why His ministers do not follow in His footsteps. In the space at our disposal it will not be possible to discuss the subject at large, and I must restrict myself to discussing the ceremony of our Liturgy.

Religion has always been hampered by the fact that vague emotion has tended to usurp the place in it of clear and reasoned thinking. And there is no aspect of religion in which sane and clear thinking is more necessary than in this one of healing. Miracles of healing, so-called, are not unknown; but what it is that enables people to heal by their mere personal proximity or by their touch is a point on which we have very little information. The Stuart dynasty are said to have had the power of the "king's touch," as it was called. It seems likely that such powers of natural healing are due to some association with the Angel kingdom, but how this association is to be brought about and maintained is still a mystery to us. No doubt the Christ could do miracles of healing, but we need to be Christs ourselves—with all the developed powers and control over nature that are His—in order to be able to go and do likewise.

The ecclesiastical custom of anointing the sick with oil is based on the well-known passage in the Epistle of St. James, V. 14-15:

> Is any sick among you? Let him call for the elders of the Church; and let them pray over him, anointing him with oil in the name of the Lord. And the prayer of faith shall save the sick, and the Lord shall raise him up, and if he have committed sins, they shall be forgiven him. Pray for one another that ye may be healed. The effectual fervent prayer of a righteous man availeth much.

The passage presents some difficulties, for it speaks somewhat confidently of the patient being cured. And it introduces the additional complication of the forgiveness of sins being involved in the process. This is only one of many examples that might be cited of the insufficiency of Scripture as the basis and foundation of Christian faith and practice. It was only at the Reformation that this curious superstition about the position of the Scriptures came into fashion. Previously it had always been understood that the Church, which gave the Christian Scriptures to the world, had other traditions, also, of value and authority. The Scriptures were not intended to be more than they are—a collection of miscellaneous records. They were never meant to be an exhaustive summary of faith and doctrine, a complete code of morals, or a directory of public worship. The Reformation substituted this idea of an infallible book for the living voice of the Church expressed through its General Councils, and Luther and his colleagues no more brought freedom of thought to Christendom than they brought peace, for their followers were bound to the letter of Scripture. Of course, the higher criticism has totally upset this idea of the infallible authority of Scripture.

The passage of St. James under discussion is really quite inadequate as an authority for anything except that its writer seemed to have known of good results being obtained through prayer and unction on the part of the Church authorities.

We have to remember that conditions of life in regard to sickness and hygiene were very different in those days from now. We can get a fair understanding of those older conditions if we have had experience of conditions in some oriental countries to-day. With us, definite possession by evil spirits is comparatively rare. It is much less rare in India, where people have less hold over their bodies, and exorcism is frequently and often successfully employed. So also with sickness. There are large masses of Indians who have comparatively little hold over their bodies, and die in great numbers during an epidemic. I have no doubt from what I have seen in India and elsewhere that spiritual healing would bring about more successful results in the conditions of those amongst whom the Bible was written than it would in these days. Not that I am sceptical of its present-day use, for I have seen remarkable results in some cases. But the responsibility for the treatment of disease lies primarily with the medical profession. One finds that with the lapse of time a good many duties with which in earlier times the Church occupied itself, tend to get separated off and to find their place under the secular administration. Medicine, like education and the administration of charity or economic relief, now belongs to the secular arm, and the role that the Church has to play in healing is purely a secondary one.

In the Roman Catholic Church unction is given only in cases of grave sickness and where there is danger of death. Unction came to be called "Extreme Unction" probably, not as most people would imagine because administered *in extremis*, but because it was the last of the unctions (following those of baptism and confirmation) given in the Christian's life. The custom of reserving it for the last rites grew up gradually. It is supposed by some that all sorts of restrictions came to be followed by, or imposed upon, those who had received it and recovered—namely, that they should not again eat flesh, or have marital intercourse, and that they should walk barefoot. We can understand how these scruples arose in regard to a body whose sense organs had thus been consecrated. The people probably grew scared to receive it, despite attempts on the part of the authorities to put things right. This is perhaps the explanation of that mysterious phrase about "a corrupt following of the Apostles," found in the Articles of the Anglican Prayer-Book. The Anglican Reformation made no provision for Unction, but there are many Anglicans in these days who have restored this "lost pleiad of the Anglican firmament" to quote Bishop Forbes.

I spoke just now of the necessity for sane and clear thinking on this subject of healing. There are a number of assumptions into which people seem naturally to rush. One common one is that ordination gives the power to cure sickness. It is true that one of the lower grades, that of Exorcist, has been associated with healing, but there is no guarantee about it. And nothing is said about it at the giving of the Priesthood. A priest can be utterly sure of consecrating the Eucharist every time that he does the rite, or of baptising. Those things have been promised to his office; they are "covenanted gifts." But the ability to conquer disease is not among these promised gifts. It comes under the category of "charismatic" gifts, those gifts of the Spirit and diversities of operations of which St. Paul speaks. Secondly, there is also the assumption frequently made that all sickness and disease is the outcome of wrong thinking, so that to cure it all we need is to get our minds right. That this is often the case probably no one in these days would deny. But it does not seem logical to account in this fashion for the thousands of cases where people fall victim to an epidemic. Has the thinking of these many people so deteriorated below the normal level that they are all ill, and by a curious coincidence simultaneously? Have they all by mental disharmony opened their bodies to germ penetration?

There is always a certain amount of nervous disturbance produced by illness. The Healing Service rectifies this for the time being and facilitates the action of the natural recuperative processes of the body. In this way it may be a valuable adjunct to regular medical treatment, but, in spite of St. James' optimism, I do not see that, judging by our experience of these things, we have any reason to assume that spiritual healing is going to cure organic disease.

Again, sickness is a matter of *karma*, and we ought not to assume that a limitation which is being brought to bear upon a person by the Administrators of that Law is going to be removed by our intervention. We cannot interfere with karma in the larger sense. But I do not take the rigid view that we cannot affect it. We can if we choose to take the responsibility, bring new influences to bear on the situation. If the karma is nearly exhausted, it is possible that through our intervention the limitation might be removed. It is here, I think, that the Christian doctrine of Grace has some contribution to make to our thinking on this matter—though I suppose that the ordinary theologian would not recognise our interpretation of that doctrine as having much to do with the original.

We can approach the matter in this way. There is no greater heresy than to suppose that each man is individually independent. We are markedly dependent on each other. There is no being more dependent than the infant. He has been dependent on his parents for his entry into the world, and is dependent for his care and nourishment. In fact, living as we do a communal life, we are perpetually reacting upon one another. The higher help the lower; and we in our turn are helped by the Great Ones. It is ridiculous for some people to say, as they do, that no one can help us from outside. There is a great sacrifice made by Those who, having attained "Perfection" or "Liberation" remain back on earth to help humanity. And because of this sacrifice, They have great spiritual power at Their disposal for that work. I look upon the work of our Lord the Christ in that fashion, and some of that spiritual power or grace at His disposal is what He gives us through the Sacraments, as channels of His grace. There is no reason that I can see why this should not operate to modify the karma of people who receive it through the Sacraments or by other means. I not infrequently have the impression when celebrating the Healing Service that the problem with which I am engaged is one of some modification or readjustment of karma—a certain reshaping of the conditions which surround the person. We have, I think, some support for this theory in the words attributed to the Christ when He asked His critics "Whether it is easier, to say, thy sins be forgiven thee; or to say, arise, and walk?" (Matt. ix, 5).

These are some of the difficulties which entangle the problem of healing and its practice in the Church. But there are worse ones of a practical nature which arise when one makes the attempt to go ahead with the work. One is the difficulty of combining enthusiasm, such as will kindle the aspiration of the patient, with a little scepticism or reserve, which will serve to allay undue disappointment if success does not accrue to the efforts of the healer. Revivalists and people of fanatical conviction often sweep people with them and so secure results that escape people of milder and more stable disposition; but the anguish of their hopeless cases is pitiful. I hold strongly that religion should not be made a matter of emotional crises, for stability does not lie that way. One wants for the Church earnest, steadfast and convinced workers, who will move steadily on with the work, arriving eventually at the stage when the question of their own development occupies them very little in comparison with the splendour of the work for others.

But there is one difficulty yet greater, which is the bane of all churches and religious movements—namely, self-interest in religion. There are crowds of people who go to religious meetings or to services to have their emotions played upon: All this has been sadly encouraged by pulpit oratory. One finds in the gatherings of Protestant bodies on the Continent of Europe a real satisfaction in being made to feel gloomy and miserable. But even in our supposedly more enlightened circles, the same element is noticeable. There is a terrible amount of selfishness in regard to spiritual things in some people. And these people will often tell one that they are quite disinterested and have only the desire for service. They often mean this quite honestly, for it is easy to be self-deluded on such matters. To be able to look within and read clearly the heart represents an advanced stage of development.

People often come up to me after lectures and talk about themselves and their interests. There is a certain well-known type that comes up and tells one that they are interested in healing. Automatically one tends to suspect plenty of sentimentality, a woolly mind unused to clear and systematic thinking, and a dominant interest in their own sensations. Such people flock to healing services and healing movements in general. They like also to join healing groups, for which they are not in the least fitted, since they drain what force there is for their own self-gratification, instead of helping to send it out to others. Mediumistic people often like this work, for they get the opportunity of vampirising from others the vitality that their own spooks draw from them.

I must confess personally to a certain dislike of healing services of the ordinary character, for they tend to collect such people. There must be a strong reaction against all this kind of thing. 'God helps those who help themselves' was the utterance of a very wise person. People of this sort are best helped by a little radical and even perhaps harsh treatment. They must be cured of their self-interest and their attitude of dependence upon others, and be helped to become positive. Above all things, the most rigorous reserve must be maintained in regard to those who come to gratify consciously or unconsciously (and it is so often the latter) some pleasure in personal contact with the priest and the service, which has its roots in sensual or sensuous gratification.

Certain rules may be deduced from a study and realisation of these difficulties. People should not be encouraged to receive healing too frequently. Exception may, of course, be made in cases of serious sickness where the patient does not show these morbid tendencies. But I have heard of people who wanted to receive healing regularly several times a week, and who preferred it to Mass. Such people should be made to understand the value of self-dependence, and that Our Lord in the Blessed Sacrament of His Love is the great Physician. That Sacrament also is to be approached, not in the attitude of 'getting,' but rather of joyous and glad offering and of merging oneself into that larger Life which is His. Hence, I think that in any case healing should be practised with reserve, and the Holy Communion rather be used for regular effort towards good health.

Another rule is that people should be made to send in their names for healing beforehand, and not be allowed to saunter up to receive treatment on the impulse of the moment. There should be some exercise or discipline of meditation given to be done the evening before, or on the day itself. The trend of this should be towards selflessness. Poetry and devotional reading may be used to elevate the mind and emotions.

Lastly, there should be insistence on cleanliness of person and of clothing on the part of the candidate, and even some dietetic regulations before the service, if thought well, and the patient is willing to co-operate.

The Healing Service itself is comparatively simple. I have always assumed that a certain latitude of usage is tolerated. I prefer personally not to do services of this kind in the evening if that can be avoided. The bodies are then apt to be tired and less unified, owing to the impacts of the day through which they have passed. My own custom has been to take the service after Mass, the patients to be treated deferring their Communion till the Healing Service.

The first cross in the section headed The Unction prepares the bodies and gets them 'to attention,' so to speak. This prayer is not unlike that which precedes the act of ordination. A solemn exorcism follows, then the anointing with oil for the sick, and lastly the imposition of hands.

Bishop Leadbeater speaks of a powerful current passing at the physical etheric level through the priest and set into motion by the representative of the Raphael hierarchy.

I have sometimes thought that our Healing Service might be compared to Absolution on a larger scale. I cannot help feeling that the confessional, so far as its regular and constant use is concerned, is unsuited to our times and outlook, though I believe it to be exceedingly useful at times. It is a rather safe form of psychoanalysis. There is a certain value in the specific mention of misdeeds, for the sections of the higher bodies connected with these faults are thus magnetically linked with the priest, and the grace of Christ's power in Absolution, passing through him, flows into those special areas and tends to heal the wounds often there to be found.

Absolution is a straightening out of kinks in the higher nature, which obstruct the direct flow of the Divine Life. Something of the same sort is done in the Healing Service, and it works like Absolution (but more effectively, perhaps) to impress upon the harmonised personality the Divine Image and Stamp which is the triple Ego. The consequence is usually a great feeling of peace and happiness, a freedom from restriction and a new hope for the future.

The effect of Unction 'in extremis' is rather different. It is extraordinarily useful, for it clears away much of the horrible influence of depression and disease which clogs the sickroom of one who has been suffering. And it certainly enables the man to disentangle himself from the body—and even, it seems to me likely, from the etheric double, so that there is less difficulty about being free from 'the grey world.'

THE ORDINATION SERVICES

IT would make too large a demand upon our space if I were to describe in detail the whole series of ordinations. It will be better to point out some general principles underlying the ceremonies of ordination, and to single out a few special points for attention. In this way, the congregation may be able to understand the scheme of work on which the ordinations are based, and to assist more usefully when they are conferred.

The form for each ordination opens with a charge by the bishop, setting forth the duties and responsibilities of the Order. There is a twofold purpose in this preliminary charge. It takes a certain amount of time, as we understand that word on the physical plane, to get a congregation into the proper attitude for a piece of spiritual work, and the reading of the charge, steadies them and arouses their interest in the particular work ahead. Secondly, the charge brings before the mind of the candidate the nature of the work to be done, the qualities that are required for it, and calls out from him an increasing enthusiasm for the beautiful ideals of service summed up in each ordination. The bishop, as he reads the charge, will be sending out the various qualities of character mentioned, and thus makes connection with a number of localised areas in the higher bodies of the candidate corresponding to those qualities. His own usual power, and that higher power which he is transmitting at the moment, flows into the candidate because of this opening up and enlisting of attention on the candidate's part. And through the many channels which are thus being made the power of the Christ will pour at the moment of ordination. The people can help by themselves giving attention to those qualities. The effect of all this is really remarkable, and it shows what an unexpected amount of reality and spiritual activity can underlie so simple a procedure as the reading of a charge.

In the matter of the Minor Orders our Liturgy shows considerable improvement on that of the Roman *Pontificale*. The Roman rite continues to work on the assumption that the duties belonging to these minor degrees are still going to be carried out by the candidates, and as this is rarely the case a certain air of unreality covers the proceedings. We of the Liberal Catholic Church have adopted the precedent of Freemasonry. History goes to show that in the middle ages 'gentlemen masons' as they were sometimes called, men of position and learning and of good family, were sometimes taken into the lodges of the operative masons, much as in these days people receive the 'freedom' of a city. These people did not learn the operative trade, as did the ordinary apprentices, and came to be called 'speculative masons.' At the beginning of the eighteenth century a certain Dr. Anderson got together some lodges and instituted a movement of purely speculative Freemasonry, from which the operative element was absent, and this was the nucleus of modern Freemasonry. Lodges of operative masons, however, still exist, having their own organisation. We in the giving of Minor Orders make this same distinction between operative and speculative work, and our ritual is consequently more clear-cut and consistent. We tell the candidate that the original functions of the office have either fallen into desuetude (like the blessing of bread and first-fruits, or the reading for the preacher) or are carried out by other people (like the duties of the Doorkeeper). And we then deduce from these duties certain lessons of conduct and of character-building, just as do the Freemasons, and as does the Roman *Pontificale*.

Even those who do not seek ordination would derive much benefit if they were to take the charges from Cleric to Acolyte as a basis for their work of character development. The scheme is wonderfully comprehensive and sequential, and it ministers to those very points which are most essential in the early period of training.

After each charge comes a prayer, in which the candidate is lifted up into the presence of Christ. The bishop makes the sign of the cross over him as he asks that he may be sanctified, and then, imposing his right hand on the head of the candidate, he solemnly confers the order. During the prayer a good deal of activity goes on in the higher bodies of the candidate. There is always at this point preceding the conferring of the order a rapid vibratory movement in the spinal column, and in general a raising in vibratory capacity of that connection between the soul and the personality, that we call in the technical language of Theosophy the *antahkarana*.[1] This prayer is supplemented by a Litany in the ceremonies for the Subdiaconate and upwards. The candidate is prostrate on the floor. The bishop repeatedly makes the sign of the cross over him during three verses of the Litany, the effect of which is to purify the bodies of the personality and to withdraw the consciousness of the candidate as far as possible to the egoic level.[2]

At the ordination itself a stream of pure and holy influence pours into the candidate from the Lord, who is the true Minister of all sacraments, and especially affects that part of the organism with which the ordination is concerned. At the grade of Reader, for example, there is a strengthening of the mental body. It is first a question of purification, and then of certain added subtlety or elasticity being given to the body. The aura of that level swells out considerably, and although it will gradually retreat to something like its former size during the hours and days that follow the ordination, nevertheless it will never shrink back to its original limitations. Added to this, the real point is that as the neophyte exerts his own efforts at right and lofty use of the mind, the growth of the mental body will take place more rapidly and with less resistance and on more harmonious lines, because of the original impulse and expansion that was given at the moment of ordination.

Following immediately upon the solemn act of ordination in the Minor Orders and at the ceremony of the Subdiaconate comes the giving of the emblems and insignia of the office. At the ordination to Cleric, the neophyte is given a surplice as the emblem of holiness, and in the Roman Church he receives the tonsure. For the other Minor Orders there is a *porrectio instrumentorum*, or *traditio instrumentorum* as it is called in theological language. The Doorkeeper receives a bell and a key. The Reader a book. The Exorcist a book and a sword. The Acolyte a cruet and a lighted candle. This giving of the instruments of office is accompanied by an explanatory and exhortatory formula. The Subdeacon receives first an empty chalice and paten, and then the cruets, lavabo basin and towel, then the amice, maniple and tunicle; and finally the Book of Epistles. The procedure in the higher Orders is varied again, but similar.

These portions of the ceremony are not only outwardly impressive and exhortatory, but have also an inner effectiveness. Once more they direct the mind of the newly ordained to the duties of this office, and while his attention is being occupied with these outer material objects and their concrete significance, the powers that have been conferred are strengthened and stabilised in their concrete expression and in their working through the personality and the physical vehicle. The same field of procedure is covered in Masonry in what is called the communication of the secrets and the investiture with the insignia appropriate to the degree.

In the higher orders from the Diaconate upwards, prayer follows the imposition of hands; and these prayers, together with anointings in the case of the Priesthood and the Episcopate, have also to do with the bringing down of the powers and their harmonious distribution. The hands are to be regarded as the special distributing agents of those spiritual forces which find expression through the physical body.

---

[1] According to Bp. Leadbeater in *The Masters and the Path* this link is unrecognized in most of us and we take the personality to be the man, ignoring the ego. (191-192) [Ed.]

[2] The personality is only part of the soul. [Ed.]

The changes which take place in the higher bodies in the case of the major ordinations, the linkings of the various principles, etc., are matters which the congregation need not perhaps try to follow. But the bishops of the Church ought gradually to be able to find their bearings in these more esoteric realms—belonging to 'the Mysteries,' because above the capacity of normally developed consciousness. Short of that, it is sufficient if we lift up our consciousness in glad devotion to the Lord. Fortunately, it is He, and not ourselves, who is concerned with the making of these stupendous changes.

VARIOUS SERVICES

The Administration of Holy Communion With The Reserved Sacrament

THE form of this, which follows in our Liturgy immediately after the order of the Holy Eucharist, provides for administration of the Sacrament out of the course of the Holy Eucharist. There are some classes of people, such as sick-nurses, night workers, mothers with children, domestic servants, whose work is apt to prohibit them from attending church at the times when the Eucharist is ordinarily celebrated. Some Low-Church Anglican and some Nonconformist Churches arrange to meet the needs of these people by evening Communion services.[1]

We, of course, adhere to the tradition that the consecration of the Host belongs to that portion of the day ending round about midday, and our Eucharists are invariably planned therefore to begin before the hour of twelve. Once the Host is consecrated, It is consecrated; and there is no reason why It should not be administered in Holy Communion at any hour round suitable.

It is recognised in all mystical tradition that there is a close connection between the course of the sun and the reaction of human nature to spiritual effort, and the earlier hours of the morning after sunrise have usually been considered the most suitable for partaking of the Holy Communion. The hours after sunset are less suitable. The body is fresh in the morning, whereas in the evening it has grown fatigued by the continual play of the consciousness upon it and of outside influences. The vehicles of the personality are more dissociated in the evening, they are less synchronised. Hence evening Communion—and the same thing applies to healing—is to be avoided, unless rendered necessary by force of circumstances.

The Divine Office

The kind of service that is represented in our Liturgy by Vespers, Prime and Complin[2] differs from the Eucharist that we have been considering at some length, as also from Baptism, Confirmation, Benediction, the conferring of Holy Orders, in that it does not involve the direct use of the sacramental channels of grace. It consists in the recitation of psalms, in the reading of the sacred scriptures, in the offering of prayer and praise. There is no doubt that this form of service had its direct origin in the worship of Israel. We read in the Acts of the Apostles that the earliest Christians frequented the common worship of the time at the Temple, besides holding their own gatherings. Features of this would gradually be transferred to their own cult; and all this gradually developed into what is called the Divine Office or the Canonical Hours.

The apportioning of these Hours was based on the Roman civil system of dividing the day up into periods of three hours. The devotions of the Hours, as observed in the Roman Church, are contained in the Breviary, and are observed daily by all beneficed clerics, by all holding the rank of subdeacon and upwards, and by those vowed to the monastic or religious life. The idea is to attune the mind by turning it periodically to God, and so gradually to make real and habitual the practice of the presence of God. Those who are interested in this idea of a disciplined life would do well to study the rules of the monastic orders.

The casual visitor to a church can form no idea of the real effect of the recitation of the Divine Office. The best way to do so is, perhaps, to visit a monastery or convent for a few days,

[1] The Liberal Catholic Church International now permits evening Eucharists. [Ed.]
[2] Also Lauds and Sext. [Ed.]

or to go to one of those cathedrals on the continent where worship has proceeded uninterrupt-edly for centuries and where a good musical and liturgical tradition has been built up. This sort of worship owes its peculiar influence largely to its cumulative effect. The regular performance of the chant enlists the influence of *gandharvas*[1] and other angels, who work best on a basis of regularly recurrent rhythms, and the feeling of intense sweetness and peace that broods over this liturgical worship, thus constantly repeated, is beyond the capacity of words to express.

There is a department of occult work which consists largely in dealing with the influ-ences that are produced in our great centres of civilisation for the upliftment of the world in general. There are certain magnetic centres in different parts of the world which can be drawn upon for this. Some are in India, and there are others like those formed by the great talismans planted by Apollonius of Tyana.[2] But groups of people, living and dead, can also make them-selves into such centres, if their work is of a suitable character. Churches are largely so used, branches of the Theosophical Society, Masonic lodges. Nor must we omit to mention how use-ful may be the drama or a performance of music, and especially the great operas like Wagner's. There are wonderful climaxes in The Ring where the higher angels sometimes bring the bene-diction of their presence. These different types of influence are all drawn upon.

The Church has its own part to play in this work, and the role is one of considerable im-portance, in view of the fact that the services are of regular occurrence and that they represent conscious and purposeful work in the way of higher things, and not simply the casual appeal to better emotions. Mgr. Robert Hugh Benson wrote during his Anglican days an interesting book entitled *The Light Invisible*, consisting of a number of stories relating to "the unseen." They were not, I believe, actual personal, experiences, but embroidered around fragments of intuition and personal experience. In one of them he describes a nun in contemplation before the Blessed Sacrament and how she was forging chains of living fire between the Host and those for whom she was praying. This is, of course, true to fact, and it would be difficult to exaggerate the im-portance of the work done by religious communities whose work includes that which is called contemplative, and who by their devotion and by their regular recitation of the Divine Office send out into the thought-atmosphere of the world great waves of spiritual influence.

This work which is done in a regular and continuous fashion by the communities is done on a smaller scale by the ordinary church through the services of Vespers, Prime and Complin, and of course through the celebration of the Holy Eucharist and Benediction. The ordinary church obviously cannot provide for the whole of the Canonical Hours; that is the work of reli-gious specialists who for that work enter the religious orders.

Vespers

Vespers is the only one of the offices of the Hours which has remained in ordinary use as a public service. It has its counterpart in the Anglican Church in Evensong. Coming, as it does, towards the end of the day, it provides a suitable opportunity for gathering people into church for a second time on a Sunday. Strictly, it represents the division of the hours corre-sponding from 3 p.m. to 6 p.m., though the time is variable according to the seasons. In the Ro-man Catholic Church it is sometimes said as early as 3 p.m., but in practice it comes to be used as a late afternoon or evening service.

---

[1] Hindu equivalent of minor deities. [Ed.]

[2] Neopythagorean philosopher (d. 98CE) [Ed.]

We may briefly examine the sequence of its constituent parts and note their effect, but its general purpose has sufficiently been explained in what has been said above.

After the Invocation, the rite begins with versicles and responses, designed to affirm the confidence of the worshippers in the divine aid and to draw the officiant and people together. The *Gloria Patri* which follows is a kind of keynote of praise introducing the psalms. These are five in number, three of praise, one of godly life and one of wisdom. It will be noted that many of the verses are taken from the Apocryphal Book of Wisdom, whose language is of peerless beauty. Legend attributed this book to Solomon. There are indications which have led scholars to suppose that it was written in Hebrew. It has some of the characteristics of Hebrew writing, but the general tendency now is to attribute to it a Greek origin, and some suppose that it may have been the work of a Hellenistic Jew. It shows distinct evidence of acquaintanceship with Greek thought. Wisdom is identified with the *Logos* coming forth into the world in the act of creation. She is treated as feminine; and because of this aspect of creative activity, is occasionally also identified with the Holy Spirit, to whom a feminine aspect has sometimes been attributed.

These psalms do not follow consecutively in the Bible, but have been put together in our Liturgy by a process of selection after the manner of a *cento*.[1] They have a beauty of their own. People sometimes wonder why a Church like ours, that has revised its Liturgy to meet the requirements of modern thought, still retains psalm and hymn singing. The answer is simple. It is difficult to find anything more suitable as a form. We have been careful to eliminate inappropriate sentiments. We no longer sing: "Moab is my washpot: over Edom will I cast my shoe." This fact ought to make it quite possible for people to get behind unintelligent prejudice and put some meaning and zest into language that is at once beautiful and charged with significance. Good poetry does not necessarily go at all well to music, nor does it usually prove suitable for common devotional recitation.

Before leaving these psalms, a word may be said about their musical setting. They are set to Gregorian music, which leaves freedom to rhythm, and they should be sung as far as possible according to the rhythm and accent of the words. The colon which marks the *caesura* or pause in the middle of the verse is important. Hebrew poetry and prose owed much of their effect to what is called parallelism, or balance between verses, or between half-verses. The colon often marks such an antithesis, and it is traditional in reciting or singing the psalms to mark this pause. Usually the pause is insufficient. In cathedrals the two sides of the choir, *decani* and *cantoris*, sometimes sing the half-verses alternately, or antiphonally, as the practice is called. The Psalm of Wisdom provides many instances of this parallelism between the half-verses. Sometimes verses are taken alternatively by the choir, and if the congregation are well-trained, they also can do this.

The psalms being over, the Little Chapter follows with its beautiful emphasis on love. The evening hymn then follows. The phrase about sunset needs to be treated with a little poetical licence if Vespers is sung either early or late. Then comes the great outburst of praise in the *Te Deum*, a hymn in rhythmical prose of great antiquity. It has been attributed in pious legend to St. Ambrose or St. Augustine, but scholars are not disposed now-a-days to endorse the likelihood of this. The original has been largely abbreviated in our Liturgy, and new verses were added by Bishop Leadbeater which are by no means out of keeping with the original.

Vespers then concludes with the various collects, the versicles and responses, and the final Benediction or the Grace. The Collects printed in the text should be said at evening, but not in the early afternoon.

---

[1] Composition assembled from various places. [Ed.]

Prime and Complin[1]

These two services are in some measure effective in working upon the neighbourhood, but much less so than Vespers. They can usefully serve as morning and evening prayers for a community or for a school. Prime is a good office for morning use, and can be used as a preparation for the Eucharist. Complin helps one to turn out of the mind before retiring to rest the cares and worries of life.

They begin as usual with the Invocation, and the versicles and responses; and include the *Confiteor* and Absolution. Then follow Psalms, optional lessons, the Act of Faith, prayers, a hymn, another psalm, and the concluding Collect, Versicles and Benediction. The choice of the words in the psalms for Prime is unusually happy and they give an excellent impression of the freshness of the new day's life. That for Complin is less characteristic; but the service leaves an effect of peace and quiet, which is quite appropriate and a good preparation for the work out of the body.

---

[1] Lauds is a morning service of praise. Sext is intended for use at noon. They follow a pattern similar to Prime. [Ed.]

THE SYMBOLISM OF THE ALTAR

(A sermon delivered at the church of St. Alban, Sydney in 1919.)

EACH of the symbols and ceremonies of the Christian Faith has a threefold meaning, and may be approached as it were from three different points of view—historical, allegorical and esoteric, or occult. Sometimes the historical meaning attached to our symbols is not altogether authentic, and has been invented to account for their existence when the inner or esoteric meaning, having to do with the purpose served by the symbol in the great work of linking together the visible world with the world invisible, has been forgotten. For example we find in the Protestant sections of the Church the explanation that the use of lights and incense originated in the catacombs, in which the early Christians had perforce to worship in secret; and that they were intended for purely material purposes as a means of illuminating and disinfecting those places of burial. That explanation of their purpose is demonstrably false, since the ceremonial use of lights and incense long antedates Christianity, and indeed was practically universal in the ancient, as in the modern world; so that to relate them to that particular set of conditions is obviously an untrue account of their origin.

To illustrate these three points of view, let us first consider the procession which passes round the Church at the beginning and end of each service. Historically we may trace this to the passage of large assemblies of people in open spaces. The religious processions of old were attended with great ceremonial pomp, and that has survived in the Christian Church to this day. Passing to the second point of view—the symbolical—we may attach a variety of meanings to such an act of worship; for we shall find in dealing with the whole question of symbolism that while there are certain allegorical explanations which spring naturally to mind in connection with certain ceremonies, there are others which lead to prolific interpretations. Some of these are forced; many quite beautiful, though often without any obviously authentic connection with the ceremonial. We may for instance explain that the procession represents man's pilgrimage through matter. It starts from the altar, the throne of God where the Divine Presence dwells; and as it winds round the nave and aisles of the church it typifies the pilgrimage of man through the mazes of his earthly existence. Finally it re-enters the sanctuary, the holy place, beneath the road of suffering, emblematical of the fourth great initiation, and reaches once more the throne of God, typifying the return of the Spirit to conscious union with the Divinity from Whom it came. Again, there is an astronomical relation, for in many Churches at penitential seasons the procession passes round the church in the reverse order to the course of the sun; whereas on all other occasions its direction is clockwise and imitates the sun's course. From the esoteric or occult point of view, we find that the procession is designed to pour out a great flood of influence upon the congregation, uniting them together in thought and feeling, harmonizing them and steadying their minds. All the earlier part of the service of the Holy Eucharist is concerned with the welding together of the congregation into a collective unity—a body corporate—so that the powers invoked at the Consecration may descend through a prepared and united channel. We may likewise trace a threefold significance in the Christian altar, which with us forms the central feature of the Church. Historically there has always been some spot at which the culminating act of worship took place. In some form or other it is found in all pre-Christian religions, and in the case of Christianity we may take it to be the direct descendant of the altar of the Jews, on which in earlier days blood-sacrifices were offered. In contradiction to these the Christian sacrifice is called the 'unbloody' or 'rational' sacrifice—the others being from the later point of view irrational sacrifices. That is not altogether true; but they were certainly of a very much lower order, one that would hardly commend itself to any civilized people.

Symbolically the altar represents our Blessed Lord the Christ; as it is beautifully put in the *Pontificale* in the Service of Ordination to the Subdiaconate: "The altar of Holy Church is Christ Himself, as John bears witness in his Apocalypse, who beheld a golden altar set before the throne of God, on and by which the offerings of the faithful are made acceptable to God the Father Almighty." That altar of Holy Church, then, is Our Lord; the cloths and corporals which lie upon it are said to be the members of Christ; and as 'the Son of Man is girded round the breast with a golden girdle,' that is to say, with the company of the Saints, so the ornaments of the altar are God's faithful people who shine with the beauty of holiness.

Then esoterically, or occultly, the altar is that special part of the Church consecrated and set apart—magnetically isolated—which is purified in various manners in order that there may be a fit and proper magnetic centre at which the great act of Christian Magic—the Transubstantiation of bread and wine into the Body and Blood of our Lord—can be effected.

Sometimes also the altar is symbolically represented as the tomb of Christ. There should properly be three cloths upon it to represent the cloths in which His body was wrapped when it was laid in the sepulchre. Sometimes it is made in the shape of a tomb; and that has a beautiful symbolical significance, for the ceremony of the Mass is in reality a dramatic representation of the Incarnation in flesh of our Lord Christ, and of His Cosmic Incarnation, the descent of the Divine Life into matter and the re-ascent of Spirit through matter. This great process may be typified by the symbolism of either birth or death, according to whether our vision is from below or from above; and thus the tomb represents the point of lowest descent when the Spirit is most heavily veiled in the robe of flesh. In the Middle Ages the Crusaders went forth to rescue the Holy Sepulchre from the hands of the infidels. That again in later mystical tradition was fashioned into a beautiful allegory in which the work of the spiritual Knights of the Cross was to rescue and redeem the physical body—the tomb wherein the Divine Spark lies buried—from the hands of the infidels, from the lower nature, the desires and cravings which desecrate it. The Christian altar is the tomb in the sense that upon it takes place the special Incarnation of the Divine Life, the descent into the physical accidents of bread and wine of the Life of Christ Himself; an act which is, so to speak, an extension under our conditions of time and space, of the great Cosmic Sacrifice by which the worlds were made, the sacrifice of the 'Lamb slain from the foundation of the world,' the primal descent of Spirit into matter.

That part of the altar which is of the greatest significance is what is called the altar stone. Indeed the whole altar should properly be made of stone, usually of marble, should consist of a large stone slab on which five crosses are carved, one at each corner and one in the centre. That is not always practicable, and is very expensive; and so in many churches the altar is made of wood. There must, however, always be in the centre of the wooden table an altar stone, a little slab of marble with the five crosses likewise carved upon it, said to represent the five wounds of Christ. These crosses may perhaps refer to the five-fold field of evolution in which the sacrifice of our natures takes place, and also to the five directions in space through which the power of the Consecrated Elements is out-poured. The stone again has its inner or esoteric significance in that a magnetic foundation is needed, a reversal of the polarity—it is difficult to express these inner things in words—to serve as a basis upon which the Elements may be laid for the downpouring of the Divine Life.

Over the altar six candlesticks stand. It is often asked why the number is six and not seven, which is the sacred or perfect number. The explanation is a very simple one; for the Sacred Host, reserved in the tabernacle upon the altar, is in the very truest sense the Body of Christ Himself, the light of the world, and It is rightly taken as the seventh of those lights. In some churches seven lamps hang before the altar, in others three, in yet others but one. The seven lamps, as also the seven altar-candles, symbolically represent the Seven Spirits before the Throne of God to Whom the Book of Revelation refers, and Who are spoken of also in other great World-Scriptures. The three lamps represent the three persons of the Blessed Trinity, of Whom the Seven are a manifestation; and the single lamp is the symbol of the Divine Presence and is ever kept burning when the Sacred Host is reserved in the tabernacle. Those six candlesticks, and the seventh, the Host, represent the seven great Rays or streams of Divine Influence, and in our churches are especially connected with those, as are the ray-crosses around the church. They represent the seven fundamental types of humanity, qualities, virtues, temperaments; and in offering incense before the altar we consecrate and identify ourselves with those seven great rays or streams of power which are ever pouring out into the world.

Finally we may consider the tabernacle which rests upon the altar, and in which the Sacred Host is perpetually reserved in our churches. It was not always reserved in this particular manner; for, often in mediaeval times It was kept in a gold or silver dove suspended from the roof of the Sanctuary and symbolical of the Holy Spirit. It is not generally reserved in the Orthodox Eastern Churches, although always in the Church of Rome. Wherever It is so reserved we have the unspeakable privilege of the perpetual Presence of Christ in the church, making it in a very special sense a holy place. Anyone who is at all sensitive will feel that a church wherein the Host is reserved is quite different in its influence from any other building. There is a sense of peace, of upliftment, of holiness, of benediction, ever radiating from that Sacred Presence; and whenever adoration is offered before the Host, It is, as it were, awakened into special activity in response to that call upon Its power. One who has the inner vision would see a great flame darting forth from It towards the person thus offering himself in worship, a flame which bears the blessing, the very life, of the Christ himself.

We speak of the Host, the consecrated bread or wafer, as the Body of the Lord; and it is important that we should have a right understanding of what that means. We cannot, of course, hope to comprehend in their entirety any of the great Mysteries of the Christian faith, but we should try to grasp all that we can. We may pause for a moment to analyse the purpose of our physical bodies—bodies composed of flesh and blood, organisms built up of various chemical substances animated by life. The purpose of the body is to serve as a vehicle (in the first place) of our own consciousness through which we may express ourselves in the physical world and to our fellow-beings, and secondly as a vehicle through which we receive from them impressions which affect our consciousness and which are ultimately communicated to the indwelling Spirit. The senses of the body are the windows through which that Spirit comes into relationship with the world around it. Just so the bread after the consecration is the Body of the Lord, in the sense that it is the vehicle through which He expresses Himself to us, through which He is made manifest, through which He pours out His life upon us, so that we, as souls, may be nourished and sustained. We should not look upon the Host as a body in the carnal sense as in any way composed of flesh and blood analogous to our flesh and blood. But it is none the less true that after the consecration His Life and Blessing is directly manifested through That which to outer appearance still remains bread, that through that Holy Bread He pours out His Life upon us, and that in the Holy Communion we are thereby enabled to come into a very close and intimate relation with Him. When in the same way we speak of the Blood of Christ, the term given to the chalice of Consecrated Wine, we may remember that 'blood' is an expression which has come down to us from pre-Christian times, and that it has always been associated with the idea of the love of God poured out in sacrifice. The same conception was found in the Bacchic Mysteries, which, though they afterwards became decadent and corrupt, were originally quite pure; in them the Divine was adored as Dionysius, the God of rose-red wine, whose blood was shed from the foundation of the world, and who typified the Divine Life and Love poured forth into matter in order that the universe might come into being. The same great symbolism is perpetuated and ennobled in the Christian Eucharist, and when we speak of the sacrifice of Christ's Body and Blood, we understand that sacrifice to be a communicating of Himself to others, to vivify, to uplift, to strengthen with His own presence and benediction those whom He has made. 'For My Flesh is meat indeed, and My Blood is drink indeed. He that eateth My Flesh and drinketh My Blood, dwelleth in Me, and I in him. As the living Father hath sent Me, and I live by the Father; so he that eateth Me, even he shall live by me. This is the Bread which came down from heaven.'[1] It is through the Holy Mysteries of the Eucharist that the Life and Love of God are directly manifested to us.

Thus the altar is the central feature of the Catholic Church. We know that in many Non-conformist places of worship where the understanding of these things has been lost, the pulpit has taken the place of the altar—the word of man has come to be substituted for the ineffable sacrifice of God. But we who perhaps understand a little more about these Mysteries, who have gone back to the knowledge which was originally the heritage of the Christian Church, naturally feel that far more important than any human preacher is the great outpouring of the Christ Himself, which takes place in the Sacrifice of the Eucharist and of which the altar is the visible representation and symbol to us.

---

[1] St. John, 6: 55-58.

WORK WITH THE DEAD

(A talk given at St. Michael's centre, Huizen, Holland, about 1928)

FOLLOWING the Feast of All Saints is the Day of All Souls, when we commemorate the dead. When we speak of the Saints, we mean a number of different things. If we look back to the rites of various Protestant sects, they called themselves the saints. 'Saint' means a person who is sanctified and they thought that they are sanctified by the Holy Spirit. There is a sense in which we are all sanctified by the Grace which we receive through the Sacraments, also by the kind of life we are living and by our own efforts; that is not exactly the sense in which the word is normally used, but it is one sense. In another sense the Saints are those you know of in history and mythology, those who have stood out in the annals of our work, who have stood for religion and God's service, though in other cases they were merely skilful controversialists and not very saintly. In yet another sense, the Saints are the great Hierarchy of those "just men made perfect," those who remained behind to look after the evolution of humanity, those Whom we call the Masters.

On the next day we turn our thoughts to the dead. You notice in the ordinary Christian Catholic tradition, they pray for the "faithful departed" those who departed full of faith, and do not pay much attention to those who did not depart full of faith. That seems to me to perpetuate a rather undesirable tradition; for those who did not depart full of faith are those who need our prayers most of all. In our Church we say, 'May the souls *of the departed*' (not the "faithful departed") 'through the love of God rest in peace.' They used to think that those who did not believe were damned and outside the pale of the Church; then they softened it down and said those were not in the covenanted Grace of God. We believe that all men 'shall one day reach His feet,' and it is not necessary to be baptized or even a Christian, or to belong to any religion, to be saved.

What I want to consider is how we can work together in the Church to help the people who are dead. You probably know in theory, if you cannot see in practice, that vast crowds of dead people, not always the same ones, but different ones, come to any service of the Church. Quite a number like to profit by the services, they find it helps and interests them; and they can realize more fully than we what is going on, though they cannot take as active a part in the singing as we do (though some can), but they can see the lights and colours, the thought-forms, and the results of the worship. They bank themselves up round the sides of the church and round the altar in tiers, hundreds and thousands of them, and not only the dead but also those who are out of the body in sleep. We don't get the people from India and Sydney except in the evening services, but they can come from America which is some distance behind our time.

All that is very interesting, but we must consider what use we can make of such information. There is not very much we can do, except on very simple lines; to sum the matter up, if you think of them and take them into your consciousness you will be helping them more specially. It is difficult to know how much people can realize this and make a reality of the dead people round us. You need not picture them in any particular place. Turn your thoughts to the idea of the dead, and make your thought quite vivid on the subject, and you can get into close touch with them. That will be a help because when you put your thought on an object to which you wish to attract that force, you make by the thought a connecting channel to that object. Provided you make a living thought, realizing that the dead are round about us, you will make a channel and much of the power will go to them and there will be a closer co-operation in the service between them and us.

It is interesting to study the effect the service has on them. This is rather a special centre for that kind of work, and there is a special atmosphere created here; it is a centre of the Masters' work and there is a daily outpouring when that atmosphere is being vivified, and the result is that people who have newly died and those who are in trouble are brought along and deposited here. It is, in fact, a kind of hospital for dead people. Where you have a place of concentrated power, they come because they need that soothing and calming influence. People who have died by suicide are brought here so as to clear up their depression, and people in sorrow and trouble are brought here for the same reason. Especially at the time of the Eucharist when we think of the dead, connections are made, and when the power of the angels goes out to those to whom it was allocated, they set to work to help them. It does not mean that the power given to such people is at once poured into them. Some part of that power is brought to bear on the person and some of it is stored up as a kind of reservoir. The angel looks after the person and all the time there is a pressure going on to clear up the causes of depression. This gradually changes one who is suffering into either an active worker, or at least into a normal person, by the gradual elimination of disturbing elements in the lower nature and by the reaching up of his consciousness to higher things. That is a definite department of the work and we can all help by just thinking of it.

There are certain tendencies of thought that it is well to guard against. There is an extraordinary tradition in regard to death. The fact that people are so uncertain when they die as to what is going to happen to them, has surrounded it with an atmosphere of fear. People on the verge of death get into a panic and frightened about what is going to become of them. This is due to the Christian teaching that still survives even among some of us. It is a subject we talk of with great awe and with bated breath, and we invest it with a reality that does not belong to it. Instead we ought to talk about it with freedom and happiness. There is a great deal of trouble and worry from which dead people are free; they don't have bank accounts, they don't have to get up early in the morning. There is a certain amount of suffering, but it does not last very long and they soon get through it. The worst suffering comes from people being frightened, and being so unfamiliar with their new surroundings. They don't know what is going to happen, and cannot settle down. It does not matter what you say to them, just as it doesn't matter what you say to people here; you may help them for a time, but it is always coming back and they are filled with fear of the unknown, and that is about the worst fear you have on the other side. Even if there are helpers, people are just as sceptical as they are here. If I gave a lecture on 'The Other Side of Death' people might say, how can he know anything about it? It is one of the things Mr. Bradlaugh suffered from. He met Mrs. Besant on the other side and acknowledged she had been right, but when the time came for him to go up into the heaven-world and she told him that he was going to die again, he refused to believe it and could not go on. It takes a certain amount of time to quieten people down, just as it takes a certain amount of time to get them out of their troubles here. We build up a kind of guardian angel, a body of thought, which works on people to give them calm and happiness. So it is a very useful part of the Church's work to look after dead people and surround them with helpful influence.

We are surrounded also by those millions who are passing through the state of *purgatory*, throwing off the lower and reaching up to the higher. Here the Church can be extremely useful also. If you really want to help them it is very desirable that your thoughts should be perfectly definite and precise, that is to say, you should formulate in your own mind what you want to do for the people. Most people are so vague. You say 'death' and get an atmosphere. You think of a shadowy person, you think of him as he was on earth but in a more shadowy condition. It is quite true they are in a more shadowy condition—that is how you can tell when they are dead. It might interest you to know how to tell a dead person from a living person on the other side. That is one thing. The matter is more rarefied, finer, more shadowy, there is less definiteness and grossness, it is more attenuated. But the great test is that a living person carries about a kind of line, or rope, with him that is sometimes called the silver cord. It is mentioned in the gradual in the service for the dead 'or ever the silver cord be loosed.' There is always behind a person who is living a line of white light which connects him with the physical body. You tell he is living by that line of connection being there, and also by the texture, whether he is shadowy or not.

You don't get far in the use of your thought if it is only vague, and you have the vague pictures you have had all your life. If you want to help a person, what would you do? Think kindly, give him calmness, speak with him, see him as you would like him to be.

Most of you would do it right because you are trained, but you must not only have a picture of calmness, you must become calmness yourself. Fill yourself with the idea of peace and calmness. Now make that stronger and stronger; more and more peaceful, thinking of the peace you have felt in this church, and now picture that enveloping the person. Most of you thought of the calmness in yourselves, that you could produce. When I asked you to think of the calmness in the church, you put the Lord's influence into it and it immediately became brighter and purer. That would do very well for helping a person. You have to get out of yourself in these things. But it is not going to help somebody in a state of great terror and unhappiness. It won't do very much. You must send him something as strong as his own unrest. What is wanted is an understanding of things as they are, not just vague ideas. You want a strong definite thought, just as strong as the state of disharmony in the person. You are all capable of doing that if you recognize how to do it in the right way. You had better not put into it so much your own thought, as the power of the Church and of the Living Presence of the Lord.

THE PRESENCE OF CHRIST
IN THE HOLY COMMUNION
AND OTHER WRITINGS

'Twas God the Word that spake it;
He took the Bread and brake it;
And what the Word did make it;
That I believe, and take it.'
                        Attributed to Queen Elizabeth I

WHAT IS A SACRAMENT?

THE best definition of a sacrament that I know is that given in the Church of England Catechism: 'An outward and visible sign of an inward and spiritual grace given unto us, ordained by Christ Himself, as a means whereby we receive the same, and a pledge to assure us thereof.' That is a little more explicit that that of the Council of Trent, which defines the sacraments as 'outward signs of inward grace, instituted by Christ for our sanctification.' In the Holy Eucharist the 'outward and visible sign' is bread and wine; and the 'inward part or thing signified,' is 'the Body and Blood of Christ.' In Baptism, the one is the washing with water; the other, the mystical washing away of sin and the descent of divine grace, the dew from heaven, whereby the child is grafted into the mystical body of Christ. In Ordination the outer form is the laying on of hands and the delivery of the instruments or insignia of the degree bestowed; the 'inward and spiritual grace' is the 'character'[1] conferred—or we might say, in the case of the major orders, the placing of the recipient in such agreed relationship with Our Lord that he can be used as the instrument through which sacramental acts are accomplished.

If we are to join issue with this definition at all, I should prefer to say that a sacrament is the 'inward and spiritual grace' rather that the 'outward and visible sign,' or that it should, at any rate, cover both. From the standpoint of reality it is the outpouring of divine grace that is the essential feature, on the principle that man is a spirit using a soul and a body, rather than a body possessing a soul and a spirit. I know that in these days people hang on to the physical world grimly as the one tangible reality; a man's body is real enough to him, but the spirit is to most people only a vague hypothesis. Similarly, the outward and visible sign of the sacrament is real and tangible, but that which it presents is too often vague and intangible—quite nicely summed up in the word 'spiritual,' which, in common parlance, means anything that we do not understand or know anything about.

---

[1] In the theological sense, character is an ineffaceable mark or distinction impressed upon the soul by the sacraments of Baptism, Confirmation and Holy Orders. It means that certain permanent changes are made by these rites in the inner nature of man. Hence, according to Western theology, it is a sacrilege to repeat these sacraments, unless *sub conditione*.

Let us, however, pass on to consider in a few words the rest of the definition. It is not essential to our subject, but it summarizes a good deal of interesting teaching. The grace is 'given to us;' it is a free gift of grace. That means that the spiritual blessing which comes to us through the sacrament is not the proportionate remuneration of any personal effort on our part. Whatever aspiration a man addresses to God calls down its appropriate response. This would seem to be a law of the spiritual world—a law of nature, it you like, provided we understand that the laws of nature are the expression of God's will operative in His world. But the grace of the sacraments is something higher than this, greater than we could earn or merit for ourselves. It is the gift of God through Christ, not the response to man's aspiration, however much that may also be included in the process.

The Apostolic Succession

The idea is important because it explains the attitude of those who hold that the efficacy of the sacraments depends upon their administration by one holding the apostolic succession of Orders. The idea is that Our Lord instituted a certain arrangement according to which He could depend upon a number of instruments working in the world, through whom His special blessing could be poured. For it is a principle in nature that a physical body is needed as a medium or vehicle if spiritual force is to be poured out on to the physical world. Certain people offer and prepare themselves; and, by ordination, changes are effected in their inner being which place them in a special relationship with the Head of the mystical body so that they can be used as instruments by Him. The 'parson' means really the 'person' (Lat. *per* = through; *sona* = sound). The word has the same sense as when we speak of a Person of the Blessed Trinity. He is the representative through whom the blessing of Christ may flow, for Christ Himself is the true Minister of all sacraments. The powers are given not for the priest's own personal enjoyment or aggrandisement, but that through him the flock of Christ may be fed.

This teaching outrages many people who are, not unreasonably, apprehensive of priest-craft. But they do not sufficiently realize, perhaps, that in the fulfilment of His scheme God is dependent upon the co-operation of imperfect workers. The greater the blessing, the greater the risks by which any such arrangement is inevitably attended. And the arrangement works the more effectively, the more the priest grows into the likeness of his Master. Arrogance and hypocrisy certainly lessen a man's spiritual influence although they cannot interfere with that irreducible minimum of efficacy which unfailingly flows from the Christ, because His scheme takes into account less the natural imperfection of the instrument than the spiritual needs of the many to whom he is to minister.

The effect, then, of ordination is that the priest or bishop becomes the channel for Christ's ministration of the sacraments. Ministers of Churches which do not carry on this original institution receive their own blessing, proportionate to the level of their own devotion and that of the congregation. They touch the consciousness of Our Lord at that level, but not at the prime source, so to speak, and, reinforced by that blessing, do what they can—and often it is much. It is not, of course, for us to presume in such a matter; but the result does not seem to be at all the same thing as in those Churches which have preserved unbroken the episcopal succession and have thus adhered to the original arrangement.

That ordination does effect such changes would, I think, hardly be doubted by bishops whose privilege it is to confer it, and by persons who receive it. I have myself, of course, received ordination, and during the twelve years of my episcopate have consecrated bishops and ordained a good many priests of some twenty-five different nationalities. I give my personal testimony for what it is worth. My own ordinations as priest and bishop completely changed me and gave me new powers of understanding; and I have frequently noticed the same thing in those whom I have ordained.

The Unity of Life

The concept of the 'free gift of grace'—the idea that it transcends anything in the nature of proportionate response to our own aspirations—turns on the principle of the unity of life. Similarly, that of the brotherhood of man turns on the fact of the Fatherhood of God. There is a universal brotherhood of all that lives because there is but one life—the Life of God which maintains all things. Man is a link in a vast chain of lives leading up from the lowest to the highest. And because of this unity of life we are all dependent on one another. That which helps one helps all, and that which harms one harms the whole body. Mutual help seems to be the law of progress in this brotherhood. As a man helps those who stand below him on the ladder of evolution, so is he helped by those who stand above him. The care and the love that we bestow upon a dog, through which quasi-human qualities are developed in him, work a change greater than that which any dog could effect for himself. Applying the analogy to ourselves, we understand that our Blessed Lord, the 'first among many brethren,' is able to look back upon the world which He has transcended and pour out grace upon it in a manner made possible by His great sacrifice.

Ordained by Christ

To resume our definition: the sacrament is 'ordained by Christ Himself.' People of a mystical turn of mind often use their language a little heedlessly. They speak of all life being 'sacramental' and this is true in the sense that all physical activities are a vehicle through which the spiritual element in man may be expressed. Life enacted in this way is lived on the sacramental principle or after the manner of a sacrament. But when they go further and speak of a family meal as being a sacrament, because the parent loves the children and vice versa, they are exaggerating. The Church reserves the word 'sacrament' for certain special rites in which the power of Christ is directly operative. These rites are so wonderful to those who understand anything about them, that we should be careful to safeguard the word.

The other two clauses of the definition can speedily be explained. The sacrament is the 'means whereby we receive' the grace. The grace comes through the sacrament—through its outward and visible sign. 'A pledge to assure us thereof.' The outward and visible sign, in the case of Holy Communion, is the taking of physical sustenance. This places our hearts and minds into accord with the idea of receiving our soul's sustenance. It is the physical token of the spiritual gift. By appealing to our senses it rightly orients our consciousness for the attentive reception of the higher gift.

THE BABEL OF THEORIES

A Glance at Early History

NOW that we have made this preliminary study of the ideas associated with the word 'sacrament,' we can turn to the more important part of our inquiry.

It seems to have been accepted from the earliest Christian times that there is in the Holy Eucharist a Real Presence of the Body and Blood of Our Lord Christ. The language of the Fathers is occasionally difficult but, on the whole, it does not seem that in the main body of the Church there was any attempt to deny a real Presence until about the time of the Reformation.[1] Luther indeed testified to the fact that all Christendom believed in it.[2]

I am not going to discuss the theory that sacramentalism is a later importation into Christianity from surrounding paganism. This theory is more in the nature of a glib attempt to account for facts uncongenial to its holders: it is not adequately supported by historical documentation, nor does it appear to be taken seriously by the generality of good modern scholars. Indeed, Dr. Gavin in a work[3] has given the *coup de grâce* to this disingenuous theory. Nor need any attention here be given to that curious document, the *Didache* or *Teaching of the Twelve Apostles*. This, when it was first discovered, was seized upon by anti-sacerdotalists as showing in an early community a 'charismatic'[4] ministry of teachers and prophets lingering on before being displaced by the later hierarchical organization. Bishop Gore holds that it emanates from 'some only half-Christian community,' and entirely lacks the familiar atmosphere of the Gospels and St. Paul.[5] The Didache is put into its right place for all time by that classic book, *Essays on the Early History of the Church and the Ministry*, edited by Dr. Swete[6]. These questions concern early history and are not germane to our subject, which is the doctrine of the Eucharist as it has been held generally in the Christian Church.

To judge from the earliest fragments of history that come to us, the literal acceptance of the Real Presence seems to date from the beginning. It was a matter of simple faith, and the rite seems to have been regarded as very sacred. Then there are attempts within the Church to explain the mystery, although these do not cast any doubt upon the fundamental fact of the Sacrament being the Body and the Blood of Christ. Later comes the thought that the bread and wine are still there in addition to the Body and Blood. Presently, the idea of transubstantiation seems to have emerged, according to which the appearances of bread and wine remain (the 'accidents' or 'species' as they are called), but their 'substance' is converted into that of the Body and Blood of the Lord. In the ninth century, Scotus Erigena is reputed to have opposed the doctrine of transubstantiation, but it is not at all sure that he was not held responsible for a book by a

---

[1] But see the references to Scotus and Berengarius occurring a little later.

[2] *Wider Etliche Rottengeister*, 1532; quoted in *The Catholic Encyclopaedia*, art. 'Eucharist,' Vol. V., p.578.

[3] *The Jewish Antecedents of the Christian Sacraments*, by Gavin, Ph.D., Th.D., Professor of Ecclesiastical History, General Theological Seminary, New York; London, S.P.C.K.; 1928.

[4] Gr. *charisma* = gift. The *charismata* are gifts or graces given to individual Christians for special kinds of work—gifts of healing, of prophecy, of the discerning of spirits (cf. 1 Corinthians xii). Nonconformists often claim, and quite rightly in individual cases, to have a 'charismatic ministry' dependent upon individual sanctification and prophetic inspiration, as distinct from the Catholic idea of Orders which is that of a ministerial office whose ability to mediate grace is guaranteed by admission to office rather than by individual merit or talents. The one idea is more impersonal than the other.

[5] *The Body of Christ*, p.97.

[6] Macmillan, 1918.

monk named Ratram who lived in the same century. The matter is chiefly of importance because of a famous controversy which, in the eleventh century, centred round a Frenchman named Berengarius who claimed support for his views in Scotus. It is difficult to decide exactly what Berengarius taught,[1] but it really is not of much importance, for he is mainly famous on account of the terms of the frightful recantation to which he was required to assent. Even Wycliff who, in the fourteenth century, denied transubstantiation, seems to have set off against it a doctrine which allowed for the co-existence of the substance of the bread and wine with that of the Body and Blood of Christ, as did Luther. It was at the Reformation that discussion grew heated on the subject.

Four Different Views

In the year 1577 one Christopher Rasperger published at Ingolstadt a book rehearsing two hundred different interpretations of the words of consecration. I do not propose to burden either the reader or myself with the arguments set out in this book, but mention the point to show how complicated is the thought of the period. Of the theories which have been propounded as to Our Lord's relationship to the Holy Eucharist, the most important lend themselves to a fourfold classification.

I. *The Real Objective Presence.* The belief is that after the words of consecration have been pronounced by a duly ordained priest or bishop, the Body and Blood of Christ are present on the altar under the veils of bread and wine.

Under this heading come three subdivisions.

(1) There are those who speak of themselves simply as believers in the Real Presence. They do not attempt to define it.

(2) Transubstantiation. The idea is that the substance of the bread and the wine is changed into the substance of the Body and Blood of Christ. The bread and wine remain unchanged as regards their species or 'accidents,' but their 'substance' is changed. Bishop Hedley says that just as 'substance' means the thing itself, so 'species' means the thing as it affects the senses.[2]

The Catholic Church does not feel called upon to follow up the ephemeral vagaries of these new philosophical systems, but bases her doctrine on the everlasting philosophy of sound reason, which rightly distinguishes between the thing in itself and its characteristic qualities (colour, form, size, etc.). Though the 'thing in itself' may ever remain imperceptible to the senses and therefore be designated, in the language of Kant, as a *noumenon*, or, in the language of Spencer, the Unknowable, yet we cannot escape the necessity of seeking beneath the appearances the thing which appears, beneath the colour that which is coloured, beneath the form that which has form, i.e. the substratum or subject which sustains the phenomena. The older philosophy designated the appearances by the name of accidents, the subject of the appearances by that of substance. It matters little what the terms are, provided the things signified by them are rightly understood. What is particularly important regarding material substances and their accidental qualities, is the necessity of proceeding cautiously in the discussion, since in the domain

---

[1] Some think that he was only protesting against a carnal presence, but he was also accused of teaching that the bread and wine were bare signs. Bishop Forbes, in his Explanation of the *Thirty-Nine Articles*, pp. 537-545, describes him as 'vain-glorious and dishonest', and shows that he was highly disingenuous in his conduct of the controversy he provoked. The Bishop is not alone in this verdict, for Bishop Gore, in *Dissertations*, p. 248, holds similar views.

[2] Bishop J.C. Hedley. *The Holy Eucharist.* p. 39.

of natural philosophy the greatest uncertainty reigns even at the present day concerning the nature of matter, one system pulling down what another has reared, as is proved in the latest theories of atomism and energy, of ions and electrons.[1]

3) Consubstantiation. This was the doctrine of Luther who believed that the substance of the bread and wine remained, together with the real Body and Blood of Christ, in and under the bread and wine.

There are numbers of people unwilling to commit themselves to transubstantiation, who hold that the substance of the bread and wine continues to exist side by side (without confusion or union of substance) with the substance of Christ's Body and Blood. Most of these would not care to use the term consubstantiation, but would range themselves simply as believers in the Real objective Presence.

II. *Receptionism.* This doctrine is best described in the words of the Anglican divine, Richard Hooker (1553-1600): 'The Real Presence of Christ's most blessed Body and Blood is not therefore to be sought for in the Sacrament but in the worthy receiver of the Sacrament.'[2] Those who hold this doctrine in a positive sense deny any objective Presence of Christ in the bread and wine.

Consecration does not change the bread and wine, but attaches to them, not a presence, but a promise—the promise that when the communicant shall partake of the bread which has been blessed, he shall be a partaker of the Lord's Body. It is at the reception of the sacrament that the communicant partakes of the sacred Body and Blood, and then only by virtue of faith. Most Receptionists would add that he receives them not in a corporal or carnal manner; that the Presence is not to the elements at any stage, but to the soul of the receiver thereof.

III. *Virtualism.* One of the problems which greatly troubled the Reformers was that of defining Christ's Presence according to the category of space. If His Body were in heaven, how could it be localized in the sacrament? It was probably as a reaction to such questionings and in order to dissociate themselves from the idea of a carnal or corporal presence that some thinkers developed the doctrine of virtualism. Its distinguishing feature is that Christ's Body and Blood are not present in literal fact, but rather their virtue and effect. There is no need, in this way, to maintain that the sacrament presents either Christ's natural body or His post-resurrection or glorified body. This doctrine crops up with some regularity from the Reformation onwards. It seemed to have been the final view of Archbishop Cranmer (1489-1556), and he maintained it in his famous *Answer to Stephen Gardner* (1551). He denied a corporal presence in the communicant even after reception. And he distinctly asserted that Christ is no more 'corporally or really present in...the Lord's Supper than He is in...Baptism.' Waterland, a famous divine of the eighteenth century, maintained a form of virtualism combined with receptionism against Roman Catholic teaching, and also against Lutheranism, Calvinism and Zwinglianism. Some of the Non-jurors appear to have held a virtualism divorced from receptionism.

Virtualism, though not identified as such, is probably held very widely at the present time by many who are reluctant to face the implications of the Real Presence—Eucharistic adoration and so on—and hold to a vague and undefined 'spiritual Presence.'

IV. *Zwinglianism.* Huldreich Zwingli (1484-1531) was the leader of the Swiss Reformation. He was opposed to Luther on many points, notably in regard to the latter's insistence upon an objective Presence in the Eucharist. The contention of Zwingli and his followers (often called the Sacramentaries, though the name was sometimes used to include those of Luther and

---

[1] *The Catholic Encyclopaedia*, Vol. V, art. 'Eucharist', p. 582.
[2] *Ecclesiastical Policy*, Book V., lxvii.

others) was that the words, 'This is My Body,' were figurative like other words of Our Lord—'I am the Vine,' 'I am the Door.' The consecrated elements are figures or symbols of the Body and Blood. An act done 'in remembrance' of Christ implies the bodily absence of Christ. There is no question of the elements being anything more than bread and wine. The rite is thus purely a commemoration of the Last Supper and of Our Lord's death and crucifixion, in which Christians are exhorted to realize their fellowship with Christ and with one another. The sacraments are signs or figures. The real Body of Christ is present by the contemplation of faith, and it consists of those who give thanks to God for the benefits conferred upon them by Christ, and who recognize that He took real flesh; that in it He suffered, that He washed away our sins in His blood, so that everything done by Christ becomes, as it were, present to them by the contemplation of faith. The bread is no more the Body of Christ than 'if a wife, pointing to a ring of her husband which he had left with her, should say, "This is my husband".'[1] The sacraments bring and dispense no grace, but are a public testimony, the badge of our profession as Christians. There are, however, some passages in Zwingli's writings which imply some manner of 'feeding on Christ' by the contemplation of faith.[2]

Views of Other Reformers

To complete our historical survey, it will be convenient, before discussing the different views here mentioned, to glance at the opinions of a few other leading Reformers.

Joannes Oecolampadius (1482-1531), a friend of Zwingli taught that the Supper was an external symbol which the faithful should receive less for their own sake than for the social example they set.[3] Bishop Forbes says that Oecolampadius 'saw nothing more in the Eucharist than a symbol whereby one is bound to sacrifice for one's neighbour, after the example of Jesus Christ, one's body and blood, as baptism is a sign by which one binds oneself to give up one's life for the faith which one professes.'[4]

Luther held that there was no option but to accept the Presence of the Body and Blood according to the plain statement of Scripture, and supported, as we have seen, the theory of consubstantiation. He hotly opposed the doctrine of Zwingli wherein he was supported by his friend Philip Melancthon (1497-1560) who regarded it as 'impious.'

Bucer (1491-1551) at times attacked both Zwingli and Luther, but tried to fill the role of mediator between the two parties. 'For a clear statement of doctrine,' says his biographer, 'he was ever ready to substitute vague formulas in the interest of unity, which even his able efforts could not establish among the Reformers.'[5] It is not surprising, therefore, that his statements appear obscure and contradictory. He appears to have held to some spiritual Presence in the Eucharist, but denies that 'we here receive and possess Christ present in some manner of this world or enclosed in or joined together with the bread and wine or under their accidents in such

[1] Opera, II., 295.

[2] The best detailed account of the teachings of Luther, Calvin and Zwingli in English is to be found in *The Protestant Doctrine of the Lord's Supper*, by the Rev. Alexander Barclay. B.D., Ph.D., Glasgow: Jackson, Wyllie & Co., 1927.

[3] Quoted from *The Catholic Encyclopaedia*, art. Oecolampadius, Vol. XI., p. 213.

[4] Forbes, p. 497.

[5] Vol.III., p. 26.

a way that He ought to be adored and worshipped.'[1] It would seem that he held the bread and wine to be unchanged; 'the bread is shown and given to the senses, and at the same time the body of the Lord, that is, the communion of the Lord, is presented and given to faith.'[2]

To relieve him of political difficulties, Archbishop Cranmer invited Bucer to England in 1549, and seems to have been influenced not a little by his friend's views. Bucer was made Regius Professor of Divinity at Cambridge where he died shortly afterwards.

John Calvin (1509-1564), who lived a generation later than Luther, occupied a position midway between the figurative school of Zwingli and what he considered the literalism of Luther. He taught an extreme form of receptionism together with a touch of virtualism. He seems to have held that the elements of bread and wine are unchanged, and, as was only consistent with his theory of predestination and election, insisted that faith was a necessary condition of reception. 'For Christ to be received without faith is no more possible than for a seed to germinate in the fire.'[3] Christ's Body is in heaven and nowhere else. 'They locate Christ in the bread; while we deem it unlawful to draw Him down from heaven.'[4] Hence he held that, by the action of faith, 'a power emanating from the Body of Christ, which is now in heaven only, is communicated to the spirit;'[5] the faithful thus receive from heaven the efficacy of Christ's Body and Blood, while for others the sacrament is only a bare symbol. The Dutch Hervormde Kerk, and the Gereformeerde Kerk still hold to the Calvinist doctrine, although in their catechisms one misses the virtualist element noted above.

The Zwinglian Doctrine

In discussing these different views, it will be more convenient to work backwards through them. We shall begin therefore with Zwinglianism.

The answer that is usually made to the Zwinglian view is one which is, it must be confessed, disarming—namely, to point out its improbability. Was Our Lord likely, at this solemn moment of their affliction, before being parted from those who had faithfully served Him, to mislead the disciples deliberately by statements that none of them understood? The parallel between this utterance and that concerning the 'door' or the 'vine' is not convincing, the circumstances of the discourses being quite different. Here we have the bread and wine solemnly blessed and distributed to the disciples, but nothing similar happened in regard to a door or a vine. And it would seem strange that this signal misconception should have misled His entire Church until the Reformation.

It seems quite plain that He meant this rite to be the means of perpetuating His Presence, and the Church, during the first centuries and for long afterwards, took this view. After all, it rests with any innovation in doctrine to win its own way: it has to prove its superiority. Zwinglianism was the outcome of the rationalizing effort, but it fails to account for the remarkable change of consciousness or experience of spiritual things that overtakes so many people at the Eucharist. There is a widespread repudiation of the 'bareness,' the 'nudity,' the 'frigidity' of the Zwinglian doctrine.

---

[1] 'Concerning the Holy Eucharist,' 1550, quoted in *A History of the Doctrine of the Holy Eucharist*, by Darwell Stone, Longmans, 1909, Vol. II., pp. 47-48.

[2] *Ep. ad Michaelem N. Hisp.*, quoted in Darwell Stone, Vol. II pp. 45-46.

[3] *Institutes of the Christian Religion*, IV., xvii., 33.

[4] Ibid., 31.

[5] Forbes, p. 499.

It must not be supposed, however, that the 'Supper' lacks solemnity. Those who believe in the Real Presence naturally enough feel that their brothers who do not find themselves able to accept this view miss a great deal in the way of opportunity and realization. But in the Protestant Churches which have lost the Apostolic Succession of Orders, there is often intense religious feeling in connection with the Sacrament, even though in many churches it is rarely celebrated. Moreover, Protestants, as well as Catholics, hold very strongly, and often with touching devotion, to the wonderful promise of Our Lord, 'Where two or three are gathered together in my name, there am I in the midst of them.'[1]

The Zwinglian view is still widely held by Protestants on the continent of Europe. It has been held by many Nonconformists in England, but would certainly be rejected by many Presbyterians and Wesleyans in favour of receptionism or virtualism.

Receptionism

Receptionism also is an outcome of that rationalist influence which seeks to explain away the 'miraculous' element in the theory of the objective Real Presence. An inescapable part of the 'miracle' is that of the changed lives and intense spiritual experience of which I have just spoken, and which many people experience before the objective Presence of the consecrated elements. It is no explanation to say that 'down here' in this world, of which we do know something, there exist just ordinary bread and wine and that in the spiritual or heavenly world, of which the ordinary man knows nothing, some mysterious process takes place. The difficulty has simply been burked by refusing to it any consideration in this world, and referring the problem to a world of unknown character where it is left unsolved.

Receptionism became a favourite view among Anglicans in post-Reformation times and is still widely held in the Anglican Church and elsewhere. Hooker, whose classic sentence was quoted in defining this doctrine, carefully abstained from indicating his own belief in regard to the objectivity of the Presence in the bread and wine and so he has been claimed on both sides of the controversy. He wrote at a critical period of change and upheaval when, as he himself explained, 'some did exceedingly fear lest Zwinglius and Oecolampadius would bring to pass that men should account of this Sacrament but only as a shadow, destitute, empty and void of Christ.'[2] He saw signs of an earnest desire for agreement and of its realization, and his thesis was that people could unite on the simple minimum basis proposed by him.

But others had not the same laudable motive and, looked at from the point of view indicated above, the theory becomes a mark of that timidity or even cowardice in religious matters with which Erastianism has infected the Anglican Establishment. The words of Bishop Forbes of Brechin are not really too strong when one realizes the ostrich-like policy underlying the receptionist doctrine.

Says Bishop Forbes:

> In England, in consequence of the great authority of Richard Hooker who, in the gradual process of working himself out of Puritanism, had on this mysterious doctrine attained to Catholic feeling while he adhered to Calvinisitic definition, this view has obtained to an extent remarkable in view of its intrinsic inanity. It does not satisfy the letter of Scripture, which distinctly predicates the affirmative proposition, 'This *is* My Body.' It contradicts the testimony of the primitive Church, as we shall presently proceed to

---

[1] Matthew xviii, 20.
[2] *Ecclesiastical Polity*, V. lxvii.

show from a long catena of authorities. It has exhibited its unsatisfactoriness in never having been able to maintain an abiding existence, either rising into the Catholic doctrine, or more commonly, degenerating into a bare Zwinglianism, and has only found favour with those who, unwilling to accept the profound mystery of the Holy Eucharist with all its consequences, are unable to bring themselves to an absolute denial of any presence of Christ, and, therefore, in this formula find a sop to the cravings of an intellect which dreads to carry to conclusion the premises which in reason only lead to the acceptance of the Catholic doctrine.[1]

Bishop Gore, whose trustworthiness as a scholar is everywhere acknowledged, says definitely that receptionism is not the primitive doctrine.

> But I do not think it is disputable that the church from the beginning did, as a whole, believe that the eucharistic elements themselves in some real sense became, by consecration and prior to reception, the body and blood of Christ in the midst of the worshipping assembly.[2]

It is difficult to fix the exact meaning of the Church of England formularies as between the theories of the Real Presence and receptionism. There are words employed which seem to suggest an objective Presence, while others seem partly receptionist. The Catechism says that the 'inward part, or thing signified,' is 'the Body and Blood of Christ, which are verily and indeed taken and received by the faithful in the Lord's Supper.' The use of the word 'faithful' suggests a qualifying factor. It may be equivalent to worshipper, or it may be taken in the more likely sense of one having the requisite faith. The insistence on faith is probably due to Continental influence and is, perhaps, linked by implication with Article twenty-nine, which deals with the problem as to whether or not the wicked are partakers of Christ in the Sacrament. It implies that 'the wicked and such as be void of a lively faith' receive the *figura* and the *res sacramenti*, that is, the outward form and the inward reality of the Sacrament, but not the *virus*, the moral effect of receiving it worthily, which is what is meant by being made 'partakers of Christ.'

But the clause in the Catechism says that the Body and Blood of Christ are 'verily and indeed taken,' as well as 'received.' This seems to throw the balance of probability as to its meaning on to the side of an objective Presence for, according to receptionist theories, it is only at reception that what the communicant has been given becomes subjectively for him (usually for his soul) Christ's Body.

The twenty-eighth Article of Religion is elusive:

> The body of Christ is given, taken and eaten, in the Supper, only after an heavenly and spiritual manner. And the means whereby the Body of Christ is received and eaten in the Supper is Faith.

Here the word 'given' seems to clinch the argument in favour of the objective view of the Presence. The concluding words of the first sentence are probably simply aimed against a carnal presence and would, in that sense, offend nobody. But the sentence can be taken in two ways. It can mean that the Body is present in the bread after the manner of a spirit, and not carnally, or that it is present to our spirits only. In fact, Jeremy Taylor (Bishop of Dromore, 1661-1667) makes this distinction and says that the Anglican view is the latter one. If, however, we are discussing a process that takes place in heaven involving only the activity of our spirits, it seems odd to talk about eating the Body. This is a looseness of speech which Zwingli would

---

[1] Forbes, p. 500.
[2] *The Body of Christ*, pp. 93-94.

never have tolerated; moreover, this concept is not really suggested by the general language of the Prayer Book.

Lastly, the sentence in the Anglican Prayer of Consecration, 'grant that we receiving these thy creatures of bread and wine...may be partakers of his most blessed Body and Blood,' although it precedes the act of consecration, is evasive and characteristically leaves room for ambiguity.

It would seem, in fact, that the Anglican formularies were meant to be ambiguous so as to permit the Church to accommodate people of different beliefs. Transubstantiation, in the pre-Reformation, carnal sense, is definitely ruled out. But the doctrine of the Real Presence can freely and lawfully be maintained in the Church of England. Archbishop Temple of Canterbury, in a Visitation Charge delivered in 1898, definitely stated that 'it is important that it should be clearly understood that it is not unlawful to hold and teach it within the Church of England.' The question was also decided by the secular courts in the well-known case of Mr. Bennett, Vicar of Frome. He was prosecuted for holding this belief, but his right to do so was upheld by the Court of Arches in 1870, and this decision was confirmed on appeal by the judicial committee of the Privy Council in 1872.

Mr. Bennett's statement was:

> I am one of those, who...myself adore, and teach the people to adore, Christ present under the form of bread and wine, believing that under their veil is the sacred body and blood of my Lord and Saviour Jesus Christ.

He spoke also of 'the real and actual Presence of our Lord upon the altars of our churches.'

Zwinglianism is condemned in Article twenty-eight; but receptionism and virtualism would be regarded as permissible in the Church of England.

To return to receptionism. Faith is a word to which many meanings can be assigned. One does not take it, in this connection, to be the dutiful but uncomprehending acceptance of that which is taught by authority. One modern definition expresses well the means by which the underlying reality of the Sacrament is appropriated—namely 'personal reliance on Christ, with surrender of the heart and will to His service.' The thought underlying this definition is beautiful, but we may well challenge the general position for, while admitting that right disposition of the heart is in every way desirable, we cannot help asking why the reality of the Sacrament should thus be tied up with these subjective workings of the mind. On this issue, I cannot do better than add to what has been said by Bishop Forbes some penetrating remarks by another clear-headed and experienced theologian, the late Canon Malcolm MacCoil of Ripon:

> The Eucharistic Presence is quite independent of the faith of the recipient. Faith creates nothing. Its province is not to create but to receive a gift external to it and offered to it. Faith is sometimes compared to an eye. But the eye does not create the light. It receives and transmits it to the brain and intellect. But a man may injure his eyes, so that they cease to be accurate conductors to the soul. The vision is thus blurred and distorted. Or he may destroy his eyes altogether and then the whole realm of light, with all its entrancing visions, is shut out from the soul. But the light is there all the same.
>
> However philosophers may dispute, we all agree that our bodily senses are our organs of communication with external facts, and that our sensations are no mere subjective impressions, but impressions resulting from contact with objective realities. The senses do not create the impressions. They only receive and convey them.

So with faith. It no more causes the Presence in the Eucharist than the eye causes the sunset. The Presence is objective—that is, outside of it and independent of it. If faith be lacking, the Presence has no more access to the soul than the glory of the setting sun has through sightless eyeballs....

Thus we see that, alike in the kingdoms of Nature and of Grace, the Presence that nourishes the soul must be objective before it can become subjective.

I will leave the receptionist theory here, except to mention that it is quite inadequate to serve as the basis of any substantial doctrine of the eucharistic sacrifice. And, since predestination and election are now dead issues while the remainder of Calvin's contention is met by what has been said above, the peculiar views for which he was responsible can be dismissed from further consideration here. What more there is to diminish our liking for receptionism is best elicited by discovering what more there is to be said in favour of a doctrine of a real objective Presence.

Virtualism

This doctrine, as we have already seen, admits of a Presence of Christ, but of His power and influence rather than of His Body, whether earthly or spiritual; and this Presence is interpreted as objective by some and after the manner of receptionism by others. The idea is well illustrated in a passage by one of the non-juring Bishops, Thomas Deacon (1697-1753).

It was at the institution of the Eucharist that our Saviour began to offer Himself to His Father for the sins of all men.... But because it would have been unnatural for Him to have broken His own body and shed His own blood, and because He could not as a living High Priest offer Himself when He was dead, therefore...He offered to the Father His natural body and blood voluntarily and really though mystically under the symbols of bread and wine mixed with water; for which reason He called the bread at the Eucharist His body, which was then broken, given, and offered for the sins of many, and the cup His blood, which was then shed and offered for the sins of many. All the sacrifices of the old law were figures of this great one of Christ; and the Eucharist or sacrifice of thanksgiving, which we celebrate according to His institution, is a solemn commemorative oblation of it to God the Father, and procures us the virtue of it.

Thus we see that by the consecration of the Eucharist the bread and mixed wine are not destroyed, but sanctified; they are not changed in their substance but in their qualities; they are not made the natural but the sacramental body and blood of Christ; so that they are both bread and wine and the body and blood of Christ at the same time but not in the same manner. They are bread and wine by nature, the body and blood of Christ in mystery and signification; they are bread and wine to our senses, the body and blood of Christ to our understanding and faith; they are bread and wine in themselves, the body and blood of Christ in power and effect. So that whoever eats and drinks them as he ought to do, dwells in Christ and Christ in him, he is one with Christ and Christ with him.[1]

I have little criticism to bring against such an exposition of eucharistic doctrine. It seems to me extraordinarily sane and lofty in tone and general concept—a refreshing change from most of the controversy. Such a view has in it everything that there is in Zwinglianism to rec-

---

[1] *A Full, True and Comprehensive View of Christianity*, 1747; quoted in Darwell Stone, op cit., pp. 482-485.

ommend it, and supplies that warm concept of an intimate life in Christ which Zwinglianism lacks. It is a bolder and more statesmanlike doctrine than receptionism, and it gives an interpretation of the bodily Presence which frees it from all grossness. Moreover, Deacon's bold idea of the Last Supper being the anticipatory offering of the Lord's Body, answers the objection made against virtualism; namely, how it explains the words, 'This is my body which is given for you' and 'my blood which is shed for you.'

But it does not clearly emerge whether a Presence is implied in this doctrine or not. The sense in which the elements are 'the body and blood of Christ in power and effect' is obscure. Are they a special channel of virtue (Lat. *virtus* = strength) or of the Presence, or only a reminder of that virtue which is available for us at all times through the sacrifice of Christ? Virtualism, as generally understood, is a bestowal of the merits of the atoning death of Christ; in fact, the bread and wine are equivalents of the absent Body and Blood. Still, among the non-jurors a theory is to be encountered according to which the Holy Spirit descends upon the elements and by His action makes them in efficacy the Body and Blood. I shall attempt to show in the next chapter how this doctrine may be legitimately expanded and approximated to a view of transubstantiation.

Consubstantiation and Transubstantiation

I have tried to keep the lines of our deliberation clear and free from entanglement with ultra-technical detail, and I do not think it necessary for our purpose to enter into any discussion on the respective merits of transubstantiation and consubstantiation. As a distinctive, self-contained theory, consubstantiation seems to have missed fire, and has never reached anything like the same eminence as the rival doctrine of transubstantiation. Two schools of thought had existed from the fourth and fifth centuries. From one school the doctrine of transubstantiation was developed—the substance of bread and wine, it said, was changed or converted into the substance of the Body and Blood of Christ. The other school tried, in its concept of the mystery, to maintain a parallel with the doctrine of the Incarnation. It taught that, as Our Lord by His Incarnation became both God and man, each nature existing side by side and unchanged, so in the Eucharist, the bread and wine continue to exist side by side with His Body and Blood.

Luther himself was persuaded of the necessity of accepting Our Lord's words in their literal sense, and taught what he called 'consubstantiation,' meaning simply that the bread and wine remained also in the sacrament. The various Lutheran Confessions of Faith which were drawn up at the time, like those of Augsburg and Württemberg, contented themselves with affirming the dual Presence, but do not speak of consubstantiation. Moreover, Luther was not always careful in his utterances, and his opponents accused him of various heresies like Impanation and Monophysitism, implying that consubstantiation meant that the bread and wine and the Body and Blood respectively became merged into one substance, just as the Monophysite or Eutychian heresy held that after the Incarnation Our Lord had but one nature. Luther was no metaphysician, and made no serious attempt to define his doctrine. Indeed, he deprecated any such tendency. Consequently, consubstantiation has never been a living factor in subsequent theology. Many theologians who hold the view of the Real Presence mentioned above, which is parallel with the doctrine of the Incarnation, would hesitate to describe it by the name of consubstantiation.

The events of the Reformation led to what is called the Counter-Reformation in the Roman Catholic Church, and to that interesting and important gathering called the Council of Trent which did so much to purge Catholic teaching of mediaeval superstition and excess, and gave some most admirable dogmatic definitions. Among these latter are some on transubstantiation. There are two principal passages which concern us in that Council's decrees and canons. I quote from Bishop J.C. Hedley's[1] standard work, *The Holy Eucharist*. The first is from Session XIII, cap. IV:

> Seeing that Christ our Redeemer hath said that that which He offered under the appearance (*specie*) of bread was truly His Body, therefore it hath ever been the conviction of the Church of God, and this holy Synod declares it afresh, that there happens a conversion (*conversionem fieri*) of the whole substance of the bread into the substance of the Body of Christ our Lord, and of the whole substance of the wine into the substance of His Blood; which conversion conveniently and with propriety is called by the holy Catholic Church Transubstantiation.

The second is from the first Canon or definition of the same chapter:

> If any one shall deny that in the sacrament of the most holy Eucharist is truly, really, and substantially the Body and Blood together with the soul and divinity of our Lord Jesus Christ, and therefore Christ wholly and entirely (*totum Christum*); but shall say that it is therein only as a sign, or figuratively, or virtually; let him be anathema.[2]

And Canon II of the same chapter declares:

> If any one shall say that in the most holy sacrament of the Eucharist there remains the substance of bread and wine, together with the Body and Blood of our Lord Jesus Christ, and shall deny that wonderful and singular conversion of the whole substance of bread into the Body and of the whole substance of wine into the Blood, the species only of the bread and wine remaining—which conversion the Catholic Church mostly aptly calls Transubstantiation—let him be anathema.[2]

These definitions are clear and to the point, and it is evident that they were made in reply to the Sacramentaries, as the schools of Zwingli and Calvin were called. The statement that Our Lord is 'truly, really and substantially' (*vere, realiter, essentialiter*) present opposes the doctrines of Zwingli, Oecolampadius and Calvin. 'Truly' is directed against Zwingli's idea that the Sacrament is a 'sign' (*signum*) only, a sign or token by which a man is known as a Christian among his fellows; 'really' against Oecolampadius who held the rite to be a figure; and 'substantially' against Calvin who denied the objective Presence but admitted an efficacy of grace limited to the predestined.

Among those who, in these days, accept the doctrine of the Real objective Presence and are outside the Roman Catholic Church, there is a general tendency not to make the question of transubstantiation a matter of faith on the one hand or of controversy on the other. Bishop Gore, who has objections to it, admits that as conceived by the Council of Trent 'it remains as little more than a verbal encumbrance due to an inopportune intrusion into church doctrine of a temporary phase of metaphysics.'[3]

---

[1] Bishop Hedley was Roman Catholic Bishop of Newport.

[2] pp. 37-38.

[3] *The Body of Christ*, p. 120.

Theologians of the Eastern Orthodox Churches, though often by no means antagonistic to transubstantiation, refrain from insisting upon any such precise definition of the mode of the Presence and ask only that a change or transmutation shall be acknowledged.[1]

There can be no doubt that it was against the concept of a carnal presence in the Eucharist that the Reformers protested, and it is certainly in that sense that the disavowal of transubstantiation in Article twenty-eight of the Church of England is to be understood. Transubstantiation as defined by the Council of Trent does not 'overthrow the nature of a Sacrament,' as is said in the Article. That there was much that was revolting in the pre-Tridentine teaching, and that many abuses and much superstition existed, is evident from the literature of the period. Says Jeremy Taylor: 'And, by the way, let me observe that the expressions of some chief men among the Romanists are so rude and crass...they thought Christ intended they should tear Him with their teeth and suck His blood....'[2]

Archbishop Ussher mentions the legend of 'a Roman matron who found a piece of the sacramental bread turned into the fashion of a finger, all bloody; which afterwards, upon the prayers of St. Gregory, was converted to its former shape again.'[3] Other instances of gross superstition will be found in Bishop Cosin's treatise against transubstantiation, and in the well-known book, *Church of Our Fathers*, written by a learned Roman Catholic, Dr. Rock.

We have already referred to the case of Berengarius. After his excursion into free-thinking he was forced to make recantation to the following effect: 'The bread and wine which are placed on the altar are after consecration...the true body and blood of our Lord Jesus Christ, and that with the senses (*sensualiter*), not only by way of sacrament but in reality (*sed in veritate*), these are handled by the hands of the priest and broken and bruised by the teeth of the faithful.'[4]

Bishop Gore describes this as 'a gross and horrible doctrine,' adding that most of the contemporary writers against Berengarius assert that the Body and Blood of Christ are to be eaten and drunk 'with the mouth of the body as well as the mouth of the heart;' and, like some of the earlier Greeks, they 'deny that the elements after consecration retain their natural properties of nourishing or becoming corrupted or being digested.... Miracles were recklessly postulated, and it was sufficient objection to any more reasonable treatment of the mystery that in diminishing the difficulty of belief it reduced the merit of faith.'[5]

An early book by Paschasius Radbert leaves no doubt as to the nature of the doctrine that was prevalent. In *his De Corpore et Sanguine Domini* (831) he writes that the bread is converted into 'the very body which was born of Mary, was crucified, and rose from the tomb,' and this book was later defended by Lanfranc in his attack on Erigena and Berengarius.

All this has to be realized if we are to understand why the English Reformers wrote so strongly against transubstantiation, as they understood it. The same considerations explain

---

[1] This view is very clearly exposed in Canon J.A. Dougals's excellent book, *The Relations of the Anglican Churches with the Eastern Orthodox.*

[2] *Works*, VI, 28.

[3] *Answer to a Jesuit. Works*, IV, p. 225.

[4] Quoted from Dr. Darwell Stone's *History of the Doctrine of the Holy Eucharist*, Vol. I, p. 247. The Latin is given in Bishop Gore's *Dissertations*, pp. 257-258. According to Dr. Stone, Lanfranc says that Berengarius subscribed to this statement; Berenganus says that he only accepted it in silence.

[5] *The Body of Christ*, pp. 117-118.

much of their hostility to the Mass and other 'Romish doctrines.'[1] There can be no doubt that many abuses had sprung up in connection with the Mass. Pilkington, Bishop of Durham (1520-1575), incidentally lets out one of these abuses; when the accusation was brought that the Mass had been changed, he answered that it had only been restored to what it was intended to be—a religious rite for the benefit of men's souls (and therefore to what the Missal contemplated), and not 'for pocky pigs, scalled horses, or scabbed sheep.'[2] referring to the custom of driving animals into church at the Last Gospel to be cured of their diseases. Bishop Forbes referred to the Synod of Rome of 648, where the Host was mixed with ink for the purpose of signing the condemnation of the Monothelite heretics.[3]

The Epiklesis

The *epiklesis*, or invocation of the Holy Spirit upon the elements, is a prominent feature in the Liturgy of St. Chrysostom, which is that chiefly in use in the Eastern Orthodox Church. In that rite, the priest, having recited the words of institution, prays God 'to send down Thy Holy Spirit upon us and upon these gifts.' He then prays in a low voice that the bread and wine be made the Precious Body and Blood and adds the words, 'changing them by Thy Holy Spirit.' It is held by some that this form of eucharistic consecration is older than that of the Western, which uses Our Lord's words of institution. Authorities seem to be divided on the subject. It certainly goes back to the fourth century and is claimed for the third. It is said that in at least one very early form the 'Spirit' invoked is not the Third Person, but the Divine Power or Virtue. It seems probable that different methods were in use from quite early times; we have evidence of different customs according to which the words of institution were employed, the Word invoked, the Holy Spirit, or the Holy Trinity. In any case, in those days the idea was vividly before the minds of all that all Christian worship was 'in the Holy Spirit.'

The proposed introduction of the *epiklesis* into the new Book of Common Prayer raises the question as to where the consecration takes place. Do the words of institution effect the consecration or is it now to be the invocation of the Holy Spirit? The Eastern Church came gradually to believe the latter, and regards the formula of institution as historical narrative. But in the fourth century the belief was widely held that consecration was effected by the words of institution. St. John Chrysostom taught this, and so did St. Ambrose. The words of Our Lord were 'caught up by His Church,' as it has strikingly been said, 'and reiterated in each Eucharist still in their ancient power. What Christ did at the Institution, He does at every Eucharist.' The one doctrine prevailed in the East, the other in the West. We need not enter into any discussion as to which is true, for certainly both are effective. The probability is that in the Eastern rite the words of Our Lord inaugurate the process of change which is carried a stage further at the succeeding words, and, at the *Epiklesis*, brought out into full expression. Precision regarding time and space is a mark of our modern Western civilization. Formerly, the rite was considered more in its entirety.

It is commonly supposed that a number of different reasons lay behind this introduction of the *epiklesis* into the alternative Prayer Book. It may be taken as a move in the direction of

---

[1] See Article twenty-two of the Thirty-Nine Articles in the Anglican Prayer Book. The Latin word used, *romaniensium*, has a technical meaning. It does not mean simply Roman Catholic, but was used by Luther and others to designate the extreme mediaeval party. 'Romish' doctrine is therefore a distinction from 'Roman Catholic' doctrines, and a vast amount of Protestant diatribe and innuendo results from ignorance of this careful distinction.

[2] Quoted from Lunn's Preface to his edition of *Barlowe's Dialogue*.

[3] Forbes, p.551.

the Eastern Church, and, contrariwise, as a veiled rebuff to Rome. Some think that a little pride of scholarship was behind the idea of reverting to a supposedly more primitive form.

The Anglican Bishop of Gloucester, Dr. A.C. Headlam, pointed out in a letter to *The Times* that the Prayer of Consecration in the older Prayer Book 'lays the whole stress on the words of institution, and is quite clearly open to the interpretation that the priest, by the recitation of these words, has the power to produce the Body and Blood of Christ. That is the extreme Roman point of view, and is exactly what appears to many of us so dangerous, perhaps almost open to the charge of being magical. The new Canon emphasizes the point that the gift, however it may be defined, comes through Divine action in response to the prayers of the Church offered through its officiating minister.'[1]

One wonders sometimes what is the state of mind which allows an Anglican prelate to write this kind of nonsense about Roman Catholics. Dangers there may be—and I think there are—attached to Romanism, but no Roman Catholic priest is conceited enough to think that he effects the consecration of the Host himself. The Bishop, to begin with, ignores the fact that the existing Anglican Prayer Book prefaces the words of institution with a prayer to the Father which obviously enlists His action. But apart from that, the letter presents a disingenuous travesty of Roman Catholic doctrine. No priest of any denomination can for an instant suppose that he is acting apart from Christ who is the true Minister of all the sacraments. Moreover, if 'magic' is to be brought into the arena, is it not just as much a magical operation that the invocation of the Holy Spirit should be supposed to affect the bread and wine as the use of Christ's words of institution? I shall speak later of this curious craze for dubbing everything that is disliked or misunderstood as 'magical,' but the Bishop is surely using dangerous weapons. The late Dr. Parker, the famous Nonconformist preacher of the City Temple, declared that the Anglican Prayer Book was steeped in Popery, and would no doubt have convicted Dr. Headlam of magic no whit less than the latter insinuates it against Rome.

The Liberal Catholic Liturgy has a form of *Epiklesis* preceding the words of institution:

> Wherefore, O holy Lord, Father almighty, we pray thee to look down on and accept these offerings, which we thy servants and thy whole household do make unto thee, in obedience to the command of thy most blessed Son, our Lord Jesus Christ:
>
> Which offerings do thou, O Father, deign with thy Holy Spirit and Word to + bless, + approve, and + ratify, that they may become for us his most precious + Body and + Blood.

---

[1] Letter, 16 February 1928.

AN INTERPRETATION

I want now to leave the beaten tracks of theology and look at the whole question in a freer spirit. Our image of the universe is different from that which prevailed in the days of the Schoolmen and the Reformers. The last century, so rich in discovery of all kinds, displaced our landmarks of thought, and our psychology moves in quite a new orbit.

Much of the difficulty which dogs the eucharistic doctrine centres round the use of the terms 'Body' and 'Blood.' It does not seem likely that the disciples in the living presence of the Lord would take the bread that He gave them at the Last Supper as His physical flesh. The Eucharist cannot be considered apart from the mystic discourse related in John vi when the Jews of Capernaum, asking for a sign, pointed out how God had sent down manna to feed the wandering Hebrews in the desert. Our Lord told them that 'the bread of God is he which cometh down from heaven and giveth life unto the world.... I am the living bread which came down from heaven: if any man eat of this bread he shall live for ever: and the bread that I will give is my flesh, which I will give for the life of the world.' The Jews, we are told, strove among themselves, saying, 'How can this man give us his flesh to eat?' Many of His disciples said, 'This is a hard saying...' and 'went back and walked no more with him.' But it was in this moment of stress that the eyes of Simon Peter were opened and he uttered the significant confession: '...we believe and are sure that thou art that Christ the Son of the living God.'

The whole of this discourse is cast in mystic terms. The supposed miracle of the manna is dismissed, and Jesus speaks of a mystical sustenance through which His followers draw their spiritual life from Him, even as He lives by the Father who sent Him. This was not the only occasion on which He spoke to them in this strain. Later on, He spoke of Himself as the 'true vine,' and gave them the beautiful simile of themselves related to Him as the branches[1]—and this just before He told them 'a little while and ye shall not see me.'[2] By the time of the Last Supper, they would be familiar with this idea of their mutual spiritual dependence.

Calvin speaks very reasonably on this spiritual nourishment:

> But to me Christ appears to have intended something more express and sublime in that famous discourse of His where He commends to us the eating of His Flesh; namely, that by a real participation in Him we be quickened; which He therefore designated under the words eating and drinking, lest any should think that the life we derive from Him is received by simple cognition. For as, not the sight but the eating of the bread gives nourishment to the body, so is it needful that for the soul to be wholly partaker of Christ it should be quickened by His virtue to life eternal.[3]

There is nothing strange or novel in the teaching. St. Paul told the men of Athens that in God 'we live, and move, and have our being...for we are also his offspring.'[4]

And does not the Apocalypse exhibit to us the symbolism of the Lamb slain from the foundation of the world—the birth of Christ in Eternity, the Life of the Second Person of the ever-Blessed Trinity poured out into His world, the Eternal Sacrifice by which it is ever nourished and sustained?

[1] John xv. 1.

[2] Ibid xvi 16.

[3] Institut. IV, xvii, 5. Quoted in Bishop Harold Browne's *Exposition of the Thirty-Nine Articles*, p. 703.

[4] Acts xvii. 28.

I bring forward these different considerations because it seems quite clear to me that Our Lord intended His Presence in the Eucharist to be understood as an objective spiritual Presence, that of His all-sustaining Life made manifest in a special way, and that the disciples must have regarded it as such.

The Meaning of 'Body' and 'Blood'

How, then, are we to explain the use of the words 'Body' and 'Blood?' A body may be defined as 'a vehicle of consciousness or life.' My physical body is my instrument of communication with the physical world. Through it I receive impacts from that world which, translated into terms of consciousness, become experiences; and I express myself through it into the external world. Moreover, the word also has an extended sense. We speak of the body-politic or organized society; of the body-corporate which acts as a single entity; of the *corpus juris*, the body or code of the laws. It means, in this sense, a system or an organized collectivity.

Is not the same idea applicable to the Sacrament? Is not the holy bread the Body of the Lord in the sense that it is His vehicle or instrument of consciousness, the medium or channel through which His Life and blessing are communicated to us?

What then shall we say of the Blood? In the sacrificial systems and mystery cults of the past special significance was attached to the blood of the victim. There is a reference to this in Leviticus xvii. 2: 'For the life of the body is in the blood: and I have given it to you upon the altar to make an atonement for your souls,' and the text goes on to forbid the partaking of blood by the children of Israel and by the strangers sojourning among them. It would seem that in the Hebrew religion, as in others, the blood represented the being of the person, and that Our Lord spoke their own language to the Jews of Capernaum. Ideas of this sort abound in the various works on folklore and comparative mythology. Further, there is a connection between the blood and wine: In the Mysteries of Bacchus (which later developed into frenzied orgies but were in the beginning probably quite pure and lofty) the juice of the grape was the emblem of the Life of the Logos poured out in sacrifice, and as sacrifice in its highest aspect is joyous and glad, great mirth and rejoicing were associated with their celebration. This symbolism runs through many cults, for the Sacrifice of the Logos is the life-blood of the world, and Christ is its heart.

It is the idea of the primal Sacrifice of the Logos which enables us most clearly to understand how the Holy Eucharist is also a Sacrifice. The primal Sacrifice takes place in the 'eternal now,' outside our conceptions of time and space. And as, in earthly time, Christ became incarnate for our sakes, so is the mystery of the Incarnation extended in every Eucharist. The primal Sacrifice was His own self-limitation in matter; in the Eucharist, correspondingly, He is at once Priest and Victim. In the Eucharist 'we not only commemorate in symbol that...eternal oblation, but verily take part in it and perpetuate thereby within the limitations of time and space, which veil our earthly eyes from the excess of [His] glory, the enduring sacrifice by which the world is nourished and sustained.'

Our Lord, we are told, spoke of having other sheep and other folds; and the student of comparative religion finds many likenesses between the great religions of the world. It is difficult to suppose that these can all be due to plagiarism or mutual influence, otherwise other religions must have plagiarized from Christianity by anticipation as, indeed, certain of the Fathers maintained. The impartial student is forced to the conclusion that there are certain basic truths and foundation symbols and myths common to all of them. There seems no real evidence for the theory, which is from time to time advanced, that the Christian sacraments, as we know them, were incorporated into the faith at a later period, having been taken over from the mystery-cults of the Mediterranean basin. There seems much evidence, on the contrary, that some of the foundations of the Eucharist are to be found in the Jewish tradition.[1] But are we to think that Our Lord was a stranger to all that was taking place in the other great religions of the world? Today, people are apt to say that the different nations worship the same God, whether one calls Him Allah or Ahuramazda. Do they not, perhaps, also worship the same Christ? Be this as it may, it is not unreasonable to suppose that Our Lord in His wisdom may have seen fit to carry into this new religious impulse something of the same symbolism that appeared elsewhere, and to adapt it to His own special purposes.

I take the bread, then, to be His Body in the sense that a body is a vehicle of life, and the wine to be His Blood in the sense that blood and wine are ancient symbols of the Divine Life poured out in sacrifice for the sustenance of the world. There is no carnal or fleshly significance to be attached to these terms. The Bread and Wine are not mere figures: the Presence is objective and real. It reaches people through their faith and devotion; but its reality on the altar under the forms of bread and wine is an objective reality and is not dependent upon the subjective attitude of one or more worshippers. The outer forms of bread and wine are the vehicles through which that Presence becomes manifest.

The advantage of this interpretation is that we are at once disembarrassed of all the complications associated with ideas of the presence of Christ's body and blood in the ordinary sense of the words. We have seen with what difficulties that doctrine became entangled. First, there was the widespread revolt against the corporal or carnal presence. Theologians, one after another, insisted that the Body in the Sacrament is the spiritual or glorified and Risen Body of Christ. But they had no explanation to offer as to why a spiritual or heavenly Body should be given to be eaten any more than a carnal body. In the later definition of transubstantiation the substances of the bread and wine are changed, not into the Body and Blood of Christ but into the substance of His Body and Blood. Then Calvin insisted that Christ's Body is in heaven. So does the 'black rubric' at the end of the Anglican Communion service. It tells us that Christ's 'natural Body and Blood' are 'in Heaven, and not here,' and that they 'cannot be at one time in more places than one.' Other theories make a distinction between the 'natural' body and the 'glorified' body. The Anglican Article twenty-eight approaches the question from another angle and directs attention not so much to the nature of the Body as to the manner of eating It 'in a heavenly and spiritual manner.' The view which I have been advocating brings with it a sense of relief. It disencumbers the question of all this literalism as to the nature and habitat of Christ's Body and leaves us with the full doctrine of the real and objective Presence.

Localization of the Presence

This view of the function of the bread and wine relieves us of any difficulty in regard to the localization of the Body of Christ which was one of the great points of contention among the Reformers. Luther took a definite view as to the omnipresence of Our Lord. Where He is as God, says Luther, He is also as Man, and where His manhood is there must His Body be. Since He is omnipresent as God, so also is His Body. This doctrine, which gives to Christ's manhood the same properties as His divine Person, is rejected by many and regarded as *a communicatio idiomatum*. Calvin, as we have seen, took a different view, holding that Christ's Body is in heaven and cannot be elsewhere. 'The Calvinistic doctrine regarding the Lord's Supper rests upon an overt principle of dualism between the kingdom of grace and that of nature; a dualism

---

[1] See Dr Gavin.

so thorough that the Lord's Supper is literally divided into two distinct acts, the one in heaven, the other on earth.'[1]

There can be no objection in principle to the idea of a localized Presence. Christ's presence was certainly localized by comparison with His universal Presence when He moved as a man among men. To say that He is present in the bread does not assert, as some take it, that He is enclosed and wholly imprisoned therein. He can be at once transcendent and immanent in regard to His vehicle, as God is in regard to His universe. Once we unburden ourselves of the theory that Christ has but one Body which is in heaven and that it is this Body which is given in the Eucharist, we are released from all sorts of difficulties. The Host is thus *a* Body rather than *the* Body; He may have Bodies upon a thousand altars simultaneously, for His consciousness is omnipresent. This may have been a difficult doctrine for the sixteenth century; it is less so for us who know that the human voice is made wellnigh ubiquitous—present at any rate in thousands of places simultaneously—by radio. That He who is omnipresent should be able to make manifest His presence when we, on our side, prepare the requisite conditions, is really not so startling. There can be, and are, degrees of His Presence, that is to say, of the manifestation of His Life. In some people 'the...Light which lighteth every man that cometh into the world'[2] is heavily veiled within its encasement of matter; in others it has begun to shine resplendently out into the world. Centuries upon centuries ago, the Mysteries of ancient Egypt taught the same idea in the myth of the breaking and scattering of the limbs of Osiris and their eventual reintegration. So the seed of divinity is scattered over the world and dwells in every human heart. Mankind lives in illusion and separateness until it awakens the Light within so that it becomes one with the Universal Light without and is reintegrated consciously into the mystical Body of Christ. Our Lord is ever thus scattering the fragments of His Life upon the altars of His holy Church, so that we, participating in that Life, may quicken and fan within ourselves the flame of our own inner divinity.

A Liberal View of Transubstantiation

There need be no difficulty, then, in accepting transubstantiation, if our philosophy of the cosmos is a spiritual one. The whole universe is an expression of God. He is the One Existence from whom all other existences are derived. In Him we live, and move, and have our being.[3] His is the One Life which animates everything. I know no better statement of the Divine Transcendence and Immanence than that magnificent proclamation of one of the Hindu scriptures: 'I established this universe with one fragment of Myself; and I remain.'[4] Man, made in the Image of God, is himself divine in essence—a spark of the Divine Fire. The Divinity that was fully manifest in Jesus Christ is being gradually unfolded in each one of us until we come 'unto a perfect man, unto the measure of the stature of the fullness of Christ.'[5] The Spirit uses a soul and body for contact with the various worlds of being through which we gain those experiences which gradually draw out into manifestation our latent divine powers.

On this philosophy, the world consists of various planes of being, reaching from the most spiritual (nearest to the primal Reality) to the most material, the physical world. All forms

---

[1] Dr Martensen, *Christian Dogmatics*, p. 441.

[2] St. John 1. 9

[3] Acts xvii. 28.

[4] *Bhagavad-Gita*, x. 42.

[5] Ephesians, iv. 13.

owe their existence to the Life of God which He breathed into His universe. If that Divine Energy were for a moment withdrawn all would be resolved back into no-being. At creation there was a differentiation into a fundamental duality of Spirit and Matter—the Life which God breathed out and that substratum of matter into which He breathed it. The planes are material, but instinct with life, their matter becoming subtler and finer as we move upwards from the physical.

Substance is the reality, force, or ensouling Life, or *noumenon*, which lies behind a physical object. It is that which stands under (Latin, *sub* = under; *stans* = standing) or behind the outer physical object, and of which that object is the expression or epiphany. Transubstantiation (Latin, *trans* = across), on this principle, means that the essence, substance, or superphysical reality and counterpart or creative force of the bread and wine is transmuted, or changed across, and replaced by a similar ensouling Life coming direct from Our Lord Himself.[1]

To put the matter into simple language; the consecrated Bread and Wine become a vehicle or channel directly connected with Our Lord, through which He expresses His Life and blessing. Because His Life—the Life of the Second Person of the Trinity—is in every man, so every man (though in lesser degree) is also a vehicle of Him. And the purpose of the Sacrament is to quicken within us the manifestation of His Life so that our efforts towards self-realization may be aided.

This view of transubstantiation rids us of a host of difficulties which have puzzled theologians. The words 'symbol' and 'figure' no longer have the negative sense of denying reality. On the contrary, a symbol is 'correspondence' (Gr. *sumbolon* = throwing together) between a physical object and a superphysical archetypal Idea of which the object is the channel or vehicle or direct expression.

---

[1] In *The Science of the Sacraments* by Bishop C.W. Leadbeater, the theory is more fully elaborated.

MATTER THE VEHICLE OF SPIRIT

IF there is one thing that strikes one all through the history of opinion about the Presence of Christ in the Holy Eucharist, it is the constant endeavour to divorce the thought of this Presence from all association with material objects. The *modus operandi* is to claim that the Presence is 'spiritual' and to protest that the idea is being 'materialized' the moment we begin to talk of a Real Presence in the consecrated bread and wine. This tendency, as we have already pointed out, is partly the outcome of rationalism and partly symptomatic of the timidity in religious matters which is especially characteristic of Anglicanism. The word 'spiritual' is like the 'blessed word Mesopotamia:' it is 'comforting' because it enables us to evade issues by transferring them to a spiritual realm of which anything may conveniently be predicated.

The exponents of this doctrine could, with some profit, consult the writings of Zwingli who was under no illusion about its merits. He writes:

> To be a body and to be eaten after a spiritual manner are inconsistent with one another, for body and spirit are so different that, whichever you take, the other cannot be.
> They say, We adore and eat the spiritual body of Christ. What, by Great Jupiter, is the spiritual body of Christ? Is any other spiritual body of Christ anywhere found in Scripture than either the Church...or our faith?... A spiritual body is just as much understood by a human being as if you spoke of a bodily mind or a fleshly reason.[1]

It is not generally realized that this attitude is also the perpetuation of an old heresy as variegated as the chameleon—the assumption that matter is evil. Among other things of which they were accused, the early Gnostics were (rightly in all probability) convicted of this error. Religiously-minded people are apt to be frightened of matter instead of recognizing it as the vehicle of spirit. Thus, to divorce the two does not in reality make for a more spiritual view of religion as they fondly imagine but is, on the contrary, a proclamation of materialism. It is an attitude which leads either to puritanism, in which matter is reprobated as evil—as something which has to be combated and avoided—or to a view of civilization based on positivism and shut off from all religious and spiritual considerations. The Protestant temperament is reluctant to face the issue that material objects are constantly used as instruments for spiritual manifestation. Thus, Dr. Barnes, the Anglican Bishop of Birmingham, floods with contemptuous ridicule the idea that it is possible to invest material objects with spiritual properties. In the first place, however, the old idea that matter belongs to the category of either 'animate' or 'inanimate' is fast losing ground with scientists. The researches of Professor Sir J. C. Bose of Calcutta, communicated on various occasions to the Royal Society, have established a strong premise that there is no such thing as 'inanimate matter,' as his ancestral scriptures—for he is a Hindu—claimed thousands of years ago. He has recorded the result of electrical stimulation on metals; he has shown that they are subject to fatigue, can be poisoned, and can be restored to normal activity by the administration of an antidote.

Secondly, there is now a fair amount of evidence for the existence of psychometry. Country folk often tell of horses which shy at a spot which was the scene of some memorable happening. Events seem to leave their impressions upon the surrounding matter or 'aether.' The objects that we wear become impregnated with our 'magnetism.' Who has not heard of the old

[1] *Opera*, II, pp. 206, 215.

trick by which a hypnotist endows water with purgative or other medicinal properties by pouring his 'animal magnetism' into it? And can it not truthfully be said that the 'magnetism' or 'atmosphere' of a speaker or musician is transmitted by radio? A broadcast church service can certainly produce religious sentiment: this is not entirely due to subjective association; something is also transmitted objectively.

The Bible itself is a material vehicle. So is the spoken word: so are prayer and worship; so are music and art. Our Lord used a material body. Naaman was cured of his leprosy by dipping himself seven times in the Jordan.

The truth is that God does make use of material intermediaries in order to communicate to us the gifts of the Spirit. He must needs do so unless their contact with us is to be purely at the level of our Spirit—of which, as yet, most of us have no consciousness. Religion has to help us at all levels of our being. It works to unify our consciousness and bring us back (Latin *religare* = to bind back) to the knowledge of our own hidden divinity. For humanity at its present stage, the physical world is the chief theatre of evolution; it is here that causes are chiefly initiated. We live in the body much as in a prison-house, and it is here, in the waking consciousness of this tenement of flesh, that help is most needed. If a power is to be made effective to physical beings, it must be communicated through a physical vehicle. And a similar correspondence applies to other levels of our being. Hence it is reasonable that the sacramental powers should be expressed through some outward and visible sign or symbol as the lowest extremity of their influence, acting as the distributing centre of that grace.

We may not wish to keep our minds fixed on the mechanical side of the process, but we need not pretend that it does not exist, or think it to be 'unspiritual.' In practice, the Eucharist is bound to lift us up into 'the heavenlies,' and, as the priest personates Our Blessed Lord, the worshipping Church blends itself in thought with the disciples in the Upper Room.

Magic

The latest fashion is to decry all this as magic and, in doing so, the disputants take advantage of the fact that it has rightly or wrongly acquired a bad name. Magic was originally the wisdom of the Magi, and is a useful thing if rightly understood. The laws of nature are expressions of the Will of God. They are statements of conditions. Science studies the working of these natural laws and teaches man how to turn them to his service. The current of a river flowing strongly in a certain direction suggests a means of saving energy in transport, as does the principle of the wheel. But it is not only a question of turning these forces to our service; there is the other side of the process, namely, the adapting of ourselves to the laws of nature. 'Nature is conquered by obedience,' is the modern adaptation of a wise remark made by Lord Bacon. The sensible man studies what conditions are favourable and what are unfavourable to any proposed work.

There is an application of all this to religious worship. Certain lines of work are laid down and, by following them, co-operation with great natural forces is assured. This gives greatly increased efficacy to the work and is in no way whatsoever undesirable so long as the worshipper does not diminish his own initiative. The traditional ceremonies of religion show evidence of a profound knowledge of human psychology and of the working of these natural laws, which is one evidence for their inspired origin.

There is, in fact, a 'science of the sacraments' but, unfortunately, its rediscovery is only in its infant stage. In primitive times magic was used to replace human effort and initiative. This was not harmful, but beneficial to the people concerned so long as they were incapable of making the effort themselves. As man grows into spiritual maturity, he learns to co-operate with nature and to use her art deliberately and consciously. In secular life, a man is not accused of magic because he uses a motor-car, a telegraph-office or printing-press. Why, then, should he be in the domain of religion?

We are above the level of the prayer-wheel, and we no longer perform rites and incantations to compel the Deity. Rather, we take advantage of what the divine wisdom has provided for us.

It is profoundly true that the divine life may be contacted everywhere. But if Our Lord has instituted a means of contacting His more direct and immediate Presence, should we not be foolish to refuse it? There is a sense in which all this is magic. Only let it be understood that magic is good or bad according to whether it is employed for selfish, personal ends, or for good and beneficent purposes. The intellectual side of this work—the effort to understand and to work purposefully—legitimate as it is, must never be divorced from the ethical and devotional. Side by side with our offering of intellect, we must offer 'ourselves, our souls and bodies' as a holy and continual sacrifice to God.

Some Protestants seem to think that because a priest believes that when he utters the words of consecration and Christ becomes present, he imagines that he has brought it about by his own magic. Such an idea is surely incredible. The magic, so far as it is magic, is Christ's, not the priest's, and we accept it with all reverence and gratitude.

Eucharistic Adoration

It is obvious that all Christians, no matter what their particular beliefs about the Eucharist may be, have in that Sacrament an ideal which calls out all the devotion and religious feeling of which they are capable. The Zwinglian sees in it a solemn contemplation of Our Lord's Passion and redemption of the world, and as a token of our common fellowship in His mystical body, the Church. The Calvinist, the Receptionist and the believer in the Real Presence, see in it a spiritual feeding upon Christ through faith. Already, however, as between the Zwinglian and the others, there is a slight difference in reaction due to the difference of belief. One is contemplating the redemption of the world by Our Lord and the deliverance of his own soul; the other believes that, in some high and mysterious way, he is being made to participate in the very being of Christ Himself. The worshipper who looks to a Real Presence brought into effective contact with the whole of his nature, physical, psychical and spiritual, must react differently again and with even greater fervour. Let it be granted that the stimulation of the highest part of our spiritual being is the chief factor, there is still the reaction of the inferior part of our being, of that portion of our nature which is most awakened and habituated to strong reaction. The behaviour of this part of ourselves brought into the immediate presence of Our Lord will naturally be different from that of one who holds, let us say, the receptionist theory. The character of the service and the nature of the cultus must inevitably be different. The kind of worship which one sees in a Roman Catholic, Orthodox, or Anglo-Catholic church is quite different from that prevalent in churches where the beliefs which determine the worship are different. There is naturally a greater sense of realism[1] in churches where the Real Presence is recognized. Some would perhaps call it literalism; but who would not be intensely realistic in every fibre of his being if he found himself standing in the presence of Our Lord as he might have seen Him in

---

[1] 'The practice of regarding things in their true nature and dealing with them as they are': Fowler, *The Concise Oxford Dictionary*.

Galilee? It is a belief which has its natural and inescapable consequences, and one does not see how these could logically be avoided even if one wished to avoid them.

Luther was not quite consistent on the question of Eucharistic adoration. He said that Christ ascended into heaven for the purpose that we might adore Him there, but that He was not present in the Sacrament for that purpose. His doctrine was that the Presence was *in usu, non extra*—that Our Lord instituted the Sacrament for the purpose of communion and for no other. Christ came to earth in the flesh, he says, not to be adored, but to minister to men, and he draws a parallel with this and His descent into the Sacrament.[1] On the question of adoration his attitude was apologetic, and he pleaded that those who did not adore should not be condemned on that account. He adhered to the custom of elevating the Host and Chalice, but later abandoned it, explaining that the act had no inherent significance and that he had not wanted to shock people by hasty innovations.

These views sound a little odd to our ears for we should scarcely suppose that we give adoration to God because He requires it of us like some boorish despot. Our position is, rather, that it is good and natural for us to give that adoration.

On this question the Roman Catholic teaching is logical and clear.

> The adorableness of the Eucharist is the practical consequence of its permanence. According to a well-known principle of Christology, the same worship of latria (*cultus latriae*) as is due to the Triune God is due also to the Divine Word, the God-man Christ, and in fact, by reason of the hypostatic union, to the Humanity of Christ and its individual component parts as, for example His Sacred Heart. Now, identically the same Lord Christ is truly present in the Eucharist as is present in heaven; consequently He is to be adored in the Blessed Sacrament and just so long as He remains present under the appearances of bread and wine, namely, from the moment of transubstantiation to the moment in which the species are decomposed (cf. Council of Trent, Sess, XIII, can. VI).[2]

Bishop Gore accounts in a very interesting fashion for the fact that eucharistic adoration was but little developed in the early Church. He quotes Dr. Hort (*Life and Letters of F.J.A. Hort*, Vol. II, p. 50) to show that

> 'Jesus-worship,' as a whole—the distinctive feature alike of Protestant evangelicism and Catholic sacramentalism—is not at all prominent in the theology of the first five or six centuries...the separate and distinctive worship of Jesus in His manhood, with all the specially tender associations of His human name—the worship which gives its special sentiment to so much mediaeval and modern devotion—was but very little developed.
>
> We cannot, moreover, conceal from ourselves that this type of devotion, whether among Catholics or among Protestants, whether in mission hymn-singing or in sacramental worship, has belonged to the emotional and devotional part of our manhood rather than to the moral and rational.

He speaks of this as a change in the colour of devotion. It is certainly a change of emphasis.

---

[1] *Vom Anbeten des Sakraments.*

[2] *The Catholic Encyclopaedia*, Vol. V, art. 'Eucharist', p. 581.

We cannot reasonably separate the worship of Jesus in the sacrament from our whole attitude towards Him. If the early Church had been in the constant habit of singing such hymns as 'Jesu, Lover of my soul,' is it not very likely it would have also have sung, 'Jesus I adore Thee on Thy altar throne?'[1]

Humanity passes through different phases of experience. There are periods when devotion is at the flood-tide in human affairs and other times when intellectualism is predominant. Intuition seems likely to be the phase of the future. Obviously, eucharistic adoration developed partly under the devotional influence of the Middle Ages, but largely owing to the increasing denial of the reality of the Presence which began at the Reformation. We have a good parallel in the change which was brought about in the discipline of the Sacrament of Penance. It was formerly the custom to make public confession but this altered as conditions changed.

A criticism that is sometimes leveled against eucharistic adoration is that, in concentrating attention so much on Christ in the Blessed Sacrament, we are apt to pay insufficient attention to His universal presence and to that mystical aspect of Christ wherein He is spoken of as reigning in the human heart. It is also thought that there may be a tendency to devote too little attention to the other Persons of the Trinity. This last criticism seems to be met by the fact that in the Liturgy there is a constant play upon the interrelation of the three Persons of the Blessed Trinity, and that prayers are normally addressed to the Father. In fact, *usum non tollit abusus*; it is senseless to say that a thing right in itself should be sacrificed because there is danger of neglecting other things. Rather let us give more attention to those other aspects of truth. The difficulty is, really, that worship is seldom envisaged as a whole and in a philosophic sense, as a systematic method of awakening and developing the whole nature of man.

Idolatry

One curious feature of the controversy about the Eucharist is the allegation that eucharistic adoration is idolatry. The Bishop of Birmingham remarked that the High Churchman, with his Eucharistic adoration, was little removed from the cultured Hindu idolater. The Bishop's harsh and iconoclastic language outraged the susceptibilities of many Christians, and other Anglican Bishops publicly rebuked him for his want of moderation. But the Hindu might equally be outraged. No Hindu of intelligence and education would think of giving to an idol the worship which is due to divinity alone. Catholic theology makes the distinction between *latria*, the worship due to God alone, and *dulia*, the reverence given to creatures because of their closer relationship with God. A lesser veneration may be given to sacred objects.

There may be—indeed there probably are—ignorant peasants who do not stop to think of the difference between the Host and Christ, but even in their case the worship, however primitive, is in effect directed to Christ. Apart from these cases, to suppose that any ordinary person worships the bread and wine is utterly ridiculous (*pace* the Anglican Black Rubric). It is Our Lord who is worshipped under the species of bread and wine, and that type of adoration is as high and pure and as completely lacking in grossness as the meditative devotion of any Quaker or mystic who divorces himself (as far as the world in which he lives allows him to do so) from forms and intermediaries. From my knowledge of 'cultured Hindu idolaters,' I should say exactly the same of them. There is, for example, a Hindu deity named Ganesha who is portrayed with an elephant's trunk. People familiar with elephants tell us of their extraordinary sagacity. Ganesha is thus the representative of wisdom, the attribute of the Second Person of the

---

[1] *The Body of Christ*, pp. 106, 107. 109.

Hindu Trinity, and the elephant-like form is simply a way of making a homely appeal to a people of agricultural traditions. That such silly charges should be made by bishops in the twentieth century against either Hindus or their fellow-Christians, shows only how difficult it is for even clever men and women to disencumber themselves of the superstitions and prejudices of the past.

I come back to the thought with which this chapter opened. We are all familiar with what is ordinarily meant by materialism. But materialism is a monster of protean form, and is none the less dangerous in the disguise in which it shows itself in the world of religion. The tendency to 'spiritualize' our concepts of religion by refusing to them any objectivity in this world is nothing but materialism. The denial of the Real Presence is one form of this pseudo-spiritual materialism which refuses to see the spiritual in our midst, and must 'locate' it elsewhere.

FIRST-HAND KNOWLEDGE

It will scarcely seem strange that one holding these views should also hold that the Real Presence is not solely a question of faith or philosophical speculation, but can become a matter of realized experience and therefore first-hand knowledge. The higher psychical faculties, the possibility of whose existence is becoming more and more recognized, are powers of the soul. Now it is a common error to suppose that we are only concerned with the life of the soul after the death of the body. In point of fact, man's physical life and soul-life are lived simultaneously. There is a science, called meditation in the West and Yoga in the East, by which the higher faculties of man can be cultivated. If one accepts the idea that man is essentially divine in nature, a spark from the Divine Flame, it follows that he possesses within himself in a latent or potential state all the attributes of divinity. It is his task to unfold and realize those faculties one by one, and the doctrine of reincarnation provides a key to the method. If, for example, we take a quality like intuition, we find it recognized that some people possess it and others do not. It is regarded as an endowment of birth. On the other hand, it can quite reasonably be maintained that this, like every other human faculty, can be developed under the necessary conditions. We have, thus, a theology of human evolution by which man gradually unfolds within himself quality after quality of character, developing his powers of consciousness, and in doing so establishing himself, self-consciously and of right, as a citizen not only of the physical world but also of the higher worlds or realms of consciousness commonly called spiritual.

Pursuing such exercises, it eventually becomes possible for a person to gain for himself first-hand knowledge on many disputed problems of religion. If he can learn to open the windows of his soul, he can see out into that soul-world where live those persons who have cast off the physical body. That prayer is effective to help the dead becomes a matter of conscious knowledge. That a change takes place at the Consecration is another. That the Presence is not limited to the period of a Communion Service is yet another. The enormous spiritual blessing that is poured out by Our Lord in the rite of Benediction of the Most Holy Sacrament is yet another. Scripture and the traditions of the Church may be, and often are, of priceless value; but men are poles apart in the way in which they interpret them. And it must be confessed that, in most cases, the evidence is much too scanty and vague to warrant a clear decision.

Bishop Barnes was perfectly right in saying that spiritual changes wrought by the consecration of the elements should be perceptible to some faculty of spiritual apprehension. But these higher modes of consciousness are difficult to develop and even more difficult to bring completely under control. Their working tends to be intermittent, and often depends upon the bodily health of their possessor. That they exist is to me a matter of knowledge. It is but reasonable to suppose that as man spiritualizes himself, he grows sensitive to spiritual influences from without. As he grows more Christ-like in his character he gains the power to attune himself to Our Lord and to respond to His influence. A spiritual priest (or layman or laywoman) ought not to find it difficult to know whether the Real Presence is fact or fancy.

That there are dangers of aberration, of self-delusion and of pride connected with the study and practice of these things, none know better than those who have had most to do with them. The pioneers of every science have to lay its foundation at much risk to themselves. The fact that this particular science is but yet imperfectly explored is, however, no reason to deny the existence of the facts on which it is based.

At the beginning of every great religion there are Gnostics or knowers who know at first hand the truth of what they teach. Truly has it been said, 'Where there is no vision, the people perish.'[1] As a Church ceases to produce men of spiritual experience, so do its teachings become narrowed and hardened, its theology grows legalistic and mechanical, and its priesthood—unable to impart knowledge by process of inner illumination—seeks to impose it by outer authority and persecutes those who resist its will. Spiritual truths are at all times capable of reverification by spiritually developed men. The ancient paths of purification, illumination and union are still open for the treading. Those who approach by the traditional path may still hope to attain discipleship. The way of the Cross of self-sacrifice means the progressive unfoldment of the Christ-Spirit within man, and it is to help forward the growth of the Christ in us 'unto a perfect man, unto the measure of the stature of the fullness of Christ'[2] that the sacraments of His Church are appointed.

I like to go back in thought to the scene of the Last Supper, the outlines of which we recapitulate in the Prayer of Consecration at each eucharist, Our Lord had been giving hints to the little band of disciples of the parting that was impending. How deep the grief that must have fallen at the thought of that separation, the anxiety, the sense of helplessness, the thought of awful and utter loneliness. Can we not picture His tender sympathy with their distress, the endeavour to re-hearten them and to inspire them for work they had yet to accomplish? For the disciple must not think of himself, but of the world's great need. The Lord speaks to them of His love and care for them, of His power that will sustain them and support them in all their difficulties. Presently He tells them of the plan that He has devised for them, a rite that shall incorporate His very being, that shall keep the sense of His living Presence perpetually in their hearts, and shall help them to maintain the realization of their fellowship with one another, that holy and all-possessing unity which they had gradually found in their common devotion to Him. How wonderful must have been those moments as in solemn thanksgiving He broke the Bread and blessed the Cup! How deep the peace and stillness of that greatest of all moments! What a panorama in the inner worlds, what hosts of angels and great ones to do homage to that memorable occasion! And above all the sweetness of His love binding them perpetually to Himself with ties that should never be broken!

It was not only once in the history of this sad world that so marvellous an experience was given to men: the rite still lives on; His love still binds men's hearts together, and we take comfort and strength in His marvellous promise, 'And lo, I am with you alway, even unto the end of the world.'[3]

ACCENDAT IN NOBIS DOMINUS IGNEM SUI AMORIS.
ET FLAMMAM AETERNAE CARITATIS. AMEN.

---

[1] Proverbs xxix. 18.

[2] Ephesians iv. 13.

[3] Matthew xxviii, 20.

PART II

THE DISTINCTIVE CONTRIBUTION OF THEOSOPHY TO CHRISTIAN THOUGHT

(Lecture delivered at the Annual Convention of the Theosophical Society at the Queen's Hall, London, 12 June 1926)

H.P. BLAVATSKY'S CONTRIBUTION

THE original contribution of Theosophy to Christian thought, through the person of Madame Blavatsky, was decidedly high spirited and vigorous. She denounced the Christianity of her time, often with much logic and penetrating acumen, and the Theosophical Society, not altogether undeservedly, acquired the reputation of being anti-Christian. But to understand properly the earlier phases of the Society's work it is necessary to cast our minds back to the conditions of thought which prevailed when Madame Blavatsky brought Theosophy to the western world.

The conflict between religion and science was at its height; and even if official Christianity could no longer make use of the *auto-da-fe*, it was still able to forge and employ the weapon of social ostracism. It will be within the memory of some still living how the early Darwinists were subjected to petty persecution in one way or another; they were reputed to be godless and atheists, and society people forbade their daughters to call at the houses of such 'dreadful people.' The letters of Darwin to Huxley are amusing, and yet make very pathetic reading.

Nowadays bishops and canons of the Establishment are sturdy evolutionists, and even the Catholic Truth Society is able to assure the public that belief in evolution is not incompatible with Roman Catholicism. Things have so changed that we find it difficult to realize how reactionary was the Christian thought of the day. The story of creation in seven days, as narrated in Genesis, was taken quite literally; and in England the Biblical chronology of Archbishop Ussher, which placed the creation of the world in 4004 B.C., found common acceptance. The doctrine of the verbal inspiration of the Scriptures by God the Holy Ghost was held in its entirety. Belief in everlasting hell-fire was everywhere prevalent; the revolt against it was only just beginning.[1] Missionary maps were drawn in which the so-called heathen countries were coloured black to show how much of the world was still wrapped in the darkness of error. The doctrine of the vicarious atonement was held in its crudest substitutionary form, and, interwoven with it, was its twin doctrine of justification by faith. According to this widely accepted theory, belief in 'the cleansing blood of Jesus' washed away all sin and, quite irrespective of good works, ensured a place in heaven.

Against such religious obscurantism, of which this is no exaggerated picture, Madame Blavatsky ranged her artillery. Every master-builder must clear away the rubbish which encumbers the site of his intended structure. And if it be 'anti-Christian' to have disencumbered Christianity of such distorted theories as these, then many among the leaders of the present generation of Christian teachers must stand condemned with Madame Blavatsky. She herself was careful to explain that it was 'Churchianity' (as she called it) to which she was opposed, not the religion of Christ.

---

[1] Canon (afterwards Dean) Farrar's *Eternal Hope* was published in 1878, and Samuel Cox's *Salvator Mundi* at about the same period. It is to be remarked that Origen and Scotus Eringena were universalists.

Eastern Wisdom and Evolution

Madame Blavatsky's work was at once destructive and constructive. She was not one of those who tear down religious faith without having something to offer in its place. The Theosophical Society was to open up to the western world the treasure-house of eastern wisdom. It was essential to show that the other great religions of the world also contained the highest revelation and that Christianity could learn much from Oriental philosophy and psychology. The idea could no longer be perpetuated that the Hebrews had the sole monopoly of divine truth and, alone among all other nations in the pre-Christian dispensation, worshipped the true God. Above all, it was necessary to insist that, in the domain of religion, natural law still held sway; for the most epoch-making event in the thought of the century had occurred—the promulgation by Darwin and Wallace of the doctrine of evolution, a doctrine that was to revolutionize the thinking of the whole world, and to which it was the mission of Theosophy to supply the spiritual corollary.

This, then, was the contribution that Madame Blavatsky made to Christian thought. It needs only to be understood in order to receive the high recognition it deserves.

THEOSOPHY A CO-ORDINATING SCHEME

IN the years which have run their course since the death of H.P. Blavatsky the theosophical teaching has steadily expanded and developed. As Theosophy has contributed much to the understanding of Hinduism and Buddhism, so also has it cast a flood of light upon the Christian religion. And let me at once make it clear that I do not claim that the ideas which I shall class as theosophical are found only within the precincts of the Theosophical Society. Many of them are by no means peculiar to Theosophists, although some are. But I do affirm that Theosophy as a coherent system of thought brings a new meaning into Christian teaching and makes a distinctive contribution to Christian thought.

Theosophy is a systematized scheme of thought, singularly inclusive and coherent. Its supreme value is that it takes many otherwise isolated facts of life and fits them into an ordered and comprehensive world-scheme. Why are we here? Whence came we? Whither going? These are questions which ought to be of interest to everybody. And religion should explain to man the purpose of his existence, why he is in the world, what he is intended to do, his relationship with the world around him, with his fellow-men, with God. Hinduism, as is well known, has its six schools of philosophy, and has always maintained the close connection between philosophy and religion. The Upanishads, for example, are permeated with philosophy. Christianity, on the other hand, has no fountain-head of philosophy in its scriptures. Christ (so far as history tells us) founded no philosophical school, as did Shankaracharya and Buddha. The earliest Fathers of the Church were Platonists, but in the Middle Ages the tendency grew increasingly strong, and finally triumphed, to separate off scholastic theology on the one hand and philosophy on the other into separate watertight compartments. Philosophizing came, in consequence, to be regarded as a secular pursuit. Hence Christianity can claim no traditional philosophy as can Hinduism, and official western religion has failed in one of its chief duties.

Our theosophical writers tell us that this poverty of Christianity in the matter of philosophy is due to the exclusion of the Gnostic Doctors from the early Church.[1] That is no doubt true to some extent. But it is well also to remember that Gnosticism included many rather wild extravagances, both of doctrine and practice.

Be that as it may, there is certainly room in Christianity for the theosophical explanation of the purpose of life with its teaching of the divinity latent in all men and the gradual unfoldment of man's divine powers through repeated incarnations. Christianity, as such, has said little about the purpose of existence. Man exists, we are vaguely told, in order that 'God may be glorified,' or 'to know God and to serve Him for ever.'[2] These clauses acquire an added significance if applied to the God within, for it is profoundly true that man's task is to glorify the God within him—to cause Him to shine forth in the perfection of His glory and splendour—and to do His service.

God Without and God Within

The theosophical conception of the world-order enables us, furthermore, to reconcile two perpetually conflicting tendencies in Christianity. In the old-fashioned doctrine of the last century God was seen as external to man. The revolt against a personal God was directed chiefly against an extra-cosmic deity having, none the less, human attributes (and of these not

---

[1] Cf. C.W. Leadbeater, *The Christian Creed*, pp. 23-26; *The Inner Life*, Vol. I. pp. 178-180.

[2] 'Man's chief end is to glorify God, and to enjoy Him for ever.' (*The Westminster Catechism*).

always the highest) who from time to time intruded himself into the cosmos in order to work miracles and abrogate the reign of natural law. In the views of the Atonement then current this idea of a God external to man also takes prominence. The literature of the subject is full of forensic theories of ransom and satisfaction. Christ's Sacrifice was made to appease the wrath of a God sitting in judgement on the human race. Against these views of an external God dealing with his creatures by means of covenants and juridical transactions, a great wave of mysticism swept in by way of reaction and laid stress on the immanence of God in His universe and in man. Suspected and ridiculed at first, mysticism has steadily won its way to recognition in religious thought. But the pendulum always swings to the one extreme after the other and the danger now is that, in the discovery of the God within, men will lose sight of the God without. Much New Thought literature, and that which passes under the name of the 'new mysticism,' tends towards unbridled subjectivism. If people are taught to look for everything inside themselves they tend to become self-centred and to lose their sense of values. Theosophy, with its doctrine of the macrocosm and the microcosm, introduces an element of sound common sense into this welter of emotional subjectivism. It is true that the Kingdom of God is within us and that we are heirs to those good things which pass man's understanding. Yet our life is but a slow and gradual process of unfolding the flower of divinity within ourselves, and that divinity is often more unfolded in other persons than in ourselves. The Christ present in the Blessed Sacrament of the Altar is usually a 'stronger' Christ than that as yet awakened in your heart or mine. And the one kindles the other into greater activity.

Direct Knowledge of God

It would be possible, granted the necessary time, to take one doctrine after another of the Christian faith and see how Theosophy extends and enriches its meaning. There is, however, one great contribution that Theosophy makes to Christian Thought—one which is indicated by the name 'Theosophy' itself—the theory that direct knowledge of spiritual things is possible to man. Any impartial critic must admit that Christian theology occupies itself with a great many subjects that are beyond the range of ordinary human understanding. The original matter of these doctrines is regarded as revealed truth; but as, in the course of time, disunion and heresy arise in the Church, doctrines come to be defined and formulated and thus gradually accumulate into a system of theology. In *The Soul of a Bishop*, H.G. Wells creates a striking situation in which the bishop (who has been much occupied with definitions of the nature of God) is given a potion to drink which sends him out of his body. He finds himself experiencing a new sense of freedom and of the spaciousness of things. Catching sight of his brain, he is struck by the absurdity of trying to express all this heightened sense of reality through 'that little box of brains.' So it is with theology. Its discussion is felt to be barren and profitless because in handling it we are employing faculties of our being incommensurate with the task. What has the lower mind to do with the mysteries of the divine existence? There is only one way of apprehending the deeper spiritual truth—that is to be, to become, the thing discussed. One does not understand love by talking around and about it, but rather by loving.

Now, Theosophy maintains that man, by virtue of the eternal Spirit within him, can know God. That this direct knowledge is possible has been the contention of the long line of philosophers called Theosophists, or mystics, stretching back to the earliest days of philosophic thought. Since man is a fragment of God (or has the divine spark in him) it is possible for him to know God whose nature he shares. And, by unfolding the powers of God within him (which is the purpose and method of evolution) he approaches slowly, yet with utter certainty, towards union with the divine omniscience, gaining in that growth an ever fuller knowledge of the universe which is the expression or manifestation of God.

This view of things at once opens up new horizons of thought. It lessens in no way the value of scripture or tradition which contain much of the original teaching of the Christ and are therefore a precious heritage. But it means that spiritual truths are at all times capable of reverification by spiritually-developed men, and that it is as possible to speak with the authority of first-hand knowledge in this twentieth century as it was in the first century of the Christian era.

Prayers for the Dead

As a simple illustration of what is meant, we may take a subject which is one of perpetual controversy among Christians—the question of prayers for the dead. The older churches—the Roman Catholic and Eastern Orthodox—encourage their people to pray for 'the faithful departed.' Protestants at the Reformation all rejected this custom. Such prayers were excluded from the Anglican Prayer Book but have been widely restored in the Anglican Church through the Catholic Revival, much to the distress of its Protestant section. It is a practice which rests on tradition rather than on scripture, for there is no clear warrant for it in scripture save in the Book of Maccabees which Protestants do not accept.[1] How simple the whole matter becomes for the Theosophist; for a comparatively slight quickening of the higher faculties latent in all men enables him to see the dead and to ascertain beyond any shadow of doubt that they are helped by our prayers and loving thoughts. I chose this particular subject by way of illustration because it is not so far removed from our grasp. There are other doctrines whose verification takes us up into far higher reaches of spiritual consciousness; and yet others—some of them relating to God—which are so far above the possibility of our comprehension that they must be included for the present in the category of pure revelation outside the possibility of our verification.

The experiences of the higher consciousness are such that points of view which down here seem contradictory are, in that condition, often realized as supplementary to each other. I have sometimes wondered if it would be really too absurd to say that one endorsed the orthodox faith and at the same time held all the heresies. This much, at any rate, is profoundly true: that the soundest student of theology or metaphysics is he who develops the higher powers of consciousness which enable him to contact direct the truths to be investigated, and not he who talks about them and theorizes intellectually.

Kenosis

I go back to Mr. Wells's remark as to how impossible it is to express the deeper mysteries of the spirit through our little brain-boxes in order to point out, in passing, that this is one approach to a problem which has greatly occupied theologians, namely, the theory of *kenosis*, according to which Christ, in taking upon Himself the human form, voluntarily 'emptied Himself' (which is what the word means) of certain Divine attributes.[2] We do well, I think, to bear in mind that the consciousness of the Great Ones embodies itself in collective as well as singular manifestations. The Second Person of the Blessed Trinity is incarnate in the whole universe, and the Christ is the special epiphany or manifestation of the Second Person to the world—the

---

[1] *Vide* also 2 Timothy 1. 16-18; iv. 19. Some infer from the narrative that Onesiphorus was dead. But this is guesswork; he might merely have been separated from his family.

[2] *Vide* the long essay on 'The Consciousness of Our Lord' in Bishop Gore's *Dissertations*.

channel through which those forces flow. It is impossible for the plenitude of that great consciousness to be expressed through any human personality, however great and splendid, for physical embodiment is in itself a limitation.

I would conclude by saying that a theology can only justify itself and aspire to permanency in so far as it partakes of the character of a theosophy. Proceeding on this train of thought, we are led to the conclusion that the same mystical experience is reached by people of different religions and that it cannot be claimed as the exclusive possession of any one faith. Theosophists have continually maintained that all the great religions have their roots in the Divine Wisdom. Well did St. Augustine say: 'The very thing, which now is called the Christian religion, existed among the ancients and never did not exist from the beginnings of the human race, until Christ Himself came in the flesh, from which time the true religion, which already existed, began to be called Christian.'[1]

---

[1] *Retractatus*, 1,13, 5.

ETHICS

ON the side of ethics Theosophy has also its contribution to make. In the first place, it helps us to compose the vexed question of human relationships by its special view of the brotherhood of man. That brotherhood, originating from the great truth that we are all sons of the one Divine Father, exists as a fact in the higher world of man's being. It is man's duty, and at the same time the indication of his progress, to bring down this brotherhood as realized experience into the lower worlds of being. There is a duality in every man. On the one side, he is the product of evolution through the lower kingdoms of Nature and the lower stages of human development, and has carried along with him many animal propensities. On the other, he is a mirror of the divine perfection, still rough and unpolished and distorting the perfect image of God, but occasionally reflecting lights of dazzling and superb splendour.

The animal residue makes for separateness and confusion, and we do well to begin our attempt at brotherliness by looking for the glimpses of the divine light in our fellows and cultivating our appreciation of these. A man who is dirty and rude is not a brotherly object at the level of his dirt and rudeness. But he is so at the buddhic level, and we had better begin there (or at whatever reflection of it we can touch); and, having seen the Divine Pilgrim in him, we shall presently be able to relegate the dirt and rudeness to their place of proper subordination.

The Sermon on the Mount

It is impossible to discuss ethics in relation to Christian thought without considering the bearing of the Sermon on the Mount upon the subject. The ethics of the Sermon on the Mount are not, of course, peculiar to Christianity. Five centuries before the Christian era, Gautama, the Buddha, taught: 'Hatred ceases not by hatred at any time; hatred ceases only by love.'[1] But the influence of this sublime ethical teaching of the Christ on the world has been marvellous and far-reaching.

Unfortunately, it has come to be regarded as of universal or general application to all Christians and, since it naturally comes into direct conflict with the foundations of our civilization, an alarming discrepancy is observable between precept and practice. In the event of war, for instance, there is a natural instinct of patriotism which prompts a man to take up arms in the defence of his country, to say nothing of the reasoned logic that, granted the imperfections of human society, the Sermon on the Mount is unpractical idealism. As Bishop Magee[2] of Peterborough said, if it were put into practice society would go to pieces in a fortnight. That Christianity should have an official code of ethics which has to be disregarded and treated as inapplicable during the most solemn crises of human life is obviously a source of weakness.

Not For the Multitude

The spiritual consciousness of man responds to a noble and beautiful ideal like the Sermon on the Mount, only it is regarded as a counsel of perfection and put into application only so far as circumstances will permit. It is here that Theosophy does us the great service of bringing logic and sincerity into our concept of Christian ethics. Dr. Besant pointed out that the Sermon on the Mount was not preached to the multitude at large, but to the disciples. 'And seeing the

---

[1] *Dhammapada,* ,dviii., 37.
[2] Afterwards Archbishop of York.

multitude,' says St. Matthew, 'he went up into a mountain: and when he was set, his disciples came unto him.'[1] St. Luke also suggests that it was to the disciples that He spoke, for though the narrative refers to the great multitude of people who came to hear Him and to be healed of their diseases, it continues: 'And he lifted up his eyes on his disciples, and said....'[2] The narrative in Luke also states that the sermon was preached on the plain, though he had previously spent the night in prayer on the mountain. Dr. Besant reminds us that 'the mountain' was a technical term of the Mysteries. It evidently refers to a condition of spiritual consciousness, and, when understood in that fashion, gives new meaning to many passages in Scripture. The Law was delivered to Moses on the mount.[3] Moreover, the Tabernacle was made after the pattern shown to Moses in the mount,[4] and the writer of the Epistle to the Hebrews also interprets this in a mystical sense.[5] Christ was transfigured on the mount.[6]

In view of all this, it is not extravagant to claim that the sermon was addressed to the disciples and not to the world in general, and was in the nature of instruction specially applicable to those dedicated to the religious life.

Path of Forthgoing and Path of Return

In her pamphlet, 'The Relativity of Hindu Ethics,' Dr. Besant shows how the ethics on the *nivritti marga*, or Path of Return, are necessarily different from those of the *pravritti marga* or Path of Forthgoing. In the original caste system of Hinduism the ethical duties of the people were graded according to their different stages of evolution and the dharma that were theirs. Those of the Kshattriya or warrior caste were different from those of the Brahman or priestly caste. It would be difficult, and perhaps dangerous, to introduce a system of graded or relative ethics into our Western civilization where democracy has confused the castes worse even than in India. But it might well be recognized that the Sermon on the Mount was never intended to apply to the man in the street. As things are now, the critics of the Churches and the adversaries of Christianity have the arguments their own way. It is demoralizing to affirm your belief in a theory which, in effect, you do not and cannot practise. A sensible declaration of Christian ethics is urgently needed which shall take into account the inequalities of human development and the fact that the state of civilization at any given period of the world's history is largely determined by the actual capacity for righteousness of the people who compose it. Until the close of the *manvantara* it is useless to expect people to be perfect.

---

[1] Matthew v. 1.

[2] Luke vi. 20.

[3] Exodus xxiv. 12-18.

[4] Exodus xxv. 40.

[5] Hebrews viii, 5; ix. 23.

[6] Matthew xvii, 1 et seq.

WORSHIP AND CEREMONIAL

CHRISTIANITY may conveniently be studied under the three aspects of philosophy, ethics, and worship. We now come to the third and last of these divisions, that of worship. As I said at Adyar last Christmas:[1] Theosophy makes its own contribution to the elucidation of religious philosophy and ethics, though in both of these departments one can go reasonably far without having to use the key of Theosophy to unlock further recesses of knowledge; but in the understanding of religious ceremonial we can advance nowhere without the aid of Theosophy.

Origin of Christian Ritual and Sacraments

Christianity is essentially ceremonial in its worship. It possesses a number of rites coming down from the earliest traditions of the religion, of which the most important are called sacraments. Occult research substantiates the belief that the sacraments were instituted by Christ Himself. It has been contended by anti-Catholic controversialists that the ritual and ceremonial element was a later importation into Christianity from surrounding paganism,[2] and this view has found some support from modern sceptical scholarship. Opinions upon the question of how far Christianity at its inception was influenced by the Mystery religions are much divided. The truth is that upon most questions of Christian origins the evidence available is too scanty to justify the sure grounding of any one of the many theories advanced. Scholars will argue from the bias of their temperament and of the age in which they live.[3] I permit myself, however, to quote the opinion of one who, although favourable to the mystic exegesis of religion, is a critical scholar and student of historical tendencies. The Rev. Dr. W.F. Cobb goes so far as to say: 'Recent research has proved as convincingly as anything can be proved that, so far from Christianity arising from an exclusive and closed system of truth in the midst of surrounding error, it is more true to say that its roots ran deep into contemporary life, and that there was little that was new in it except the higher life which came down to earth in the person of its Founder.'[4] Further, 'If it be urged that Christianity bears every mark of having been originally a growth inside Judaism before it underwent a process of "acute Hellenisation," and that therefore it is illegitimate to seek to explain its origins from outside Judaism, we reply that at the beginning of our era Judaism itself had yielded to the eclectic movement which was the dominant intellectual force in the Roman Empire between the death of Alexander the Great and the birth of Jesus Christ, and had opened its doors to every religious impulse which was to be found between India and Spain. So far, then, from the fact that Christianity appeared as an offshoot from Judaism being any proof of its exclusive character, it is much more a proof to the contrary. Judaism had become the host of all the speculations of all the existing religions....'[5]

---

[1] 'The Revival of the Mysteries', Convention Lecture, Adyar, December 1925.

[2] *The Two Babylons*, by the Rev. Alexander Hislop and *Paganism in the Papal Church* by W.J. Wilkins.

[3] Reincarnation gives support to the idea that groups of people who make vocal special tendencies of thought incarnate in periodic cycles. The Montanists are much in evidence nowadays.

[4] *Mysticism and the Creed*, p. 20.

[5] Ibid., p. 21.

Manifestation Demands Form

Now the objection commonly made against the sacramental system is a twofold one, though it would be truer, perhaps, to say that it is vaguely felt rather than clearly reasoned. First of all, there is a widespread objection to forms and ceremonies, to which is commonly added a dislike of 'bowing and scraping,' whatever that may mean! This objection is illogical. So long as we have to deal with manifestation, so long have we to deal with form; where there is spirit and matter there is life and form.[1] We cannot escape from forms and ceremonies until the divine breath is again indrawn and the manifested universe ceases to be. Every action of ours in the course of the day is really a ceremony. Think of the marvellous ritual of the body, of which the breath, the beating of the heart and constant change of self-expression are typical. The Quaker who thinks that he has dispensed with all forms and ceremonies in religion has not really done so. He has only substituted others of a simpler, and perhaps less effective, kind. What is really meant, then, in the common phrase about disliking forms and ceremonies is a dislike of certain special forms and ceremonies. Indeed, I suspect that sometimes the person who professes most loudly to dislike forms cares most about them and is consequently critical of imperfect ones. The dislike is, in some cases, brought over from a past life of persecution by the Church; usually it is due simply to ignorance and a want of understanding, much on the same principle that insular people find foreign customs peculiar and irritating.

Spiritual not Divorced from Material

The other objection to the sacramental theory is less crude though usually not very clearly defined. It exists—and, in fact, is extremely widespread in these days—as a vague idea that true religion is something 'spiritual' and therefore independent of physical rites or objects. 'God is Spirit; and they that worship him must worship him in spirit and in truth,'[2] is the favourite text quoted in support of this idea. The question really turns on the point whether the spiritual is divorced from the material and the superphysical from the physical. To suppose that there is this divorce between the realms of spirit and matter is to become an accomplice to the heresy of the Manichaeans who are supposed to have held that matter was inherently evil.

As Dr. Steiner pithily says: 'In the end it all resolves itself into the fact that man ordinarily carries body, soul and spirit about with him, yet he is conscious only of the body, not of the soul and spirit, and that the student attains to a similar consciousness of soul and spirit also.'[3] While in physical incarnation our superphysical processes are largely initiated from the physical body, and it is through and from that body that we have to work. Hence religion, far from leaving the physical body out of consideration, must, in fact, devote much attention to it; and the mediation of divine grace by physical objects is eminently reasonable as a theory.

---

[1] It is interesting to note that the theosophical theory is adumbrated by Coventry Patmore among his mystic aphorisms. People 'forget that science is certainly acquainted with at least one kind of substance which is not matter, and which has none of the properties of matter; I mean ether. What hinders, then, that there should be many kinds of substances, each, more subtle than that below it, as ether is more subtle than matter; and why not correspondent ranges of being until you reach the absolute and underivative substance God?' (*The Rod, the Root and the Flower*, p. 85). [Modern science no longer feels the need for the "ether" as a way of accomplishing 'action at a distance;' e.g., electromagnetism works in vacuum. [Ed.]]

[2] John iv. 24.

[3] *The Way of Initiation*, p. 142.

Mysticism and Occultism not Incompatible

In practice, nobody contends that the material cannot be the vehicle of the spiritual. People flock to hear a popular speaker whose words of burning idealism make real to them the life of the spirit; and music, painting, architecture, sculpture and the beauty of the landscape can all convey inspiration in the physical world. There is no justification for the idea that physical things are not channels of spiritual power or that inspiration must come direct from within and not from without. There are springs of spiritual life which well up within the individual soul, but there are also sources of that selfsame life in the world outside, whether in objects or in people. To attempt to limit the operation of divine grace to some closed internal process of the soul is irrational. The mystic tends, as a rule, to centre himself far too exclusively on his own internal experiences. I once heard it said, in reference to the Theosophical Society, 'You can never make a Society out of mystics, for each mystic is a law unto himself; you can only make up a working body out of occultists,' and the remark has ever since remained impressed upon me. I suspect that there are many more balanced occultists than there are balanced mystics, for, while I have met many occultists who could understand and sympathize with the way of the mystic, I have never yet met a thoroughgoing mystic who had any patience with the way of the occultist. After all, the two ought not to be incompatible; why should not a man be both occultist and mystic? The Roman Catholic Church, whose norm of worship is sacramental, can show great heights of mystical achievement. Indeed, I should be inclined to suggest that it is through the regular use of the external steadying power of the sacraments that inner mystical development of the religious type can most safely be cultivated.

Theosophy Explains the Modus Operandi

Theosophy is able to explain the *modus operandi* of the sacraments with clarity and precision because it gives us an understanding of the superphysical worlds. 'One reason why the whole idea and practice of the Eucharist strikes so many people as unnatural, meaningless and anachronistic is...that the rest of life is so unlike it,' says a Nonconformist writer.[1] People whose outlook on life is bounded by the physical plane fail quite naturally to understand ceremonies whose whole foundation rests on the interaction of the visible and invisible worlds. It is as though they were trying to solve a jigsaw puzzle from which several of the component parts (represented by the superphysical worlds) were missing.

Sense Objects as Media of Superphysical Forces

On these grounds the use of lights, colour, incense, sound and music, architecture, vestments, gestures and symbols in the ceremonial processes of religion is rational because all are, or can be, vehicles and channels of special forces. If it be objected that there is much complication in all this, the answer is obvious. The advocates of simplicity in all things are voicing a natural reaction from the confusion and ostentation of modern civilization. But they often seem to forget that man is a complex being who, for the proper education of his faculties, often needs a complex environment. Do we find any trace of simplicity in Nature—in the panorama of the star-decked heavens, in the verdure which clothes the earth, or in the animal life with which it teems? And if one man be complex, how much more so an aggregation of some hundreds of

---

[1] Rev. W.G. Peck, *The Value of the Sacrament*, p. xv.

men! Moreover, true as it is that a highly-developed man can dispense with outer aids and work by the developed power of the God within, yet he is what he is only as the product of a highly complicated past. The complexity exists in himself instead of in his envirorment.

The Meaning of a Sacrament

Let us turn now to the rites called sacraments. Probably the best definition of a sacrament is that given in the Anglican Prayer Book—'an outward and visible sign of an inward and spiritual grace given unto us, ordained by Christ himself, as a means whereby we receive the same, and a pledge to assure us thereof.'[1] Perhaps it would be more appropriate to say, 'an inward and spiritual grace given to us through an outward and visible sign,' thus making the sacrament essentially the grace rather than its vehicle. The word 'sign' may here be understood as sigil, or equivalent of 'symbol,' which last word comes from the Greek *sumbolon*, meaning 'thrown together' and thus means a 'correspondence' between the visible and invisible worlds.[2]

Theology takes cognizance of two factors in the external composition of a sacrament, namely, the 'matter' and the 'form.' The 'matter' is the material used, such as water, bread, wine; the 'form' is the words pronounced which determines the meaning of the act. It should be noted that the 'outward and visible sign' ('matter' and 'form') always stand in relation to the spiritual change which the sacrament effects. Thus in Baptism the pouring of water signifies the washing away of sin, and also the descent of heavenly blessing, the dew of divine grace. The fact that the physical actions have a natural meaning is of interest in that they suggest to the mind and heart thoughts which are in harmony with the spiritual process accomplished and thus open the way to its action on the recipient. This is the purpose of the *porrectio instrumentorum* or the delivery of the 'working tools.'

Baptism

The theological idea of Baptism is that it remits 'original sin' inherited from the fall of Adam. The Theosophical explanation of this is that the child brings over from past lives tendencies towards either good or evil. Baptism arrests the development of the germs of evil while giving an impetus to those of good, so that the good may have a better chance of prevailing over the evil. The neophyte is at the same time 'grafted into the Mystical Body of Christ' or, in other words, admitted to the fellowship of that mystical organization, existing not alone on the physical plane but also in the higher worlds, which serves as the vehicle for the power and blessing of the Christ.

Confirmation

In Confirmation, which is intended to be administered after the Ego has entered into the normal measure of his relationship with his vehicles, the link with the Christ is further extended. There is, once more, a cleansing of the personality, and then a strengthening of the Ego

[1] A Catechism.

[2] The same idea is involved in the distinction between 'accidents' and 'substance' in the doctrine of transubstantiation. The 'accidents' (Lat. *ad* = to, and cadere = to fall) are the outer phenomenal physical manifestation of bread and wine. The 'substance' (Lat. *Sub* = beneath, and *stans* = standing) is the superphysical basis or subsistence thereof. It is the 'substance' which is changed 'across' (Lat. *trans*); the accidents remain.

in the atmic, buddhic and causal vehicles by the power of the Holy Spirit. Of this, the laying on of the bishop's hand, the signing with the cross of sacrifice, and the anointing with consecrated oil is the outer symbol. Oil is at once a fuel, suggesting the fire of the Holy Spirit, and a healing balm.

Holy Communion

In the Holy Communion the matter is bread and wine; the form is the words of consecration. As bread and wine feed and nourish the physical body so does Christ's life, of which they become the vehicles, nourish us spiritually. Christ is thereby incorporated in us and we in Him; we become for the time being *alter Christus*, and should strive to act as though we were He.

Holy Orders

In Holy Orders the linking of the candidate with Our Lord, which was begun at Baptism and continued in Confirmation, is carried on to still closer degrees of union. In *The Science of the Sacraments*, Bishop Leadbeater gives a chart of the details of this process, showing how the various Orders affect the higher principles of their recipients. This is how it comes to be that the Christ is the true Minister of all sacraments, not the human personality who, in the exercise of his office, is His instrument. This is the real explanation of what is called the doctrine of the Apostolic or Episcopal Succession.[1] It is the Lord Himself who baptizes, confirms, and administers the Sacrament of His Body and Blood. In reality, nothing could be more impersonal than this conception of sacramental procedure; to emphasize still further the submergence of the priest's personality, he is so clothed as to suggest in every way the office and not the man. In this sacrament, the 'matter' is the imposition of the bishop's hand or hands and the delivery of the instrument of the offices conferred.

Absolution, Unction, Marriage

Of the remaining three sacraments, Absolution straightens out the distortions in the relation between the lower and higher self caused by wrongdoing. It does not enable a man to escape from the Karma of his acts, but it does help to raise him from that state of spiritual death which we are told is 'the wages of sin.' Unction fortifies against sickness or prepares for death, and Marriage unites the contracting parties in due spiritual sympathy.

The Sacraments Ordained by Christ

The definition of a sacrament says that it was 'ordained by Christ.' When we speak of sacraments we mean certain rites in which Christ is operative in a direct and special sense. The Second Person of the Holy Trinity is present everywhere in His universe, yet in the consecrated

---

[1] Madame Blavatsky is often quoted as rejecting this doctrine in *Isis Unveiled*, Vol. II, p. 124. An examination of the text shows that the doctrine there rejected is that which is properly known in theology as the Supremacy of St Peter, and has no connection whatever with the doctrine of the conferring of Holy Orders. On the question of St Peter's connection with Rome scholars are divided. Bishop Leadbeater stated that in the early Church the head of each community was called Peter (the Rock), and that the difficulty which faces clairvoyant investigators is that of finding so many Peters. (*Vide The Hidden Side of Christian Festivals*, p. 291.)

Host we have a special intensification and localization of that Presence; He is more immediately present. It is well to emphasize this point, for much modern mysticism loses itself in vague and sentimental talk about all life being sacramental, and equates a sacrament with a symbol or simply with the expression of life through form. A family meal may be the scene of much glad affection and corporate feeling but it is not therefore a sacrament in the technical sense of the word.

Our definition goes on to say that this 'inward and spiritual grace' is 'given unto us.' We receive a free gift of grace. It is the idea of the unity of all life. As we help those who stand below us on the ladder of evolution so can we be helped by those who stand above us.

There is no need to comment on the remainder of the definition, save to mention that occult research supports the *ex opere operato* theory of Catholic tradition which does not make the virtue of the sacrament depend upon the subjective disposition of the recipient (*ex opere operantis*). The spiritual response of the worshipper has much influence on what he receives from the sacrament; but the consecration of the bread and wine takes place objectively on the altar and not by virtue of its reception with faith by the worshipper.

Evelyn Underhill on Magic

It is the custom of modern apologists for the sacramental system to disclaim all sympathy with any 'magical' view of the sacraments. When Bishop Leadbeater describes the sacraments as 'the magic of the Christian Church' he excites frenzy and exacerbation in the tents of the orthodox. Yet it is, after all, only a question of names. As Evelyn Underhill aptly says: 'In magic...we have at any rate the survival of a great and ancient tradition, the true splendour and meaning of whose title should hardly have been lost in a Christian country; for it claims to be the science of those Magi whose quest of the symbolic Blazing Star brought them once at least to the cradle of the Incarnate God.' And again: 'Orthodox persons should be careful how they condemn the laws of magic for they unwittingly conform to many of them whenever they go to church. All formal religion is saturated with magic.'[1]

Magic, rightly understood, is but the science of using the forces of nature and of supernature. If natural law be the Will of God in operation it cannot be undignified or profane to study its *modus operandi*. Bishop Leadbeater, in his *The Science of the Sacraments*, writes with much detail of the mechanism of the sacramental processes, but no critic would be impartial who asserts that his attitude towards the holy realities involved is in any degree less reverent or spiritual than that of a Roman Catholic or Anglican theologian. The attempt to involve your opponents in the opprobrious practice of magic is no new chapter in the history of the *odium theologicum*. Athanasius 'was formally condemned of rebellion, sedition and a tyrannical use of his episcopal power, of "murder, sacrilege, and magic;" he was deposed from the See of Alexandria and prohibited from ever returning to that city.'[2]

Eastern Yoga and Western Mysticism

If I have chosen to show how Theosophy vindicates the principle of sacramental worship, it is because it is an unpopular cause and can, therefore, bear with a little championing. But Theosophy also helps us to understand that other aspect of worship which looks for God in

---

[1] *Mysticism*, p. 182.
[2] Newman's *The Arians of the Fourth Century*, p. 284.

the shrine of the human heart, and it shows that these two are not antagonistic to one another but complementary. Nowhere is the science of mystic contemplation more understandingly treated than in the oriental scriptures. If one takes up a book like Father Poulain's *The Graces of Interior Prayer*, one glimpses the Yoga of the East in Western garb and realizes how true is the claim of the eclectic Theosophist that mystical experience is the same in essence the world over and knows no barriers of race or creed.

Personally, I must confess to a dislike of that emotional subjectivism prominent in the writings of so many western mystics; it is a pleasure to turn from it to the homely philosophy of Angelus Silesius or the marvellous perception of Novalis or Coventry Patmore. If we contrast the exercises of meditation derived from theosophical sources with those prescribed in books of Christian piety, the balance of method and common sense seems to me to be decidedly on the side of the former. On all questions connected with the new psychology, New Thought and psycho-analysis, Theosophy, as Dr. Besant has said, 'is truly as a lamp in a dark place, as all who are willing to use it will find.'[1] Moreover, it brings to the subject the vitally important warning that exercises to unfold the powers of the consciousness and attempts to reach union with God can only safely be undertaken *pari passu* with the systematic purification of the vehicles, the method of which receives intensive treatment in theosophical literature. Otherwise there is danger of hysteria and neuropathy. The higher forces, coming down into a brain and a nervous organization unprepared to receive them, are liable to shatter them.

Of the contribution that Theosophy makes to our understanding of the position and office of the founder of the Christian faith it needs a tongue more eloquent than mine to tell. The identification of the Christ with the head of all faiths and the inspirer of all religious progress, who comes out into the world in each successive age or dispensation to reproclaim the essential truths of religion and morality in a form suited to that age, and who, in due course, will be among us again, is a message of sublime inspiration.

---

[1] *Foreword to Theosophy and the New Psychology.*

PART III

THE SACRAMENTS AND THE THEORY OF 'ECONOMY'

GENERAL CONCEPTS

THERE is, perhaps, no better definition of a sacrament than that given in the Catechism of the Anglican Prayer Book, namely, '...an outward and visible sign of an inward and spiritual grace given unto us, ordained by Christ Himself, as a means whereby we receive the same, and a pledge to assure us therefore.' The outward sign is a token or a figurative representation of the inward grace. The flowing of the water in baptism represents the mystical washing away of sin. The giving of bread and wine in the Eucharist is the symbol of our spiritual nourishment. And this outer sign so directs our outer attention and understanding that our whole being is made receptive to the grace that is outpoured.

This grace is 'given unto us.' A sacrament differs from other rites of the Church in that it carries with it 'a free gift of grace.' In prayer, and in choir offices like Vespers, there is a natural action of cause and effect at work. The response depends on the effort made by the worshippers. The same law of cause and effect continues to be operative in the sacrament, but the factor of grace is now introduced. What takes place is utterly beyond and out of all proportion to our human endeavour. This mighty outpouring of power is linked up with and made possible by virtue of that 'enduring sacrifice by which the world is nourished and sustained.'

The one criticism of the above Anglican definition which may suggest itself to someone who likes to view the universe *sub specie aeternitatis* is that the sacrament is identified primarily with the grace rather than with the sign or symbol through which that grace is transmitted.

The doctrine of the sacraments has been worked out with admirable precision in the Western Church. For their due administration a number of conditions are necessary. These can be outlined as follows:

I. The sacrament itself is viewed under the aspects of matter and form. (a) The 'matter' is the physical material and, perhaps, action used. In Baptism it is the pouring of water; in the Eucharist it is bread and wine; in the sacrament of Penance it is the due confession of sin.[1] (b) The 'form' is the accompanying form of words. In Baptism it is the words, 'I baptize thee' (or, as a variant in the Eastern Churches, 'The servant of God is baptized') in the Name of the Father, and of the Son, and of the Holy Ghost;' in the Eucharist it is the familiar formula used at the consecration of the host and of the chalice.

II. A second requirement is concerned with the person of the minister. For the Eucharist the minister of the sacrament must be of the rank of priest; for Holy Orders, a Bishop is essential. In the case of Baptism the minister should be a priest; failing the priest, a deacon may baptize; and, in cases of necessity, a layman or a laywoman may baptize. (Roman Catholic theologians say that a woman should not do it in preference to a man unless she be better instructed in the proceedings.) In the sacrament of Holy Matrimony the priest gives the nuptial blessing but the contracting parties themselves are the ministers of the sacrament.

III. A third requirement is that of 'intention.' What is required is the intention to do as the Church does. There have been theologians who maintained that for the sacrament to be valid the officiating minister must have in mind the detailed and orthodox view of the operation of the rite in use; the Council of Trent, however, decided the question in the earlier sense and, consequently, this is the official doctrine of the Roman Catholic Church.

---

[1] In early times, it is said to have been ashes used as a visible sign of penance. [Ed.]

Character

There are two other factors which remain for consideration. They are known as 'character' and 'jurisdiction.' Of the seven sacraments three impress character on the person who receives them. They work in him a permanent and indelible change, and on that account must not be repeated. These are the sacraments of Baptism, Confirmation, and Holy Orders. The other four—the Holy Eucharist, Matrimony, Penance, and Unction—may be repeated. If there is doubt about one of the character-conferring sacraments having been validly administered, the said sacrament is given *sub conditione*. The phrase used in conditional baptism, for instance, is 'If thou are not already baptized, then do I baptize thee....'

Jurisdiction

The view of the Western Church is that sacraments administered in Churches which have preserved the Apostolic Succession are valid provided that there is no reason to doubt the sufficiency and intention of the rite. The Roman Catholic Church denies the validity of Anglican Orders but admits that baptism is duly administered by clergy of the High Church party at any rate; their baptism ranks with that of laymen. Bishops of the Roman Catholic Church and of other historical Churches are vested with an administrative authority or jurisdiction over the diocese or area to which they are appointed. Sacraments administered within that sphere of jurisdiction by outsiders rank as 'irregular.' If an ordained priest of one such 'schismatical' Church—let us say of the Eastern Orthodox Church—were to submit to Rome and were to be approved for the priesthood he would not be re-ordained but would simply be regularized and vested with the jurisdiction hitherto lacking.

'Ex Opere Operato' and *'Ex Opere Operantis'*

The ideas briefly summarized in the foregoing paragraphs are those of the Roman Catholic Church. They would be subscribed to by the Anglo-Catholic party as well as by many 'moderate' churchmen of the Anglican Church. And they are held by Old Catholics in general and by some other separated bodies who have kept intact the apostolic succession of Orders. One cannot speak with exactitude and unreservedly about the Old Catholics, since from time to time Protestantism has made incursions upon some sections of that body. Of the various Protestant bodies there is no need to speak here.

The theory of the sacraments which we have been considering is described by the Latin words *ex opere operato*. What is meant by the phrase is that Christ Himself is the true minister of all sacraments and that, when the conditions above formulated are fulfilled, the sacraments work of their own virtue and power. It was St. Augustine who worked out this thesis with masterly skill and precision; basing it on the testimony of St. Paul: 'Yet not I but Christ liveth in me.'[1]

There is a contrary theory which has been widely held in the Anglican Church, according to which Our Lord is not truly and really present in the consecrated elements, for example, but rather in the heart of the faithful receiver. This theory goes by the name of *ex opere operantis*, and it implies that it is the disposition of the believer that is the condition of the sacramental presence and virtue.

---

[1] Galatians II, 20.

The Teaching of the Orthodox Church

The Eastern Orthodox Church repudiated Rome in the eleventh century because of the increasing claims of the Papacy. It consists of a number of autocephalous national Churches. There is an Qecumenical Patriach of Constantinople and there are Patriarchs of Alexandria, Antioch, Jerusalem, and Moscow. The Church is widely spread over a number of countries such as Russia, Greece, Yugoslavia, Romania, Bulgaria, Ukraine, Palestine, and Egypt. There are also so-called heretical and schismatical Churches.

The doctrinal history and outlook of the Orthodox Church is different in many respects from that of the Roman Catholic Church. It has no centralized papal authority; there has indeed been little intercourse or exchange of ideas between the various Churches until lately. The Eastern Church has shown marked reluctance to embark upon dogmatic definition. This has had its good side but it has also led to some inconsistencies of action to which we shall presently refer. The man who sets himself to study Orthodox theology is faced with the fact that one point of view argued with great skill and documentation by certain outstanding theologians will be repudiated with equal certainty by others.

The Orthodox Church claims to be the one true Church. The Roman Catholic Church is considered to have separated herself from the true fold because of her 'arrogant claims, innovations in dogma, worship and discipline.'

> If...we enquire...whether our [the Anglican] Sacraments and, indeed, whether the Sacraments of the Papalist, Assyrian, Armenian, and other 'heterodox' Churches, are valid, the Eastern Orthodox are bound to answer that, since there can be no true Sacraments outside the Church, they cannot consider the question of their validity as a *principle* at all.[1]

Zekos Rhossis remarks:

> ...a bishop who falls from the true universal church of the first eight centuries and changes the faith by novelties can never transmit to others the genuine episcopal office and true ordination.

This statement is based on the theory that the grace of the Holy Spirit is wanting from such ministrations, so that clergy who break away from the one Church become laymen. They are severed from the Body of Christ and from the fellowship of the Holy Spirit. This opinion is based on the concept of the exclusiveness of divine grace in the Church, outside of which (since divine grace does not exist) the sacraments are inoperative.

A natural reaction is always likely to set in against extreme and austere doctrines of this sort. Douglas quotes from a book by W.J. Birbeck entitled *Russia and the English Church*, containing the correspondence between William Palmer and M. Khomiakoff ranging over the years 1844-1845. Khomiakoff writes:

> Inasmuch as the earthly and visible Church is not the fullness and completeness of the whole Church which the Lord has appointed to appear at the final judgement of all creation, she acts and moves only within her own limits and...does not judge the rest of mankind and only looks upon those as excluded, that is to say, not belonging to her, who exclude themselves. The rest of mankind, whether alien from the Church or united to

---

[1] J.A. Douglas: *The Relation of the Anglican Churches with the Eastern Orthodox*, London 1931, p. 52.

her by ties which God has not willed to reveal to her, she leaves to the judgement of the Great Day.

The idea of a Mystical Church transcending the boundaries of any worldly organization is one familiar in the literature of religion.

The theory of the invalidity of sacraments administered outside the visible body of the Church dates from early times. There is no need to cite authorities at any length, but a few references may be given. The Anglican Father F.W. Puller testifies to this in his well-known book, *The Primitive Saints and the See of Rome*:

> The Post-Nicene Fathers for the most part teach that baptism administered by heretics is invalid, even though the right formula be used....

St. Basil is quoted as saying that 'the bestowal of the Spirit ceases by the severing of the order...and those that have broken away, having become laymen, have neither authority to baptize nor to ordain, nor yet are they able to pass on to others the Grace of the Holy Spirit from which they themselves have fallen away.'

WESTERN FORMULATION OF DOCTRINE

THE many schisms and conflicts with authority appearing in the early history of the Church rendered inevitable the formulation of the conditions under which Orders could be conferred and exercised. The Western Church developed a well-grounded distinction between Orders and Jurisdiction. In our study of Roman Catholic doctrine we have already seen that the sacraments of Baptism, Confirmation and Holy Orders are said to impress upon those who receive them 'character.' This character is seen as something different from grace and jurisdiction. The Roman Catholic Church acknowledges that character is conferred by the administration of these sacraments in heretical and schismatical churches which have retained the succession of Orders.

This validity of the sacraments is based on the fact that it is Christ Himself who is the true minister of all sacraments. The sacraments are not affected intrinsically by the worldly conduct of either minister or recipient. This view of the question is put forward with clearness and precision in the Thirty-Nine Articles of the Anglican Prayer Book. Article 26 reads: 'the unworthiness of the ministers...hinders not the effect of the Sacrament.' Question 19 of The Catechism of the Council of Trent teaches similarly. St. Augustine maintains that 'the Baptism of Christ is holy, even though administered by adulterers, for His holiness cannot be polluted and His divine grace is present in the Sacrament.'[1] Devine, in a Roman Catholic textbook entitled *The Sacraments Explained* quotes another passage from St. Augustine:

> Judas baptized, and yet after him none were rebaptized. John the Baptist baptized and after John they were rebaptized, because the baptism administered by Judas was the baptism of Christ but that administered by John was the baptism of John; not that we prefer Judas to John, but that we justly prefer the baptism of Christ, although administered by Judas, to the baptism of John, although administered by the hands of John.

Fortunately, the conclusions of Western theology are specially clear on the subject of Holy Orders, owing to their emergence from centuries of thought and experience during which the issues could be disencumbered of bias and party feeling and treated as questions of principle. St. Augustine's masterly defence of baptisms and ordinations administered by heretics settled that question for later generations, and was so conspicuously logical that it became the starting-point from which the doctrine of the sacraments was gradually systematized. Circumstances then forced into prominence the question of ordinations procured by simony or other sinister artifice. Time again decided in favour of the more spacious view. I quote from Wilhelm and Scannell:[2]

> The doubt continued...until the question was discussed with great clearness by Robert Pullen, whose opinion as to the validity of heretical, intruded and simoniacal ordinations was accepted by Alexander of Hales, St. Bonaventure, St. Thomas and Scotus.

What is lacking in schismatical Orders according to this perfectly logical thesis is not character but the gift of grace, which alone makes for salvation. This view was worked out in masterly fashion by St. Augustine and developed by subsequent theologians. It is the view and practice which has prevailed and has been everywhere accepted in the West. The Western

---

[1] *De Baptismo*.

[2] *Manual of Catholic Theology*, revised edition, 1908, Vol. II, p. 503. This is a favourite textbook in the Roman Catholic Church.

Church admits that even Jews and heathen are capable of administering validly the sacrament of Baptism in cases of necessity. Schism, therefore, is not healed by re-ordination but by contrition and the giving of jurisdiction by the competent authority.

The Principle of Economy

The Eastern Church developed a different method of procedure. It retained the primitive idea as to the invalidity of all sacraments outside its own pale; and it has continued to put into practice a form of procedure which dates from primitive times. This can be traced back to the time of St. Basil (c. 330-379). Dyovouniotes says that

> since the fifth century...the Eastern Church has applied with regard to the sacraments of schismatics and heretics who adhere to her the principle of economy, which has been in use in the Church from the beginning.

The word 'Economy' is derived from the Greek *oikonomia*. St. Basil speaks of 'an economy of many things' as justifying the recognition of certain extraneous baptisms; he also accepted certain episcopal Orders and he urged a certain Gennadius[1] not to avoid communion with the schismatic Bishop Proclus 'on account of the economies of the case...which at times must be strained a little beyond what is necessary.'

This Greek word carries with it a certain subtlety of meaning. It means, fundamentally, 'order' or 'arrangement.' We speak of the 'economy of nature' and the 'economy of the body,' in the sense of their workings. The word eventually came to be synonymous with administration; thus, we speak of 'political economy' and of 'economy' in finance. The term is analogous, in its ecclesiastical application, to the technical theological terms of 'indulgence' and 'dispensation.' Gavin suggests that it means 'the carrying out of the spirit rather than the exact and rigid letter of a law,' and he quotes a 'prominent Orthodox ecclesiastic' who likened it to 'the figure of a ship in a storm being lightened of valuable cargo for the purpose of saving human life.'[2] Neither of these two suggestions seems to meet the case. In actual practice Economy means that the Church may choose to validate acts which previously, from the Eastern point of view, have been null and void, by causing the Divine Grace to flow into them. The reconciliation is effected by the use of the holy oil of chrism in the case of persons received into the Orthodox Church who may have lapsed into schism or have received baptism or ordination at the hands of schismatics.

When one comes to study the history of the application of the principle of Economy in the Orthodox Church one is struck by the entire absence of any consistency in the proceedings. 'This diversity,' as Gavin rightly remarks, 'has laid her [the Orthodox Church] open to the charge of having no principle at all in such matters.' A few instances will suffice. The Synods of Constantinople held in 1261 and 1481 decided that converts to Orthodoxy should simply be chrismated. In 1629 the Synod of the Russian Church decreed that Western Christians, whether Roman Catholic or Protestant, should be rebaptized; and then in 1666-1667 reversed the decision. In subsequent times the Russian Church has dispensed even with chrismation. In 1718, with the consent of the Qecumenical Patriarch, it actually decided in favour of the recognition of Calvinist and Lutheran baptisms. In 1756, four Greek Patriarchs decided not to accept Western baptism; yet in spite of this, numbers of Roman Catholics and Protestants were accepted 'economically' in the ensuing century.

---

[1] Probably St. Gennadius I of Constantinople. [Ed.]

[2] F. Gavin: *Some Aspects of Contemporary Greek Orthodox Thought*, Milwaukee 1923, pp. 296, 297.

There have been numbers of cases of inter-communion between the Orthodox and the Anglicans, each receiving sacramental ministrations from the other. The Protestant Episcopal Bishop of Fond du Lac celebrated at the Orthodox Cathedral in Belgrade with Orthodox bishops and clergy present. On the other hand, in 1840 a bishop of a Uniate Church (one using the Orthodox rites but in communion with Rome) was rebaptized and re-consecrated. In 1920, a Roman Catholic priest was re-ordained as deacon by the Metropolitan of Nis. One of our own Liberal Catholic priests concelebrated with an Orthodox priest, at his invitation, in one of the British Colonies.

Economy and Non-Episcopal 'Orders'

There is one aspect of the Economy thesis which seems to merge into the region of the fantastic. It is stated that Economy can be applied to validate cases where the apostolic succession of Orders has been broken.

Yet it must be understood that the Church, as the dispenser of divine grace, can recognize the Orders and the sacraments in general of schismatics and heretics even if they have not been performed canonically and even if the Apostolic Succession be broken; and for reasons which may seem to her good and necessary the Church may reject the Orders and the sacraments in general of heretics and schismatics who do preserve the canonical order in the administration of the sacraments and possess unimpaired the Apostolic Succession.[1]

Theoretically her discretion as to such acceptance is complete, and by it she could re-invalidate sacraments which were deficient in rite and even in purpose. For example, she could accept Orders conferred by a Presbyterian.[2]

Dyovouniotes states quite unequivocally: 'That the Church, as steward of the divine grace, can recognize the ordination and sacraments in general of heretics and schismatics, among whom these are not canonically performed or the apostolic succession has been broken.'[3]

The usual divergence of opinion shows itself on this point. There were Orthodox churchmen present at the Lambeth Conference of 1930 who told the Anglican Bishop of Gloucester, in reply to a question put by him, that they did not endorse the theory just enunciated. The Patriarch of Alexandria said that the Church 'had no power to recognize ordinations in Churches where the apostolic succession had been broken.' Dyovouniotes goes on to say quite characteristically:

While the Patriarch of Alexandria...asserts that the Church can only recognize valid Orders as invalid, and not invalid Orders as valid, D. Georgiades asserts that the Church can only recognize invalid Orders as valid, and not valid Orders as invalid. These two opposite and one-sided opinions when united together constitute the true teaching of the Eastern Church, according to which the Church as steward of the divine grace can recognize invalid Orders as valid and valid Orders as invalid.

[1] Gavin, pp. 298-299.
[2] Douglas, p. 177.
[3] Dyovouniotes: Article on 'The Principles of Economy,' in *The Church Quarterly Review*, April 1953, pp. 98-99.

SOME COMMENTS ON THE DOCTRINE OF ECONOMY

THE Eastern Orthodox Church has many attractive features. It holds fast to what it considers to be the essentials of the Faith, yet it avoids the aggressive dogmatism so often characteristic of the Roman obedience. Its clergy are usually found to be kindly and hospitable. There is much that is wonderfully beautiful and dignified in its liturgy and in its ceremonial, but it gives the impression of not having moved with the ages. The liturgy is exceedingly lengthy—the sung celebration of the divine mysteries is likely to occupy three hours; furthermore, as is said in the Preface to our own liturgy, 'the Greek liturgies come before us like a sea of beautiful language, but they do not appear to be constructed on any framework whatever of coherent and consecutive thought.' At the more solemn moments of the Eucharist the celebrant is veiled from the people by the lowering of a curtain or by the closing of a door (there are some exceptions to this normal procedure) a custom which is assuredly a heritage of the esotericism of the Mysteries, as is also the custom in the Latin rite of saying the Canon of the Mass 'in Secret.' We find something of this reflected in the Orthodox theology which, while it has avoided the dangers of over-definition, lacks the coherence which we associate with all forms of modern thinking. However, many of its leaders are changing through contact with other Churches.

Let us now briefly examine the theories summed up in the word 'Economy.' Members of the Liberal Catholic Church will, in the first place, dissent from the assertion that the divine grace is not operative through the sacraments of Churches other than the Orthodox. To say that the sacraments of the great Roman Catholic Church are invalid and that their Eucharists are not true Eucharists, is to deny the continued experience of thousands of people. Yet we have also to join issue with the Roman theory that, while 'character' is conferred through 'schismatical' ordinations, the accompanying grace is withheld. Our own point of view would be that neither character nor grace is wanting where the true succession of Orders has been preserved, whether the Church style itself Old Catholic, Anglican, or Liberal Catholic. This attitude is abundantly justified by real and continuous experience.

The situation is other when we come to consider those Churches—Presbyterian and Nonconformist—which have not guarded the succession of Orders. In such cases *the ex opere operato* doctrine is not applicable. But we may be sure that in their rites a due measure of grace on the principle of *ex opere operantis* is at work. The worshipper in such cases will receive a blessing in proportion to his devotion and spiritual effort; and those who have experience of such bodies know that evangelical belief is often productive of the deepest sincerity and devotion. So much for general principles.

From this point of view the recognition of Orders or Baptism by economy is simply equivalent to an act of regularizing or granting lawful jurisdiction. There is enshrined within each Church organization a kind of collective consciousness, marvellous, often, in the richness and splendour of its atmosphere. By formal act of admission into that body-corporate a person is brought into relationship with that storehouse of blessing. In our own Church we have a simple Form of Admission where conditional re-baptism or confirmation does not need to be administered, as in the case of adult Roman or Old Catholics.[1] By this form of admission the candidate is brought into relationship with and into the fellowship of our Church. Priests in Orthodox and Roman Catholic Orders who have been admitted to office in our Church have, of course, been accepted in their priestly rank without any question of conditional ordination. Our

[1] Since 2001, the Form of Admission may also be used to admit to membership in the Church those who have been efficaciously Baptized, but not yet Confirmed. [Ed.]

usage in regard to Anglicans is different. There is evidence of baptism in the Anglican Church having been carelessly administered by a mere flicking of water in days gone by. That may, perhaps, be relegated to past history. We do, however, attach value to the use of the sacred oils alike in baptism and confirmation, and for that reason we make a practice of administering baptism *sub conditione* to those joining us from the Anglican Church. It is not that for one moment we consider the previously administered baptism invalid, but rather as lacking the plenitude of grace. For the same reason Anglican priests are ordained by us *sub conditione*. Moreover, the repetition of Confirmation and Orders in this conditional form maintains our status with the Roman Catholic Church which denies the validity of Anglican Orders.

Most of us would probably affirm that there are degrees of validity in the matter of the sacraments; that, for instance, while baptism by a layman is technically and actually valid—or to use another word, sufficient—it has not the same efficacy as that administered by a priest. The Latin word *validus*, like many other Latin words, translates itself through various shades of meaning. 'Efficacious' is perhaps a faithful rendering of the word, while 'strong' is one commonly received. So, then, there are degrees of efficacy and strength. If one makes distinctions of this sort they should not be interpreted as reflecting in any sense on the original outpouring of divine grace. That grace, so far as its normal and regular working is concerned, has to be transmitted through physical channels, and it rests with us to provide the most suitable physical conditions. In the case of all candidates for Orders the Liberal Catholic Church insists that there shall be due evidence of right baptism.

What are we to think about the recognition in terms of Economy of sacraments which are not valid from the Western point of view—let us say, to return to a case already cited, of Presbyterian Orders? My own view is that the divine grace flows wherever possible through the form used and adapts itself in some measure to that form. But the case now under review introduces a serious difficulty. If a Presbyterian minister were to be received into the priestly order simply by a process of chrismation, it is conceivable that Our Lord would use this external rite as the means through which the priestly character hitherto lacking would be conferred. But it would seem essential that a bishop should officiate and that he should have the acceptance or the bestowal of the priestly rank in mind—that he should have the right intention. That is to say, according to the Orthodox theory he would, indeed, be supplying through process of Economy that which had hitherto been lacking. Economy from a distance by correspondence, or transmitted through the personal intermediation of the priest, would hardly seem to meet the case.

What has to be borne in mind is that, in the case of each of the sacraments, the divine grace has to be communicated to a physical body on this physical plane through a physical intermediary. It is with a view to opening up these physical, as well as other higher channels, to the blessing and power of the Lord, that the Liberal Catholic Church attaches, as has just been explained, value to the use of the holy oils in Baptism and Confirmation and in ordination to the priesthood. 'Down here,' on the physical plane, we are conditioned by physical plane laws and conditions. It rests with us to provide the requisite physical conditions. And we need to be scrupulously careful in such matters, since it is this world which is the most encompassed by form and the most remote from the primal source of Reality.

THE ANGLICAN CHURCH AND ECONOMY

SINCE Pope Leo XIII, in his Bull *Apostolicae Curae* of 1896 condemned Anglican Orders as invalid the Anglican Church has turned its attention increasingly to the Eastern Church. A number of Anglicans have become 'infected' (if one may be pardoned the expression) with the Economy theory. Others of its most stalwart scholars—and there are many of these in its ranks—refuse to have anything to do with it. Not very long ago an Anglican priest wrote a letter to *The Church Times* in which he referred to Orders derived through Archbishop Vilatte and Archbishop Mathew as 'Orders' in inverted commas. I sent him a copy of the open letter entitled *The Lambeth Conference and the Validity of Archbishop Mathew's Orders.*[1] The Lambeth Conference had decided at its session in 1920 that persons deriving their Orders from the Mathew or Vernon Herford line of succession, or from other *episcopi vagantes* (as they rather nicely phrased it), should in the event of their being accepted for work in the Anglican Church be re-ordained *sub conditione.* I pointed out at the time that no sound scholarship or tradition of true ecclesiastical usage lay behind such a direction; what was applicable was the giving of jurisdiction, not the repetition of Order. From the Anglican standpoint such clergy would need 'regularization.' Anglican Orders are not invalidated by the plentiful misdemeanours of Reformation and eighteenth century divines, nor Roman Orders by the many scandals of the Papacy and Sacred College of Cardinals.

The pamphlet points out, also, that certain persons ordained by Dr. Mathew had been admitted to office as ministers of the Anglican and Old Catholic Churches without re-ordination. One bishop deriving consecration from him, the Prince de Landas Roches et de Berghes, took part in the laying on of hands at the consecration of a Protestant Episcopal bishop in New York. Moreover, Bishop Mathew's episcopal status was fully recognized when he was received into union with the Orthodox Patriarch of Antioch by the Archbishop of Beyrout, Mgr. Gerassimos Messara.

The Anglican priest in question said in answer to my representations that the Anglican Church had power to refuse recognition of such Orders 'by Economy.' And I have been told recently that the Bishop of London, who appears to be charged with the consideration of such cases, now insists on absolute re-ordination. It would seem that the theory of Economy has assailed that episcopal stronghold. It is a pity; for Dr. Winnington-Ingram has done yeoman's service to the Catholic cause in the Church of England. But Economy is a two-edged weapon, as will be evident from what follows.

A scheme has been afoot in India for a number of years having as its purpose the fusion of various Churches; these include the Anglican Church, an existing confederation known as the The South India United Church, and the Wesleyans. The scheme provides for the gradual fusion of their ministries, episcopal and nonepiscopal. Meanwhile, the Anglican authorities in India, by a majority vote, authorized their members 'to join in the Lord's Supper celebrated by ministers of the uniting Churches' at certain meetings To put the matter plainly; the bishops of the Anglican Church in India, Burma and Ceylon by this majority vote condoned the participation of Anglicans in an invalid communion.

The Oxford Mission to Calcutta submitted the matter to seven of the most eminent theologians of the Anglican Church in England, who replied that the proceeding was 'a clear violation of Catholic order.'[2] Such a service celebrated by ministers not episcopally ordained took

---

[1] Included in this collection. [Ed.]

[2] *The Church Times*, 29 April 1952.

place in June 1932. The Archbishop of Canterbury, commenting on the situation, made a speech in which he talks of Economy:

> There are certain great principles for which any who speak in the name of this Church must stand; but in special circumstances it may be necessary, sometimes at least, to acquiesce in anomalies and irregularities; things done, as our friends of the Orthodox Church would say, by way of economy which may be necessary to carry out so great an experiment.[1]

Following on this appeared a letter signed by the Bishop of Gloucester, by Bishop Palmer (formerly of Bombay), by the Bishop of Oxford and others. They said: 'We believe that the Church has authority to dispense with that [the rule of episcopal ordination] as other ecclesiastical rules, if the well-being of the Church and of the individual Christian demands it.' They then cite the saying already quoted that 'The Church, as steward of the Divine Grace, can recognize invalid sacraments as valid and valid Sacraments as invalid.'[2]

The Church Times rightly pointed out 'that the bishops of a local synod have power to dispense from regulations of their local synod, but certainly not from fundamental principles of the whole Catholic Church.'[3] Next, Bishop Palmer wrote that it is 'obviously a rule of procedure' that no one shall celebrate the Eucharist except a bishop in the apostolic line of succession or a priest ordained by him.[4] Bishop Headlam of Gloucester talked about 'a narrow and over-rigid interpretation of the Christian theory of the ministry...which would be definitely rejected by the Orthodox Church.'[5] To this a lay correspondent from Bombay made the simple and trenchant answer that 'whereas the validity of celebration by episcopally ordained ministers is a matter of certainty, any other method of celebration introduces an element of uncertainty to which we have no right to leave so vital an issue.'[6]

The movement in this country eventually reached self-expression in a letter to The Times[7] signed by twenty English bishops in support of the Indian scheme of compromise. On the following day, The Times printed another letter in favour of the scheme signed by numbers of Anglican priests and dignitaries. Dr. B.J. Kidd, the Warden of Keble College, Oxford, then wrote a letter[8] which had been prepared in answer to a request for information on the part of the Bishop of Colombo (a High Churchman) as to whether the principle of 'dispensation' in Western Canon Law or 'Economy' in the writings of Greek theologians could be applied in such a case. In a covering letter Dr. Kidd said:

> We are as anxious as the bishops who have written to you to 'promote the union on the basis of the traditional ministry' of the Catholic Church; but we hold that episcopal ordination is not a mere 'rule' of the Church but part of its constitution, and to depart from it is 'not within its competence' and will interfere with the really Catholic character of the scheme.

[1] 1 July 1952.

[2] 26 August 1932.

[3] 8 July 1952.

[4] 29 July 1932.

[5] 19 August 1932.

[6] 14 October 1952.

[7] 28 December 1952.

[8] 31 December 1952.

The document sent to the Anglican Bishop of Colombo was signed by H.L. Goudge, Regius Professor of Divinity, Oxford; B.J. Kidd, Warden of Keble College, Oxford; K.E. Kirk, Fellow of Trinity College, Oxford; W.B. O'Brien, Father Superior-General of the Society of St. John the Evangelist (commonly know as the Cowley Fathers); F.W. Puller, S.S.J.E.; Darwell Stone, Principal of Pusey House, Oxford; N.P. Williams, Lady Margaret Professor of Divinity, Oxford.

The signatories to this letter dealt with the right of dispensation and quoted Canon E.G. Wood, 'the greatest modern authority on Canon Law,' who declared that Canon Law could only be repealed by the same or equivalent authority that proclaimed it. It was not within the competence of the Indian bishops to abrogate it. The letter then went on to say:

> It is probably because of the weakness of this appeal to the Western theory of 'dispensation' that the advocates of the suggested permission have recourse to what is known in the Eastern Church as the theory of 'economy,' and regard this theory as supporting a wide conception of the dispensing power of the Church. A Greek theologian Professor Dyovouniotes, has been cited as expressing Orthodox Eastern doctrine on this subject.

The opinion of the Professor, which we have already discussed in this article, is then quoted. 'There are several conditions,' they went on to say, 'which destroy any argument based on such utterances:—

'(a) There is no authoritative Eastern Orthodox doctrine on the subject of economy.

'(b) Discussions on this subject, though found in the theologians of the Greek Church, appear to be avoided in the literature of the other component parts of the Orthodox Eastern Communion; for instance, in Russian dogmatic treatises.'

(c) It was pointed out under this section that among the Greek theologians who accept the principle of Economy there is diversity of opinion as to its scope.

(d) The opinion of the Patriarch of Alexandria, which has already received attention in this article, was cited.

Finally, under (e) they said: 'The principle of economy is unknown in the Western Church; and, in particular, has never been accepted in the Church of England.'

PART IV

VARIOUS SUBJECTS

RELIGION AND THE PURPOSE OF CEREMONIAL

(From a booklet, *Present-Day Problems*, published 1950)

What is Religion?

I have pointed out elsewhere that in any study, etymology is often a useful aid. This is especially true in regard to the technical terms of religion. The word 'religion,' for example, is generally held to be derived from the Latin *religare*, 'to bind back.' It is a common idea in religious tradition that man has lost the knowledge of his birthright. There is the Christian tradition of the fall of man. Hindus speak of our having lost our way in illusion or *māyā*. Religion is intended to teach us our Divine origin and birthright and to help us to gain realization at first-hand of the divine element in us. It 'binds us back,' or re-knits us in self-consciousness to that divine principle.

The work of religion divides itself conveniently into three departments—philosophy, ethics, and worship. Each of these ministers to the needs of man. Philosophy, when rightly handled, gives him an understanding of the world in which he lives. It shows him that there is a purpose in life, that there is a divine plan or scheme of development in which he takes part. It explains to him the meaning of the world in which he lives and how to profit by the experiences with which life provides him.

Ethics deals with man's relation to man and to the world around him.

Worship means literally the ascribing of 'worth-ship' to God—that is, the lifting up of our hearts in gratitude and reverence to God. It teaches man to realize his own inner divinity and to effect union with the divine life without. It includes a system of training by which the whole nature of man is purified and uplifted. Rightly understood, it deals with the upliftment and full expression of human consciousness.

Hence we see that worship consists of a set of spiritual exercises whose purpose is to bring man into conscious relation with God, with his own 'higher self,' and with his fellow-men in the entirety of his and their consciousness. One side of this consists of exercises to be done in solitude, taking the form chiefly of prayer or reflection and meditation; another of collective or 'congregational' effort. From one point of view, worship serves for personal spiritual edification, and can be thought of as having the same legitimate motive as education. It would not be thought selfish for a man to educate himself. From another point of view, the effect of worship is to unite us in closest spiritual association with our fellows, and also to send out into the world floods of spiritual power, making for the upliftment and reheartening of all those who come within their sphere of influence. As a man grows in the understanding of religion, he uses it less with intention for his own spiritual development (though that continues, naturally, to take place) and more with the purpose of pouring out blessing and help upon the world around him.

On Ceremonies

If one seeks for a definition of 'ceremony' in the dictionaries and encyclopaedias, one sometimes finds the word limited to religious usage. But we speak of the 'master of ceremonies' at a dance or social gathering, which reminds us that the word has also secular applications. One dictionary defines it as 'observance, or etiquette, or formality, or prescribed rule.' The fact is that we cannot express ourselves in any fashion on the physical plane without using some form of ceremony. This statement applies in some respects also to other planes. The familiar talk of 'doing away with all forms and ceremonies' may sound very gratifying but it is difficult to achieve when one really comes to face the facts of the situation. It is the kind of remark that is heard from people who have never attempted to think out for themselves the logic of ceremonies. There can be no expression of consciousness in the worlds of form except through some 'formality', that is to say, through formal action or ceremony. People would do much better to study and examine impartially things they do not understand, rather than dismiss them on the strength—or, rather, weakness—of illogical prejudice.

There is one idea which is especially involved in the more technical meaning of 'ceremony.' A bus or a motor-car is a product of human ingenuity applied to lessen bodily fatigue and to increase the area of a man's influence and activity. Its use is a ceremony, and nobody quarrels with this. There are ceremonies of court or civic etiquette with which people are entitled to quarrel because they may be out of date—the dress of a court lackey, for example. To remedy matters we do not, however, abolish ceremonies connected with his equipment; we change the dress and employ another form of ceremony. We can choose between ceremonies but, without lapsing into inactivity, we cannot abolish them.

I have before me the picture of a gathering at Ommen. The trees, the sky, the open spaces, the grouping of the multitude around the speaker, the speaker's attitude and dress—all these were to many, surely, an ideal spectacle. It was a form of ceremony to stage this gathering in the open air amid the witchery of nature. It would have been another form—with a loss perhaps of beauty but a possible gain in certain practical considerations—to have had it in a hall.

Let us turn to another scene—a concert at the Queen's Hall in London. It is a musical ceremonial with astonishing power to move the heart and to lift the spirit to sublime heights of consciousness. For this kind of ceremony great technical skill and intelligence are needed. The processes involved are largely hidden from the ordinary man, and it requires training and education in the specialized art of music for a man to be able to derive full benefit from what he is hearing.

There are ceremonies taking place everywhere in the world around us. Nature has her own ceremonies in the changing of the seasons, in the wind, the rain, the alternation of sun and moon. Moreover, it is natural to man in the extremity of feeling to express himself in gesture where words fail; and there are nations who give natural vent to this form of self-expression and are more demonstrative in the response of their bodies than their more repressed and stolid brethren.

Ceremonies of Religion

All actions, then, are ceremonies but, as in the case of the motor-car or orchestra, there may be a specialized grouping of activities, the product of high and concentrated intelligence, which is of enormous help and service to mankind.

It is on this basis that I want to discuss the ceremonies of religion. If one studies the primitive ceremonies of certain races, one finds devices which are labour-saving in a decidedly humorous fashion. The Tibetan prayer-wheel is a case in point. The sacred formula is written on slips of paper attached to the wheel which is rotated by hand, water or wind. Sometimes it is written on streamers which are allowed to float in the breeze. This apparatus is supposed to secure great merit for its promoter. Among the Zuni Indians, sticks with a feather attached are employed. The plumes are supposed to convey the prayer to the stick which represents the deity. These devices are perhaps not entirely valueless, as elemental creatures get attached to them and keep a certain influence at work. But the underlying idea is obviously to replace human effort and hard work by mechanical means. They must not, however, be confused with the scientific use of the rosary in which the sense of touch regulates the length of time, leaving the mind free for intense concentration upon the chosen intention.

There is an active reform movement at work in India to replace these mechanical aides to worship with intelligent and heartfelt devotion on the part of the worshipper. It is unfortunate for the true understanding of ceremonial in India that the mechanical automatic repetition of ceremonies has long been the prevalent custom and has obscured the idea of active and intelligent human co-operation. The same attitude is widespread though in less crude form, among the less educated classes in Europe who 'assist at Mass' in a negative and routine way.

Words as Vehicle of Thought and Emotion

It has been the special work of the Liberal Catholic Church to set quite a different standard in regard to the meaning of worship. The congregation is taught to take the language of the liturgy as an indicator or guide in the work of self-expression. Each sentence contains one or more leading ideas, which indicate the direction, or sense, in which the feeling and thought of the congregation is to flow. The mention of the word 'love,' for instance, is a signal for a collective self-expression in terms of love; the congregation thinks and feels love. This form of expression can be elaborated as the worshipper learns his work. There are technical terms which suggest certain ideas. 'I will go unto the altar of God,' for example, is a phrase which carries with it a marvellous significance. The altar is suggestive of sacrifice. The word 'altar' is the signal to the group of trained and intelligent worshippers to direct their thoughts to the supreme sacrifice of the self-limitation of the Logos. There comes a stage in human experience when we learn to become more interested in other people and in humanity as a whole than we are in ourselves—a stage when we are able to divest ourselves of all personal and selfish interests; at this stage it is possible, in an act of complete and joyous self-abnegation, to identify ourselves in thought and in feeling with the supreme unselfishness of the Logos.

The Occultist and the Mystic

We read in the literature of the East, and of meditation generally, of the turning inwards of the consciousness. There are various practices connected with this—the withdrawing of the consciousness to the heart, for instance. This is all useful but open to danger unless kept constantly in balance by the complementary practice of turning outwards. Introspection can be dangerous, largely because one is exploring uncharted territory and, in the process, is apt to lose one's bearings and one's standards of judgement. Meditation of this sort may lead people to be self-centred and self-interested; it may cause them to lose their practical hold on life and their sense of proportion in their relationship with their fellow human beings. It is a practice which must be undertaken with great discretion, and the wise student will exercise constant care to correct it by outward-turned effort and practical work. To become outward-turned as a matter of habit is the surest way of conquering morbidity and depression.

The way of the Occultist seems to me to consist in learning to control and to work freely with the consciousness directed either within or without. Becoming 'outward-turned' does not imply the neglect of that branch of work which concerns the initiation, or the bringing into being within one's waking consciousness, of various mental, emotional and still higher qualities. That is an essential part of the Occultist's training and it is indispensable to active and intelligent co-operation in church services. For this work, the consciousness is largely inward-turned. In the earlier stages of his work, a man's mind and emotions depend for their action largely upon outside stimulation. The ordinary person is not capable of arousing within himself at will a strong feeling of love. He is dependent upon stimulation from outside—the sight of a loved friend, for instance. One task which has to be mastered in order to gain efficiency in church work is that of learning to induce within oneself at a moment's notice any of the fundamental virtues such as love, sympathy, devotion, strength. Merely to think about these things is not sufficient. One must be capable of awakening strong emotion on demand and of pouring it out as a contribution to what is needed in the church service or for helping people in ordinary life.

The difference between the Occultist and the Mystic is that the former learns to employ his consciousness at will in both directions whereas the Mystic works chiefly at introversion and prefers to ignore the outer phenomenal life.

I have heard the idea put forward that the Mystic endeavours to touch experience outside the conditions of time and space whereas the Occultist frankly works within those categories. This may be true as regards the Mystic's wishes and aspirations. To escape from the limitations of time and space (like the attainment of ultimate liberation) is a consummation a long way ahead of most of us. Ideas of this sort are heard not infrequently; I take it that they are used not in the technical and absolute sense but in a relative sense. In such a way, liberation—a bursting of bonds and restriction—is possible at many stages and is a real and living experience.

Collective Work

There is another vista of work and progress which opens up as soon as one has responded to the ideal of being normally outward turned. It has to do with group or collective work, and is well illustrated in connection with congregational worship. It will be within the experience of many that there is a condition of consciousness in which one feels oneself united with one's fellow-beings. There are approaches from outside to this state at the level of what is called the causal body but it is more readily grasped at the buddhic level. I have worked with church congregations to get them to express themselves in their interpretation of the liturgy, not simply as individuals, but to attempt to blend their consciousness with that of their fellow worshippers so that every leading word that is sung and every emotion or thought that is expressed is the product of the entire congregation. It is impossible to exaggerate the spirit of unity, of love and friendliness engendered by a work of this kind, or to what an extent the power contributed by a congregation working in this collective fashion transcends what is done along the more ordinary separate methods. The devotion and enthusiasm of a congregation can be maintained by this method without the least difficulty, and the people themselves grow rapidly into a realization of what is happening and gain much spiritual experience for themselves at firsthand.

Religion Based on Knowledge of Natural Law

In the foregoing remarks I have tried to show that a liturgy provides opportunity for people to express their thought and emotion according to a preconceived and well-planned scheme, and with a clear purpose in view as to the results to be obtained. The worshippers can and do derive great spiritual help from this work for themselves, but the higher attitude is that of being outward-turned and of regarding this work as done for other people or for humanity as a whole, and of blending in with and being modeled after the Eternal Sacrifice of the Logos. And, finally, we saw that the whole process could be greatly intensified and raised to a higher level if the people would cease to think of themselves and their own welfare and realize themselves as working on behalf of a great body-corporate.

We have already seen that human intelligence is able to plan for the welfare and wider usefulness of man. The motor-car was taken as a case in point; it enables a man to benefit by wider intercourse with his fellows and to diminish the difficulties caused by separation in space. The principle which underlies all inventions of this kind is that of learning to single out and to make use of certain laws of nature and to adapt the working of these to the particular ends in view.

Now the same principle underlies what we may call religious ceremonial as exemplified in the services of religion or of an institution like Freemasonry.

The Holy Eucharist and Natural Law

A Church service, especially a service like the Holy Eucharist, may strike the uninstructed spectator as a hopelessly complicated affair. Why such an intricate ceremony? Is not the spirit of Christ the very apotheosis of simplicity? These and similar criticisms are constantly heard. The spirit of Christ is, indeed, essentially simple, but man in his natural and undeveloped condition is chaotic and complicated. It is typical of all spiritual growth that the higher one rises the more one passes out of complexity into simplicity and out of diversity into unity. The course of the Eucharist is perhaps outwardly a little complicated and bewildering to the newcomer, but a moment's reflection will explain this difficulty. One has, in the first place, to deal with a number of people at many different levels of development, and to unite such people, in itself, involves some complexity of procedure. But one has only to pause for a moment to consider what the Eucharist is intended to do, to find the answer to this and to other difficulties on the part of people unfamiliar with the subject.

The Eucharist sets out to do nothing less than to repeat or, at any rate, to extend in terms of time and space, the Incarnation of Our Blessed Lord. Such a task is not to be achieved without some effort on our part and there is a minimum of time and procedure required for its application. It is a little arrogant to ask that so sublime a wonder should be subjected to our conditions. The man in the street has yet to learn that in affairs of religion—the most elevated and sacred with which we are privileged to concern ourselves—it is a question of adapting ourselves to its requirements and conditions rather than vice versa.

The Stages of the Eucharist

I have written elsewhere[1] in detail about the Eucharist and it is unnecessary to repeat it here. I propose, however, to devote a little space to a consideration of the different stages into which that service may be divided. The Eucharist is perhaps the supreme ceremony given to mankind on the physical plane. It comprises within itself a whole cycle of spiritual development, shown forth in its symbolism and worked out in the forces it liberates upon and within the worshippers. Indeed, we cannot respond to its full possibilities at our present stage of evolution. A short examination of its principal features will suffice to show how marvellous is its whole conception and what vast possibilities it offers to the devout and intelligent worshipper.

---

[1] *New Insights into Christian Worship*, included in this volume.

The first thing that must be done in any public gathering for religious purposes is to purify and unite the people. Not only do they come from a great variety of occupations with their auras full of all sorts of ideas and emotions and of influences picked up from their surroundings, but they show among themselves wide differences of temperament, of degrees of receptivity and of age of evolution. Obviously the first thing to be done is to give them a spiritual bath, so to speak, and weld them together into whatever degree of unity is possible. The service starts off, therefore, with congregational singing and with purification with holy water, as we approach the altar of God—the place of sacrifice of the personality The Confiteor and Absolution follow. All this does a great deal to turn out of their auras the foreign influence of the outer world and to bring them into tune with the Higher Self. The earlier part of the service is devoted to singing or to vocal self-expression in praise of God, and to prayer. Passages from the Scriptures are then read which enlist the mental element, and finally the recitation of the Creed or similar passage, rightly accomplished, brings into activity and expression the causal body. Thus the whole being of the worshipper, from his waking consciousness in the physical body to the Ego, has been purified and brought into active self-expression.

There is now a complete change in the nature and intention of the service. At the Offertory, bread and wine are presented as tokens of the fruits of the earth. Elementals of earth, air, fire and water take part; and we join with Nature in our offering of praise and gratitude. With it, we unite 'ourselves, our souls and bodies, to be a holy and continual sacrifice' to almighty God. The angelic hosts are invited to join in the outpouring of praise and thanksgiving.

We now come to the Prayer of Consecration. The link between ourselves and the elements of bread and wine is broken so far as all lower and personal connections are concerned, and they are blessed and set apart as channels for the divine grace. We mention special objects for which the Holy Sacrifice is to be offered, and we remember those, both living and dead, for whom we want to pray. Reference is made to the stupendous sacrifice of the Logos, to the Hierarchy, to the institution by Our Lord. And it is He who now changes the elements into the vehicles of His life and power. The Body is the vehicle of life; the Blood is the life poured out in sacrifice. Various processes take place in distributing the power over the world and to the people present. There is an assembling of men and angels into a closeness of consciousness, and the Holy Communion follows. The service closes with ascriptions of praise, with prayer, with the solemn and grateful dismissal of the angels, and with the final blessing.

I do not propose to comment upon this. People must study it and experience it for themselves and realize what they can of the wonder and the beauty of this marvellous condescension of the Lord to His people. Those who come to understand even a little of the significance of this rite know that they could spend many incarnations participating in these sacred mysteries before entering into the fullness of what they have to offer. I know of no quicker or surer way of entering permanently into the consciousness of our dear Lord. And I know of no more effective means of uplifting the world and of bringing inspiration to the many who are struggling and striving often in terrible difficulty and isolation.

THE WORK OF THE CHURCH

(From addresses given to a gathering of priests at Huizen, 1929)

A New Idea of Church Worship

It is commonly accepted that it is natural for man to give worship and glory to God, and that it is 'meet and right so to do.' It is also thought that this action is beneficial to the people themselves. We believe, in this Church, that the members of the congregation are greatly helped by our services, but I think that we are peculiar among the Churches in holding that the services are conducted principally for the helping of the world outside. However, this conception of church worship has become more and more widespread as people have begun to take into account the power of thought. Reasoning from the phenomenon of thought-transference, they are coming to realize that every time we give birth to a definite thought, a certain corresponding power flows out from us and influences other people. It is but a short step from that to the realization that the result of a service performed by trained congregations may be inestimable; it may produce a tremendous sweep of power able to travel to a great distance. It may influence for good the whole neighbourhood where the church is situated. The degree of influence depends very much on the whole quality of the worship, on our attitude during the service and the extent to which we participate in it, and on the kind of thought we send out. It depends, in fact, on the training of the people and their ability to raise their consciousness to higher levels.

The Liturgy

The first requisite for this kind of work is a liturgy, on which people can easily concentrate and whose language provides a means of happy and enthusiastic self-expression. When Bishop Leadbeater and I were at work on compiling our liturgy, we took a great deal of trouble in selecting the language carefully in order to make this possible. I do not pretend that from every standpoint the liturgy is ideal, or that it does not contain anything to which people might object.

For instance, we retained the ancient creeds, some of the clauses of which cannot be taken literally and with which some of us do not feel ourselves in agreement. There were certain difficulties which had to be considered. The creeds were put together by the General Councils of the Church and it is a matter of etiquette that a small body of people like ourselves should not take upon itself to alter documents of that standing. We wished to keep our connection with the Christian Church at large and therefore we retained those forms which are a mark of our fellowship with other Churches. We considered that it would be more satisfactory to retain them, bearing in mind the force of ancient tradition and the great body of thought which has been generated through the centuries which lies behind them and, at the same time, to allow freedom of interpretation so that people should not feel in the least dishonest in using forms and phrases which are a little archaic. We also eliminated sentiments not acceptable in these days, such as the fear of God and an exaggerated sense of unworthiness; we tried to make it a liturgy of joyous aspiration. It took a great deal of time and effort to get the liturgy to the point where people would be able to take a keen and active part in the worship and express themselves sincerely.

Having got the liturgy, the first thing we have to do is to encourage the congregation to try to express themselves whole-heartedly through it. One important point is that we should put as much meaning and power as we can behind the words we use. We have language as a common vehicle for the expression of our thoughts in order to communicate with one another, but few of us normally use it with more than a casual significance, and fewer still realize the full value of the words they employ. When a word like 'love' or 'justice' is used, it has a whole content of meaning which is based on the life-experience of the person who uses it. We try to get all present to read into the word all that they can through the vivid exercise of their imagination which enables them to contact the power which lies behind the words.

Let us take, for example, the hymn, 'All hail the power of Jesus' Name!' One finds that hymns vary a good deal in quality. Some have no very profound meaning and it is difficult to put any significance into them. Others are particularly fine from the literary point of view; they are rich in imagery, and we can open ourselves up to higher states of consciousness and express a great deal through them. Consider for example, the two lines,

> All hail the splendour of His might,
> And crown Him Lord of all.

These words give us the opportunity for definite acts of consciousness. 'Hail' means a lifting up of the whole being in adoration, in reverence and wonder at the majesty of the Being to whom our thoughts are turned. In the Litany of the Benediction Service, there is a word in the last line of each verse which gives us a similar opportunity for such self-expression—'We hail Thee' and 'We Thy Church adore Thee.' It is the corporate consciousness of all present which performs the act of adoration of the Christ. The words are flexible and offer a special opportunity for the power to flow through them. Having thus given careful consideration to the wording of the liturgy, we ask the congregation to try to mean to the utmost what they say and to offer it for the purpose for which it is destined.

In this work we use various levels of our consciousness at one and the same time. First, there is the intellectual grasp of the phrase, the ordinary meaning of the words; secondly, there is the content of our experience in the world of both thought and emotion—the whole idea to which we are giving expression. Thirdly, there is the corporate aspect of our aspiration; we are working as one body, one fellowship, and the power is increased and enriched by the realization of our unity. We are His Church, the channel of His power in the world, and in that corporate capacity and in the consciousness of our power and of our mission we offer our adoration to Christ. We use these forms of language to express the highest and noblest thoughts and feelings that are within our power of control and expression on those occasions. It takes a good deal of effort to grow into this attitude, and it requires some study of the language of our liturgy before we can use it effectively.

Working as a Unity

In other churches, the clergymen do most of the work, although there is the singing of the choir and a feeling of devotion in the congregation. But if one observes the people carefully it is generally found that they are expressing themselves individually, their minds dwelling on their own past experiences, and that they give their own personal meaning to the words—if they are thinking very much about them at all. As a rule, one does not find any great depth of thought; church-going has become a habit with them and although, in certain cases, they experience some degree of reality, it is not with them that exercise of Yoga which we in this Church try to make it.

In this Church we feel it to be most important to give people scope for intense and sincere self-expression, and we take up our work, not as separate individuals but as the one mystical body of Christ. We should each one contribute what he has to give, not each on his own behalf, in his own habitual state of mind, not expressing his own outlook based on his own experience in the past, but each identifying himself with the whole body of people and saying what he has to say on its behalf. We try to lift ourselves up in thought and aspiration to God, we try to touch the Divine consciousness and to pour ourselves out to Him in adoration. And we do it as far as possible as one action, with one consciousness and on behalf of the whole body, thus lifting up the whole congregation, and not only the visible congregation but also co-operating with the angels, with the departed, with the forces of nature—this whole corporate consciousness is lifted up in aspiration.

All this is in the nature of a new experiment which we have tried in the Liberal Catholic Church with considerable success. It has, of course, more marked results when carried out by people who have had some training in meditation and who are able to penetrate into the significance of the great root emotions and ideas. It also helps to have studied the expression of thought and emotion in terms of language and of music. A very wonderful result could be achieved if everybody were to approach the service from this point of view.

Self-Initiated Experience

Now all this presupposes a certain amount of study and training. In the case of most people a large amount of their thought and emotion is not self-initiated, but is stimulated from outside themselves. In the early stages of human development, we depend on the external stimuli of our environment, of our amusements and entertainments to keep us going. Most of us depend greatly on other people and on the stimulus we get from outside for arousing emotion and thought. But in this work, something more than that is needed and that is experience which is self-initiated. It is easy to feel affection for some one we love when that person comes into the room; it is more difficult when he is far away. What we have to do, then, is to take the idea behind the words in the liturgy, such as 'pity,' 'love,' 'tenderness,' 'sympathy,' and, so far as we are able, to 'flash out' that quality not by dint of stimulus from outside or from other people, but because we have reached a certain stage in the understanding of those particular qualities of character within ourselves and have learned to answer to them at once; we are able to call upon sources of divine power within us and to express those qualities at a moment's notice when they are suggested by the words we are using.

To be able to express ourselves in this way through a liturgy requires a considerable measure of self-development; it requires that we should have familiarized ourselves with different aspects of life in order to acquaint ourselves with the full meaning that lies behind the words. When this is done collectively, not as individuals but on behalf of the whole body corporate, the power that can be poured out over the world is intense and wonderful indeed.

Stages of the Eucharist

The Eucharist can be divided into sections in order to enable one to understand more clearly what is being done.

PURIFICATION. A heterogeneous set of people comes into the church—people of different types, of different interests and ages, some in good health, some in bad, with different degrees of intelligence and with varied experiences. From one point of view, all this is very valuable because many aspects of humanity are emphasized. But all these people have to be drawn together in order to achieve a certain harmony and unity in the expression of a general devotional aspiration. Therefore an intelligently devised service like the Eucharist begins scientifically with a process of purification and with the welding of the people together. It is necessary as far as possible to free the congregation from the extraneous influences of the outside world in order that they may be in as refined and purified a condition as possible in the church. We begin with the Asperges, the sprinkling of holy water and the recitation of a canticle, which throws off the ordinary habits of thought and brings the people together. The *Confiteor*, which in other Churches is an expression of unworthiness, is in ours a reaching up to our essential nature, an identifying of ourselves with the Higher Self instead of thinking ourselves 'miserable sinners.' This is followed by the Absolution which is intended to put the consciousness straight with the Ego.

When we have made the effort to purify and unite the people, we pass on to the definite work which we have to do together. The Introit and Gloria, the Collects, Epistle, Gospel and Creed build up the eucharistic structure; they also build up the unity of consciousness. The thought we should have in mind during this part of the service is a high and pure ideal of common effort and aspiration, lifting our consciousness as high as we can.

FIRST OFFERING. With the Offertorium comes a new aspect of the service. We turn to the forces of nature and offer the bread and wine to be used as the channels of the Presence; in this first instance they are offered as tokens or representatives of the fruits of the earth. The powers of fire, earth, air and water are drawn up through the altar stone. We attract the influences of nature from outside especially if we work consciously and realize our unity with it and call its forces into co-operation with us in our worship. We may also include the material parts of our bodies inasmuch as they are derived from nature. All these are offered as 'a sacrifice, pure and acceptable' in the sight of the Lord.

SECOND OFFERING. At the Orate Fratres we pass on to the second state of the offering, that of 'ourselves, our souls and bodies.' To the natural body and the forces of nature we add the richness of human consciousness, high and lofty feelings, will, and intuition.

THIRD OFFERING. In the Sursum Corda and the Preface we call on the collaboration of the angels.

FOURTH OFFERING. Then comes the Consecration. We now separate ourselves from the lower elements and anything that is not high and pure, and the offerings are prepared to become channels for the spiritual power of the Lord and vehicles of His Presence. We lift our consciousness high, thinking of the Cosmic Order, the universal Sacrifice of the Second Logos; and in the prayers which follow we recall the Last Supper and the institution of the Holy Sacrament. In this final stage, the bread and wine become the Body and Blood of the Lord, the vehicles for the life-force poured out in sacrifice for us and for the whole world.

Knowledge of God

One result from work of this kind is the proof we can obtain for ourselves of 'the existence of God.' If we desire to know that God exists and to have some experience of divine power, this is one of the best ways of achieving it. I do not, of course, mean that it is a direct demonstration of it, but it is possible to experience a great downpouring of power to which we can make ourselves sensitive. There are all sorts of mystical experiences. There are wonderful revelations of divine power in the beauties of nature and we find ourselves lifted into the immensity of things and filled with the marvellous wonder of it all. But as a scientific method for achieving this experience, I do not know of anything better than the sacramental form of worship. For when we divest ourselves of selfishness, thinking of the good of the whole and putting aside our own personal satisfaction, a great down-flow of power, which is quite different from our ordinary consciousness, comes in response. Much that before was theoretical will become matters of real experience and we shall know the truth of it for ourselves.

Influencing the World

I should like to end with the thought with which I began—that none of this is for ourselves alone. Our Church insists that worship does not only concern the individuals taking part in it, but that the world in general, including the kingdoms of nature and our fellow human beings who do not come near the church, is greatly helped by the outpouring that takes place through the Holy Eucharist. It is a wonderful privilege to be able to send out this power into the world, and when we learn to work in this particular way, touching high levels of thought and emotion through the beautiful language of the Liturgy and with the power of the Lord Himself flowing through it, we can carry out a powerful and efficient work for changing the thought atmosphere of the world. This effort does a great deal to melt away the disharmony and discord of the world. A number of people working in this way can do a tremendous lot, and the higher the level they reach the more effective the work they do. When this work goes hand in hand with the practical, physical work that is also necessary, it becomes a powerful means of helping humanity and for forwarding God's plan of evolution.

THE HOLY EUCHARIST

(Sermon at Sydney, 22 April 1927)

The derivation of the word 'Mass' is a matter of some dispute. It is supposed by most authorities to be taken from the words, *ite, missa est*, which occur at the end of the service, meaning 'Go. It is sent' (the sacrifice is sent) or 'Go. You are dismissed.' Other people consider that the word is akin to the Old English word *messe* surviving in the military 'mess' and, in that sense, the 'messe' or the 'supper' of the Lord.

The Mass is spoken of as a Sacrifice, and it is worth considering in what sense this is so. It is held to be a perpetuation—not a repetition but a continuation—of the Eternal Sacrifice upon the Cross. This Sacrifice refers to the putting down into manifestation in matter of the Divine Life, as Plato explained when he spoke of the Logos as being stretched out on the cross. It is that limitation of God in matter 'in the beginning'—the slaying of the Lamb 'from the foundation of the world,' as the Book of Revelations has it—that Eternal Sacrifice outside our concepts of time and space, in the great eternal now in which our past, present and future are all synthesized. The physical body imposes upon our consciousness certain limitations of time and space in which we see everything in a certain continuity of flow and sequence. So this Sacrifice, repeated day after day, shadows forth within our conception of time and space that Eternal Sacrifice which is the pouring down of the Divine Life into the world, by which it and all that therein is, is nourished and sustained. In that sense the Mass is the Sacrifice.

Again, the mystical teaching is that Christ is Himself the Victim and the Priest. This is the transcendence of God and also His immanence. He is above His world transcendent and is therefore the Priest—the one who offers the sacrifice. He is also immanent in the universe; His life is poured down into matter and He is therefore the Victim who is offered.

We speak, too, of the Real Presence in the Sacrament. It has already been explained what the doctrine of transubstantiation means—the changing of the substance of the bread and the wine in the archetypal world; the switching, so to speak, of these superphysical counterparts aside and the direct manifestation through the outer appearance of bread and wine of the ray from the Second Person of the Blessed Trinity.

But it is sometimes urged by those who do not understand this interpretation of things that since God is omnipresent—is everywhere in His universe—the idea of a Real Presence in the Blessed Sacrament is impossible. It is, of course, quite true that everything is God and that His life expresses itself through every form in the universe, but what we have here is a special intensification of that Presence. He is more directly with us, more directly expressed through the consecrated Bread and Wine, than through those more ordinary manifestations called bread and wine. It is in that sense that there is the Real Presence in the Blessed Sacrament.

The service itself is divided into three sections: the Preparation, the Canon, and the Communion.

The Preparation consists of certain versicles and responses, psalms and hymns, the object of which is to prepare the congregation, to attune their hearts and their minds in preparation for the great act which is to follow in the Canon.

In all church worship, we come to give honour and praise to God. Worship does not consist in listening to sermons and addresses, but rather in pouring out one's heart to God and in giving Him praise and adoration. This is the idea which is carried into effect in this earlier part of the service in which the congregation are encouraged to lift up their hearts to God in praise and worship and so attune their minds and their hearts to the outpouring of spiritual power that is to follow.

At the beginning of this section is the *Confiteor*. (We have kept the Latin titles for some of these sections so as to show the essential identity of our service with the older liturgies.) Here we have the confession of our unworthiness, our imperfections and shortcomings, followed by the Absolution given by the priest.

> God the Father, God the Son, God the Holy Ghost, bless, preserve and sanctify you; the Lord in his loving-kindness look down upon you and be gracious unto you: the Lord absolve you from all your sins, and grant you the grace and comfort of the Holy Spirit.

In this sacramental absolution there is a straightening out of the disharmony of the inner nature caused by wrongdoing. Power is given to those who are duly ordained to the priesthood to restore the condition of inner harmony so that the person thus restored (who has profited by what is sometimes called the ministry of healing) is able to make a new beginning in the full power of the God within him flowing down through his personality or lower vehicles—the full power, that is, of as much of that inner divinity that is unfolded within him.

The Confession is intended to attune us so that we may profit fully by the outpouring of Divine Grace; in proportion as we are in earnest in confessing our imperfections and resolving to make a new beginning, so will the Absolution be effective in our case.

Now we come to the Canon of the Mass. It is so called because that is the old term for what is sometimes called the 'rule' in things. This is the important and more permanent part of the Mass and it should not be altered without the very gravest consideration, because it is really here that the 'magic' for the special outpouring of spiritual power begins to come into operation.

We begin with the versicles and responses:

> P. The Lord be with you.
> C. And with thy spirit.
> P. Lift up your hearts.
> C. We lift them up unto the Lord.
> P. Let us give thanks unto our Lord God.
> C. It is meet and right so to do.

Then comes the Preface:

> It is very meet, right and our bounden duty, that we should at all times and in all places give thanks unto thee, O Lord, holy Father, almighty, everlasting God.
> Therefore with Angels and Archangels, with Thrones, Dominations, Princedoms, Virtues, Powers, with Cherubim and Seraphim and with all the company of heaven, we laud and magnify thy glorious name, evermore praising thee and saying: Holy, holy, holy, Lord God of Hosts, heaven and earth are full of thy glory; glory be to thee, O Lord most high.

Here we unite ourselves with the whole company of heaven in praising and magnifying the glorious Name of God. I think there is no finer act of worship than this lifting up of our hearts—of our whole nature—into union with God Himself.

After the Sanctus, commences the long prayer of consecration:

> Wherefore, O most loving Father, we thy servants do pray thee, through Jesus Christ, thy Son, our Lord, to receive, to purify and to hallow this oblation which we do make unto thee....

and the officiant makes three signs of the cross over the bread and wine thus purifying the first fruits, or the offering which has been made to God.

This purification is accomplished by the making of the sign of the cross, the sweeping through of the flow of magnetic power. Then, in the remainder of the prayer, the idea of the great Sacrifice is brought out, of God manifesting through the hierarchy of His glorious saints, those made perfect, the Great Brotherhood which rules and directs the world.

The priest spreads his hands over the offering. This was the old Jewish way, and possibly used in other rites, of communicating something of the sacrificing priest to the victim which he was offering.

The Angel of the Presence appears, and soon afterwards are said the words of consecration whereby the divine Power is caused to flow to the outer vehicles of bread and wine, Then follow a few moments of silence in which we offer ourselves in dedication to Almighty God. Certain hymns are now sung. This singing of a hymn before the consecrated elements has a very wonderful result, for any adoration offered before them brings a great return of power, proportionate to the effort made. When this hymn is sung with real devotion, the power that flows out through the consecrated elements comes upon us and renews and vivifies our whole being.

Our first act after the Consecration is to offer this 'most precious gift' to God who has given it to us, and with it our gratitude for the grace that He has poured upon us.

Then, through the consecrated elements, 'meetly celebrating the mysteries of the most holy Body and Blood,' the priest prays that he 'may be filled with God's mighty power and blessing,' thus himself taking the place of the Angel of the Presence.

The same power is mediated to the congregation:

> Likewise we pray thee to sanctify thy people here present with these thy heavenly gifts, and through these mysteries do thou hallow, quicken and bless them, that both in their hearts and in their lives they may show forth thy praise and glorify thy holy name.

Then comes an ascription of praise with which the Prayer of Consecration concludes:

> ...for we acknowledge and confess with our hearts and lips that by him were all things made, yea, all things both in heaven and earth; with him as the indwelling life do all things exist and in him as the transcendent glory all things live and move and have their being:

Then comes the ascription to the two other Persons of the Blessed Trinity, in which we draw ourselves into union with their power:

> To whom with Thee, O mighty Father, in the unity of the Holy Spirit, be ascribed all honour and glory, throughout the ages of ages.

After that we enter into the third part of the service—the Communion. The priest breaks the Host in half:

> O Son of God, who showest thyself this day upon a thousand altars and yet art one and indivisible, in token of thy great sacrifice we break this thy Body.

This resembles the old Egyptian rite in which 'the body of Osiris was 'broken for us.' It refers to the One Divine Life put down into the universe, into the separated units of consciousness. Our work is to reunite the scattered parts, the broken portions of the Body, by our conscious fellowship with one another in God.

The sign of the cross is made three times over the chalice at the words '...thy strength, thy peace, thy blessing, which thou dost give us in this holy sacrament, may be spread abroad upon thy world;' the power is radiated out around and beyond so that all those outside, coming within its sphere of influence, may also receive help and spiritual upliftment.

A fragment of the Host is dropped into the Wine, with the words '...as thou, O Lord Christ, wast made known to thy disciples in the breaking of bread, so may thy many children know themselves to be one in thee even as thou art one with the Father.'

The liturgy is the drama of the human soul which, coming forth from God, is labouring and striving in this world of pilgrimage and exile towards reunion with the divine source from whence it came.

The Communion of the people follows and the service concludes with the Blessing and the recitation of the Last Gospel,[1] the opening words of which also come down to us from ancient times:

> In the beginning was the Word, and the Word was with God, and the Word was God...

The Liturgy presents a very wonderful opportunity for the refreshing of our whole nature, for the opening up of our spiritual life, for making ourselves channels through which the power of God can flow. What we learn to do in the services in our church we can carry into effect in the outer world and so make ourselves centres of blessing and help wherever we may go.

1 The Last Gospel is no longer part of the usual usage of the Liberal Catholic Church, although it is retained in the optional Latin version of the Rite. [Ed.]

THE HOLY TRINITY

(Sermon at the Church of St. Alban, Sydney, 22 May 1921)

THERE is a general tendency at the present time to make a strong distinction between belief and conduct. People often say that it does not matter what a man believes so long as he acts rightly. They think that in the past too much emphasis was laid upon the question of belief apart from the necessity for righteousness as the real test of life.

The doctrine of the Holy Trinity is one which is fundamental to Christianity. It may, indeed, be regarded as the deepest mystery of the Christian Faith in that it teaches the nature of the Godhead itself.

It is sometimes asked why Christianity lays so much stress upon this doctrine. People have attempted to portray the mystery of the Trinity in wonderful and beautiful terms with all the resources of language that they can summon to their aid. But still it remains a mystery; it is said that this is one of those teachings which we cannot hope to understand but must take upon faith.

There is a certain rightness in the tendency of modern man to differentiate between belief and conduct. It is true in one sense that a man's conduct often does not reflect his belief; there is also another sense in which belief underlies all conduct, hence a man's beliefs as well as his stage of development are both important. But we might say, with all reverence, that it would make no difference whatever to the ordinary man if he believed in a fourth Person to the Godhead, because the doctrine of the Trinity has to do with a higher stage of progress than that with which he is concerned.

But the Athanasian Creed declares: 'Whosoever will be saved: before all things it is necessary that he hold the Catholic Faith.' Of course, the word 'saved' does not mean what many people take it to mean. The Latin word *salvus* means 'state of health' and is akin to the English word 'salve.' Whosoever, then, would be in the way of making healthy progress it is before all things 'necessary that he hold the Catholic Faith;' that he rightly understands the universal principles so far as they concern himself. That is eminently reasonable. But this doctrinal statement is almost entirely taken up with the Trinity because in the Christian Church we are dealing with the three great Powers that flow from the Godhead and our progress turns upon a right understanding and a right use of these three fundamental powers or manifestations of God that are at work in the universe and in man.

It is unfortunate that in the Christian Church belief has come to be so much a matter of lip statement. It has been held that there are certain doctrines which must be taken upon faith, which we cannot hope to understand, which are a matter of divine revelation, and that the acceptance of those doctrines is necessary to what has been called 'salvation.'

In the Liberal Catholic Church we leave our members perfectly free in matters of belief, because we recognize that a man's belief depends very much on his stage of evolution. As he grows in spirituality, so will he grow in understanding and in knowledge of the great facts in nature. So while we have certain teachings and beliefs which we present to our people, we do not insist upon an acceptance of them until they themselves can see them to be true. If they are wise, they will take them as working hypotheses and try to make them living realities in their lives.

That is the work that lies before us—to try to make these teachings of the Christian Church matters of understanding and not merely matters of faith.

How are we to do that in regard to the doctrine of the Trinity? The fundamental position is this: man is made in the image of God, and as God Himself is a triplicity of Persons so also that triplicity is reflected in man. Man has therefore within himself the power of knowing these three aspects of the Deity.

The method of attaining that knowledge has been set before us from ancient times in the scriptures, in 'the Three Paths' spoken of by the mystics—the path of purification, the path of illumination, and the path of union. If we examine what takes place at each of these three stages we shall see that they come under the three aspects of the Deity successively. In the path of purification we are especially concerned with the work of the Holy Spirit; in the path of illumination with the work of God the Son; in the path of union with the work of God the Father.

It is the work of the Holy Spirit to sanctify us; the work of the Son is to preserve; but it is not very clear how the aspect of the Father works because that stage lies so far beyond us that little stress has been laid upon it in conventional Christian teaching.

Our first work, then, is the work of purification. It is a matter of controlling our emotions and our thoughts and of purifying and refining our whole nature; in other words, of sanctifying ourselves, raising ourselves into a state of holiness or health so that we may be fit to press on to the stage of illumination; that we may pass from the influence of God the Holy Spirit to the influence of God the Son.

One of the titles sometimes given to the Second Person of the Godhead is 'World Teacher.' Most people would say that teaching is the passing on of knowledge, and would connect it with the intellectual nature of man which comes under the special guidance of the Holy Spirit. But a difficulty sometimes arises from a misunderstanding of the teacher's task. It is not to lay facts before the pupil but to encourage him to exercise his own faculties in order to grasp fundamental realities by his own efforts; the true teacher will quicken initiative and enterprise in the student in order that he may learn to use his own powers and come to see things for himself.

Wisdom is not a mere matter of intellectual theory; it is not something which can be put into the mind by another person. Centuries upon centuries of evolution separate the man of intellectual theory from the man of pure wisdom. The pupil reaches truth by the inner illumination of the Spirit. This comes especially under the second Aspect of the Trinity and is part of the work upon the path of illumination, the opening up of the inner resources of a man which will help him to touch at first hand the sources of knowledge for himself.

All knowledge exists somewhere or other in the universe, in the projection from the mind of God, from the creative impulse which brought the worlds into being. The great facts in nature exist as archetypes and the man who is truly original is the one who touches these sources of knowledge for himself. To be original does not mean doing or saying something which has not been done or said before. Because a fact is true it is likely that thousands of people will touch that same truth. Originality consists in reaching the truth yourself. It does not matter whether one or a thousand people have arrived at the same thing, it is none the less original so far as you yourself are concerned.

When we come to the third path—the path of union—there is not very much that we can say on the subject because it lies so far beyond most of us. But as we purify ourselves and as we open up the inner illumination of our nature we shall begin to touch the stream of influence which flows from the First Person of the Blessed Trinity.

It is very natural, then, that the Christian Church should lay so much emphasis upon the doctrine of the Trinity, because when we rightly understand the progress that lies ahead we realize that it consists in the opening up of these three aspects of the spiritual nature that are in each one of us. It is only because the Churches have forgotten the knowledge that they once possessed, because they have been indifferent to their birthright, because they did not properly understand the glorious heritage which was theirs, that people find the doctrine of the Trinity a strange one in these days. If we were people of vision, if we rightly understood the great things which are ours, we should not be asking whether the doctrine of the Trinity is true or not; we should know its truth in our own spiritual experience. I do not mean to say that at our present stage we can fully understand the mystery of the Godhead, but we can begin to understand those reflections of the Godhead in the spirit of man. We shall not need to echo the words of Tertullian: 'It is certain because it is impossible.' We shall say rather, 'I believe because in my own experience I have found some of these great things to be true; therefore I accept this teaching as a revelation, as a working hypothesis, to be more fully understood and realized as I make further progress.'

That is the work which we set before our people in the Liberal Catholic Church. It is for this reason that we do not seek to fetter the intellect even though we have certain definite teachings to lay before our people. These can only be verified as they grow in spirituality. And there is no greater help to this growth into the reality of things than the power which flows through the sacraments, especially through the Blessed Sacrament of Christ's love which is celebrated Sunday by Sunday in this church. As we open ourselves to the love of Christ which flows out through the Holy Sacrament we shall find His spirit opening in our natures and we shall begin to comprehend things which before were only matters of intellectual theory.

THE HOLY GHOST

People with any measure of sensitivity will know the difference in influence between a service of Benediction and a service of Confirmation or Ordination or any service at which the *Veni Creator* is sung. In the first service it is the influence of the Second Person of the Holy Trinity which is predominant; in the other it is that of the Holy Spirit. This is, of course, a sort of pragmatic test based on practical experience and experiment and does not come within the borderline of speculation and metaphysics. This influence of the Third Person is especially noticeable on Whitsunday, the day on which the Church gratefully commemorates the gift of the Holy Ghost, and when the colour of the vestments is red, emblematical of the 'tongues of fire.'

The word 'ghost' has a root that signifies spirit, angel or messenger. The Holy Ghost is the name given by Christian theologians to the Third Person of the Trinity. As in the case in most theological formulations the doctrine was only gradually elaborated and worked out.

In the early part of the Old Testament, Jehovah ranks as a tribal deity—a god among other gods. Later, he is presented in terms of monotheism, but he is still the god of Israel alone. It is Jehovah who intervenes in the affairs of this small nation and who speaks direct to Moses and the prophets. Later, there developed a tendency to see him as transcendent and as working through a Spirit of Wisdom: side by side with this, there were hints of the Logos active through the Word. A large and beautiful Wisdom literature emerged. The Book of Proverbs has the following passages: 'Doth not wisdom cry? and understanding put forth her voice?... The Lord possessed me in the beginning of his way, before his works of old. I was set up from everlasting, from the beginning, or ever the earth was.' (viii: 1, 22, 23) In some passages, Wisdom possesses man; in other passages man holds communion with her. This doctrine of the Logos was later to influence Christianity.

The early Christian teaching regarding the work of the Holy Spirit was far from explicit. In the first four centuries, Christianity was mainly 'binitarian,' it recognized two Persons of the Trinity—the Father and the Son. Origen, for example, held that the Spirit was a creation of the Father through the Son and that His field of work was in the Church while that of the Son embraced the universe.

There was also much overlapping and confusion of function between the Second and Third Persons. Divine operation is sometimes attributed to the Wisdom or Logos activity, at other times to the activity of the Spirit. In much of the New Testament, the Holy Spirit is simply the power of God working through Jesus Christ. It has been pointed out that St. Paul does not differentiate between 'being in the Lord' and 'in the Spirit.' (cf Romans viii:1-11; Philippians i:19)

The same overlapping of ideas survives to this day in the doctrine of the Eucharist. In the Western Church it is the Lord Jesus Christ who consecrates the elements of bread and wine at the words 'This is my Body,' 'This is my Blood.' The Eastern Orthodox Church, on the other hand, after reciting the words of institution, invokes the Holy Ghost for the act of consecration. The Liberal Catholic Church also uses an *epiklesis* but places it before the words of consecration.

In the course of development we find an early writer named Victorinus advancing the idea that the Holy Ghost is the copula or joining principle of the Trinity. Proclus taught that all movement implies three stages, the beginning, the going out of self, and the return to the original source. This is akin to the Indian idea of the Self, the not-Self, and the relation between the two. There was one view of this which was abstract and static. What finally emerged in Christianity was a dynamic view; the Holy Ghost is not simply a relationship, rather it is the relationship of the Father and the Son that eventuates in the Holy Ghost. As one writer has put it: 'If God be Love, He must go forth in love.' Similarly, to revert to the Indian teaching, the interaction of Self and not-Self results in acquired dynamic virtue or character. It was along such lines of reasoning that the Holy Ghost came to be regarded in terms of creative activity.

The function of the Persons of the Trinity is worked out with great precision and clarity in theosophical literature. The reader can consult Plate II in Bishop Leadbeater's *Man, Visible and Invisible*[1] and also Mrs Besant's *A Study in Consciousness*. Man, made in the image of God, reflects in himself the three dominant attributes of the three Persons of the Trinity as will, wisdom, and creative activity, and these interact in various ways in the physical waking consciousness. The Deity is a triple manifestation on the highest plane of the world in which we live. The Second Aspect is manifested one plane lower and the Third Aspect two planes lower. The same process of descent into manifestation is reflected in the being of man on the buddhic and higher mental planes.

These successive phases of descent mark at each stage a closer relationship with man and with the general field of evolution. Hence it is that the Holy Ghost is most intimately related with normal human evolution. There is a reference to this in John xvi, 12-15; 'Howbeit when he, the spirit of truth, is come, he will guide you into all truth...He shall glorify me: for he shall receive of mine, and shall shew it unto you.' The creative activity of the Holy Spirit is ever at work in the Church, guiding Christians into spontaneity and helping them to unlock the resources of their own being. Dr. W.R. Matthews, the Dean of St. Paul's Cathedral, London, in his book *God in Christian Thought and Experience* (pp. 200, 201) writes:

> The activity of the Spirit may best be expressed in the most general terms, as that *nisus* in things and in persons which seems to drive them forward towards a higher degree of perfection.... What in the lower types of being appears as a tendency or striving, becomes in persons a conscious act of will which is guided by the idea of value. The movement of 'return' is no longer one in which the objects appear to be acted upon, or to be the passive participants in a general trend; the individuals are now moved from within by the spontaneous response of the self to ideal ends. Thus it is said of the Spirit both that 'He shall take of mine and shew it unto you' and that 'He shall guide you into all truth.' These two activities of the Spirit are identical. The Spirit moves the will of personal beings by presenting to them the Son in whom they see the truth of their nature, and its ideal perfection. And when they perceive Him they desire to move towards Him.

[1] See also Plate I in *The Christian Creed*.

THE ASSUMPTION OF THE VIRGIN MARY

There is no shadow of doubt as to the historical existence of Our Blessed Lady, or that she reigns as a mighty angel and lives wholly for the helping of mankind and for the glory of God. The mystical interpretation of all this has played a large part in Christian history.

Christianity is an Oriental religion just as much as Buddhism, Hinduism, Mohammedanism or Zorastrianism, and in order to understand it we must learn to look at it as an Oriental would. In the Eastern religions symbolism plays an important part. Symbols are used and studied with a vigour and delight which it is difficult for most Westerners to understand. Every time these stories are told, even though they have an historical basis, their symbolism is also recalled to mind.

Philosophically, God in the Absolute is eternally One, but in manifestation He is always Two—life and substance. We sometimes call it spirit and matter, or force and matter—it is all the same, for all these things are manifestations of God and of His power. When Christ, the only begotten of the Father, springs forth from His bosom and looks back upon that which remains, He sees it as a veil which in India is called *mulaprakriti*, the root of matter, or the Mother-matter; It is not really matter, but the potentiality of matter; not space, but the within of space, that from which all proceeds, the containing element of deity of which space is a manifestation.

This is the original substance underlying that of which all things were made. This is the Great Deep of Cabbalistic philosophy, and so it is also the heavenly wisdom which encircles and embraces all things. Now Our Lady has been identified with *Sophia* or heavenly wisdom; many titles from the book of the Wisdom of Solomon have been applied to her. She is spoken of as the mother of fair love, and of patience, perseverence and of holy hope; she is addressed as the rose of Sharon and the lily of the valley, and by many another beautiful and poetical name. She is the soul, macrocosmic and microcosmic; she is Daughter, Mother and Spouse of God. Daughter, because she also comes forth from the same eternal Father; Mother, because it is by the interaction upon and through her that the Christ-spirit is born, and Spouse, because the dynamic aspect of Deity works upon the negative or feminine aspect and in that way evolution takes place.

In the first of all Trinities (for there are many trinities at different levels of evolution) the Father represents the Absolute or what we may without irreverence call the static mode of Deity, while the Holy Ghost represents the dynamic or Will in action, and therefore His emblem is the equal-armed cross or swastika. The Mother aspect of Deity manifests as the aether of space, the *koilon*, without which there could be no evolution, and yet it remains virgin and unaffected after evolution has passed. Into this, the Christ, or the energizing Logos or Word, breathes the breath of life.

In this symbolism, Our Lady is the essence of the great sea of matter and so is seen as Aphrodite, the Sea Queen, or Mary the Star of the Sea, clothed in the blue of the sky and of the sea, just as in the Greek manifestation of the same idea Pallas Athene wore the same colour. Because it is only by means of our passage through matter that we evolve, so is she also, from another point of view, Isis the Initiator. She is the Virgin Mother by whom the Christ is born in us; just as Jesus was born in the outer world, so is she the causal body, the soul in man, the Mother of God in whom the divine spirit enfolds itself within us. She is the Immaculate, for the symbol of the womb is the same as that of the cup; she descends as Eve into matter and generation, and, as Mary, is assumed beyond matter into life eternal.

On earth, she is truly *mater dolorosa*—the Mother of Sorrows—because sorrow and trouble come to us through our connection with matter; but when she rises above the lower self she is our Lady of Victories, the glory of the Church triumphant, 'clothed with the sun, and the moon under her feet, and upon her head a crown of twelve stars.' We must identify ourselves with this glorious evolution and become part of it if we would gain from it the benefit which God intends us to gain.

> I must become Queen Mary,
>   And birth to God must give,
> If I in heavenly blessedness
>   For evermore would live.

On the Feast of the Assumption we celebrate the final drawing up of matter into the Absolute when evolution is over, so that God may be all in all. That is the symbolical side. The historical side is the assumption of the mother of Jesus into the angelic host. Christ, being divine in nature, ascends by His own power and volition, even as of His own will He sprang forth in the beginning from the bosom of the Father; but Mary, the soul, is assumed, drawn up by the will of Him who is at the same time her Father and her Son; for the first Adam (says St. Paul) was made a living soul but the last Adam—the Christ—is Himself a quickening or life-giving Spirit. So in following Adam, who typifies the mind, all die; but in Christ all are made alive.

Realize, also, that our highest concept of deity combines all that is best of the characteristics attributed to both sexes. It is natural that men should separate in their thought these two aspects of God; that strength, wisdom, scientific direction, the 'destroying' aspect of deity should be thought of as masculine, and that love, compassion, harmony, beauty and tenderness should be thought of as the feminine side of the divine. But all is God from whatever side you may look at it. It is called sometimes God and man in the person of Christ, but in other religions it is thought of as Father-Mother.

Different forms of the divine power flow forth, and in the older religions there were gods and goddesses with their priests and priestesses. The great teachers in the later religions did not choose to make this division prominent, and so in Christianity and Mohammedanism there are priests only and the forces which are poured forth through the services of the Church, although they include all the qualities, are yet so shaped and arranged as to run through the male form.

But it must be remembered that in the ancient world the feminine aspect of the deity was held in the very highest honour. The festival of the Assumption of Our Lady had its origins in a harvest festival held at a time when the celebrations in honour of Astarte would not be interfered with by hail or storm. Thus the very day of our Christian festival was fixed by the older religion.

The physical body of Our Lady was not, of course, caught up through the clouds into Heaven. That is only the Oriental way of stating the fact that she was raised above human evolution and became what we should call a mighty angel. That is why the Church offers to her, not *doulia* the reverence paid to the Saints—but *hyperdoulia*, the greatest and deepest reverence that is given to her alone. But even that comes no way near to, or conflicts, with *latreia*, the divine worship which is given to God alone.

Our Lady receives the love and devotion of her adherents, but she receives it as a channel through which it passes to Christ, her Son and King, while she is also the channel for the outpouring of His love which comes in response. Thus, she is also *Consolatrix Afflictorum*, the consoler of those who are afflicted or in sorrow.

We have good reason, then, from the points of view both of symbolism and of fact, to keep the festivals of Our Lady and to rejoice and be thankful for the love and wisdom which have provided this line of approach through her. We are thankful to Christ who gives it, and to Our Lady through whom it comes. So we join in the world-wide chorus of praise and repeat the angel's words: 'Hail Mary! full of grace; blessed art thou among women.'

> Ave Maria! thou those name
> All but adoring love may claim.
> > Yet we may reach thy shrine.
> For He, thy Son and Monarch, vows
> To crown all lowly lofty brows
> > With love and joy like thine.

SOME ANSWERS TO QUESTIONS

1. *'Brethren, pray that my sacrifice and yours may be acceptable to God the Father almighty.' Does the priest remain turned towards the people until they have answered, or does he at once begin to turn back to the altar?*

It is not necessary, nor is it in keeping with the symbolism to wait until they have finished their response. The response is addressed to the Lord rather than to the priest. This is one of the two occasions in the Mass (the other being at the final Blessing) when the priest turns completely round in the form of a circle. The work of the moment is the sweeping up of the response of devotion and self-dedication made by the people, and the celebrant carries that offering of spiritual energy with him, symbolically and actually, as he turns.

The sacraments, as 'means of grace,' have as their purpose the quickening of evolution. We use here the word 'quickening' in its older sense, as when the Nicene Creed speaks of 'the quick and the dead.' In this sense, quickening means the awakening into fuller and (in the later human stages) more self-conscious existence.

The bread and the wine have just been offered as tokens of the fruits of the earth. It is the offering made on behalf of nature, and each Mass helps forward in some measure the evolution of the lower kingdoms. At the stage now under consideration the offering is made of 'ourselves, our souls and bodies.' The more we can learn to regard ourselves as an integral part of the human family—in other words to reach what has been called 'cosmic consciousness'—the more widespread is this offering, later to be worked upon by the Lord Himself. The divine grace outpoured later has the effect of quickening all creation. The more intelligent and sincere and integral the co-operation of the clergy and congregation with the Divine Will, the wider and deeper will be field of operation.

2. *Following the singing of the Adeste Fideles a blessing is invoked on the people and three crosses are made over the Host and Chalice. '...do thou + hallow, + quicken and + bless them....' Please explain.*

The process will be understood more easily if we study the significance of the various crosses made during this second part of the Canon. The action is clearly described by Bishop C.W. Leadbeater in his book *The Science of the Sacraments*. The process at work can be followed by studying the wording of the Roman Missal, but it is expressed a little more clearly in our text.

When the first set of crosses ('...this pure + Host, this holy + Host') is made the priest pours into the consecrated elements the offering of himself and of the people and the attendant angels. The crosses correspond to the fivefold being of man as represented by and expressed through his will, intuition, synthetic thought, concrete thought, and emotion. This offering is a pouring in of all that we have to give, and is linked up with the earlier stage of the Eucharist when we made the offering on behalf of the lower kingdoms of nature, and of 'ourselves, our souls and bodies.' The foregoing has now been intensified, and the priest takes up all the devotion of the congregation, living and dead, and of the nature spirits and angels that are gathered round, also of all beings at a distance with whom he has linked the sacred oblation, and he pours it all into the chalice to be offered at the throne on high.

We come to another set of crosses. The priest now takes the place of the Angel of the Presence in the triangle with the Host and the Chalice. Again, the priest prays that the people may be blessed, and he sends out over the congregation three waves of influence. Here the term 'congregation' covers all those far and wide with whom he has linked up whether in terms of aspiration or for purposes of helping. 'Hallow'—First Person of the Trinity; 'quicken'—the Holy Spirit; 'bless'—the Second Person. The Second Person is mentioned last because He is now represented by the priest.

3. All over the world, Mass is being offered. Is this a spiritual structure into which we are pouring force? Can we think of this as going on continuously, and of ourselves as joining in?

This question opens up a vast and fascinating field of thought. The ordinary worshipper usually thinks only of what is going on in the church in which he is present, and not of other places and congregations. The first step for him is to get away from his semi-passive and dreamy way of looking on at things although even this attitude is not without its benefits for he gets uplifted, purified and strengthened as the result of being present at the service and of the small contribution he makes to it. But worship becomes altogether different and much more powerful as people learn to mean and to become those qualities and virtues which are expressed in the liturgy. And our liturgy is so framed that the worshippers are lifted out of the attitude of being occupied with themselves and their own salvation.

The question put here suggests a higher stage of worship in which our conceptions of time and space undergo considerable modification. There is a passage in the Canon of the Mass which reads: 'Uniting in this joyful sacrifice with thy holy church throughout all the ages, we lift our hearts in adoration to thee, O God the Son....' This is intended to bridge over our separation in time, and to link us up in the fellowship of Christ's people who have participated in the Christian offering and memorial of the Great Sacrifice for some two thousand years. It need be no more difficult for us to bridge over the separation of space, although the mastery of space on the physical plane makes considerable demands on our resources. But in terms of thought and emotion, space or separation is not a question of distance but of sympathy or antipathy, of unity or separateness. In the ordinary course of life we are familiar with measurements of time and space. The chronometer marks one standard of time, the milestone or yard-measure the corresponding standard distance. These instruments of science measure the conditions imposed on us by the form or matter side of manifestation. But our standards of consciousness are entirely different. In the company of an interesting speaker time will fly, as the expression has it; in the company of a bore, or under the strain of a sleepless and restless night, time is protracted. In the same fashion, a walk may be short and exhilarating, or long and tedious, according to the whim of the body or to the company in which it is taken. The more we reach out into spiritual experience, into the realization of the omnipresence of God, the more readily and freely are we able to transcend the material limitations which were the conditions of our earlier growth.

The ability to work consciously with a number of other people, at a distance and in several places simultaneously, is part of what is meant by our 'oneness in Christ' and by the unity of His 'mystical Body.' The prayer 'that they all may be one' (John xvii, 21) is grievously misunderstood by the rank and file of churchmen who generally believe it to mean that they must hold the same beliefs and carry out the same rites. Variety exists so that the endless diversity of the divine life may be brought out into adequate expression and be made fully manifest. But the man who can reach up into Christ's Presence knows himself to be one with all others and with all other modes of self-expression. It is not that all these phases of self-expression are of equal value and worth, but that they are phases of experience through which countless individuals are rising into the knowledge of the oneness of the divine life.

How is this oneness to be reached? I know of no better training, for those who can answer to its call, than the reverent use of the Holy Eucharist. We have in that rite the supreme example and activity of the Christ Himself.

The Holy Sacrifice can be envisaged in three sequential phases. First there is the primal Sacrifice of the Logos. This is beautifully depicted in the familiar words: '...we lift our hearts in adoration to thee, O God the Son, consubstantial, co-eternal with the Father, who, abiding unchangeable within thyself, didst nevertheless in the mystery of thy boundless love and thine eternal sacrifice breathe forth thine own divine life into thy universe and thus didst offer thyself as the Lamb slain from the foundation of the world, dying in very truth that we might live.' That sacrifice is re-enacted in a secondary phase or correspondence in the coming into the world of Our Lord Jesus Christ, and of other great Teachers of humanity who have caused the light of their presence to shine in the world and have bequeathed to mankind the various religions for its upliftment, guidance and instruction. And thirdly, that we may be aided in our task of transforming ourselves into His likeness, the eternal sacrifice of Our Lord Christ is perpetuated for us in terms of time and space in the Blessed Sacrament of the altar as 'a means of grace.' It is also an extension of the great mystery of the Incarnation.

In the Eucharist it is not difficult to learn to forget ourselves, for we have in it the supreme example of the Lord who is continually pouring Himself out in sacrifice for the helping of the world. It is a question of learning to be able constantly to give, to become naturally more interested in others and in causes that make for righteousness in the world, than in ourselves; to be aflame with love for the world and for our brother men. That way lies the royal road to uniting ourselves with the one great Life.

Once that state of consciousness is reached we no longer think of ourselves as isolated units in the world, but as one with our fellow-men yet having each his own special contribution to make to the great plan. On the same principle, the church in which we offer our worship is not simply an isolated building or centre of worship; it is one of the thousands of centres of worship through which Our Lord is sending out His blessing over the world, and it is our task to make that centre one which can be specially useful in His service. It may have the allotted task of allaying fear and mistrust among the nations. It may have the task of wiping out rivalries among the warring classes and castes. It may have the task of spreading the light of truth abroad in this age of doubt, difficulty and distress. It may serve all these purposes and others besides. We can glimpse a plan in which the many churches form one great organism through which Our Lord can work out His purpose for His world. There will be some churches with hundreds of worshippers whose work it will be to spread the divine blessing over large areas. There will be others, counting fewer workers, whose privilege it will be to add richness and wisdom and wealth of spiritual realization to the offering of worship which rises from all parts of the earth before the Throne of God.

4. Is it true that cremation is sometimes an alarming experience for the deceased?

When the cord between the dense physical body and the etheric double is broken, there can be no further physical sensation in the higher bodies. Some think that it is this process of disentanglement from the corpse which is meant by the phrase in the Requiem Eucharist: 'Or ever the silver cord be loosed....' If the dead man does feel anything it is the product of his own imagination. People do not realize how much of the after-death surroundings of the ordinary man are illusory, that is, self-created by thought. An entertaining instance of this occurs in Sir Oliver Lodge's *Raymond*, a book containing communications from his deceased son. It speaks of whisky distilleries and cigar factories on 'the other side' but Raymond discloses that the whisky and cigars are sadly lacking in substantiality. A.P. Sinnett once told of a dead man who claimed to live in a house with the ordinary scenic panorama before him, but who admitted, on closer questioning, that the scenery changed every now and again.

Any story of suffering during cremation is explainable on this hypothesis. It also sometimes happens that people who have just died lapse into a period of unconsciousness and will float about in this condition near the grave. Hence the stories of haunted churchyards.

5. *How do you explain the fact that some people are disturbed by a 'red service?'*

The only explanation the occurs to me is oversensitiveness of the nervous system. Each of the four colours used at different seasons and festivals of the Church has its special effect. The influence flowing through the services changes in some measure according to the season or feast. Many people will be sensitive to the fact that a greater wealth and volume of power will flow through the services at Easter, Christmas and Pentecost than on one of the routine Sundays after Trinity. The colour is arranged to fit in with the variation of influence. These changes of season and of influence help in the development of character, which is one of the purposes of worship; they represent a scheme of specialization. White, which is used on great festivals like Easter and Christmas and at ordinations, is the synthesis of all colours and the power is then characterized by joy. The whole of our being—as much of it, that is to say, as is awake—is at work. There is then no question of specialization. Red and violet are the extremes of the spectrum; each is powerfully specialized. Violet is actinic and cleansing, and is therefore used at introspective seasons like Lent and Advent. Red does in the range of outward-turned activity what violet does in the complementary inward-turned. It represents the flowing out of the creative activity of the Holy Spirit. The martyrs consecrated their lives by the supreme act of martyrdom, and their feasts express something of this power of consecrated action. This power reaches its fullness at Pentecost. Green is midway between the two poles of the spectrum, and is the colour associated with sympathy and understanding. It is used at those periods when we are trying to build into our characters, and to work out in practice, the lessons inculcated by the seasons of the Christian Year.

To come back to the question asked. The cutting out of the grey of fear and misery and of the exaggerated reiteration of human sinfulness has worked to make our churches into living centres of power. If any sensitive person goes into any of our churches he will notice within it the same matured and consecrated feeling as is found in the older cathedrals. I have known some unusually sensitive people who found our services difficult to bear because of the sense of power they carried with them, no matter what colour was used. Red is a colour known to be exciting to the nervous system, and it is probable that in the cases mentioned the persons are sensitive to this exteriorization of power.

6. *'Whose sins thou dost forgive, they are forgiven; and whose sins thou dost retain, they are retained.' Is it allowed to 'retain' sins and, if so, in which case?*

This raises the whole question of confession and absolution. The note in our Liturgy which prefaces the formula for these acts contains the following sentences:

> In the Liberal Catholic Church auricular confession is entirely optional and is not required as a preliminary to the reception of holy communion. It is intended primarily for those who may feel their conscience to be troubled with some weighty matter. Its frequent and systematic practice is not encouraged, since it is felt that under such conditions the detailed confession is apt to become a matter of routine and its spiritual value in the life of the individual thereby defeated. For all ordinary purposes the general confession in the Holy Eucharist should suffice.

As to the question of 'retaining' sin, I can think of a simple example. Suppose a person comes to confession and says that he had stolen something. The priest might rightly say: 'I think that you should go and tell the person concerned, and you may come to me for absolution afterwards, which will gladly be given in Our Lord's Name.' We can see that there might be a number of cases where the person must do his physical-plane duty to the individuals concerned before he can receive the grace and consolation of the Church.

7. *How do you know that you are doing good in the services of the Church?*

The scheme of worship aimed at in our Church is to a large extent original. I do not mean to say that work of the same kind has not been done by outstanding personalities in other Churches, but [neither the][1] Roman nor the Anglican liturgy lends itself in the same way as ours to the work which we have in mind. Our liturgy has been carefully planned; so far as we are able to judge, the right sequence of action has been laid down in the ceremonies, and the language has been so framed that it keeps to a lofty idealism on the one hand and, on the other, puts into the hearts and minds of the worshippers ideas which they can conscientiously express. During the Roman Mass, the congregation does not usually participate actively and intelligently in what is taking place. There may be a wealth of true devotion but it is not always conjoined with the action at the altar. The Anglican Prayer Book contains wonderful stately language, to much of which we are ourselves indebted, but its Communion service has been described as 'the baldest eucharistic rite in Christendom.' One finds in many High Churches large sections of the Roman rite or other equally unofficial rites being intercalated, often secretly.

We have sought in our Church to make the worship a common act on the part of those in the sanctuary and in the congregation. This method provides every opportunity for the individual worshipper to grow into spiritual realization and maturity. The output of power in terms of emotion and thought can be wonderful when many people, trained in this method, are worshipping together. The various qualities of character expressed in our liturgy—love, wisdom, beauty—represent an objective power with which the worshipper finds himself in contact. The secret of growing into the experience about which the questioner asks is to forget oneself in the presence of the splendid ideals which are being expressed, of the congregation of devout and dedicated worshippers, of Our Lord Himself and of His holy angels, and of our Father in heaven.

---

[1] The original text contains the words 'such cases have been' instead of what is included in brackets. It is not clear what Bp. Wedgwood had in mind. [Ed.]

MEDITATION FOR BEGINNERS[1]

Withdraw into yourself and look. And if you do not find yourself beautiful as yet, do as does the creator of a statue that is to be made beautiful; he cuts away here, he smooths there, he makes this line lighter, this other purer, until he has shown a beautiful face upon the statue. So do you also; cut away all that is excessive, straighten all that is crooked, bring light to all that is shadowed, labour to make all glow with beauty, and do not cease chiselling your statue until there shall shine out on you the godlike splendour of virtue, until you shall see the final goodness surely established in the stainless shrine.

Plotinus on the Beautiful
(Translated by Stephen MacKenna)

INTRODUCTION

It is significant of the spiritual tendency of the Theosophical Society that there is a steady interest in meditation, and many now desire help and guidance as to its practice. Within the Inner Section of the Theosophical Society (called the Esoteric School) very definite and helpful instruction is available for earnest and approved students; but there are many who, perhaps for domestic or other reasons, do not feel free to undertake the heavy responsibility implied in joining this—for to enter the Esoteric School implies that Theosophy is thenceforward to become a dominant factor in the life. Such members often wish to learn how to meditate, and it is with the hope of aiding this large class of earnest and spiritually-minded people that these present suggestions are put forward. Also, it may be pointed out, it is only possible to gain admission to the Esoteric School after three years' membership in the outer Society, and during this preliminary period much of the necessary spadework may be accomplished, with the result that the aspirant will be better fitted for the training of the Inner Section and of greater service to its corporate life.

The present hints are written more especially for Theosophists, although they may be found helpful by others who have not yet embraced the philosophy of life summed up under the name of Theosophy. This course has been followed quite advisedly, for the author believes that it is of little use to set to work upon the serious practice of meditation until the teachings regarding the control and use of thought and emotion set forth in Theosophical books have been mastered, and until the aspirant has emerged from the dilettante stage of occultism. Until then he will derive more benefit from quiet reflection upon devotional books or from the practice of the earlier methods laid down in the various exoteric religions. For more advanced students, following other methods of study, the author does not profess to write.

---

[1] This book exists in various revisions by various editors. The differences are caused, at least partly, by who is perceived as the target readership. The version included here was aimed at an audience of Theosophists, as is clear from the text. [Ed.]

WHAT MEDITATION IS

Meditation consists in the endeavour to bring into the waking consciousness, that is, into the mind in its normal state of activity, some realization of the super-consciousness, to create by the power of aspiration a channel through which the influence of the divine or spiritual principle—the real man—may irradiate the lower personality. It is the reaching out of the mind and feelings towards an ideal, and the opening of the doors of the imprisoned lower consciousness to the influence of that idea. 'Meditation,' says H.P. Blavatsky, 'is the inexpressible longing of the inner man for the Infinite.'

The ideal chosen may be abstract—it may be a virtue, such as sympathy or justice; it may be the thought of the Inner Light, of that Divine Essence which is the innermost reality of man's nature: it may even be recognized only as a vague and dim sensing of the highest that is in us. Or the ideal may be personified as a Master, a Divine Teacher—indeed it may be seen as embodied in anyone whom we feel in any way to be worthy of our respect and admiration. Consequently the subject and type of meditation will vary widely according to the temperament and 'ray' of the individual. But in all cases it is essentially the uplifting of the soul towards its divine source, the desire of the particularized self to become one with the Universal Self.

FIRST STEPS

The first step in meditation consists in cultivating the thought, until it becomes habitual, that the physical body is an instrument of the spirit.

Those who have only just made the acquaintance of Theosophical thought find it difficult at first to reverse their point of view; to them the soul and spirit are unreal. The planes and bodies, of which Theosophical writers speak in their endeavour to convey clearly and with scientific precision some little glimpse of the mysteries of man's being, are memorized in terms of some textbook diagram, each name being conjured up with an effort of memory. The physical body is the one tangible reality and the superphysical the shadowy and vague, a mere intellectual conception. But gradually and almost imperceptibly this feeling is lost; a feeling of realisation of the superphysical begins to work down into the physical brain and to enliven what was previously merely an intellectual theory. The reason for this is not far to seek. To read Theosophical books is to place oneself in touch with powerfully stimulating forces in the world of mental archetypes; to read of higher bodies tends by directing the attention to those bodies to awaken self-consciousness in them. Interest in and study of the astral plane and the astral body gradually waken the student on that plane during physical sleep. The stimulation of the higher bodies into greater activity is also assisted by being within the aura of superphysically developed people. As a natural result this expansion of the inner nature begins to modify the waking consciousness, the knowledge of the Higher Man slowly filters down into the physical brain, and the student will find his outlook on life undergoing great change. An extension of consciousness becomes noticeable, new vistas of thought and feeling open up before him, his surroundings in life assume a fresh significance as he awakens to them, and the truths of Theosophy begin to change from intellectual theory into spiritual experience.

Such, briefly stated, is the rationale of the gradual expansion of consciousness, which comes within the early experience of most Theosophists who are really in earnest; and we may, in passing, hazard the idea that the three years that must elapse before a student is eligible for the Esoteric School are prescribed not only that his steadfastness in Theosophy may be tested but also that time may be allowed for this change in the superphysical bodies, through which he may come intuitively to feel himself as the Higher Man using a physical instrument.

Now this process and awakening may be materially quickened. 'Help Nature,' says *The Voice of the Silence*, 'and work on with her; and Nature will regard Thee as one of her creators and make obeisance.' A modern scientific writer has echoed the same truth in the words 'Nature is conquered by obedience;' we have but to understand the laws of nature, and then, rightly selected and applied, they become our obedient servants. That which takes place slowly and gradually in the ordinary course of time may be deliberately hastened by intelligent and well-directed effort. Hence the student's first exercise in meditation may fittingly have in view this aim of consciously realizing the Higher Man.

The following practice is one which the present writer employed with good results, until it became unnecessary to continue with it.

Meditation on the Bodies

Let the student begin by thinking of the physical body; then consider how it is possible to control and direct it, and thus separate himself in thought from it—regarding it as a vehicle, and picture himself for a few moments as living in the astral body. Let him reflect, in turn, that he can control his emotions and desires; and, with a strong effort, repudiate the astral body and realise that he is not this body of surging and struggling passions, desires and emotions. Then let him picture himself as living in the mental body; and reflect again that he can control his thoughts, that he has the power of setting his mind to think on any subject he pleases, and again with an effort repudiate the mental body. The student should now let himself soar into the free atmosphere of the spirit where is eternal peace, and, resting there for a period, strive with great intensity to realize That is the real Self.

Let him now descend again, carrying with him the peace of the spirit through the different bodies. Let him picture the aura of the mental body raying out around him, and let the influence of peace suffuse it, as he affirms that he is the Self which used the mental body as an instrument in his service. Then descending into the astral body, again let the peace ray out through the aura, as he affirms that he is that which uses the emotions as his servants; and lastly, let him return to the physical body, recognizing it as an instrument, and as a centre of the divine peace, wherever it may pass in the world.

The exercise may at first seem strange and fruitless, for the physical body is still the great reality, and thought and feeling are still the great reality, and thought and feeling are still apt to be regarded as products of the physical brain. The beginner must remember that he is seeking to undo the thought-habit of years, and therefore must not be impatient for immediate results. Possibly much time may elapse before his intuition assures him with unerring certainty that there is a higher power within him, guiding his actions and shaping his course through life. Quite naturally, he may dread the possibility of self-hypnosis, the thought that he may by slow degrees be deluding himself into beliefs which are fanciful and have no foundation of reality. To the well-balanced mind the earlier stages are by far the most difficult, for there is a natural caution about venturing into the unknown, and a tendency to beat a mental retreat at each suspicion of danger. None the less, it is only reasonable to give due trial to a system expounded by the greatest minds of antiquity, prescribed in all the great religions and witnessed to by eminently sane and sincere people of the present day. And a little steady and persistent practice is bound to lead to certain results. How definite those results will be and with what degree of rapidity they will be apparent will naturally depend upon the temperament, the industry and the possibilities of the individual.

A More Elaborate Form of the Above

As the beginner grows more familiar with the meditation outlined above, he may begin to elaborate it, according to the bent of his temperament. He may find it helpful, for instance, to consider the simile pianoforte and a pianist. As the pianoforte produces sound and ordered music, so the brain and physical body give expression to thought, feeling and ordered activity. But it is the pianist who expresses himself through the medium of the instrument. In the same way the physical body (in its voluntary activities) does but vibrate in response to the Higher Man.

Detaching himself in thought from the physical body and examining it in the cool discrimination of the mind, he should endeavour to realise that it is only a vehicle, an instrument, a vesture of flesh. In order that the consciousness, which is the manifestation of the spirit, can contact the physical world it must inhabit a tabernacle of physical matter, kith and kin with that physical world, for only a physical vehicle of consciousness can make vibratory relationship with physical matter. By the multiplicity of experiences to be gained from the physical world and the gradual shaping of the physical instrument to respond to them, the spirit unfolds its innate powers from latency into potency.

He may then consider how it is possible to control and direct it, how it responds to the behests of the governing intelligence—the I. Thus separating himself in thought from it, he should next picture himself for a few moments as living in the astral body.

Let him reflect, in turn, that the astral body is not his real self. He can control his emotions and desires, he can regulate the play of feeling. His emotions are but one aspect of his consciousness working in and limited by the astral body, which, in its turn, is a tenement built up from the material of the astral plane, that the indwelling consciousness may come into relation with it. He himself is not this body of struggling surging emotions, passions and desires. In his calmer moments he knows that he is above the surge of emotions. His fits of passion, of jealousy, of fear, of selfishness and hatred—all these are not himself but the play of emotions which have slipped beyond control, as a greyhound may slip his leash. In his heart of hearts he knows that as much of this is already under his control, so by dint of patient perseverance and earnest endeavour all may in course of time be brought within due bounds, and mastery of the emotions be gained.

Thus standing as it were outside of his emotions, looking down upon the whole sphere of their activity, let him next picture himself as living in the mental body.

It is not difficult for the beginner to separate himself from his physical and emotional bodies—he has been taught in the practice of ordinary morality to check and control action and violent emotion; but he has probably never been taught much of the power of thought, and accordingly he finds it difficult to realise at first the possibility of controlling his thought.

Yet he has the power to set his mind upon any subject he pleases, and by dint of perseverance he may learn to keep it fixed thereupon. And eventually he may gain such control of the mind as to be able to dismiss from it at will any unwelcome thought.

And so, passing through the various stages, he may raise himself into the contemplation of That which is beyond words, ineffably real and sacred, reaching the very shrine of his own being, the altar upon which the Divine Shekinah itself is made manifest, and bearing with him that radiance into the outer world of sense.

When the student by his meditation and by his oft-repeated thought during the day has grown to regard himself as the Inner Man, working outwards into the world through the instrumentality of a physical body, he may then pass on to more elaborate and scientific forms of meditation. He should begin to work with fuller understanding of its various details and stages, regarding it as at once a means of spiritual refreshment and growth and a science of wrestling with the wayward mind and feelings.

CONCENTRATION

Meditation is often divided into three stages: Concentration, Meditation, Contemplation. It may be still further subdivided, but it is unnecessary to do so here; on the other hand the beginner should bear in mind that meditation is a science of a life-time, so that he must not expect to attain to the stage of pure contemplation in his earlier efforts.

Concentration consists of focusing the mind on one idea and holding it there. Patanjali, the author of the classic Hindu *Yoga Aphorisms*, defines Yoga as 'the hindering of the modifications of the thinking principle.' This definition is applicable to concentration, though Patanjali probably goes further in his thought and includes the cessation of the image-making faculty of the mind and of all concrete expressions of thought, thus virtually passing beyond the stage of mere concentration into that of contemplation.

To be able to concentrate, then, it is necessary to gain control of the mind and learn by gradual practice to narrow down the range of its activity, until it becomes one-pointed. Some idea or object is selected upon which to concentrate, and the initial step is to shut out all else from the mind, to exclude therefrom the stream of thoughts alien to the subject, as they dance before the mind like the flickering pictures of the cinematograph. It is true that much of the student's practice must be in the initial stages take this form of repeated exclusion of thought; and to set oneself to do this is excellent training. But there is another and far sounder way of attaining concentration; it consists in becoming so interested and absorbed in the subject selected that all other thoughts are *ipso facto* excluded from the mind. We are constantly doing this in our daily lives, unconsciously and by force of habit. The writing of a letter, the adding of accounts, the taking of weighty decisions, the thinking out of difficult problems—all these things so engross the mind as to induce a state of more or less wrapt concentration. The student must learn to accomplish this at will, and will best succeed by cultivating the power and habit of observing and paying attention to outer objects.

Let him take any object—a penholder, a piece of blotting paper, a leaf, a flower—and note the details of its appearance and structure which usually pass by unnoticed; let him catalogue one by one its properties, and presently he will find the exercise of absorbing interest. If he is able to study the process of its manufacture or growth, the interest will again be heightened. No object in nature is in reality entirely dull and uninteresting; and when anything seems so to us, the failure to appreciate the wonder and beauty of its manifestation lies in our own inattentiveness.

As an aid to concentration, it is well to repeat aloud the ideas that pass through the mind. So; this penholder is black; it reflects the light from the window from some portions of its surface; it is about seven inches in length, cylindrical; its surface is engraved with a pattern; the pattern is branch-shaped and is formed of a series of closely-marked lines—and so forth *ad libitum*.

In this way the student learns to shut out the larger world and to enclose himself in the smaller world of his choice. When this has been done successfully he has achieved a certain degree of concentration—for it is evident that there are still many and various thoughts running through the mind, though all on the subject of the penholder. The speaking aloud helps to slow down this stream of thought and to hinder the mind from wandering. Gradually by practice he learns to narrow down still further the circle of thought until literally he can reach one-pointedness of mind.

The above practice is somewhat in the nature of drill instruction; it requires a degree of strenuous application, and, moreover, may appear somewhat cold to the student, since it arouses little emotion. Another exercise in concentration may therefore be taken concurrently, but before describing this we may say that the former exercise must needs be mastered at some stage of the student's career. Some degree of mastery therein is a preliminary to successful visualisation—that is, the power of mentally reproducing an object in accurate detail without it being visible to the eyes—and accurate visualisation is a necessary feature of much of the work which is done by students trained in occult methods such as the deliberate construction of thought-forms and the creation of symbols by the mind in ceremonial. Accordingly the student who is really in earnest will not neglect this branch of work on account of it being difficult and requiring application. He will also set to work at visualisation, observing and carefully scrutinizing an object, and then with the eyes closed endeavouring to build up a mental picture of it.

The second method, above referred to, is that of concentrating not upon a physical object but upon an idea. If some virtue be taken it has the advantage of arousing the enthusiasm and devotion of the student, and this is a very important consideration in the initial stages of his practice, when perseverance and steadfastness are often sorely tried. Moreover, the effort builds that virtue into the character. In this case the concentration is chiefly that of the feelings and less conspicuously a mental process. The student strives to reproduce in himself the virtue, let us say sympathy, at which he is aiming, and by dint of holding himself to a single emotion, by the power of the will eventually succeeds in feeling sympathy. It is easier to be one-pointed in feeling than in thought, for the latter is more subtle and active; but if intense concentration of feeling can be induced, the mind will to a certain extent follow suit.

MEDITATION

Having thus considered concentration we can now pass on to the second main division of our subject—namely, meditation. Meditation is the art of considering a subject or turning it over in the mind in its various bearings and relationships. Properly speaking, the stage of meditation does not follow directly upon the complete one-pointedness of mind which we have discussed above, it rather succeeds that stage of comparative concentration which has banished from the mind all ideas alien to the one subject under consideration; but efficiency in concentration will be required as each branch of the meditation is taken up. We need not occupy space with further definitions of meditation, but may at once pass on to certain schemes of practice which will illustrate its nature and method more clearly than theoretical dissertation. We have touched above on the thought of sympathy and may well use it as a subject of meditation.

Meditation on Sympathy

Reflect that like all other virtues this is an attribute of the Divine Consciousness; try to understand its nature and function in the world; consider it as a binding power uniting one particularized self to another. Compare it with love: sympathy implies understanding of another and the power to place oneself in his position; love need not imply this understanding; on the other hand for its complete expression sympathy requires the strong inner motive power which love alone can supply. Picture the divine sympathy as poured forth into the world through the ideal man—the Christ or the Master—and then as directed towards one's self individually.

The student should then with a strong active aspiration merge himself into the stream of this ineffable influence radiating from the Master, and to seek to reach the object of his devotion. (Here the stage of contemplation may be attained). He should then think of this virtue as applied in his daily life, to his friends and loved ones—even to those with whom there is need for better understanding; let him picture them one by one before him and wrap them round with the influence which is pouring through him.

Another and more elaborate meditation may be given for the benefit of those who are unable to dwell for any length of time on a single thought.

Meditation To Expand the Consciousness

The student should raise his consciousness and contemplate the immensities of the universe; the picture of the starlit heavens, the soft radiance of the sunset, or the thought of the cosmos enshrined within the infinitesimally minute atom, will aid him in this, and he may, if he so desire, use the method of rising through the bodies described earlier in this book. Let him then direct his thoughts in loftiest aspiration to the Logos of our system and picture the whole system as contained within the bounds of His consciousness: 'In Him we live and move and have our being.' He may then follow out the line of thought developed in the pamphlet by Mrs. Besant entitled *On Moods*—namely, that though we might naturally think of the loftier members of the Hierarchy as being most distant from us and almost beyond the reach of our halting aspiration owing to their remoteness from petty human interests, the reverse is actually true, and we are literally in closest touch with the all-embracing consciousness of the Logos. The student may find it helpful to think of the increasing size of the aura as spiritual development is achieved; of that of the ordinary man, of that of pupils and initiates, of the aura of the Master and the close relation of consciousness between the Master and the close relation of consciousness between the Master and his pupils and others whom he is helping, of the aura of the Lord Buddha which according to tradition extended three miles about His person, and so rising in thought he may conceive of a being whose aura of field of consciousness encompasses the whole of our planet and of One who thus embraces the whole of our planet and of One who thus embraces the whole of the system to which we belong. Literally is it true that every action, every feeling and every thought to which we give expression are part of Him; nay, our very memory is part of His memory, for is not all remembrance but the power to touch the akashic records of nature, which is but the expression of Himself?

The student may then pass on to think of some of those qualities which we may associate with the manifestation of God in His world—let us take justice and beauty and love; that the justice of the Supreme is shown forth in the invariable laws of nature, the law of the conservation of energy, the dictum of Newton that action and re-action are equal and opposite, the law of karmic retribution which gives unto each man the just reward of his deeds. Let him think of what belief in karma really implies—the hand that strikes a grievous blow is one's own dead past come back to life again; and from such reflections let him win content with that which is or which may befall him. Let him think also of the innumerable relations under this law made between man and man, the weaving of God's plan in the universe, and see in those complex relationships the immutable law of perfect justice.

Passing next to the aspect of beauty he may study the exquisite plan of the Great Architect and Grand Geometrician of the Universe, and looking with closer attention at all created nature may perceive the universality of that aspect of the Supreme which expresses itself in beauty or harmony. Turning from beauty of nature to that created by man he may soar aloft on the wings of the imagination and contemplate the masterpieces of that human art which borders on the realm of divinity, because in very truth the materials in the hand of the artist are the divine powers of nature. Thus, in music, the mighty structures of sound reflect in many hues those archetypal forces of nature which stream forth through the blazing hosts of the Gandharvas, revealing to man the power of the hidden Word and raising him aloft once more to the kingdom of his divine heritage.

And in the compassionate love of the Supreme all human relationships of tenderness and love have their source. To the eye of the spirit the beauty of woman gives no cause for carnal desire, but is rather a reason that she should be respected as a child of God and a manifestation of His supreme beauty. There is but one love throughout the universe, given by the Divine Father into the custody of His creatures; it is the one primal force which in its elementary creative aspect produces multiplicity of form and in its higher aspect draws souls together towards unity in the One Life.

CONTEMPLATION

To the beginner attempting the foregoing meditations they will at first probably appear little more than intellectual exercises, more or less interesting according to the bent of his temperament and capable of arousing a certain degree of feeling. But as he perseveres in his efforts and enters more into the wonder and beauty of the great concepts he is considering, he will gradually acquire something of that personal spiritual experience which spans the gulf between the man of knowledge and the man of wisdom, and he will attain to some realisation of that inner peace and exaltation of the soul, of which St. Alphonsus de'Liguori speaks when he describes meditation as 'the blessed furnace in which souls are inflamed with Divine love.' For meditation harmonises the bodies in which we work, enabling the light of the spirit to shine down and illumine the dark recesses of our waking consciousness. It stills the turmoil of our personalities—the mind, the emotions, the restless activity of the brain—and by reasons of the synchronous vibration of the lower bodies enables the ego to influence the personality. And as the student thus grows richer in spiritual experience, he will find new phases of consciousness gradually opening up within him. Fixed in aspiration upon his ideal, he will presently become aware of the influence of that ideal raying down upon him, and as he makes one desperate effort to reach the object of his devotion, for one brief moment the floodgates of heaven itself will be opened and he will find himself made one with his idea and suffused with the glory of its realisation. These are the stages of contemplation and union. The former is the reaching upwards, when the more formal figures of the mind have been transcended, the latter is the attainment of that state of ecstasy of spirit, when the limbs of the personality have fallen away and all shadow of separateness has vanished in the perfect union of object and seeker. It were idle to attempt further description of such experiences, for are they not beyond the reach of formulated utterance? Words can but serve as signposts pointing out the way to that which is ineffably glorious, so that the pilgrim may know whither to direct his steps.

THE SEARCH FOR THE MASTER

The meditations outlined above will serve as a good groundwork for the beginner, and, if conscientiously followed, are bound to lead to good results. What precisely will be the value of those results will depend, of course, on the individual. But the growth into the inner life of spiritual experience may be hastened by taking advantage of certain opportunities which are the privilege of the Theosophist. No earnest student can be long a Fellow of the Theosophical Society without realising that the keystone of our whole spiritual edifice is the conception of the Masters, and that their power is the very life-blood of the Society. We are told that the Society was founded by the Brothers of the Great White Lodge, to be in a special sense their instrument in the world; if this be true, the opportunities of the Theosophist must be transcendently wonderful. It rests with the beginner to prove this great fact for himself, as others have proved it before him.

It was stated once by Mrs. Besant that a Master said that when a person joins the Theosophical Society he is connected with the Elder Brothers who direct its work by a tiny thread of life. This thread is the line of magnetic *rapport* with the Master, and the student may by arduous effort, by devotion and unselfish service, strengthen and enlarge the thread until it becomes a line of living light. The Masters take as pupils those who offer the necessary special qualifications. The fact that there are few who attain this exceptional privilege need in no way deter the earnest student, for there are many below the stage of pupil in whom the Master takes an interest and whom he will aid from time to time either in a general way or with special attention. Indeed, it may be said that there is a constant pressure of the Masters' force behind the Society, so that members who will open themselves to it may become channels through which it will flow, enabling them to do in the Master's name works greater than their own.

Realising all this, the earnest Theosophist in shaping his spiritual endeavour will in all probability desire to reach the Master, as the loftiest ideal within the range of his spiritual aspiration. How may he address himself to this task? First, by faithful service—both to his daily life and to the Society which is the physical instrument of the Masters. Taking that for granted—and more will be said about this anon—how shall he proceed? The next step will depend on his temperament. He may picture to himself an Ideal Man, synthesising in him the qualities and endowments of character which most strongly attract him, and endeavouring to perform all actions in his name and to reach him in his meditation.

Others choose also a more concrete method and strive to reach the Great Ones through those who are their pupils and disciples in the outer world. Take those, for instance, who stand before us as the widely acknowledged leaders of the Theosophical movement. Those leaders represent to many of us the Masters who stand behind the Society, and are the channels to the Society of their mighty influence. It is true that some people dislike intensely the attitude of hero-worship and devotion to persons; such dislike springs too often, alas! from hopes in the past, disappointment and blasted, while in other cases it is undoubtedly more fundamental and a matter of temperament. The human instrument may, and generally does, show many imperfections; the seeker certainly should not emulate these, but neither need he be troubled about them, for it is not that which he reverences the idea within the actual? 'What, know you not that your body is the temple of the Holy Ghost, which is in you, which ye have of God?' I *Corinthians* VI, 19) The characteristics that we admire in a man are the manifestations of the Divine Light shining through him, and that feeling of admiration is the response within ourselves to the ideal we see expressed in the other. Consequently, we can well afford to ignore what we consider the faults in others, and, whilst avoiding the foolish exaggeration of placing them on a pedestal be grateful for the glimpses of the divine light they reveal to us. The advantage of this method of reaching the Master is that it gives to the student some ideal constantly within reach, definite and tangible to him. There are many who echo the cry of Lamartine that he had need of a God near and personal to him, a God Whose arms could encompass suffering humanity and Whose feet could be kissed by repentant sinners. The same thought, though with a different application, is expressed in the well-known text 'for he that loveth not his brother whom he hath seen, how can he love God whom he hath not seen?' (I *John* IV, 20) Every regularly accepted chela of a Master, and still more every victor who has passed through the portals of initiations, is a channel of the Master's influence; through him the Master can be reached. The Master has taken certain definite responsibility for him, and he is an outpost of the Master's work in the world. Consequently any service done for him, is done also, in a sense, for the Master, even though it be merely in such small ways as in easing his labour or caring for his physical comfort, to say nothing of larger ways.

The bearing of all this will be perfectly plain to the student who has set his face seriously towards the goal with determination in his heart. In many ways he can place himself in close touch with, say, one of the great leaders of the Theosophical Movement. He can bring his mind into tune with that leader through the latter's lectures and writings. A photograph may help him in his meditation; and at regular intervals throughout the day he can fix the image in his mind and send thoughts of love, devotion, gratitude and strength. On two points he should exercise scrupulous caution—namely, that his mind is pure and lofty and not filled with worldly thoughts as he directs it towards his ideal—to this end a few moments may be given to a preliminary tuning-up or cleansing process; and secondly, that there should be no selfish expectation of help, of benefits or favours to be received in return. It is a point worth remembering in meditation, that if one seeks to draw down the ideal to oneself in personal possession, or is semi-consciously looking for personal gratification or the sense of power of other selfish results, the effort will not be crowned with due success: what is needed is an act of pure unselfish aspiration, the soaring upward, with no thought save that of giving, to the object of one's adoration. Only when free from the taint of personal selfishness does the student's thought play at a sufficiently high level to open him to the inflow of higher influence.

Much success may ensue along these lines of effort; for the law is sure, and since the nearness of the ideal renders intensity of enthusiasm more likely, proportionately great will be the result. If the motive be kept utterly pure, and the thought of the Master constantly in the mind, the student may one day perceive that the influence he contacts issues through, rather than from, the person who embodies his ideal, and so he may gradually raise himself into direct consciousness of the Master's presence. It may be that at a lecture or a ceremonial or devotional gathering, he will become conscious of a Presence greater than that of the physical instrument, for the Masters frequently are pleased to bestow in person their benediction upon such meetings of earnest members.

In such ways the student will find that whereas at first the Masters were to him merely an intellectual conception—a logical necessity in his scheme of philosophy—gradually, as his bodies grow more responsive to higher influences, they will become a living reality in his life, recognised and perceived by the heart as well as by the head.

THE BUILDING OF CHARACTER

Few words need be said upon this aspect of meditation, for it is comprised within what has already been stated. Meditation upon a virtue causes a man to grow gradually into the possession of that virtue; it is the deliberate setting of the bodies to vibrate in response to the thought of that virtue, and the establishing of a habit of response thereto, for with every repetition of the thought its recurrence is made easier. It is finely said in a Hindu Scripture 'What a man thinks on that he becomes; therefore think on the Eternal.' Especially should the image-building faculty of the mind be utilised, side by side with strenuous efforts at the practice of the virtue desired. If a student lack courage, he should picture himself in circumstances requiring its display, and carry on a scene to a gallant conclusion. As in actual life occasions offer themselves for courageous conduct, the thought of courage will more and more readily fly to the mind, and effort at practice will remedy the original defect.

It is well to take the various virtues as subjects of meditation, and by the exercise of the mind and power of the imagination train oneself to be able to *feel* them at will.

In the struggle to eradicate his faults one suggestion may prove useful to the student. The habit of brooding over faults does not lead to healthiness of mind, but is apt, rather, to encourage morbidness and depression, which act as a wall, shutting out spiritual influences. As a practical expedient, it is better to ignore faults of disposition so far as may be done, and to concentrate one's whole aspiration and endeavour towards building the opposite virtues into the character.

A well-known writer and preacher has forcefully expressed this truth. 'Remember you cannot see both sides of the coin at once. When you are discouraged by the striving of the animal nature, and utterly disgusted with yourself, and hating yourself as wholly unregenerate, the noblest exercise for your mental faculty is to force yourself to turn over the coin of yourself, and think intensely into the other side. Say, "I am The Lord's, my true ego is his Divine Spirit...".' (*Light on the Problems of Life*, by Archdeacon Wilberforce)

Success in the spiritual life is gained less by fierce wrestling with the lower nature than by growing into the knowledge and appreciation of higher things. For once we have sufficiently experienced the bliss and joyousness of the higher life, by contrast the lower desires pale and lose their attractiveness. It was said once by a great Teacher that the best form of repentance for a transgression was to look ahead with hopeful courage, coupled with a firm resolve not to commit the transgression again.

PHYSICAL AIDS TO MEDITATION

Although the more important part of meditation has to do with the direction of the will, thought and feeling, it is obvious that we cannot dispense with the physical body, so that some hints as to physical plane procedure will not be out of place; indeed this must necessarily be among the things that will engage the mind of the student who is entering upon the practice, as distinct from the theory, of meditation.

POSTURE

Just as certain thoughts and emotions will express themselves in characteristic movements and gestures of the body, so, by a reversal of the process, positions of the body may tend to induce states of mind and feeling, and to assist the student in dwelling on them. It is a matter of harmonizing the physical with the higher bodies and with the play on it of the external forces of Nature.

In beginning meditation the student may adopt either of two postures recommended by experts in these matters; he may sit upright in a comfortable armchair, the back of which does not slope unduly; the hands may be clasped and rest on the legs or be laid lightly on the knees; and the feet be placed together or crossed with the right over the left. The position should be easy and relaxed, the head not sunk upon the chest but lightly balanced, the eyes and mouth closed, and—as suggested by a well-known Indian writer on yoga—the spinal column, along which there is much magnetic flow, erect. Or else he may sit in a similar position on a couch, stool on floor, cross-legged, in eastern fashion. The locking of the extremities of the body is also recommended by authorities as preventing the outflow of magnetism, which is a natural phenomenon, from the fingertips, feet, et cetera. The cross-legged position is in some slight ways the more effectual, since magnetism thereby liberated is said to rise around the body in a protective shell. But it is an exceedingly inconvenient posture for most western people, though in the East—whence most of our modern yoga teaching originates—it is the natural manner of being seated, and it has been wittily remarked by one writer that 'the initial difficulties are many, but they are considerably enhanced by those who think it necessary to assume fantastic eastern postures to annoy the body, which should be quiescent, if it is to be successfully ignored.' (*Meditations*, by Alice C. Ames)

One position which should not be adopted, except in very rare cases, is that of lying down, for its natural tendency is towards sleep. Further, the brain cannot respond sympathetically to the higher vibrations of the superphysical bodies if the circulation of the blood be sluggish, hence the value of a cold tub or brisk walk before the morning practice.

BREATHING AND OTHER MATTERS

The postures of the body above recommended not only admit of, but may even be said to induce, full abdominal breathing, such as is practised by well-trained singers. There is an intimate connection between profound meditation and breathing. George Fox, the Quaker, and some other Quietists claim to have received the gift of 'internal respiration.' It is found in actual practice, that as the body becomes harmonized in meditation the breathing grows deeper, regular and rhythmic, until by degrees it becomes so slow and quiet as to be almost imperceptible. This effect having been noticed, the process was reversed in *hatha yoga*, and by deliberate regulation of the breathing it was sought to harmonize the functions of the body, and finally the workings of the mind. But the student should be warned against indiscriminate practice of breathing exercises spread broadcast in westernized yoga literature. To begin with, it is always more dangerous in psychic culture to work 'from below up;' to play pranks with the physical body instead of taking to heart the profound teaching of *The Voice of the Silence*: 'The Mind is the great Slayer of the Real.... Let the Disciple slay the Slayer.' The student will be better advised to learn control of thought along the lines of *raja yoga*, leaving his efforts at meditation to work their natural effect on the development of his physical body and the shaping of the psychic organs. Furthermore, that which can be practised with impunity in an eastern body cannot always with equal suitability be tried on a western body; and some of these breathing exercises are exceedingly dangerous and fraught with disastrous consequences. It may be said in passing that there is no objection to simple deep breathing, provided undue strain is not placed upon the heart and lungs and no attempt is made to concentrate the thought on the various centres of the body.

The student may find it helpful to burn a little good incense, for this purifies the atmosphere from the occult standpoint: he may also gain assistance from beautiful colours and pictures in his surroundings, flowers and other means of uplifting the mind and feelings.

He will also find it useful to observe certain dietetic restrictions, even going to the length of complete abstinence from alcohol and flesh-food. The taking of alcohol *pari passu* with the practice of strenuous meditation is apt to set up inflammatory symptoms in the brain - but the whole question is fully dealt with in Theosophical literature. (See Annie Besant's *Man and His Bodies*, C.W. Leadbeater's *Some Glimpses of Occultism*, Chapter X.)

TIMES

Another point not to be neglected is the question of hour. It is well—though not a *sine qua non*—that the times selected should be regularly adhered to. Much of the initial difficulty of meditation springs from the automatic consciousness of the various bodies—called sometimes the elementals of the bodies—resisting with a sort of instinct, which if blind is nevertheless often extremely forceful, the attempt to impose upon them new habits. Three periods of the day are stated to be most suitable magnetically—namely, when the sun is rising, at its meridian and when setting. These were the times selected by ancient devotees, though naturally they must be modified to suit the conditions of modern life. In addition to these times, it is well if the habit can be cultivated of turning the mind for the moment at the stroke of every hour during waking life to the realization of oneself as the Spiritual Man. This practice leads to what in Christian mystical theology is called self-recollectedness. It is the object of the student to train the mind to revert automatically to spiritual thoughts.

It is not well to meditate immediately after a meal or late at night; in the one case the process of thought withdraws the blood from aiding the digestive functions, in the other the bodies are tired and the etheric double more readily displaceable, and, moreover, the negative influence of the moon is operative, so that undesirable results are more liable to occur.

POSITIVITY AND PSYCHIC DEVELOPMENT

The system of meditation here laid before the student has as its object spiritual, mental and ethical development, and the control of the mind and feelings. It does not aim at developing psychic faculties 'from below upwards.' But its natural result may be to open up a form of intuitive psychism in persons of sufficiently sensitive organisation, which will show itself in increasing sensitiveness to the influence of people and places, in the recalling of fragmentary memories of astral plane experiences from sleep, in greater susceptibility to direct guidance from the ego, in the power to recognize the influence of the Masters and spiritually developed people, and so forth.

There is one special contingency which the student following the methods of positive self-development here outlined should carefully avoid, and that is the development of passive mediumship and spirit control through negative methods of meditation—for, whatever may be the merits of spiritualism, the two systems are quite incompatible. For instance, in some books of westernized yoga the student is instructed to begin meditation by rolling his eyes upwards and keeping them so fixed. The effect of this is to impose a strain on the visual mechanism and so to deaden the brain somewhat, with the result that a negative state of auto-hypnosis is induced, and semi-trance may supervene, accompanied by certain psychic manifestations. A similar result is obtained by the use of a crystal.

It is also apt to puzzle the student when writers tell him to open himself to spiritual influences and at the same time be positive. The difficulty arises through a confusion of stages. Positive effort is needed as a preliminary, and the passive condition follows later. The positive intensity of effort uplifts the consciousness to play through the higher levels of its different vehicles, or—to look at the matter differently—harmonises the vehicles, bringing them into synchronous relation with each other, so that the higher influence can play down; and only then is it safe to relax the upward straining in the realization of the peace thus attained. Perhaps, after all, the phrase 'opening oneself to spiritual influences' in such a condition means nothing more than maintaining an attitude of intense stillness at a high spiritual level. The present writer once heard a similar point well illustrated by Monsignor Robert Hugh Benson. He instanced the picture of a seagull poised against the gale; truly to the onlooker the bird seemed passive and immobile, nevertheless one knew there was a powerful effort continuously maintained in wing and pinion.

Now it is obvious that this intense stillness marks a stage separated by years of persistent effort from the attitude of people who assume they can reach great spiritual heights while flat on their backs in a warm and comfortable bed or even in a piping hot bath! Such persons mistake for meditation what is merely bodily enfeeblement and an idle drifting of thought upon some soothing and agreeable topic. Not thus is the kingdom of heaven taken by storm!

Real mediation means strenuous effort, not the sensation of happiness which arises from a state of semi-somnolence and bodily luxury. The man who is beginning real concentration of thought should not at first exceed five or ten minutes at a stretch, otherwise he is apt to overtax the brain. Very gradually the interval may be lengthened to fifteen, twenty and thirty minutes.

RELAXATION

Since meditation involves effort the student will do well to remember that the natural effect of concentrating the mind is to produce tension of the muscles in the body. The familiar habit of knitting of brows is evidence of this bodily automatism. This tension of the muscles not only induces great bodily fatigue, but acts as an obstacle to the inflow of spiritual forces. Therefore the student should periodically in his meditation, and repeatedly during his daily life, turn his attention on the body and deliberately—'let go' in relaxation. People of strong and intense natures often find difficulty in expressing themselves either in speech or letter owing to a habit of imposing too great and sudden a pressure on the brain. They should learn to let the brain take the load gradually, as an electrician would say. A moment of complete relaxation would rid them of the difficulty. In much the same way if a lecturer suffers from brain-fag and sudden forgetfulness of his sequence of ideas or inability to get a word, by far the wiser course is the bold one of letting go absolutely in momentary relaxation, rather than straining to remember, for the latter effort merely increases the tension round the brain.

The student should also remember that concentration is not a matter of physical effort. The moment the mind turns to a thought it is concentrated upon it. It is difficult to express in words what, after all, must be experienced to be understood; but concentration is less a matter of forcibly holding the mind on a certain thought than of letting the mind continue to rest on that thought in perfect stillness and quietude. Further the student may realise, and apply for what it is worth in his own inner experience, the idea that the mental body and not the brain is the seat of thought, and that though in the initial stages effort must seem to centre on the task of quietening the brain, nevertheless concentration really concerns the mental body more than the physical brain.

THE WAY OF SERVICE

The Theosophical student should always remember that right motive is of primary importance in all work that he undertakes, and that only by dint of unselfish motive and the sincere desire to benefit humanity can the Masters be reached. It need not be that any intense love for humanity in the mass possess the aspirant in the earlier stages; we may safely assume it is sufficient if he seek to act unselfishly towards those in his immediate environment, for as he perseveres he must inevitably become increasingly sensitive to the cry of suffering humanity in its collective aspect.

Yet it is well that the Theosophist who is awakening to some realization of the spiritual life should understand that meditation and service are complementary to each other and that the best results will accrue when they are combined. We are not in the Theosophical Society just for what we can get out of it; we are members because the teachings of the Eternal Wisdom have sunk deep into our hearts and are moulding our lives anew. It is the mark of the spiritual man to give freely to others rather than to demand for himself; therein only is true happiness to be found. Hence our attitude towards the Society should be in the nature of a continual interrogation: What can I do to help?

The newcomer into the Society is given his opportunities and according to his capacity is judged by the use he makes of them. Small services well rendered often bulk larger than ambitious undertakings fitfully carried out. The student who is likely to progress is the one who is found faithful in small things, who is willing to clean windows and light fires in the Lodge room, to undertake various small duties at meetings, to be unfailingly regular in attendance at Lodge, or other meetings in which he has promised to take part, to train himself to lecture and write. No more need be said about this; a hint to the earnest student is sufficient, and the parable of the talents is extremely applicable to Theosophical work.

Along such paths of service will the way to the Masters be disclosed; for service willingly given must be the watchword of the aspirant and he will learn to forget himself and his own progress in the joy of ministering to the needs of others. Let him seek to perform every act of service in the Name of the Master; and so let him work onward in perseverance and steadfastness to the day when he shall know the Master face to face, and from the depths of his being offer himself in glad surrender to his Lord.

But let him not think that the relation between Master and pupil is in any way one of coercion or one in which the pupil's individuality is submerged in the flood of power from the

Master. On the contrary, the Master's influence is not a hypnotic force from without but an inexpressibly wonderful illumination from within, irresistible because so deeply felt as in perfect accord with the pupil's highest aspiration and as the self-revelation of his own spiritual nature. The Master is himself in fullest measure a channel of the Divine Life and that which flows from him awakens into activity the seed of divinity within the pupil. Indeed the student who finds inspiration in scientific study may discover a suggestive analogy in the electric phenomenon of induction. It is because of the identity of nature in the two that the influence of the Master stimulates in the highest degree all the noblest and finest qualities in the pupil. The love of the Master for a disciple may be likened to the sunshine which opens the lotus bud to the fresh morning air, and very truly may it be said that one smile from the Master will call forth such an outburst of affection from the pupil as would only be gained by months of scholastic meditation on the virtue of love.

May these few hints on meditation win some to the knowledge of the Great Teachers and to the service of humanity in their name.

ACCENDANT IN NOBIS DOMINUS IGNEM
SUI AMORIS ET FLAMMAM
ÆTERNÆ CHARITATIS

APPENDIX[1]

A CERTAIN technique which some find of value is to use a modified form of meditation in order to find a real solution to personal problems. Such problems inevitably arise as the student seeks to penetrate the inner life, for new stresses are brought to bear on the personality, and these reveal faults and imperfections perhaps hitherto concealed or inactive.

Instead of refusing to allow the thoughts and feelings resulting from these imperfections to come into the conscious mind, it is well deliberately to allow them to rise to the surface. Here they can be looked at and, gradually, the deeper aspects of them can be explored and exposed. Then, when the root of them is clearly seen, one is in a position to change them. Such a technique is not new but goes back at least as far as St. Ignatius Loyola's *Exercitia,* which was finished in 1548 and has been used, by the Jesuits at any rate, ever since.

The student should take as the theme of his meditation the problem that is disturbing him, settling himself down deliberately to contemplate it. A preliminary affirmation can be made to the effect: "I am doing this in the light of spiritual Truth and for the purpose of changing a trait in myself that I consider undesirable." He then recalls the circumstances in which, perhaps, he became angry or frightened or self-conscious. He allows his mind to wander freely round the incident, studying all that he did or said and felt, the people involved, and his reactions to them; and he considers all that he *might* have done or perhaps *wished* to do but for fear of the consequences; or what he feared might happen—and did not happen—and so on. Perhaps he will find that he recalls other similar situations, incidents in childhood, even events that at first sight may seem unrelated to the one under immediate scrutiny. These he notes in his mind for future reference. After a time he may get tired, and he can then recall himself to his starting point of self-dedication and finish his meditation. On a later occasion he picks up the thread again, and this time may find himself penetrating more deeply into the situation, for in the interval his unconscious mind will have been working on the problem. Eventually, after repeated attempts, he may discover himself free from his trouble. He may reach a point of full conscious awareness of how it originated, or he may not: this is not important—what counts is that one is no longer afraid, or angry, or jealous. Sometimes even one may not be aware that the trouble is overcome one realizes that circumstances had arisen previously always called forth the habitual reaction and that one had, so to speak, "forgotten" to react.

Another proof that this method is proving effective is when the individual becomes gradually aware beforehand that he is in a frame of mind tending to lead up to a reactive state. This is of value in that, being forewarned, he may learn to *relax* to the impact rather than meet it head on a violent collision upsetting his emotional life. It is like using the technique of judo (which is a by-product of Zen Buddhism) rather than boxing in order to overcome the emotional "opponent." The student will find that he is still often taken unawares, but by steady persistence and the use of much patience, rather than by seeing spectacular results, he will gradually loosen the bonds of even his worst habits. For, as he becomes the observer of his personal behaviour, it is as if the energy hitherto causing an emotional reaction gets increasingly diverted into other and more useful channels. This seems to be the correct way of carrying out Patanjali's instructions to yogis to "build the opposite" into their characters. It takes place when forces previously centred round personal desires, aversions or passions become focused on a different and higher level of being where man is no longer concerned with asserting or defending his small, separate self.

[1] This Appendix appears at the end of a 1961 Edition of *Meditation for Beginners.* Authorship is not stated but it is presumably Lawrence J. Bendit, the editor of the edition. [Ed.]

This technique is often difficult, unpleasant and humiliating to one's pride. But it represents a direct attack on personal difficulties and undesirable feeling habits, and many can vouch for its effectiveness in bringing about a real and profound change in personality and outlook. This in turn makes life easier and happier because as the inner life changes, so does the external world begin to appear kinder and less harsh and the people one meets much pleasanter. The change, however, is in oneself; and because one is beginning to find peace within, so is one creating around oneself an environment that reflects that peace. Thus, by helping oneself, one is also helping one's fellows—which is the sole aim of the spiritual quest.

THE FACTS REGARDING THE EPISCOPAL SUCCESSION
IN THE
LIBERAL CATHOLIC CHURCH

A number of attacks have been made on the Liberal Catholic Church, mainly in connection with the origin of its Episcopal Succession. It is well that the public should clearly understand the source of these attacks and the reason for the venom behind them.

THE SOURCES OF THE ATTACKS

Those in two London journals were directly inspired by Archbishop Mathew and a handful of his adherents. Others were made by the Jesuits, notably in their organ, The Month. In one case, details of information were obtained from our friends in a London book depot by a man who posed as an innocent and sympathetic enquirer. The rest have emanated from rival Theosophical Societies in America (e.g., in the Chicago Divine Life), and from a few discontented or aggrieved members of the original and world-wide Theosophical Society, who have not yet learned its elementary principle of tolerance to other opinions and religious beliefs. The Jesuit attacks are cunningly devised to discredit a movement whose Orders are as valid as their own, but which stands for entire freedom of thought and belief. They misrepresent our motives and actions, but are not, in the main, mendacious. The others are flagrantly mendacious, and, in the last group, are aggravated by the grotesque ignorance of the writers on the technical and historical points discussed—as, for instance, when they talk of priests ordaining other priests or bishops! One short (and anonymous) pamphlet, recently issued in Sydney, contains no fewer than thirty-four direct falsehoods and misstatements. Such misstatements—made without any attempt to learn the motives actuating the persons attacked, or the real significance of their doings—are liable to be received as "history." The following information is therefore placed on record.

It is true that the Liberal Catholic Church originated from a movement marred and even made ridiculous by many vicissitudes. In no way is the Liberal Catholic Church responsible for these; rather, it is their victim.

THE CONSECRATION OF BISHOP MATHEW
AT UTRECHT IN APRIL, 1908

The Old Catholic Bishops declared at Utrecht in 1920 that this consecration "Was surreptitiously secured by the production of false testimony." This may be so; but Dr. Mathews complicity in the proceedings has never been proved. On the other hand, in a letter to *The Guardian* (June 3rd, 1908) the Old Catholic Bishops completely exonerated him, saying "our confidence in Bishop Mathew remains unshaken after carefully perusing a large number of documents bearing on the matter." For some time he worked in friendly relations with Anglican societies, like the Society of St. Willibrord; but at the close of 1910 he broke off relations with the Continental Old Catholics, who, however, made no official pronouncement about the affair of the consecration till 1920.

We have no solicitude in this matter, for at the time of ordination none of us knew of the events at Utrecht, and in any case we should have been satisfied with The Guardian's statement. Only one point is of significance, so far as we are concerned. The Old Catholic Church, though it has repeatedly dissociated itself from all connection with Archbishop Mathew, has in practice always recognised the validity of his orders. One priest whom he ordained left him at the breach with Utrecht in 1910, but continued to work in London as the official representative of Utrecht without any reordination. The Anglican communion also has in its ministry certain clergy accepted on the strength of their ordination by him. One of these is a London vicar. The Lambeth Conference did not pronounce upon the validity of Orders derived from Archbishop Mathew. Our *Statement of Principles* does not claim that our Orders are "negotiable" among Churches which accept the doctrine of the Apostolic succession. It says that we have "preserved" Orders which are so negotiable, namely, those of the Dutch Old Catholic Church, which have been acknowledged as valid by the Roman Catholic, Eastern and Anglican Churches. As to our own, they have never been made the subject of formal examination, therefore it is premature to speak on the subject.

OUR BREACH WITH ARCHBISHOP MATHEW

I first met Archbishop Mathew in 1913, and found him outwardly a most charming man. I had originally contemplated taking Orders in the Church of England, but held back on account of my "unorthodox" views. The difficulty was not so much that of subscribing to the outer formularies, as with the interpretation I placed upon them. I approached Archbishop Mathew with a view to ordination, telling him that I was a member of the Theosophical Society and giving him full opportunity of enquiring into my tenets. He made few enquiries of me personally; but I had sent him Mrs. Besant's book, *Theosophy*, in the Jack series, and papers relating to other organizations of which I was a member. He later ordained other members of the Theosophical Society. I have been accused of concealment in this matter in *Divine Life* and *The Occult Review*. I answered the charge in the latter journal, taking proof to the Editor in the shape of the correspondence between Archbishop Mathew and myself. Archbishop Mathew preserved a discreet silence thereafter in *The Occult Review*.

In the autumn of 1915 he instituted a "heresy hunt," and demanded our resignation from the Theosophical Society. This being a violation of the conditions under which he had admitted us to ordination—namely, that there should be no interference with the Theosophical work to which we had devoted ourselves—we declined to submit to his demand. The remainder of the "non-Theosophical" clergy in Great Britain (with the solitary exception of one priest, who had not been active in the movement), including the Dean, stood by us. The issue presently widened, and the clergy decided to dissociate themselves from a leadership which they had come to regard as irresponsible. One reason which actuated our friends was a farcical letter written by Archbishop Mathew to the Anglican Bishop of London, offering him reordination and "recognition."

It has since been declared that I and everyone of my Theosophical friends made a written statement of withdrawal from "the Old Catholic Church." The point has no importance, but happens not to be true. In the first place, Dr. Mathew called his movement "The Catholic Church of England;" secondly, at least one of our clergy (and I think another) and certain laity did not so withdraw. In view of the breach of faith which forced it, my own resignation was from further connection with Archbishop Mathew, and was phrased as "a declaration of independence" (borrowing the phrase used by Archbishop Mathew himself in relation to Utrecht). Finally, he wrote to me that he "terminated" the movement he had begun.

Archbishop Mathew then tendered his "unconditional submission" to the Roman Church. The announcement appeared in *The Times* during the last days of 1915. When we had entered his movement, we had found to our surprise that the number of active adherents might be counted on the fingers of one hand. Archbishop Mathew had quarreled successively with the Dutch and Anglican Churches, and lost one after another of his Auxiliary Bishops and clergy. We had opened an oratory, and got together a fair congregation, who learned greatly to value the ministrations at our altar. They asked us not to abandon the movement. We, on our part, felt that there were great opportunities for a movement on broader lines, combining the Catholic form of worship with the widest intellectual liberty and respect for the individual conscience.

BISHOP WILLOUGHBY AND THE SUCCESSION

It was now that we were faced with a great difficulty. Had we been founding a new sect, we could have proceeded without let or hindrance. But it is a cardinal article of our faith that ordination is not merely a figurative or symbolical rite, but conveys definite power, necessary for the administration of the Sacraments. For this we hold the Episcopal Succession to be necessary, as do the Roman Catholic, Eastern and Anglican Churches.

I must now interrupt the narrative to recite certain events.

In four years Archbishop Mathew had consecrated no fewer than seven bishops, all of whom left him to join other movements. The succession thus hung on one thread. In September, 1914, he addressed a letter to his clergy saying that in view of his advancing years it seemed to him desirable that "immediate steps should be taken to preserve the valid episcopal succession in our portion of the Church from risk of loss." The election then held resulted in the consecration of the Rev. F.S. Willoughby, MA, Cantab., by Archbishop Mathew on October 28th, 1914. I had nothing whatever to do with the issue of this circular, with the election or consecration of Mr. Willoughby to the Episcopate, or with his subsequent dismissal from the movement, as at this period I was in India. My name came second in the voting; it was understood that I was to be consecrated on my return, so that there might be bishops to the canonical number of three.

After he had acted as Auxiliary Bishop for seven months, Bishop Willoughby was attacked in a London journal. Archbishop Mathew summoned him at a few hours' notice to defend himself Bishop Willoughby declined to appear, claiming that the affair had long since been disclosed to the Archbishop. A farcical sentence of degradation was pronounced by Archbishop Mathew.

The circumstances under which Mr. Willoughby had resigned his living in the Anglican Church were known substantially to Archbishop Mathew from the outset, as is proved by his extant letters; but he did not think it worth while to mention these to any of his clergy when he received Mr. Willoughby into our Church. In fact, they were not made acquainted with them until the final *débâcle*, except for a passing hint given by Archbishop Mathew to one of the clergy that if he heard any rumour of scandal about Bishop Willoughby he was not to believe it.

These letters written to Mr. Willoughby by Archbishop Mathew are in the possession of our Church, lodged in a safe deposit in London. They were shown to the Editor of *The Occult Review*, who at once admitted my point. In the letter to this magazine (June, 1918) I wrote: "one of which has been shown to you, Sir." The Editor let the statement go unchallenged, and Archbishop Mathew never replied.

The responsibility for Bishop Willoughby's consecration therefore rests entirely with Archbishop Mathew.

Let me add that he was not expelled from the Church of England or "unfrocked" (as the author of certain objectionable articles that appeared in America assumed). He executed a deed of voluntary relinquishment of his benefice. Subsequently he was in friendly correspondence with his diocesan. Again, it is only fair to say that he has denied the aspersions which were cast upon him in his absence from the parish, and so far as my information goes, persons of tender years were not implicated in these charges. His wife, a noble woman whom I knew, stood staunchly by him throughout. What he has since suffered in persecution defies description. Hunted by malice and revenge out of one situation after another, harassed by an unscrupulous and sensation-mongering press, left to starve save for the charity of a few faithful friends, and now attacked by these so-called Theosophists—the very stones they cast might cry out in anguish and rebuke.

I now print a statement by Bishop Willoughby which appeared in the Universe, an English Roman Catholic journal having a very wide circulation:—

A LETTER FROM BISHOP WILLOUGHBY

Sir,—I trust you will allow me a few words of personal explanation in reference to Father Thurston's very severe strictures upon me in the current issue of the Month. Hitherto, in reference to Press attacks, I have been silent, partly because they appeared in quarters in which I thought it useless to venture on any request for justice, and partly because I was hampered by professional confidence all along the line in clearing myself in a court of law. The newspapers were not the real enemy, but the cunningly devised distortions of fact with which they were fed. As a Catholic, an attack in the very centre of the Household of Faith cannot thus lightly be regarded by me.

The whole affair of Stockton happened when I was absent from home. Behind my back, and entirely without my knowledge, a "trial" was held by the Bishop's official. No one possible chance was given for me to face my accusers in cross-examination, and the matter of enquiry thus cunningly got through *absente reo* was published broadcast in the town before I knew anything about it. Consequently I was powerless.

Having executed the deed of voluntary resignation of my benefice I approached Archbishop Mathew. I wrote to him fully about the circumstances of my quitting my work in the Establishment, and hold his letters in reply, which clearly confirm this fact as I state it. He never communicated this matter to his clergy. He ordained me almost at once. Later I was elected by the clergy and consecrated Bishop, principally with a view of keeping the succession from hanging on one thread. I worked hard, and I can say that all the clergy, save one, are my personal friends to this very day.

The peculiar genius of the Archbishop for changing his workers is evidenced by the fact that I was the eighth Bishop he consecrated within a little over four years. When the average time had elapsed my turn came to be removed, I went, and gave myself up to the matter of re-considering my difficulties as to the Catholic Church. The maneuvers with the Press and "the thanks of the Old Catholics" to the newspapers for their treatment of me were all planned and conveyed by one single person acting entirely alone, who wrote under a very far-fetched and not quite accurate title of anonymity in this connection.

Shortly after this came another of what Father Thurston calls not inaptly the Archbishop's "somersaults." With full knowledge of their opinions, and with absolutely no reservations as to their tenets on their part, he had ordained certain enthusiastic members of the Theosophical Society to the priesthood. This was previously to my joining the movement. Without a word of warning Dr. Mathew calls upon them quite suddenly to leave the Society. They naturally refused to submit to what they considered on his part a wanton and calculated breach of contract. The remainder of the non-Theosophical clergy in Great Britain, with one exception, stood by them, and finally all these unanimously agreed to repudiate once and for all this irresponsible leadership. The result of this decision was that the public prints announced just one more of Dr. Mathews "submissions" to the Holy See!

One of the very best of the laity formally brought this state of things to my notice. I keenly felt this outrageous treatment inflicted so treacherously upon a number of folk whom I knew to be absolutely sincere in their religion. My course of action appeared perfectly clear. It seemed only honourable and right on my part to come back and give them the Episcopate they had given to me. Accordingly I did so. That was my final communion *in sacris* with them before my joyful and willing submission to the Catholic Church.

One word more. The article nowhere contemplates the fact that possibly some of these good folk may have some little sincerity in their belief, and actions. I am sorry it should be so. I have never shared their beliefs, but those I have met have invariably been folk of high spiritual outlook and keenly intent on following the Truth as far as they see it. After all, as regards the genesis of their Episcopate, the greatest occupant of the See of Hippo would also come under Father Thurston's lash, and his people would have to suffer its infliction for allegations against their Bishop! Do let us believe in the glorious possibility of repentance, and in the amazing power of the Sacrament of Penance. "Charity hopeth all things"—and at least let us hope such things of the persons engaged in heresy, even if, as in duty bound, we have to say the hardest things in the hardest manner of their errors. Events in this world roll on and succeed one another. A timeless eternal now is not for us. Consequently, care in even dutiful writing should be exercised as to rules of time, lest the great law of charity be forgotten by us.

In Dr. Mathews day he distinctly advised his people at any time in case of need to resort to Catholic Churches and share spiritual privileges with Catholics. Bishop Wedgwood has altogether set his face against this, and assures me from a very intimate knowledge of all his flock that the lengthy warning at the end of Father Thurston's article is altogether "a tilting at a windmill."

I did not accept Bishop Willoughby's offer of consecration for four and a half months. I wished to avoid the obvious consequences; but, more important, I was under the impression—for which I have since heartily apologised—that he had concealed the state of affairs from his Consecrator. The letters afterwards disabused me of this injustice. The statement made by Archbishop Mathew that I applied for consecration to the Old Catholic Bishops "in Holland and America" is untrue. I did approach some of the bishops who had previously been consecrated by him (and one of another line of succession); but, as had been anticipated, without success. All had allied themselves with other communions. Bishop Willoughby was the sole channel available, and the one which Archbishop Mathew himself had provided. The choice of consecrators for a person holding "unorthodox" views is necessarily restricted.

All the clergy in Great Britain who had been active in the movement (with the exception of one whose co-operation we neither invited nor desired) stood with us at the time of Archbishop Mathew's "unconditional submission" to Rome. He called his movement "The Catholic Church of England." This had always seemed to us not a little presumptuous; and we therefore adopted the name of "Old Catholic Church in Great Britain," which he had not been using. The Church of Utrecht had no clergy officiating in Great Britain. We later took the name of "Liberal Catholic," partly because "Old Catholic" was frequently confused in America and Australia with "Roman Catholic," but chiefly because the outlook of our movement ceased to be that of historical Old Catholicism. The same might be said, however, of other branches of the Old Catholic Church, still in communion with Utrecht, whose interests have extended to wider problems than the decrees of the Vatican Council.

Archbishop Mathew wrote to *The Universe* (December 31st, 1915), expressing himself as "absolutely and irrevocably" convinced of the necessity of actual union with the Roman See, and accepting "without hesitation or doubt" the Infallibility of the Pope. Elsewhere, in *The Tablet* (January 8th, 1916), he said: "It is my firm resolve, which nothing will ever alter, to obey the commands of the Holy Father."

That four months later he should start work again with more episcopal progeny and a "Western Orthodox Uniate Catholic Church" would appear incredible to anyone not acquainted with the strange workings of his mind and the vicissitudes of his career. But it is humorous that our American "Theosophist" opponents should take him seriously and solemnly publish his repudiation of us on behalf of "the English Old Catholics." Equally foolish is their publication of a similar repudiation by the microscopic but adventurous body in America associated with the name of Archbishop Vilatte.

The unfortunate Archbishop Mathew died at the end of 1919. One would gladly have respected the old adage to speak no ill of the dead; only the evil that they do most unfortunately lives after them, and is kept aflame by interested parties. I hold it a clearer duty to protect our clergy and congregations from calumny and slander.

THE UNWORTHINESS OF THE MINISTER

The agitation worked up over the incidence of Bishop Willoughby in our line of Succession is highly artificial.

The bishop, in laying on hands, does not add his imperfections of character, real or imaginary, to those of the candidate; he hands on the Episcopate. Anglican Orders are not polluted by the plentiful misdemeanours of Reformation divines, or Roman by the many scandals of the Papacy and Sacred College of Cardinals. Were it otherwise the Orders of no Church would be unsullied. All this is clearly and very properly recognised in theology. Article 26 in the Anglican Prayer Book lays it down that "the unworthiness of the minister…hinders not the effect of the sacrament." Question 19 of the Catechism of the Roman Council of Trent teaches similarly. St. Augustine, in a telling passage, maintains that "the Baptism of Christ is holy, even though administered by adulterers, for His holiness cannot be polluted and His divine grace is present in the Sacrament" (*De Baptismo*).

The fundamental fact of the whole sacramental system is that Christ, and not man, is the true minister of all sacraments, and His power can and does work, irrespective of the private fancies or particular unworthiness of the human instruments He uses in the interests of His people at large. Imperfections, mental, moral and physical, errors both of life and doctrine, necessarily exist in an imperfect world; but they are as naught compared to His power. To hold otherwise is unduly to exalt the human element in comparison with the divine.

Let me quote some sentences from a writer in Swete's *Early History of the Church and the Ministry*—one of the finest products of modern Anglican scholarship:

...if the sacraments ministered by evil men simply convey no real grace to the recipient, then we must conclude that no one can be absolutely sure that he has been truly baptized or ordained, since no one can be absolutely sure of the inner character of the bishop or priest who has ordained or baptized him.... But obviously in practice it would not be easy to fix the point at which the characters of the clergy and the consequent validity of their ministration would remain immune from suspicion. And St. Augustine saw the truest answer to the whole difficulty. We need not be over-careful and troubled about the worthiness of the ministrant in relation to the sacraments ministered by him, simply because he is only a minister, an agent of a Master whose power is behind every act done in His name.... Augustine reminds him that God acted through Judas, who was sent to preach with the rest of the apostles....(Pp. 186-187)

THE VALIDITY OF BISHOP WILLOUGHBY'S CONSECRATION

One other matter remains for consideration. Archbishop Mathew has stated that there were certain "providential omissions" at Bishop Willoughby's consecration which rendered it of doubtful validity. He forgot the Imposition of the Book of Gospels and the Litany of the Saints. No theologian would regard these as in any degree essential. Bishop Willoughby called attention to the omission immediately after the ceremony; but both he and Archbishop Mathew held the matter not to be of sufficient importance to be worth following up. Several witnesses can prove this. I stated all this in the *Occult Review* letter, which was left unanswered. Even the Jesuit Father Thurston, writing in *The Month* (September, 1920), remarks: "The elements omitted do not seem to have been of a very vital character." Bishop Willoughby acted as Archbishop Mathews Auxiliary for seven months; performed ordinations and confirmations on his behalf, wore the episcopal habit, etc. Such reckless accusations reflect on nobody but their author. When Bishop Willoughby was received into the Roman Catholic Church, he was required to give an undertaking not to exercise episcopal functions.

In the same letter to *The Occult Review*, I dealt with the question of theological "intention." I and my colleagues find no cause to be "unorthodox" on the subject of Holy Orders. It lay with Archbishop Mathew to prove that we were incapable of the "necessary intention," instead of simply making an unfounded assertion "out of the blue" in order to hinder our work.

CONCLUSION

That our Church should be made a storm-centre is not surprising. We stand between, not two, but four, fires. The Church people find us too theosophical. Theosophists find us too "Churchy." Catholics and ritualists consider us too free in our beliefs; Protestants too Catholic in our worship. We, however, believe firmly in our principles; and the hope and courage that people derive from the teaching of our Church, the inspiration they gain from our worship and the phenomenal growth of our membership, are the true test of the work we do.

The world would certainly be happier if each man could but learn to show towards others the tolerance he claims for himself.

Let me conclude by saying that not one of our clergy receives any financial remuneration for his services. The whole of our work is voluntary.

THE LAMBETH CONFERENCE
AND
THE VALIDITY OF ARCHBISHOP MATHEW'S ORDERS

An Open Letter to His Grace the Archbishop of Canterbury

(The Most Rev, and Rt. Hon. Randall Thomas Davidson, D.D.. D.C.L. LL.D., etc.)

From

The Right Reverend J. I. Wedgwood

Docteur (Sciences) de l'Universite de Paris,
Presiding Bishop of the Liberal Catholic Church.

My Lord Archbishop,—The Lambeth Conference of 1920 felt itself called upon to consider the status of the late Archbishop Mathew and to raise some question as to his Episcopal Orders. The Liberal Catholic Church, which derives its succession through him, is not among those bodies who attach only a symbolical or figurative value to the rite of Ordination. We regard the Episcopate as a channel of peculiar grace and faculty, instituted by Christ, and consequently pertaining to the *esse* and not merely to the *bene esse* of His Church. In justice, therefore, to our congregations, as well as to our many friends in the Anglican Church and elsewhere, we feel that the widely-read utterances of the Conference should not be allowed to pass unchallenged.

This Open Letter is addressed to Your Grace not in any personal sense, but as President of the Lambeth Conference, and with every feeling of respect. I regret that it should be necessary thus to add to the, burden of public controversy, but our efforts towards a settlement of the question by private negotiation have failed, despite the assistance of one of the English Bishops (a member of the Committee), who saw the difficulty created by the Report and consented to act as mediator.

The observations of the Conference are open to criticism on various issues. I will deal with these under separate headings.

SOME DETAILS OF HISTORY

The late Archbishop Mathew is accused of having obtained His consecration at Utrecht surreptitiously by the production of false testimony. There can be no question that he was consecrated under a misapprehension, and that some of the events leading up to the consecration are exceedingly reprehensible. I hold no brief for Archbishop Mathew—indeed, I and my colleagues of the time ceased to have any confidence in him; but I am bound to say that his complicity in these events has never been proved. We have no solicitude in the matter, for at the time of ordination the events at Utrecht were known neither to me, nor, so far as I am aware, to any of Archbishop Mathew's candidates with whom I was acquainted. We knew, on the other hand, that he had been recognized as the Old Catholic Bishop for Great Britain, both by the Anglican authorities and by the ecclesiastically-minded public at large.

Your Committee make it appear that the Old Catholic Bishops "on the discovery of the facts[1], broke off intercourse with him." Nothing of the sort happened. On the contrary, they waived aside his offer to retire into private life, and publicly exonerated him in the following letter, which appeared in *The Guardian* of June 3rd, 1908:—

AN OLD CATHOLIC BISHOP FOR ENGLAND

Sir,—We, the Archbishop and Bishops of the Old Catholic Church of Holland, and the Old Catholic Bishops of Germany and Switzerland, having heard with much concern of certain events connected with our English branch of the Old Catholic Church, wish to say that we have been in correspondence with a suspended Roman Catholic priest in England since the year 1902.

This priest visited the Bishops of Bonn, Haarlem, Deventer, and the Archbishop of Utrecht, and we believed him to be in perfect accord with us. He accompanied Bishop Mathew on his visit to the Archbishop of Utrecht. On April 7th, in the present year, he, with others, signed the petition to the Bishops begging us to consecrate the Right Rev. A. H. Mathew.

All the documents were sent by this priest to Bishop Herzog, accompanied by numerous letters, urging upon us the immediate need of a Bishop, not only for the requirements of his own congregation, but for those of other clergy and congregations specified by him. We had no reason to suppose that we were mistaken in complying with his request. We wish now to state that our confidence in Bishop Mathew remains unshaken after carefully perusing a large number of the documents bearing upon this matter, and we earnestly hope that his ministrations will be abundantly blessed by Almighty God, and that he will receive the cordial support of the British people and Church in the trying circumstances in which he has been placed.

In the name of the Old Catholic Bishops of Holland, Germany and Switzerland.

The Secretary,
✠J. J. VAN THIEL,
Bishop of Haarlem.

This solemn declaration speaks for itself. It is difficult to think of the Bishops commending to another nation and Church—still less to the blessing of God—a man upon whom remained the least vestige of so terrible a suspicion. They now say that his version of the affair is to be believed. If they have had cause (from their point of view) to regret the consecration, one can only answer that regrets, however keen, do not make facts; and no new facts have come to light since this original declaration. If Bishop Matthew were guilty no one would wish to condone his action; but the public is clearly entitled to distinguish between facts and suppositions. In the absence of further proof, it seems a fair conclusion that the Old Catholic Bishops ought not to press their case.

THE UTRECHT LETTER OF 1920.

Their latest *pronunciamento* (published in the *Internatioinale Kirchliche Zeitschriff,*[2] April-June, 1920, pp. 94-96) does not advance the cause on either side, and is, in some respects, an unfortunate document. It passes over the *Guardian* letter of 1908 as though it had never been written; it rakes up the affair of the consecration after a lapse of a dozen years—four months

[1] This statement should not be laid to the charge of the Old Catholic Bishops; it is a very inaccurate rendering of the German text of their letter.
[2] Bern, Staempfi et Cie.

after the death of the person incriminated; and it asserts that the Bishops broke off relations with Bishop Mathew in 1910, when their own official documents prove that it was he who effected the severance.[1] The whole document reads as though it owed its existence to some outside pressure.

There would be no occasion to mention the Utrecht letter were it not that your committee give an unfortunate twist to its contents. It eventuates in two short Resolutions, which are as follows:—

"1. We declare that the episcopal consecration given in the year 1908 to the Roman Catholic priest, Arnold Harris Mathew, was surreptitiously secured by the production of false testimony, and would never have been given (as was shown to the same priest) if the consecrators had known that the terms asserted in the said documents and desired by our Episcopate for a consecration were nonexistent.

"2. And we declare that we stand in no ecclesiastical relationship whatever with the bishops and clergy who derive their ecclesiastical faculties directly or indirectly from this act of consecration consummated in 1908."

No hint of invalidity is to be found in these Resolutions. On the contrary, the second explicitly recognises as bishops and priests those whose Orders come from Archbishop Mathew. It is true that in the prolegomena which introduce them a doubt is once raised; but this question is at once dismissed with the remark that the Bishops "will not enter" into it "here"—a silence which is sufficiently eloquent[2]. It is your Committee who give a fictitious importance to the question by an unjustifiable interpolation in their rendering of the second Resolution:—

"They also state that...they 'have no ecclesiastical relations' with those persons who claim to have received ordination or consecration from the aforesaid person."

There is nothing at all in the original about people claiming to have received ordination or consecration. It accredits them with receiving it.

II

THE QUESTION OF VALIDITY

We now pass to the really important issue—the only one which may be said to concern the Liberal Catholic Church. Certain interested parties have already begun to assert that the Lambeth Conference denied the validity of our Orders. I propose to show, in the first place, that this argument would be suicidal. and secondly, that the Conference does not even discuss the question of validity.

---

[1] See the *Oud Katholiek Jaarboekie voor 1913*, which narrates that Bishop Mathew notified the Archbishop of Utrecht of his withdrawal from the Old Catholic communion. Also the official statement made on behalf of the Bishop of Haarlem at a meeting of the Society of St. Willibrord, at which he was present, held in London on November 7th, 1913 *(Church Times,* November 14th); "Bishop Mathew had officially broken all connection between himself and the Old Catholics." One looks in vain in the text of this statement of 1913 for any reference to the affair of his consecration and any hint as to its validity.

The reasons for this withdrawal were given by Bishop Mathew in a pastoral letter of "Declaration of Autonomy and Independence" dated December, 1910. His complain was that the Dutch Bishops had begun to tamper with Catholic teaching and practice in order to curry favor with German opinion and to minimize their differences with Calvinism and Lutheranism.

[2] Is it symptomatic of a strong case that issues should be raised, only to be immediately ignored? One would think that this could evoke nothing but prejudice.

A DILEMMA

The Lambeth Resolution and Report, both claim to be based "on a review of all the facts." One important fact, however, still calls for review. In the ministry of the Anglican Church are a certain number of priests ordained by Archbishop Mathew; they were accepted on the strength of their ordination by him, without any thought of reordination, and at the time of writing their ministry continues unchanged.

I do not wish to inconvenience these Gentlemen by publishing their names, and there is no need to do so, for the facts will not be disputed. One of them was licensed to a curacy in the diocese of London in 1913, and is now a vicar therein. Crockford[1] describes him as "in Old Catholic Orders." Another, who was given episcopal and presbyteral Orders by Archbishop Mathew, holds a cure in Iowa. Another, who was invited to the U.S.A. by the Bishop of Fond du Lac in 1914, has since 1916 been chaplain to a Home in the State of New York. One Bishop, consecrated by Dr. Mathew, assisted at an episcopal consecration in New York Cathedral in 1915; his name appears in the *Living Church Annual* for 1921, followed by the words "Old Catholic" in parentheses. I may mention that you have another working as a parish priest in England, who, as a preliminary to admission, had to give an understanding not to exercise episcopal functions. These cases will suffice: I cite them because the circumstances are fully known to me personally.

The Anglican Church can ask nothing fairer than to be judged by its own practice; and in this matter it certainly is on the horns of a dilemma. Either—

(a) Orders derived from Archbishop Mathew are valid beyond question, or
(b) The Anglican Church is indifferent to the matter of Ordination.

The Liberal Catholic Church is content to leave the matter thus. It is clear that in the sight of the Anglican Church no other vindication of its Orders is needed. But I do not wish simply to close the matter with a *tu quoque* argument, and prefer to let our case stand on its own merits.

"ORDER" AND "JURISDICTION"

Before examining the Report, it may be well in the interest of the general reader briefly to explain the principles governing the status and acknowledgment of Orders. Theology recognises two clear issues, those of "order" and "jurisdiction." The one has to do with the intrinsic validity of Orders, the other with the legitimacy and scope of their exercise. Orders may be valid, but (from the standpoint of the adjudicating Church) "schismatical" or "irregular," and their exercise therefore illicit. That exactly defines the attitude of the Roman Church towards Old Catholic Orders, as is illustrated from a well-known Roman Catholic book, "Questions and Answers on the Catholic Church,"[2] by A.B. Sharpe, M.A. bearing the *imprimatur* of the Roman Catholic Archbishop of St. Andrew's and Edinburgh.

"112. Are the orders of the 'Old Catholics' valid? They are derived from the Jansenists, of Holland, and are therefore valid, though unlawfully conferred." (p. 93.)

It is only defect of "order" which is remedied by reordination. The Western Church is

---

[1] *Crockford's Clerical Directory* [Ed.]
[2] London, Sands & Co., 1913.

altogether averse (even to the extent of considering it sacrilegious) to repeating Sacraments, like Ordination, which confer indelible mark or "character" on the soul. It rightly holds that as an act of reverence, the resources of human enquiry should first be exhausted before our Lord's attention is invoked to a ceremony for the doing of something which may already have been done.

Defect in jurisdiction is quite a different issue, and is healed by license on the part of a bishop to officiate in his diocese; this license would rectify the status of orders considered unlawful or schismatical by the bishop in question and by the organization he represents. In the Roman Catholic Church there is a preliminary "absolution from censures" held to have been incurred through the person having been (consciously or unconsciously) in schism.

VALIDITY OR EXPEDIENCY?

Let us now turn to the Report. Here is the crucial Sentence:

> The circumstances of Bishop Mathew's consecration are so uncertain, and his subsequent isolation is so complete, that, without casting any sort of reflection on the validity of Old Catholic Orders, or discussing the theological question of abstract 'validity,' we feel that, as a matter of practice,... the only proper course would be for them...to be ordained *sub conditione.*

It is difficult to know how to deal with this pronouncement, because, in the first place, the argument is a *non sequitur,* and begs the question, and secondly, the Committee so confuse the issues that one is faced with a perplexing uncertainty as to what they do mean.

As they recommend conditional re-ordination, one ought to assume that the present issue is one of validity—only the Committee brush that aside. In such case, we should be on well-trodden ground, and the course to be followed would be amply determined by precedent. It would consist in a judicial enquiry, first into the facts of the case, and then into the question whether from the theological standpoint those facts in any way invalidate the Orders. Your Committee, however, enquire into neither. Instead, they resort to some entirely new system of "pragmatic theology" which apparently disdains or evades principle, and takes as its criterion not ultimate truth, but expediency. The conditional re-ordination is proposed "as a matter of practice." I cannot escape the conclusion that the most probable reason for the Conference's inability to "recognise" our Orders is simply that those Orders come from a source of which they disapprove. That no more affects their validity than the fact of an event being unpleasant renders it unhistorical.

The allusion to Archbishop Mathew's "isolation" is hardly more fortunate. Isolation relates to "jurisdiction," and might indeed be a bar to intercourse; on no principle of theology can it affect "order." Did the Church of England herself cease to retain the Apostolic Succession when the Reformation threw her into complete isolation? As a matter of fact, Archbishop Mathew's "isolation" was the reverse of "complete," and his position placed him at no disadvantage in relation to the Church of England. Eight months after his breach with the Old Catholics he was received into union with the Orthodox Eastern Church.

It is difficult to realise that a Committee of no little eminence, to say nothing of the 252 Bishops "assembled from divers parts of the earth," should be guilty of confusion on these points, and should recommend re-ordination where the obvious implication is a process of giving jurisdiction. But one can scarcely resist the conclusion that your Episcopate speak a lan-

---

[1]. In April 1913, during the libel action *Mathew versus The Times,* the Bishop of London gave evidence as to the recognition by the Church of England of Old Catholic Orders in general, and Bishop Mathew's in particular.

guage of their own in these matters. For example, the Bishop of London[1] wrote a letter, dated August 23rd, 1918, to a Sydney clergyman containing the following sentence:—

"We have only admitted as valid one of Bishop Mathew's ordinations: that was the man he ordained when in full connection with the Old Catholic Church in Holland."[1]

Is there any need to point out that if one ordination he could administer was valid, subsequent ones must be equally valid? Once more, the confusion between validity and jurisdiction.

How infelicitous is the entire treatment of this unhappy but really simple case is again seen when we turn to the Resolution 27 of the full Conference. The Conference actually drop the "matter of practice" phrase—forgetful, apparently, that it is the sole basis of the Committee's recommendation and gravely send out to the Anglican Episcopate and to the world in general an opinion thus voided of all justification whatsoever.

It seems ungracious to take advantage of Your Grace's own well-known liberality; still, I feel I ought not to pass over the case of a lady, confirmed by one of my Auxiliary Bishops, who went to live in Cardiff, where the ministrations of our Church were not then available. She discussed the question of attaching herself to the Church of England; but the local Bishop ruled that in view of the Lambeth Report she would have to receive confirmation *sub conditione*. She asked my advice, as a result of which the Vicar laid the matter before Your Grace, who (I am told by, the lady in question) left him free to use his discretion in the matter.

THE VERDICT OF THEOLOGY

Finally, it becomes our duty to take up "the theological question of abstract 'validity,'" which the Committee raise but to dismiss. Fortunately, the conclusions of theology are specially clear on the subject of Holy Orders, owing to their emergence from centuries of thought and experience, during which the issues could be disencumbered of bias and party feeling, and treated as questions of principle. St. Augustine's masterly defence[2] of baptisms and ordinations administered by heretics settled that question for later generations, and was so conspicuously logical that it became the starting-point from which the doctrine of the Sacraments was gradually systematised. Circumstances then forced into prominence the question of ordination procured by simony or other sinister artifice. Time again decided in favour of the more spacious view. I quote from Wilhelm & Scannell[3]: "the doubt continued...until the question was discussed with great clearness by Robert Pullen, whose opinion as to the validity of heretical, intruded and simoniacal ordinations was accepted by Alexander of Hales, St. Bonaventure, St. Thomas and Scotus." The present issue, of course, ranks in this category.

Any student of history will see that if intrigue, *force majeure* and subversions of the truth, major or minor, are to be regarded as invalidating a consecration, very few lines of succession can hope to pass muster. One writer, Lagarde, in *The Latin Church in the Middle Ages,* tells us that "in the eleventh century bishoprics were frequently, and in every country, made an object of traffic." In 614 the Frankish episcopate at Paris forbade the purchase of episcopal consecration or obtaining it through the influences of princes, and several Councils condemned such traffic.

---

[1] Quoted in *The Christchurch St. Lawrence Monthly Paper,* August, 1920.

2 *De Baptismo.*

3 *Manual of Catholic Theology,* revised edition, 1908. Vol. II, p. 503. This is a favourite textbook in the Roman Catholic Church. Other authorities could be cited, but the point will hardly be challenged.

Amid the tumult of controversy disputants are apt to be restrictive in their judgments, forgetting that the plan of God moves in a wider orbit than "the fretting of man's mind." In the present case it might be argued that the Holy Spirit could not be at the mercy of a fraud, however skillfully concealed and put into effect. But such an objection is precisely of this limited order. It takes into account only the misdemeanour of a single individual, and would sacrifice the thousands of earnest and faithful people who might later approach his ministrations. Assuredly fraud brings its due recompense, but this and validity are two distinct issues. The question is parallel with that of the unworthiness of the minister, which is very soundly treated in the 39 Articles of the Church of England (Article 26), as well as by the Council of Trent.

The one determining feature of the case is that the consecration did take place. It was performed at Utrecht on April 28th, 1908, by Archbishop Gul assisted by the Bishops of Haarlem and Deventer and the German Bishop Demmel.

III

THE VERDICT OF THE OLD CATHOLIC CHURCH.

That Archbishop Mathew was consistently recognised as a bishop of the Church of Utrecht can easily be shown.

He took part in the consecration of Archbishop Kowalski at Utrecht in 1909[1], and in the following year was invited to assist at the consecration of the two Mariavite Suffragans. In July, 1910, the Swiss Old Catholic organ *(Der Katholik)* spoke of this organisation as being possibly "a welcome haven for many Roman Catholics in England, who, though dissatisfied with papal jurisdiction, would be indisposed to sign the 39 Articles." Subsequent years mark no change. The Rev. C.W. Bollmann, who had been ordained by Bishop Mathew, but left him at the breach with Utrecht, ministered in London as the official representative of the Dutch Church until his internment in 1915. His services were held (with the license of the Bishop of London) at the Anglican Church of St. Mary, Claring Cross Road. The Dutch Old Catholic Yearbook repeatedly gives reports of his progress. I met him at the Old Catholic Congress at Cologne in 1913. He received no form of conditional reordination. To this may be added the case of a Dutch lady, Mevrouw Vryberg van der Hell, née Baronesse van Heerdt, who for some years was one of the most prominent lay people in the Dutch Church and a regular communicant. No difficulty was ever made as to her status, although, after having been baptised *sub conditione* by me, she was in 1913 confirmed by Archbishop Mathew. She was required to show her certificates of baptism and confirmation to the priest at the Hague, the circumstances having been made known to Mgr. Gul, whom she met on several occasions.

It is fortunate that these cases are on record, for they show that the Dutch Church maintained the same attitude towards Archbishop Mathew's Orders after 1910 as before. In Appendix II will be found documents showing the acknowledgment of his Orders by the Roman Catholic Church. Also, his episcopal status was fully recognised when he was received into union with the Orthodox Patriarch of Antioch by the Archbishop of Beyrout (Mgr. Gerassimos Messarra) in person, on August 5th 1911

---

[1] Prof. Androutos, whose book on Anglican ordinations is well known, gives it as the opinion of the Eastern Church that bishops consecrate *per modum unius*, and that therefore the cooperation at an episcopal consecration of one who is no bishop invalidates the entire proceedings. The theory will hardly gain acceptance in the West, but it would involve the Mariavite succession in the present case. The same applies to the consecration at New York, in which Bishop de Landas took part.

IV

THE CREDENTIALS OF THE LIBERAL CATHOLIC CHURCH

The Lambeth Conference further announces that it is unable to regard the movement of the late Bishop Mathew and his successors as "a properly constituted branch of the Church." This opinion is quite subordinate to the question of Orders, and does not call for more than passing comment. Let me state our position.

We administer the seven Sacraments in their integrity and plenitude.

We allow our people the widest measure of intellectual freedom in the interpretation of Creeds, Scripture and Tradition. In this we go somewhat further than you, though we erect into a principle what with you is virtually conceded as a matter of practice.

We regard the claim of the Episcopate to territorial jurisdiction as an anachronism,[1] and consider that the bishop exercises jurisdiction over those who voluntarily adhere to his rite. Your Resolution 35 goes half-way to meet this proportion; and the consecration of Bishop Cabrera by Irish Bishops, and of Missionary Bishops by the American Church to territories already occupied by the Roman hierarchy, is based on the identical principle. Our Bishops take the title of no see, but style themselves "Bishop of the Liberal Catholic Church in" the territory under their administration. The Liberal Catholic Church has no wish to proselytise from among the adherents of any other Church, and as an earnest of this welcomes all to regular and full participation in its services without asking or expecting them to leave their original Church. Its chief appeal is addressed to the thousands who, in these days of materialism and religious ineptitude, stand outside the existing Church organisations and religious societies, and are bereft of the help they could otherwise receive. Its congregations are mainly composed of men and women who had ceased to attend Church.

We use a liturgy brought into harmony with present-day outlook and requirements. The need for revision of the Book of Common Prayer is generally conceded among your clergy.

I do not know that these distinctive features of our work deprive us of Churchly status, or (apart from questions of size and influence) would entitle us to any less consideration than your own communion on the part of the historic Churches. Certainly they do not render our Church any less "properly constituted" a body than the various Nonconformist organisations to whom the Conference has so generously stretched out the right hand of fellowship.

When Archbishop Mathew made his abortive act of "unconditional submission" to Rome at the close of 1915, his movement passed into the hands of myself and my colleagues. There could then be no question of forsaking the lay people whom we had collected around us, and who had learned greatly to value the ministrations of our Church. We did subsequently approach the Archbishop of Utrecht, quite sincerely stating that the English movement felt it owed *amende honorable* to the Dutch Church, although (with one exception) none of our clergy had been in the movement at the time of the breach with Utrecht. Despite favourable comments on our work that had appeared in the Old Catholic periodicals of Holland, the wounds evidently rankled too deeply to permit of even the courtesy of an acknowledgment, let alone a reply. We therefore considered ourselves absolved of any inherited participation in the events of the unfor-

---

[1] There are seven Patriarch of Antioch; four, of different rites united with Rome, viz the Latin, Melchite, Maronite and Syriac Patriarchs; and three who repudiate the papal jurisdiction, viz, the Orthodox, the Armenian and Jacobian Patrarchs. The fact that in the early Church one bishop did not hesitate to intrude into the diocese of another if the latter fell under the imputation of heresy further complicates the situation, if precedent is to be invoked and territorial monopoly claimed, Is not the position of the Roman hierarchy in England justifiable on such principles?

tunate past, and reluctantly decided that our movement must work independently. It took the name of "Liberal Catholic," not wishing that there should be imputed to the Church of Utrecht principles of liberalism in religion which might be distasteful to it.

CONCLUSION

Throughout this Open Letter I have not attempted to exceed the recognised limits of theology. But we live in an age of change; a new psychology is fast arising, and it is more than probable that the older standards of judgment will be discarded as men gradually develop the powers latent within them. Theology has been called the queen of sciences, but up to the present its methods have been purely theoretical and speculative. May it not be possible to judge of the validity of Orders by direct observation of the effects they produce, and so to establish a new basis of surety? If, under the veil of bread and wine, Christ be really present on the altar, ought it not to be possible for spiritually-developed people to feel His Presence? There are those today, who are not without first-hand knowledge in these matters; and we who exercise Orders ought not to lack evidence of the power conferred on us through the imposition of hands. I may fairly claim that the clergy and the vast body of the laity of the Liberal Catholic Church can testify on the basis of their own spiritual experience to the reality of the Orders it inherits. Those Orders are a precious gift, which it strives to use faithfully for the perfecting of mankind, "for the edifying of the body of Christ."

The world at large is tired of sectarian controversy, and not unjustly reproaches the Christian Churches for so constantly disputing with one another, instead of devoting their time to larger problems. In face of the sin and the great anguish of the world, is it not possible to forget, or by mutual goodwill to adjust, our differences? How petty are the things that divide us, how mighty is the Voice that summons us to work in the LORD'S vineyard! The Lambeth Conference made an appeal for Christian unity, touching in its sincerity and memorable for its large-hearted charity. "The harvest indeed is plenteous, but the labourers are few." May I not, therefore, echo an ancient challenge "Sirs, we are brethren, why do we wrong one to another?"

I have the honour to be, My Lord Archbishop,
Your Grace's most obedient servant,

✠ J. I. WEDGWOOD,
Presiding Bishop of the Liberal Catholic Church.

ROMAN CATHOLIC OPINION.

The following is a translation of part of a document connected with the excommunication of the parties concerned, which appeared in *The Times,* and was the basis of the libel action *Mathew versus The Times* (April, 1913). The italics, in both this and the subsequent document, are mine:—

> For some time past we have known it has been to you a source of grievous scandal and of deepest sorrow of mind that the priests and of the clergy of the Diocese of Nottingham, seeking the things that are their own and not the things that are Jesus Christ's, and led away by their ambition, after several attempts to procure for themselves the rank of the Episcopate from men who are not Catholics, have lately reached that pitch of audacity in which, *having obtained the fulfillment of their wishes,* they have arrogantly informed us of their *episcopal consecration.* Nor was this information left without authentic testimony, for the person who was the chief author of this sacrilegious misdeed—a certain pseudo-Bishop named Arnold Harris Mathew, was not ashamed to confirm the *fact* in letters full of self-assumption, which he addressed to us.

(It was elicited from Father David Fleming, of the Franciscan Order and an official of the Holy Office, during the hearing of the libel action, that the term "pseudo-Bishop" is a technical term applied to bishops whose consecrations might be valid, but who are not in communion with the Holy See.)

Decision of the Sacred Congregation of the Holy Office, communicated to...by the Most Rev. Edward Ilsley, Archbishop of Birmingham:—

(Dated from Rome, November 21, 1912.)

To the Most Illustrious and Most Reverend Lord Archbishop of Birmingham.

> Most Illustrious and Most Reverend Lord,—In a congregation held on Wednesday, the 13th inst., after consideration of the prayers of..., who seeks absolution from the censures into which he has fallen, for that he *hath received Sacred Orders* from the pseudo-Bishop Mathew, and hath behaved schismatically, and after weighing of those matters which are explained concerning the petitioner in a letter, the Most Eminent and Most Reverend Lords Cardinals, together with myself, Inquisitors-General, decreed that the petitioner shall live as a layman, with permission to receive the sacraments in the manner of laymen, after previous absolution from censures. While I make known to your Lordship these matters, I implore for you every joy and happiness.

Your Lordship's most obedient servant in the Lord,

M. CARDINAL RAMPOLLA.

To these official documents may be added the information that prior to their reception into the Roman Catholic Church clergy ordained by Archbishop Mathew have been required to sign an undertaking not to exercise their Orders, that in private intercourse their status is unhesitatingly recognised, and that one of them, Fr. Migliole, an Italian, was received into the priesthood in Italy without further ordination.

THE BEGINNINGS OF THE LIBERAL CATHOLIC CHURCH

Beginnings of the L.C.C.

The Editor[1] has asked me to put pen to paper and write some account of the beginnings of the Liberal Catholic Church. The story has not been told in its entirety before, so I gladly do as he asks. I shall have to request the indulgence of readers if a certain amount of *autobiography*, or talk about oneself, enters into the narrative. The train of events is mixed up with my early life. I shall try to keep that autobiography as short as possible.

From quite an early age I was interested in the church organ. I remember being taken as boy of about seven into an old church at Folkestone and bursting into tears when I heard the organ being played. Later at school I was given lessons in organ playing, and I began to study the complicated mechanism inside the organ and the treatment of its many kinds of pipes. Later I wrote some books on the subject, of which a *Dictionary of Organ Stops* has run into seven editions. Another hobby was chemistry. On leaving school I was sent, on the advice of Sir Henry Roscoe, a famous chemist of the time, to University College, Nottingham, in England, to study analytical chemistry with a view to taking it up as one's profession.

My interest in church music led me to a *high* Anglican Church in that town. I got deeply interested in the Catholic presentation of Christian doctrine and worship, became an altar server and started reading books on theology. The choirmaster of that church, St. Alban's, Nottingham, Dr. Beckett Gibbs an authority on the Solesmes system of plainchant, is now (1936) in charge of music at St. Ignatius' Episcopal Church, New York. So soon as my studies in Nottingham were finished I was sent to York Minster, one of the largest and most beautiful of the historic English cathedrals, as an articled pupil of the organist there, Dr. T. Tertius Noble, now (1936) of St. Thomas' Episcopal Church, New York. I spent four years with him. During that time I was up in the organ loft twice in the day and helped in the training of some of the junior boys in the choir. I acted as server in two Anglican churches in succession and as choirmaster in one of them, in which the Solesmes system of plainchant was and is still used.

I finally decided to read for Holy Orders in the Church of England. But there is an old proverb: "Man proposes. God disposes." (People who think that the Devil is behind theosophy are at liberty to impute the responsibility to him!) Mrs. Besant came along to York to lecture there. I had heard her once before, at Nottingham. I said to the Vicar in whose church I was working and in whose house I was living: "I'm going to hear that woman again, but she won't get me this time." He came with me to the lecture. Three days later I joined the Theosophical Society and was summarily banished from the church. The Vicar could not have such a heretic as a church official! We are the best of friends these days, and I told him recently that he had acted in my best interest and that I knew that I could never have been happy in the Anglican church.

From that time forward I renounced all thought of church work and of a church career, and having just enough income on which to live decided to devote myself to work in and for the Theosophical Society. From 1911-1913 I acted as General Secretary of the Society in England and Wales, relinquishing that office to become Grand Secretary of the British Jurisdiction of the Co-Masonic Order. So much for preliminary history.

---

[1] The editor of *Ubique,* then the American Provincial magazine.

In 1913 a letter appeared in one of the London daily newspapers dealing with the habits of birds. The letter caught my eye especially because it was signed by Archbishop A.H. Matthew, of whose existence as an Old Catholic bishop in England I knew vaguely. Something impelled me to write to him to ask for particulars of the Church of which he was head. He sent a very friendly answer. The idea of taking Orders re-entered my head. I told him something of the story of my life, of my interest in church work and of the studies I had made.

During the interchange of letters which followed I was honest with him about my relation with the Theosophical Society, and as some indication of one's belief sent him a copy of Mrs. Besant's little book, *Theosophy*, published in the *Jack* series of *The People's Books*. He asked me to go and see him, and at once accepted me. I was rebaptized and reconfirmed by him *sub conditione*, given the Minor Orders, those of Subdeacon and Deacon, and finally ordained by him as a priest on July 22, 1913. These ceremonies all took place in an oratory which I equipped in my rooms at 1 Upper Woburn Place, London, opposite the Headquarters of the T.S. where I worked as General Secretary. I mention details such as these because in attacks of a most unscrupulous kind which were later to follow it was alleged that I had concealed the fact of my being a Theosophist from him.

The following two years saw the ordination to the priesthood by Abp. Mathew of other members of the Theosophical Society. Their names are: Bernard Edward Rupert Gauntlett (July 1, 1914), Reginald Elphinstone Astley Loftus Farrer (August 1, 1913) and Robert King (August 1, 1914). Rupert Gauntlett belonged to a family who owned a large paper manufactory and worked in that firm. Reginald Farrer had independent means. Robert King was and is well known as a theosophical lecturer and authority on psychic faculties.[1] Following upon these names should be mentioned Fredrick James (April 4, 1915); he had been a member of the T.S. until the previous year. The ceremonies took place for the most part in the oratory in my house. (The dates following the names are those of ordination to the priesthood.)

At the same time as Robert King and Reginald Farrer, an ex-priest of the Anglican Church, not a Theosophist; Frederick Samuel Willoughby, M.A. (Cantab.) was passed through the ceremonies from Confirmation to the Priesthood, all being administered, of course, *sub conditione*. He and Reginald Farrer were baptized *sub conditione* on the same day, July 18, 1914, in my oratory and in succession to one another, one by Abp. Matthew, and the other by myself.

Bishop King and I were discussing these events recently—we have remained close friends for nearly 30 years—and he reminded me that it was on the first anniversary of my ordination to the priesthood that I took him to Bromley in Kent to see the Archbishop, and that much of the conversation on that occasion had turned round the habits of birds, about which the old Archbishop had a wide range of information.

Another member of the Theosophical Society was also ordained at this period of the Church's history, that is, during the period of Abp. Mathew's headship, namely Theodore Bell, of Harrogate. Quakers were numerous round about Harrogate and York, and he came of a Quaker family. The parents, William and Elizabeth Bell, were leading Theosophists in Harrogate and were proprietors of the chief drapery establishment in that town. Theodore Bell was baptized by Reginald Farrer, confirmed by Bishop Willoughby, and at the hands of Bishop Willoughby, and received the several ordinations up to the priesthood (November 13, 1914) at the hands of Bishop Willoughby. He has for some years worked in the United States as a priest of the Protestant Episcopal Church and has achieved some renown in that field of work. His

---

[1] Bishop King died in 1954.

brother, Robert William Bell, is also well known as a priest of our Church, serving at Tekels Park, Camberley.[1]

In the autumn of 1914 I went to Adyar, India to the Headquarters of the T.S. on the invitation of Mrs. Besant, and in the following year visited Australia. I was at the time Grand Secretary of the Order of Universal Co-Masonry for the British Jurisdiction, and I went there largely in connection with that work. It was in that year, 1915, that I had the privilege of initiating C.W. Leadbeater into Freemasonry. I talked with him about my ordination and he came to various celebrations of the Eucharist by myself. He was greatly impressed by the power for good which such ordination bestowed and with the splendid scope that the celebration offered for spreading spiritual blessing abroad on the world. In the meantime Abp. Mathew had consecrated F. S. Willoughby as Bishop. In September 1914 he had addressed a letter to his clergy saying that in view of his advancing years it seemed to him desirable that "immediate steps should be taken to preserve the valid episcopal succession in our portion of the Church from risk of loss." The election then held resulted in the consecration of the Rev. F. S. Willoughby on October 28, 1914. My name came second in the voting and it was understood that I was to be consecrated on my return, so that there should be bishops to the canonical number of three. It is a rule of the Church that three bishops shall officiate at an episcopal consecration. Consecration by a single bishop is valid; the rule requiring three is partly aimed against clandestine consecrations and to ensure that all shall be done *coram populo*. Also it is well that in an independent movement the chain of episcopal succession shall not hang on one or even on two links.

The Old Catholic Church

At this stage of our narrative it will be fitting and most convenient to say something about the movement which Abp. Mathew represented. There is no need to write in any detail about the origin and history of the Old Catholic Church. An outline of that is given in our *Statement of Principles,* and the story can be read in various books which treat of church history. At the beginning of the 18th century a number of Dutch clergy centering round the Chapter of Utrecht found themselves in resistance to what they regarded as unlawful interference on the part of Rome. It is claimed on their side that they were fighting against Jesuit intrigue. They were able to secure the episcopal succession from a bishop in Roman Orders, and thenceforward maintained themselves in a state of independence from Rome. In Holland they came to be known as *The Old Roman Church.* They retained the Latin Rite, since their differences were at first ones of discipline and not of doctrine. The Pope was prayed for as patriarch of the West until 1910.

The movement known as *Old Catholic* is of later and different origin. It dates from the time of the formulation by the Roman Catholic Church of the doctrine of *Papal Infallibility,* a doctrine promulgated by the Vatican Council of 1870. A number of prominent scholars on the Continent of Europe went into revolt at what they regarded as a serious innovation in doctrine. The Dutch *Old Roman Church* came to their aid and consecrated Prof. Reinkens of Bonn as their bishop in Germany. He in his turn consecrated a certain Dr. Herzog as bishop of the Swiss *Christian Catholic Church* (as they called and call themselves) in 1876. And the movement eventually spread to some other countries. There is [in 1937], for instance, in U.S.A., a *Polish National Catholic Church* in union with Utrecht, whose first bishop, Antonius Stanislaus Kozlowski, was consecrated in 1897 by the above-named Bishop Herzog of Switzerland. He was succeeded by Bishop Francis Hodur, consecrated at Utrecht in 1907. There are other so-

[1] Father R.W. Bell died in 1964.

called *Old Catholic* or *Old Roman Catholic* Churches which are not in union with Utrecht.

I ought now to say a few words about Abp. Mathew's relations with Utrecht. On taking up work in the English movement we discovered to our surprise that the number of active adherents in that country could be counted on the fingers of one hand. Archbishop Mathew had quarreled successively with the Dutch Church and the Anglican Church, and had lost one after another of his Auxiliary Bishops and clergy. It was owing to our efforts that an oratory was opened in London in Red Lion Square and a permanent congregation gradually gathered there.

It does not fall within the range or purview of this article to discuss at any length the difficulties with Utrecht or the misunderstanding under which Dr. Mathew had been consecrated. They are dealt with in a pamphlet by myself issued in 1920 in the form of an *Open Letter* to the Archbishop of Canterbury and bearing the title, *The Lambeth Conference and the Validity of Archbishop Mathew's Orders.* It had been thought that some Roman Catholic congregations in Great Britain were proposing to join the Old Catholics and on these grounds the consecration took place. No such exodus from the Roman Church did follow.

On the discovery of the facts Bishop Mathew offered to retire into private life, but the Old Catholic bishops in a letter to the English journal, *The Guardian,* dated June 3, 1908, exonerated him from all complicity in the proceedings, saying that their "confidence in Bishop Mathew remains unshaken after carefully perusing a large number of documents bearing on this matter," and they commended his ministrations to the blessing of Almighty God and to the support of the English Church and people.

In 1910 Bishop Mathew broke off relations with the Old Catholics. He gave as his reason the fact that the Old Catholic Bishops had begun to tamper with the Catholic faith. As we have already seen, the Dutch Church had been most conservative in regard to changes. It was otherwise in regard to other branches of the movement. They had tampered with Catholic teaching and practice in order to find favour with and to diminish their differences with Lutheranism and Calvinism. There is to this day a good deal of difference between the Dutch Liturgy on the one hand, and the German and Swiss Liturgies on the other hand. Incense is commonly used in Holland; it is much less used in Switzerland and has almost disappeared from the German churches. And the general outlook of the Dutch Church has been affected in no small measure by the more Protestant tendencies of these other Churches. Various changes were made in the Dutch vernacular Liturgy of 1910. I mention these points to show that Abp. Mathew, as a man of thoroughly orthodox outlook, did not act as he did without some justification behind him.

Our Breach with Abp. Mathew

The real trouble with Abp. Mathew was his instability of character. He was outwardly charming and the most courteous of men, and it was difficult for one who knew him to think of him as being consciously or intentionally dishonest. But he was constantly changing his outlook on things. His mind behaved like a weathercock, blown about by the exigencies of the moment and the emotional reaction awakened by them. One of the many priests who had left him once said to me that he fixed six months as the average time that a man was likely to remain with him. Our turn came along in due course.

I was on my way back to England from Australia when I received word of two crises. One was concerned with the sudden dismissal of Bishop Willoughby from the movement in consequence of an attack made on him by a certain weekly journal noted for public arraignments of this kind. Abp. Mathew summoned him at a few hours' notice to defend himself. Bishop Willoughby declined to appear, claiming that prior to his entry into the movement he had discussed with the Archbishop quite freely the circumstances which had led him to resign his living in the Anglican Church. A farcical sentence of degradation was pronounced. The other sudden movement was that we all had been required to abjure our theosophical tenets. A priest who had been ordained by him who was not active in the movement and whom none of us had ever met had been impressing upon the Archbishop the iniquity of our beliefs.[1]

I arrived home to learn that Robert King and Rupert Gauntlett had been consecrated bishops by Bishop Willoughby. The latter was on the verge of making his submission to the Roman Church. He himself was not concerned one way or another with the doctrinal dispute. The remainder of the non-Theosophical clergy in Great Britain (with the solitary exception of the priest just mentioned) stood by us. Bishop Willoughby said that he owed his consecration to the suffrages of the clergy concerned and he regarded it as an honourable obligation to hand back to the movement the episcopate to guard and perpetuate which he had been consecrated. The two were to hold the succession in trust for me. Bishop Willoughby was still free when I got back to England. I waited four and a half months before accepting his offer of consecration. I wanted, if possible, to avoid later difficulties by obtaining the episcopate from another source. Four of those who had been consecrated by Abp. Mathew were approached by me, also a certain Bishop Vernon Herford, deriving his episcopal Orders from another line of succession altogether and who was and is concerned with the giving of Sacred Orders to Nonconformist ministers;[2] but, as had been anticipated, without success. The main reason for my reluctance to accept consecration at the hands of Bishop Willoughby was removed when he showed me his correspondence with the Archbishop which bore witness that he had been open and above-board with him. These letters are now in the files of our Church.

In the meantime the issue with Abp. Mathew had widened, and the clergy active in the movement decided to dissociate themselves from a leadership which they had come to see to be lacking in any sense of responsibility. Abp. Mathew then tendered his "unconditional submission" to the Roman Church. The announcement appeared in *The Times* during the last days of 1915. In a letter to a widely circulated Roman Catholic journal he expressed himself as being "absolutely and irrevocably" convinced of the necessity of actual union with the Roman See and as accepting "without hesitation or doubt" the Infallibility of the Pope *(Universe,* December 31, 1915). He wrote me at this time that he "terminated" the movement which he had begun. To one not acquainted with his capacity for changing his mind it would seem incredible that after so solemn and public a pronouncement he refused Rome's conditions and went through the *jeu de theatre* of resuming the headship of the movement at the invitation of the priest to whom we have referred. The later movement never made any headway in this country. Abp. Mathew died in 1919.

The Reorganization of the Church

I was myself consecrated bishop on February 13, 1916 by Bishop Willoughby, assisted by Bishops King and Gauntlett. Our Oratory was much too small for the occasion and we made use of the Co-Masonic Temple in London. There was present a large congregation, a number of whom added their names as witnesses to the *Instrument of Consecration* signed by the bishops. In the photographs taken after the ceremony Dr. Seaton, the Dean of Abp. Mathew's Chapter, is to be seen in the front row with the bishops.

[1] Bernard Mary Williams, later the erratic "Archbishop of Caer-Glow," who died in 1952.
[2] Bishop Herford died in 1938.

Our situation was not an easy one. We had not entered the movement with any idea of starting another Church. Nothing was further from my mind. It had been a disappointment to me that I could not enter the Anglican ministry, and when the opportunity presented itself of assuming "the sweet but heavy burden of the priesthood" under these conditions of greater freedom I gladly and happily embraced it. Had there been any thought of founding an independent church one would have taken information as to Abp. Matthew's relationship with the other Old Catholic Churches and would certainly have decided to seek opportunity elsewhere. But things were not to be so. We found ourselves in relation with a devout and earnest congregation who had learned to value greatly the spiritual privileges which the movement afforded them. Experience had shown us that inevitably we should come to grief with orthodox leadership. There was no option but to go ahead, no matter how formidable and distasteful some of the outer consequences of that course were likely to prove. The decision to carry on was therefore taken.

A few months later I was once more on my way to Sydney to take counsel with C. W. Leadbeater. The worldwide journeying was decidedly expensive, but I realized some capital in order to make it possible. Bishop King was left in charge of the work in England and admitted some good workers to the priesthood. Mr. Leadbeater saw great possibility for usefulness in the movement and placed his services unreservedly at our disposal. He was consecrated bishop on July 22, 1916, having previously received conditional baptism and confirmation and the earlier Orders, again conditionally, at my hands.[1]

There now began one of the happiest and most interesting phases of my life. The many and sundry rites of the Church were carefully studied and through these researches were laid the foundations of our existing *Liturgy* and of the valuable and interesting book later published by our great colleague, *The Science of the Sacraments*. My own studies in theology now proved useful. I was able to formulate question after question, and the principles governing the working of the holy sacraments and the offices of worship of the Church were gradually elucidated.

I may mention one interesting investigation as a case in point. It turned round the question of what is called *intention*. The main reason why the Roman Catholic Church regards Anglican Orders as null and void is that the Reformers, according to this judgement, had no intention to ordain sacrificing priests in the Catholic sense. There lived in England in the days of my youth an ultra-Protestant Anglican Bishop of Liverpool, a certain Dr. Ryle, who carefully told his candidates before their ordination that he was not going to ordain them as sacrificing priests but purely as ministers of the Gospel. The enquiry now made showed quite clearly that the intention to do what the Church intends to be done suffices and that idiosyncrasies of personal belief do not seriously intervene in the situation. It is the good of the many which is taken into consideration, not the misplaced belief of an individual. in other words, *it is not Bishop Ryle who ordains but the Lord Christ.*

We agreed that in the work of the revision of the Liturgy there should be no question of departing from the general outline of Christian thought and worship. Ours was a Christian church and we intended to keep it such. And we followed the general plan of the Roman Liturgy which had been in use in our Church and which we found to be the most suitable as a basis for work. I had myself been ordained and consecrated according to the Roman rite. The book used was entitled *The Old Catholic Missal and Ritual*. It had been published in 1909 by Bishop Mathew and bore the imprimatur of Gerardus Gul, the Archbishop of Utrecht. It

---

[1] C.W. Leadbeater was then a priest in Anglican Orders but had been inactive since 1884. He served as Presiding Bishop of the Church from 1923 until his death in 1934.

incorporated, of course, the trifling changes which distinguished Old Catholicism from Roman Catholicism. We had used this book in our general services, though in accordance with Abp. Mathew's wishes I said my private daily Mass in Latin. The forms given in this book were used for the ordination and consecration of Bishop Leadbeater—they are those found in the *Pontificale Romanum.*

We set to work to eliminate the many features which from our point of view disfigure and weaken the older liturgies. References to fear of God, to His wrath and to everlasting damnation were taken out, also the constant insistence on the sinfulness and worthlessness of man and the frequent appeals for mercy. The services were made as clear and free from repetition in their structural sequence as possible. And every opportunity was given to the congregation to join in the worship with all the resources of mind and will and emotion and self-dedication they were able to command. The sentiments put into the mouth of the worshipper are such as those who are filled with the spirit of devotion and service can honestly and sincerely utter. There is no need to speak further of this side of our work, for it is outlined and discussed in the Preface to our *Liturgy* and has been written about elsewhere.

One other change of method remains to be mentioned. The historical liturgies follow the custom of the time in identifying man with his physical body and activities. They speak of "my soul" and "my spirit." This outlook works to restrict man in the play of his faculties. It leads him to pray and ask for the gift of various virtues as though they were not inherent in him. Our method of treating man as a spiritual intelligence using a physical body leads to greater effectiveness and to far greater freedom and readiness and power of self-expression. It stresses the idea of co-operation with the Divine Father rather than that of supplication, and being outward-turned in the service of God and His world soon enables a man to realize something of the boundless resources of his own being. They are his by right and not simply by grace.

This work at the *Liturgy* took much time and effort. Early in 1918 a small volume was published in London. It contained *The Liturgy of the Mass,* together with a *Form for the Administration of Holy Communion out of Mass, Form for the Communion of the Sick,* the *Order of Vespers* and of *Benediction of the Most Holy Sacrament.* The book was headed with the name, *The Old Catholic Church* and was "Prepared for the use of English-speaking Congregations of Old Catholics." The complete edition of the Liturgy was published in the following year and the note authorizing its use and signed by myself is dated *The Feast of St. Alban, 1919.* We had by then changed the name of our Church to Liberal Catholic, and for the word *Mass* had substituted *Holy Eucharist.* Certain small alterations were made in the wording of the earlier book. There was, for instance, a phrase at the beginning of the Canon of the Mass: "We desire to offer this Holy Sacrifice in praise to Thee and that it may avail to lift the heavy burden of the sin and sorrow of the world." This was now left out. A later edition with some additions incorporated was issued in 1924.[1]

I was myself responsible for the wording of most of the forms of service. Bishop Leadbeater and I collaborated in the writing of the Collects, though he was mainly responsible for them. Bishop Leadbeater selected the verses for the psalms and canticles, and the passages serving for epistles and gospels. Mr. E. Armine Wodehouse originally wrote the lovely hymn at the end of *Benediction,* "Closed is the Solemn Hour," for a ceremonial movement named *The Temple of the Rosy Cross,* of which Mrs. Besant, Mrs. Hotchener (then Russak) and I were the principals. He wrote also the Litanies which figure in the Benediction rite and in the Forms of Ordination. These were to have been based on those to be found in *Hymns, Ancient and Mod-*

---

[1] A third revised edition of the Liturgy appeared in 1942. It was reprinted in 1987 and 2002. [Ed.]

ern. Readers who care to look up numbers 464, 470 and 472 in that book will see that only a few sentences were actually taken from that source. These Litanies are a very beautiful and happy addition to our book of worship.

I have so far discussed changes in the *Liturgy* and mode of worship. One other matter calls for mention in this record of our early work. We decided to be scrupulously careful in our choice of bishops and in the circumstances of their consecration. During four years and four months Abp. Mathew had laid hands on no fewer than eight bishops, and his bishops left him and submitted to other Churches (where some of them worked as priests) as readily as did his priests. The title of Archbishop is with us set aside.[1] It was originally decided to drop the title of Father attached to priests. There are no longer *Canons* in our small ranks.[1] And no jurisdiction is claimed in regard to territory. We have done our best to be sensible and to cast off the earlier tradition of extravagance. I was myself responsible for the writing of the *Statement of Principles.*

The work on the Liturgy was interrupted by a good deal of traveling about needed for the founding of our movement in different countries. This is not the place to speak of those journeys. But the following facts may be of interest. On my journey to Sydney as a newly-consecrated bishop I stopped at Adelaide in South Australia and ordained to the priesthood on July 6, 1916, David Morton Tweedie, now bishop in Australia. He was the first of our men to be ordained priest in Australia.[2]

In 1917 I went to New Zealand in connection with church and Masonic work. During that visit John Ross Thomson and William Crawford were ordained priests at Auckland on February 18 and 25 respectively. Both are now bishops.[3] I returned to Sydney and on June 24, assisted by Bishop Leadbeater, consecrated to the episcopate The Jonkheer Julian Adrian Mazel.[4]

Later on in the same year I returned to England via U.S.A., staying for some time at Hollywood and visiting other towns in the States and in British Columbia on the journey. The first priest to be ordained in U.S.A. was my dear and honoured friend, Charles Hampton. He was ordained at Los Angeles on August 19, 1917. Dr. Edwin Burt Beckwith of Chicago was ordained in New York on September 16, 1917. Some years later, on July 18, 1926, by courtesy of Bishop Cooper I had the honour of consecrating him bishop in the Church of St. Michael, Huizen, Holland, assisted by Bishops Cooper and Pigott.[5] Also in New York I ordained as priest Ray Marshall Wardall on October 4. He also is now a bishop.[6]

On January 18, 1918 in London I gave conditional reordination to the priesthood to Frank Waters Pigott, now our Presiding Bishop.[7] I returned to Australia a few months later, traveling again via U.S.A. On the way through I stopped at Chicago and ordained Edmund Walter Sheehan, now a bishop, as priest.[8]

The following year, 1919, our *Liturgy* as we now know it was at length published. My copy of this first edition bears on the title page the following note: "This copy was used at the consecration of the Rt. Rev. Irving S. Cooper at St. Alban's, Sydney, on July 13, 1919." I had

---

[1] Some of these decisions have been altered through the years.
[2] Bishop Tweedie died in 1941.
[3] Bishop Thomson died in 1938 and Bishop Crawford in 1962.
[4] Bishop Mazel died in 1928.
[5] Bishop Hampton died in 1958, Bishop Beckwith in 1929.
[6] Bishop Wardall died in 1954.
[7] Bishop Piggott was formerly an Anglican priest. He died in 1956.
[8] Bishop Sheehan died in 1988.

the privilege of acting as consecrator on that occasion, and was assisted at the ceremony by Bishops Leadbeater and Mazel. Bishop Cooper was the first bishop for whom the form of consecration printed in our *Liturgy* was used. Mazel, like Bishop Leadbeater, was raised to the episcopate according to the Roman rite.[1]

I mention these American cases, first because I am writing for an American magazine, but also because I keep in my heart a living gratitude for the unfailing kindness and warmth of welcome which was everywhere shown to me in your country. Bishop Cooper's presence at Sydney while the work on the Liturgy was being finished was useful and timely. He put before us the needs and the outlook of a country which is not much tied to tradition.[2]

The later development of the Church comes more within the range of knowledge of our members and clergy in the large number of countries in which it is now at work. How much it has meant in the lives of numbers of people there are many to testify. It may be small so far as membership is reckoned in terms of numbers, but it makes its own distinctive contribution within the fellowship of Christian churches and serves its own good and intrinsic purpose as an instrument in the service of our common Lord and Master.

---

[1] Bishop Cooper was the first Regionary Bishop for the U.S.A. A photograph of his consecration appears in *The Science of the Sacraments,* p.436, and in *The Ceremonies of the Liberal Catholic Rite.* Plate VII. He died in 1935.
[2] It was at this time, in 1919, that Bishop Cooper commenced work on his book, *Ceremonies of the Liberal Catholic Rite,* first published in 1934. The latest edition is dated 2001. [Ed.]

INDICES
Index of Subjects

Index of Names